Roy Porter

English Society in the Eighteenth Century

Penguin Books

Penguin Books Ltd, Harmondsworth, Middlesex, England
Penguin Books, 625 Madison Avenue, New York, New York 10022, U.S.A.
Penguin Books Australia Ltd, Ringwood, Victoria, Australia
Penguin Books Canada Ltd, 2801 John Street, Markham, Ontario, Canada L3R 1B4
Penguin Books (N.Z.) Ltd, 182–190 Wairau Road, Auckland 10, New Zealand

First published 1982

Made and printed in Great Britain by
Richard Clay (The Chaucer Press) Ltd
Bungay, Suffolk
Set in Monophoto Bembo by Butler & Tanner Ltd
Frome and London

Contents

Editorial Foreword

Historians respond to the problems of their time almost without being conscious of the process, and the focus of their study changes with the changing times. In the nineteenth century all countries of Europe and America were preoccupied with the origins of national identity, with the need to forge a living past that would give meaning not only to the present but also to the future: Ranke, Macaulay, Michelet, Bancroft and other great historians of the nineteenth century were so preoccupied. As Britain's national identity seemed to be inexorably involved with the evolution of constitutional rights, with liberty, freedom and, particularly, democracy, it is not surprising that an ever growing number of professional historians should devote all their skills and interest to constitutional, legal, and political history and that these subjects should dominate university syllabuses when they were first designed in the late nineteenth century.

The First World War, the Great Depression, and the economic disasters which followed gave great impetus to the study both of diplomatic and economic history, the one generally attracting the conservative, the other the radical historians in the 1920s and 1930s. After the Second World War interest in diplomatic history faded first or, rather, transmogrified itself into International Relations and Strategic Studies. Economic history drifted into a professional morass and developed a confused identity – the quantifiers and the econometricians moved in and so did the sociologists, especially American sociologists, hoping to establish an ideology which would refute the Marxist interpretation which had flourished within the realm of economic history.

But the problems of Western industrial society have become much more complex since the Second World War. Fantastic economic growth, and it has been fantastic this last thirty years, has created its own social tensions and, even more important, the very nature of highly industrialized society, apart from its growth, has created new conflicts. Institutions which have lasted for ten thousand years, not only in the West but also in the East, have suddenly seemed to be in jeopardy. In the last two decades there has been a mushrooming of interest amongst historians in the problems of demography, of the nature of the family, of the position of women, children, slaves, and servants, of the uses of leisure, of the influence of printing, of the expansion of the arts, of the importance of the images society creates for itself, and of the interpretation of class not in economic but in social terms. A new panorama of social history has spread before the eyes of scholars and led them to subjects which historians of previous generations would have thought of interest only to antiquarians.

Naturally, other forms of history are not dead, even though some of them are corpse-like, but there can be little doubt that the historical imagination, for better or worse, has become intoxicated with social history: for example, the volume of work on death in the last ten years is prodigious and it is matched by the quantity of studies on childhood or marriage.

The danger of social history, which in spite of its present explosion has, in some of its aspects, long roots reaching back through G. M. Trevelyan to Macaulay and Sir Walter Scott, has been the tendency to drift into descriptive history, of how people lived and spent their days with little or no attempt to analyse why their lives, their beliefs, their activities were what they were. Also, the evidence social historians, even very good ones, used in the past, was impressionistic – diaries, letters, personal memories, together with material collected from folk-lorists and antiquarians. Naturally, most of this evidence related to the literate class, always, until very recent times, a modest segment of the nation.

In order to give this material greater rigour, sociological theory, either of Marxist or capitalist bent, has been used and, often, in discussion of death, birth, education of children, or the position of women, it has been infused with modern psychological analysis. Although this has given rise to some nonsense, particularly in the history of childhood, it has given the subject, on the whole, greater intellectual weight.

As with economic history, there has also been a powerful movement which has attempted to quantify the evidence of the past in order to give a statistical basis for some of the fundamental questions of social history – average size and nature of the family, whether nuclear or extended; the age of marriage for men and women; death rates and ages at death; even an attempt has been made to quantify literacy. Huge mountains of data have been assembled and computers have hummed away merrily at great expense but the results remain extremely tentative. Before the nineteenth century record-keeping was erratic and its reliability was not easy to test. There is, too, one unknown factor of great importance – how many of the population were never recorded at all, neither their births, marriages, nor deaths? Indeed, most of the results obtained are easy to criticize and must be treated with considerable scepticism. Even so, generalizations about the family and about its size, about marriage, about bastardy, about age of death, all are firmer than they were and, because they are, help us to understand the life of the country in greater depth.

Although statistics may give shadow and depth to the picture, they cannot paint it, and social history still depends upon a great range of records. Formerly, it depended most of all on letters, diaries, and imaginative literature but, although these are still of the greatest value, more attention has now been given to artefacts: to the study of houses and gardens, to newspapers, bills, and trade cards, to carriages, instruments, games, and toys, indeed to everything that may throw a light on the way life was lived or the way it hurried towards its future or clung to its past. By extending its range and its depth, by encompassing a multiplicity of scenes, social history has become a far more complex and intellectually exciting discipline than it was.

Over the last ten years the flow of monographs and articles on the social history of England has increased, mushroomed like an atomic explosion, and the time is more than ripe for an attempt at synthesis.

J. H. Plumb

Acknowledgements

A work of this kind must inevitably be largely a distillation of the research and interpretations of others, and a dialogue with them. I cannot acknowledge all their work here (though I list some of it in the section of Further Reading). I hope I haven't anywhere used their work in vain. The following scholars and friends have read this book at various stages (some more than once): John Brewer, Robert Brown, W. F. Bynum, David Cannadine, Estelle Cohen, Linda Colley, Mark Goldie, Joanna Innes, Chris Lawrence, Sue Limb, Gillian Morris, Michael Neve, Jacqueline Rainfray, Keith Snell, David Souden, John Styles, Sylvana Tomaselli, and Christopher Wright. I have benefited immensely from their help, though I am of course entirely responsible for the outcome. Jack Plumb has given me every encouragement with the project; I hope the result will not seem a travesty of 'Plumb's century'. The first part of this book was written in the peaceful surroundings of Churchill College, Cambridge, and during the latter stages I have basked in the time for research and the facilities offered by the Wellcome Institute for the History of Medicine. I should like to express deep gratitude to Verna Cole and Frieda Houser for ever-cheery help with typing; to Tim Harris and Chris Husband for help with references; to Mrs Jean Runciman, who has read the proofs; and to Nick Collins, who has compiled the index.

Roy Porter, February 1981

Conversion Tables

1 inch = 2.54 centimetres
1 yard = 0.914 metres
1 mile = 1.609 kilometres

1 pound weight = 0.454 kilograms

1 gallon = 4.546 litres

1 acre = 0.405 hectares

12 pennies (d.) = 1 shilling (s.)
20 shillings = 1 pound (£1)
21 shillings = 1 guinea

Given the recent rates of inflation, it is hardly practicable to give modern real-worth equivalents of eighteenth-century monetary units. Multiplying eighteenth-century sums, however, by approximately 60 will give a rough-and-ready 1982 equivalent. In this period, rock-bottom wages for males were about eight shillings a week, but a man fully employed all the weeks of the year would not have been able to support a family on such a sum (earnings in the region of some £30–£40 a year would be needed for that). A careful family could hope to keep itself out of debt on a pound a week, and most of the petty bourgeoisie would have incomes of between £50 and £100 a year. About £300 was the least that would keep a gentleman in any style.

As to outgoings, for much of the century a full loaf of bread cost about 4d. and a pot of ale 1d.; a meal could be bought in a London tavern for about 1s. 6d. A new two-up and two-down brick cottage would cost about £150.

Introduction

Interpretations of eighteenth-century English society have been very varied. Many Victorians were repelled by its 'soullessness', seeing it as rationalist, cynical, and materialist. More recently, certain historians have admired it as an age of wise traditionalism, of elegance and wit, or of Squire Western rumbustiousness, and the effect of such characterizations has been to portray Georgian England as a golden age, creating a great divide between past and present. This side of the watershed of the French Revolution lie modern times: our world of the masses, democracy, progress, opportunity, alienation – or whatever; on the far side, there is the world we have lost, utterly lost, best evoked by George Eliot in *Adam Bede* over a century ago, recalling even then the irrecoverable times of the early 1800s:

Leisure is gone – gone where the spinning wheels are gone, and the pack-horses, and the slow waggons, and the pedlars, who brought bargains to the door on sunny afternoons. Ingenious philosophers tell you, perhaps, that the great work of the steam-engine is to create leisure for mankind. Do not believe them; it only creates a vacuum for eager thoughts to rush in. Even idleness is eager now, eager for amusement: prone to excursion-trains, art-museums, periodical literature, and exciting novels: prone even to scientific theorizing, and cursory peeps through microscopes. Old Leisure was quite a different personage; he only read one newspaper, innocent of leaders, and was free from that periodicity of sensations which we call post-time. He was a contemplative, rather stout gentleman, of excellent digestion – of quiet perception, undiseased by hypothesis: happy in his inability to know the causes of things, preferring the things themselves. He lived chiefly in the country, among pleasant seats and homesteads, and was fond of sauntering by the fruit-tree wall, and scenting the apricots when they were warmed by the morning sunshine, or of sheltering himself under the orchard boughs at noon, when the summer pears were falling. He knew nothing of weekday services, and thought none the worse of the

Sunday sermon if it allowed him to sleep from the text to the blessing
– liking the afternoon service best because the prayers were the shortest,
and not ashamed to say so; for he had an easy, jolly conscience,
broadbacked like himself, and able to carry a great deal of beer and
port-wine – not being made squeamish by doubts and qualms and
lofty aspirations. Life was not a task to him, but a sinecure; he fingered
the guineas in his pocket, and ate his dinners, and slept the sleep of the
irresponsible; for had he not kept his charter by going to church on the
Sunday afternoons!

Fine old Leisure! Do not be severe on him, and judge him by our
modern standard; he never went to Exeter Hall, or heard a popular
preacher, or read *Tracts for the Times*, or *Sartor Resartus*.

For excellent reasons, another school of historians is now out
of sympathy with such evocations of the magic of the past, and
has rightly emphasized the 'modernity' of so much of Georgian
life. Eminent Georgians were not, after all, lovable paternalist
eccentrics; not all squires were bucolic, wenching Nimrods:
they were profit-hungry capitalists. Labourers were not
forelock-touching and deferential, but as tenacious of their
rights as any modern trade-unionist.

All this is salutary. Yet it is just as much a mistake to assimilate
the eighteenth century by denying its differences. The Georgian
century formed a distinctive moment in the making of modern
England. It was a society which was capitalist, materialist,
market-oriented; wordly, pragmatic, responsive to economic
pressures. Yet, its political institutions and its distribution of
social power, unlike those of more modern times, were un-
ashamedly hierarchical, hereditary, and privileged; economic
activity was on a human scale (though often not wearing a
human face); change was generally occurring at a pace people
could adapt to; custom still enjoyed great authority; and deep-
rooted particularism, grounded on community loyalties, shaped
what remained a face-to-face society. All this was possible
because people were not breathing down each other's necks, for
by our standards England was – in 1700 and still in 1800 –
empty. Competition for living space, natural resources, and
livelihoods was not so cut-throat, or so sternly dictated by
impersonal economic iron laws as it was to become. Runaway
population rise and tumultuous industrial change, building up

in the last third of the eighteenth century but not coming to a peak until the nineteenth, were to change all that.

The following chapters attempt to interweave themes and chronology. In Chapter 1, I offer a flavour of Georgian society by highlighting its particularity and diversity: the poles of experience between rich and poor, young and old, male and female, town and country, North and South; between England and other places where English-speaking people lived; between England and the other nations of Europe. Regions became more mutually integrated and dependent during the century, largely owing to the growth of market relations, yet England also remained a patchwork of distinctive local communities – a fact that must silently temper all the generalizations I venture. In Chapters 2 and 3, I depict the different social groupings and their interrelations, stressing their hierarchical inequalities, their frictions, yet the fundamental stability of the overall structure. The social entrenchment of the propertied was reinforced because they effectively monopolized the inflexions of power: land, status, patronage, office, and political and legal authority within the state. In Chapter 4, I further emphasize how social solidarity was internalized by inherited patterns of reproduction and continuity: the dovetailing of family life with economic life, home with work-place; the roles of household, labour, and community in integrating individuals into their social position; the conditioning effects of education and religion.

In Chapters 5 and 6, I turn to explore the generation of *change* and its impact in the economy and in society. Overcoming traditional distaste and 'paternalist' scruple, the titled, rich and powerful increasingly gave their backing to the pursuit of wealth and its accompanying consumerist culture. The newly acceptable acquisitiveness and opportunism had certain socially accommodating and integrative effects, helping to create a consensus amongst the affluent and the aspirant. Yet new moneyed wealth (with its poor relation, new poverty) was also a social solvent. Gaps were opening between successful capitalists and the proletarianized, between patrician and plebeian cultures. These simultaneous processes of cultural consensus and cultural atomization are further explored in Chapter 7, which examines the attempts of the 'polite' to validate more egoistical life-styles within this 'opportunity society' under the cloaks of liberty, progress, and refinement. 'Civilization' could be held as both a carrot and a stick before the lower orders. Chapters 8 then scrutinizes the acceleration of industrialization, seen as the progeny of the earlier unhindered development of a market economy – but as a wild and unruly progeny.

Pioneered by the *nouveaux riches* and their development of new manufacturing towns, industrialization was a challenge to old ways. It threatened the unity of home and work-place, the traditional family working unit; it also threatened to replace the 'moral economy' with political economy, and values such as 'politeness', 'tradition', and 'deference' with marginal utility. In the concluding chapter, I therefore pose the question of how far, by endorsing capitalism, the scions of Georgian society were digging their own graves and producing a parricidal brood – industrialism, a self-confident manufacturing bourgeoisie, a desperate proletariat, and political disaffection. I conclude that what the challenge of these new forces – fanned by the French Revolution – chiefly reveals is the tenacity and elasticity of the Old Order.

One way in which the Georgian century teetered on 'modernity' is that – more than previous ages – it tried to weigh and measure itself. This primitive auto-analysis opens up the tantalizing prospect of quantified history. Yet most attempts by Georgian political arithmeticians to draw a statistical anatomy of England are unreliable (revealing mainly for what they tell us about their compilers' assumptions). Sophisticated attempts have been made recently to use raw eighteenth-century data as building bricks for quantified profiles of social trends (particularly in the pioneer work of the Cambridge Group for the History of Population and Social Structure, which uses parochial documents to trace literacy, population movements, and family patterns). Such 'number-crunching' is immensely valuable. Yet it cannot escape being based on irremediably defective foundations. In their registers, parish clerks recorded Anglican baptisms, marriages, and burials. We can only guess (and some guesses are better informed than others) what proportion of births got registered as baptisms, of unions as marriages, of deaths as burials; or indeed what proportion of the population was Anglican. In any case, these proportions doubtless varied from place to place and from time to time. We have official excise returns for trade imports and exports, but no records for contraband; we can enumerate criminal prosecutions but not lawlessness. Moreover, deference to statistics runs the risk of creating mists of mythical 'averages' which veil the significant contours. To have much faith, for example, in measures of 'average wages' in eighteenth-century England would be misguided. Not only was there no average person, but for few did the recorded money wages alone represent total 'income' or 'livelihood'. Even assessing wage differentials from region to region, or from decade to decade, makes sense only if we can be confident (and usually we cannot) that we are comparing like social realities with like. I offer figures in this book, but usually for graphical purposes rather than as strict and reliable indices. In my terminology, I have tried to avoid pseudo-scientific technical jargon when discussing matters such as social composition. English society was disparate, fluid, and spangled with contrasts and anomalies. No single social scientists' vocabulary or historians' shorthand captures that complexity in its entirety.

I have quoted a lot from eighteenth-century writers. I do not offer these voices from the past as 'proof' of my points. Contemporary observers had their own axes to grind – and often they were just simply wrong. However, what people experienced, believed, and uttered is no less a part of social history than what they ate. Furthermore, the comments of foreign visitors (again, often biased: many were Anglomaniacs) at least indicate what in English society seemed special to continental eyes.

This is a book essentially about England. Obviously it would have been desirable to have written a social history of England together with the English-speaking peoples but (although I have made occasional mention of other parts) that is a task of a different order. I have kept money values in contemporary units, but added a conversion table. I have discussed the period from about the Glorious Revolution (1688) to about the Peace of Amiens (1802), and this is what I refer to when somewhat cavalierly using the epithets 'Georgian' and 'Hanoverian'. I have modernized punctuation in some quotations, but retained original spellings. Lastly, in writing this book I have become acutely aware how easy it is for a male historian to write as if only adult males existed – or at least as if only they made history. However, I have kept to the conventional use of 'he' or 'his' when people of both sexes are being referred to. Circumlocutions and neologisms such as 'he/she', 's/he' or 'his or her' help little, and phrases such as 'Englishmen' and 'the common man' are too rich a part of the language's heritage to be lightly jettisoned.

1. *Contrasts*

England is a rich sea, but strewn with many reefs, and those who voyage there would do well to take precautions. [Casanova]

England 'is different in every respect from the rest of Europe', thought Casanova, and all foreign commentators agreed that in some ways at least England was unique. *Vive la différence* was most Englishmen's toast. Theirs was a breezy, bigoted, chauvinism which embarrasses us now. 'I do not think there is a people more prejudiced in its own favour than the British people,' wrote the Swiss visitor César de Saussure in the 1720s; 'they look on foreigners in general with contempt, and think nothing is as well done elsewhere as in their own country.' The body politic puffed itself up with patriotism. 'I glory in the name of Briton,' boasted George III. Foreigners – 'French dogs' above all – were jostled in the streets: 'Before they learn there is a God to be worshipped,' wrote Fougeret de Montbron, 'they learn there are Frenchmen to be detested.' Even the cosmopolitan Edward Gibbon thanked 'the bounty of Nature, which cast my birth in a free and civilized country, in an age of science and philosophy, in a family of honourable rank, and decently endowed with the gifts of fortune'.

Success bred confidence. Britain's *arriviste* pride was swelled by her glorious and lucrative triumphs in the War of the Spanish Succession (1702–13), the Seven Years' War (1756–63), and from 1793 in the Revolutionary and Napoleonic wars (even if, as Admiral Vernon had warned, 'our fleets are defrauded with injustice, marred by violence and maintained by cruelty'). 'No nation,' judged the Sussex shopkeeper Thomas Turner in that *annus mirabilis* of victories, 1759, 'had ever greater occasion to adore the Almighty Disposer of all events than Albion, whose forces meet with success in all quarters of the world.' Success turned the plain-dealing, choleric, insular John Bull from a blundering butt of ridicule into a swaggerer. Victory made Jolly Jack Tars national heroes, however much ministries were abused. English boys – Samuel Johnson was an exception – ached to go to sea. In 1782 the yeoman's son William Cobbett saw the sea for the first time, and the Channel squadron riding at anchor at Spithead. 'No sooner did I see it than I wished to be a sailor' (he enlisted, but by mistake ended up in a marching regiment). The great English patriotic songs – 'God Save the King', 'Rule Britannia', 'Hearts of Oak', and 'The Roast Beef of Old England' – were all penned during this century: not just composed, but struck up lustily when the opportunity offered. Choruses of 'God Save the King' greeted George III at the theatre – more out of patriotism than love specifically for the Hanoverians. William Hogarth, who signed himself 'Britophil', caught the mood with a flattering – though double-edged – series of national stereotypes. People loved his beer-guzzling, roast-beef-eating, four-square Englishmen, the 'dread and envy' of starveling, bare-foot, onion-nibbling French peasants, oppressed by lecherous Popish priests and mincing courtiers. Abroad the English saw the Continent through eyes prejudiced by these caricatures: they saw poverty, superstition, tyranny. 'I think nothing so terrible as objects of misery,' confided Lady Mary Wortley Montagu on her travels in northern France in 1718, 'and all the country villages of France shew nothing else.'

The English postured as the 'plucky littl'un' coming from behind, a David to the Bourbon or Habsburg Goliath. Through much of the seventeenth century, Albion's island had bobbed fitfully on and off the European power map. Eclipsed by the Sun King, Charles II had been a client, James II a tool. Even during the eighteenth century, England's native resources and manpower remained puny compared to those of Bourbon France, Habsburg Austria, or Romanov Russia. In 1700 there were well over three Frenchmen to every Englishman (in 1800 the ratio was still over two and a half to one). There were twice as many Italians as English, and fewer English even than Spaniards. The English saw themselves as a free, civilian, industrious people – not slaves to military despots – yet a people who, if forced, could roll up their sleeves, beat ploughshares into swords, and fight. England's peacetime standing army was pygmy by continental standards: in war in 1794 its strength was 45,000 compared to Prussia's 190,000. Certain Opposition ideologues and backwoodsmen, fearing tyranny, wanted to abolish it altogether, devolving the bearing of arms on to local citizen militias, such as Edward Gibbon served in. Unlike sailors, soldiers were rarely popular, and the armed forces were recruited in a hand-to-mouth way. In war, the Royal Navy requisitioned ships and sailors from the merchant marine, and press-ganged men in ports. British warships long remained inferior in design to the French or Spanish ones, some disintegrating at sea, making 'Gravesend voyages'. Yet this offhand approach did not stop Britannia ruling the waves in a century of global and scarcely checked imperial expansion.

Englishmen saw their vices as virtues and indulged them with brio. They liked being thought bloody-minded roughnecks. 'Anything that looks like a fight,' observed the Frenchman Henri Misson, 'is delicious to an Englishman' – something even a lord could confirm. 'I love a mob,' explained the Duke of Newcastle; 'I headed one once myself.' Even the top people duelled (it took gentlemen to make a duel). In 1712 the Duke of Hamilton and Lord Mohun met; both died. In 1789 the Duke of York fought Colonel Lennox. In 1798 Prime Minister William Pitt and George Tierney, a leading Whig, exchanged shots. In 1770, following a pupil rebellion, the Riot Act had to be read at Winchester School. At Rugby the young gentlemen mined the head's study with gunpowder. Yet fighting was rated manly, and pugnacity (alias 'love of liberty') preferable to servility. Better to be 'governed by a mob, than a standing army', thought Charles James Fox.

The English – so foreigners saw them – ate to excess, drank like lords, and swore like troopers (amongst 'cunning women', cursing was still a fine art). Henry Herbert, ninth Earl of Pembroke, was 'so blasphemous at tennis that the primate of Ireland was forced to leave off playing with him'. Though Dr Johnson 'could not bear anything like swearing', he was in a minority, since in his day even fashionable ladies habitually swore; the air of their levées was as blue as their stockings later became. The German pastor Karl Moritz joked that a traveller arriving in

London might believe everyone was called 'Damme'. The native idiom had not yet been disinfected by delicacy. House-hunting early in married life, the Newcastle man Henry Carr told a friend that his wife 'wanted a canny hole of her own to fart in, to use a Northern expression'. And every gallant had his gal: 'where is male chastity to be found?' bemoaned John Wesley (himself no stranger to the lusts of the flesh).

Few cared. Tourists hacked at 'Shakespeare's chair' in Stratford (the German philosopher Lichtenberg paid 1s. for a sliver), and chiselled souvenir flakes off Stonehenge. Cathedral walls are scrawled with eighteenth-century graffiti. The helpless were fair game. The fifth Earl of Berkeley seduced the seventeen-year-old daughter of a Gloucester tradesman – and then had seven children by her, eventually marrying her. Yet such no-nonsense behaviour was admired for its gusto, pluck, and 'bottom'. In the countryside the same earl, waylaid by a high-wayman, unhesitatingly shot him. In the Commons, Prime Minister Sir Robert Walpole munched Norfolk apples to show he was at heart just a plain-dealing squire; he was proud to be thought 'no saint, no Spartan, no reformer'. When they could not be passed off as virtues, certain vices such as hypochondria or cantankerousness could be put down to the island's climate, or to those other darling traits of the English character, eccentricity and contrariety. 'We are precarious, uncertain, wild, enduring mortals,' rhapsodized that normally crusty gentleman, John Byng, 'and may we so endowed continue, the wonder and balance of the universe.' In the guise of a Spanish tourist, the poet Southey commented in 1807:

The English love to be at war, but do not love to pay for their amusement; and now that they are at peace, they begin to complain that the newspapers are not worth reading, and rail at the French as if they really wished to begin again. There is not a people upon the earth who have a truer love for their Royal family than the English, yet they caricature them in the most open and insolent manner. They boast of the freedom of the press, yet as surely and systematically punish the author who publishes anything obnoxious, and the book-seller who sells it, as we in our country should prevent the publication. They cry out against intolerance and burn down the houses of those whom they regard as heretics. They love liberty; go to war with their neighbours, because they choose to become republicans, and insist upon the right of enslaving the negroes. They hate the French and ape all their fashions, ridicule their neologisms and then naturalize them, laugh at their inventions and then adopt them, cry out against their political measures and then imitate them; the levy in mass, the telegraph, and the income tax are all from France. And the common people, not to be behind hand with their betters in absurdities, boast as heartily of the roast beef of Old England, as if they were not obliged to be content themselves with bread and potatoes. Well may punch be the favourite liquor of the English – it is a truly emblematic compound of contrarieties.

But did the English have anything to be proud about? In 1700 theirs was still a minor rustic nation of hamlets and villages. Outside London it had no town to match even Bologna, Liège, or Rouen in size. Nearly 80 per cent of the population lived in the countryside, and almost 90 per cent were employed either in agriculture or in processing rurally produced raw materials. By later standards, England was empty: its population in 1700 of barely 5 million is about the same as the present-day population of Surrey, Kent, and Middlesex. Millions of acres were waste, heath, bog, or fen. Roads were perhaps worse than the Romans had left them:

> Cleveland in the clay
> Bring two shoes and carry one away.

The harvest was still, in 1700, the heartbeat of the economy. Would there be enough bread to eat? And how much would it cost? The weather held the answer. And, according to whether it shone or poured, the country reposed or rioted, business boomed or drooped, interest rates and capital investment levels see-sawed. Industry fed off the soil: timber, hides, hops, flax, madder, saffron, horn for knife-handles, bones for glue, were among its essential raw materials. And most industry was cottage industry: spinning, lace-making, stocking-knitting, tanning, smithying, and coopering went on in villages more than in large towns. Family life and work danced in step with the phases of the year. From harvesting, fruit-picking, or fishing to chimney-sweeping, work was seasonal. Social life – with its feasts, fasts, and fairs, its post-harvest bonfires and enforced winter unemployment – syncopated with the rural rhythms of toil and tribulation, abundance, and leisure.

Few got fat off the land, and many scratched Lenten livings off hungry soil. All-weather outdoor toil took its toll: it was a grind of immeasurable fatigue. Gregory King, the pioneer statistician, estimated near the end of the seventeenth century that about half the families in England were not earning a subsistence. And yet one critical watershed *had* been passed. English husbandry had undoubtedly under-used resources, for Gregory King thought a quarter of the land was unproductive in 1688, and Arthur Young, touring the North nearly a century later, could still comment, 'It is extremely melancholy to view such tracts of land as are indisputably capable of yielding many beneficial crops, lie totally waste.' But – as everybody noted – the rural economy was far better capitalized, and more businesslike and productive, than almost any on the Continent, where east of the Elbe serfs were still legally yoked to the soil, and debt-ridden, share-cropping peasants starved on subdivided holdings elsewhere. Famine had caused mass mortality in Stuart England, and subsistence crises still traumatized many parts of Europe (including Ireland) well into the eighteenth century. Between 1696 and 1697 famine killed about one third of the population of Finland, and close on a million people died of starvation in France in 1769. Throughout the century the rural economies of many regions of Europe were still suffering from over-population and under-production: chronic indebtedness, exhausted soil, paltry grain yields, uneconomic fragmentation of holdings, and population pressure spelt mass misery and periodic disasters. But the English had earned a pardon from this death sentence. People did not starve to death *en masse* in England any more. Bad harvests produced short-falls of grain, but not absolute dearth. Indeed, grain was exported on an increasing scale in the first half of the century. Shortages were brief, local, and of particular crops only, and their effects were cushioned by better transport of supplies and the capitalization of the grain trade. Grain rioters in England protested not against the absence of corn, but against its dearness, maldistribution, and profiteering, or about being reduced to eating rye bread instead of wheaten.

By the turn of the eighteenth century England had in this one respect escaped the 'biological *ancien régime*', the remorseless pressure of population upon rigid land and food supply, which had dogged Europe since the eve of the Black Death. Food output was becoming more elastic, thanks to such early agricultural breakthroughs as the spread of convertible husbandry, new rotations, fodder crops, and fen drainage. Yet microorganisms were still the absolute princes of English people's bodies. Medicine was not yet winning the battle against disease and death. In twentieth-century England death is the visitor of the aged; in 1700 almost the reverse was true. Far more people died young than old. Up to one in five babies died in their first year; perhaps one in three infants died – of various fevers – before the age of five. In the 1740s in certain London parishes about three in four children died before the age of six. The deaths of children had to be accepted. Mrs Thrale, wife of the great London brewer, 'regarded the death of various daughters at school with great equanimity'. Up to a point chances of survival improved with age. England had a very youthful population profile – over half the nation in 1700 was under twenty-one – but a population ever vulnerable. Overall life expectancy was about thirty-five years.

The grim reaper was no snob: in fact, he paid more calls on the poor than the great. Pauper children died like flies, especially during the generation of severe epidemics and the Gin Craze in the 1720s. But the gentry were not immune: all Edward Gibbon's six brothers and sisters died in infancy (he himself barely survived a sickly youth – 'I swallowed more physick than food'), and none of Queen Anne's children lived to grow up. Tens of thousands of mothers died in childbed. Plague had mercifully quitted England before the century began (no thanks to doctors; possibly rats had become immune to the disease), and medicine disarmed smallpox through inoculation and vaccination before the century was out. But fevers, the 'panzer divisions of death' – typhus, dysentery, measles, influenza – rampaged unchecked in epidemic waves, shattering the flimsy defences of the medical pharmacopoeia. Death struck out of the blue. The *Northampton Mercury* reported in 1771:

Last Thursday se'nnight a most Melancholy Accident happened; two Farmers went to a Neighbour's House to view a sick Calf, the

Weather was then most intensely cold; while they were handling the
Calf it went mad, and slaver'd on each of them; alarmed at this, they
by Advice of Friends, set off to bathe in the Sea; but on the Tuesday
following they were brought back dead in a Cart, to the Terror of the
whole neighbourhood.

But if death was a mystery of Providence there were also the
endemic evils society condemned people to, meted out according to their class, sex, or trade: industrial diseases such as silicosis
for potters, cancers for chimney-sweeps, and anthrax for butchers; rickets and scurvy for scarecrow paupers; rheumatism for
farm labourers – but also gout and dropsy for hard-drinking
squires and spinal deformities for their swaddled babes and
tight-laced, wasp-waisted daughters. Cosmetic poisoning defaced the fashionable – Lady Coventry reputedly died poisoned
by lead-based cosmetics.

It was the powerful who sliced up the cake of the nation's
wealth. For 1688, Gregory King thought that the least a family
(say, a man, his wife, and three children) could live on, without
getting into debt or taking poor relief or charity, was about
£40 a year. He believed that peers' families netted about £2,800
(an underestimation: their purses were perhaps twice as big),
but most of the working population lived below the bread-line.
For instance, 364,000 'labouring people and servants' had family
incomes of £15 a year; 400,000 'cottagers and paupers' were on
£6 10s. a year; 50,000 seamen on £20; and 35,000 soldiers on
£14: together, over half the families in the country. His calculations suggest that the top 1.2 per cent of the population
possessed 14.1 per cent of the national income; the bottom 67.1
per cent a mere 29.9 per cent of it.* The figures in King's
pioneer political arithmetic are not gospel: his sources were
limited and he had axes of his own to grind. But his general
profile stands. King thought that most family units in the
labouring classes were irremediably in a poverty trap because
they could not earn as much as they needed for subsistence.
With no irony intended, King labelled these people,
the country's labour force, 'persons decreasing the wealth of
the country'. 'Suppose the rich grind the face of the poor, what

*In 1980 the top 1 per cent owned 25 per cent of all personal wealth in England.

remedy against such oppression can be found in a Christian country?' No one answered John Wesley's question.

Poverty meant lives of deprivation and dependence: relying on bread as the main foodstuff; freezing in shacks and cellars; having animals occasionally living under the same roof as humans (at least they gave warmth); enduring the petty tyranny of poor-law overseers; undergoing back-breaking toil for pittances under brutal masters, with ahead only the prospect of a pinching old age, neglected, or in a poor-house. Everyone below the plateau of skilled craftsman was undernourished. This was a biological fact but one with social causes – a consequence of the way in which the powerful, wielding the knife of the law, carved up the national wealth. Indeed, the politics of property and poverty became more explicit during the century. Take taxation. As governments sought greater revenue, decisions were made to swing the tax burden from the land tax (paid by landowners) to indirect taxation – taxes on consumables (such as salt and beer) which hit everyone. Thus, more of the ordinary man's money got syphoned off into the Treasury, where it largely financed war and paid interest to opulent fund-holders who had invested in the National Debt.

The poor were a festering problem – though not the Achilles' heel – of Georgian governments. Yet hardly anyone – not even most reformers and radicals – doubted that there always would, or indeed *should*, be rich and poor: the dependent relationship seemed as natural as that between husband and wife or master and servant:

> God bless the squire and his relations
> And keep us in our proper stations

was the prayer not just of squires. 'Mankind are happier,' the petty bourgeois Dr Johnson was sure, 'in a state of inequality and subordination.' Parsons such as Archdeacon William Paley tried the Herculean labour of convincing the poor they were really the lucky ones: 'Some of the necessities which poverty imposes . . . are not hardships but pleasures.' Certainly the horrors of grinding toil and chill penury were expunged for a very few by meteoric ascent: John Taylor, beginning work as a journeyman, rose to become a button manufacturer and founder of

Lloyds Bank, leaving a fortune of £200,000. But to most working men, women, and children, work, deprivation, and suffering were the basic facts of life.

The social hierarchy was another basic fact. Few questioned that there should be aristocrats and 'shopocrats', nobility and 'mobility' ('nobs' and 'mobs'), lords, esquires, Mr and Mrs, down to plain Hodge; that at the theatre, polite society should sit in the stalls and the commonalty make pandemonium in the gallery (claques and fribbles catcalled in the pit); that, in town, the Quality should reside in squares and rows, while the middling sort dwelt in courts, and the poor festered in alleys and warrens; or that in a large house the better-off should bask on the first floor, while servants and the down-at-heel shivered in dingy garrets and cellars. Accent and idiom, dress, address, and addresses echoed status differences. 'Upside-down world' satires such as *The Beggar's Opera*, which caricatured Walpole and the great as gangsters, or the radicalism which taunted King George with the names 'King David' (a Yorkshire counterfeiter) or 'Captain Ludd', exposed the hollow world of titles but underwrote those same adamantine hierarchies in their sleep.

The regime of the great was little anchored in genetics: unlike their Habsburg cousins, they were not worshippers of blue blood. But it had biological consequences. The wealthy were healthier and lived longer; sexually they probably matured earlier; being taller, they literally looked down on the poor. Their lives were lived by a different clock – for example, the poor rose, ate, and slept early (lighting was costly), the rich late. The show of superiority and deference was emphasized by the encrusted rituals of bowing and scraping, head-baring, standing, curtseying, and knuckling foreheads.

Yet suffering was *everyone's* lot sooner or later, low- or high-born. Physical pain, a great leveller, was always awaiting its cue. There were no anaesthetics, and alcohol was the best pain-killer. People had to cope philosophically, and religiously, with disease (but the English were also noted for suicide). In 1776 Parson Woodforde had John Reeves the local farrier draw a tooth, 'but shockingly bad indeed, he broke ... one of the fangs of the tooth and it gave me exquisite pain all the day after, and my face was swelled prodigiously ... Gave the old man that drew it however 0-2-6. He is too old, I think to draw teeth, can't see very well.' Pain's henchmen were discomfort and danger. The unfortunate traveller shared his bed with strangers and fleas, and his roads with gibbeted corpses and highwaymen. 'I was robbed last night as I expected,' wrote Lord North, the Prime Minister, in 1774; 'our loss was not great, but as the postillion did not stop immediately one of the two highwaymen fired at him – It was at the end of Gunnersbury Lane.' Horace Walpole, shot at in Hyde Park, wryly observed, 'One is forced to travel, even at noon, as if one was going to battle.' Yet people travelled more and more.

It was a raw life. Practically all youngsters were thrashed at home, at school, and at work – and child labour was universal. Blood sports such as cock-fighting were saluted as trials of skill and courage. Criminals were publicly whipped, pilloried, and hanged. Jacobites' heads were spiked on Temple Bar till 1777. Work-animals were driven unremittingly: England was notoriously 'hell for horses', and things did not improve with industrialization and the craving for speed.

People were not squeamish about inflicting or bearing physical pain. Cudgelling was a favourite West Country sport, and village football sometimes led to deaths. Sailors boasted of the thousands of lashes they had borne. Turbulence simmered and occasionally boiled over. Benjamin Franklin, writing in 1769, was staggered:

I have seen, within a year, riots in the country, about corn; riots about elections; riots about workhouses; riots of colliers, riots of weavers, riots of coal-heavers; riots of sawyers; riots of Wilkesites; riots of government chairmen; riots of smugglers, in which custom house officers and excisemen have been murdered, the King's armed vessels and troops fired at.

Life was cheap and people had to have strong stomachs. In 1764 two drunken bricklayers were casually lobbing bricks at each other in Gray's Inn Lane. One was struck on the right temple and killed. In the same year a Tooley Street porter drank three pints of gin for a 2s. 6d. wager and expired half an hour later. Until 1789 women were occasionally burned alive at the stake for murdering their husbands (the crime of petty treason), though a kind hangman might strangle them before the flames reached them. When a seven-year-old girl was hanged in Norwich for stealing a petticoat, no one protested. Condemned felons were often more concerned to be 'launched into eternity' in style at the gallows than to try to escape: the crowd demanded a brave end. But mobs could also take the law into their own hands. In Bristol in 1735 James Newth, condemned to hang for murdering his wife, poisoned himself, and the mob saw him buried instead of strung up. Incensed, they dug up the suicide's body and, as the *Gentleman's Magazine* put it, 'dragged his guts about the highway, poked his eyes out, and broke almost all his bones'.

No doubt gentlemen enjoyed reading that report, for executions were not just plebeian entertainments. George Selwyn, the necrophiliac rake, notoriously got sexual pleasure from hangings. There were permanent wooden grandstands round Tyburn Tree, called Mother Proctor's Pews, and their owner had good congregations. When Earl Ferrers was hanged in 1760 Mother Proctor took a collection of £500: Englishmen loved a lord, even unto death. Crowds also flocked to see convicted whores stripped to the waist and whipped. Papists and witches were still greatly feared. In 1700 a mob at St Albans did a reputed witch to death. A newspaper in 1751 reported:

Last Saturday a ragged beggar came to a Public House in Puckle-Church in Gloucestershire, to ask Charity of some countrymen who were drinking there, who told him, in a joking manner, they used to hang all Beggars and would hang him; he told them he was not fit to die; but they taking hold of him, he begg'd they would do him no harm; however they got a Rope, put it about his Neck, and drew him up to a Bacon Rack, and bid him cry Bacon; to which they hung him so long, that he seem'd without Life, his tongue extending from his Mouth, so let him fall again, and perceiving they had carried their Folly too far, and being frightened with the Apprehension of what might ensue, carried the Beggar to a neighbouring Field, and laid him under a Hay-Rick for dead. He recovered his senses, and making mournful groans, a Woman heard him, and upon approaching the Hay-Rick, the poor Man gave her instruction by signs, how he came in that Condition, and pointed to the House where he receiv'd the Injury, and died soon after.

The Hanoverians inherited a hard-working, hard-living, plain-speaking nation which only gradually became concerned with refinement. The Duchess of Northumberland entered in her diary for 6 May 1760: 'Went home; voided a large stone. Tired to death. Went to ball; tired to death. A Bad Supper. Miss Townshend drunk.' People almost never bathed. Before cottons became cheap, clothes were difficult to wash; children in particular were often sewn into theirs for the winter. There had to be rat-catchers royal and flea-catchers royal. In the 1770s Andrew Cooke advertised himself as 'Bug Destroyer to His Majesty'. Chamber-pots were providing in dining-room sideboards for men, to save breaking up the conversation. Back in the 1660s Pepys had thought nothing of defecating into a fireplace (servants cleaned up the mess), and had himself caught Lady Sandwich 'doing something upon the pot' in the dining-room. Food hygiene was no better than personal hygiene. The omnipresence of animals meant the streets were full of dung. What we have above all lost from the world we have lost is the stench; eyes were less offended than noses, for much was invisible in a world lit by candles and rush-lights.

There was a high tolerance of inconvenience and squalor. People co-existed with these by pursuing pleasures and passions. Emotion was near the surface. The English leapt to cheer and jeer, and despite Lord Chesterfield's strictures they laughed and cried out loud. People jested and capered, sang and shouted a lot; they hurled themselves into fun-making, love-making, noise-making. They joined in rough sports, liked horse-play, and rode hard. As a national institution the stiff upper lip came later (though many, Dissenters in particular, took comfort in being earnest).

Alcohol gave stimulus, release, oblivion. The *Gentleman's Magazine* for 1770 listed ninety-nine ways of calling a man drunk, from the genteel 'sipping the spirit of Adonis' to the vulgar 'stripping me naked'. To gain a reputation as a blade one had to be at least a three-bottle man. Sheridan, Pitt the Younger, and the Greek scholar Porson were all reckoned six-bottle men, and Dr John Campbell supposedly could drink thirteen bottles of port a day. Blackstone wrote his *Commentaries on the Laws of England* with a glass of port as his companion – but Oxford dons were notorious for what Gibbon called 'their dull and deep potations'. The third Cambridge professor of history died after a drunken fall. Eminent gentlemen, from Addison and Boling-broke to Charles James Fox and Lord Eldon, were all bottle-struck. 'Drunk as a lord' was a very apt phrase. And they drank competitively. As man-about-town William Hickey put it, 'I was always ambitious of sitting out every man at the table when I presided.' Hard drinking obeyed no social boundaries. In his youth, Samuel Johnson remembered, 'all the decent people in Lichfield got drunk every night, and were not the worse thought of'. The shopkeeper Thomas Turner's diary shows people of substance in rural Sussex no less befuddled in the 1750s. After one head-splitting revel, he remorsefully recorded, 'we continued drinking like horses, as the vulgar phrase is, and singing till many of us were very drunk, and then we went to dancing, and pulling wigs, caps and hats; and thus we continued in this frantic manner, behaving more like mad people than they that profess the name of Christians'. And of course the intoxication of many of the London poor in the Gin Craze was lethal: 'Drunk for a penny, dead drunk for tuppence; straw free.'

As a solace of the flesh, gluttony was honourable. In an agricultural society, where food was home-produced, hand-some eating was a token of success, and hospitality admired. Englishmen tucked in and took pride in their boards and bellies. Until the elongated fashions of the Regency dandies and the Romantics, who made consumptive thinness *à la mode*, men and women were pleased to be corpulent and were as resigned to gout as to the laws of cause and effect. 'Sir,' said Dr Johnson, 'I mind my belly very well, for I look upon it that he who will not mind his belly will scarcely mind anything else.' 'He lived in a strange voluptuous manner, caring for nothing but his guts,' was Thomas Wilson's verdict on Bishop Hildersley. 'The goose is a silly bird,' worried Samuel Ogden, Dr Johnson's favourite sermon-writer, 'too much for one, and not enough for two.' Wiser Cambridge dons, however, clearly found fowl medicinal: Thomas Gray recorded how Dr Ridlington, a Fel-low of Trinity Hall, dying of dropsy, 'prescribed himself a boiled chicken entire and five quarts of small beer', and re-covered. But it was roast beef which was the Englishman's sacramental meal, immortalized in Hogarth's prints (Hogarth expired soon after finishing a steak), Fielding's song 'The Roast Beef of Old England', and the Sublime Society of Beefsteaks. Parson Woodforde, whose diary is a meticulous record of his belly, scratched this last entry the day he died: 'Very weak this morning, scarce able to put on my clothes and with great difficulty get downstairs with help. Dinner today, roast beef etc.' Life's pains were people's fate. But, from the splenetic don to the bent-backed hedge and ditcher, at daily Hall or annual harvest-home they could hope to forget.

The topography of social relations was as imposing and established as the hills, partly because it was – in Laslett's phrase – a 'face-to-face society'. People were set into the social strata not primarily by choice, or by 'faceless' bureaucracy and paper qualifications (except for a record of baptism, marriage, and burial in parish registers, people did not automatically figure in official files), but rather by their personal connexions with others, especially authority figures: fathers, masters, husbands, patrons. People had to shift for themselves. There was no welfare state, or army of social workers, guaranteeing care from cradle to grave. How one made out depended on skills in the games of deference and condescension, patronage and favour, protection and obedience, seizing the breaks and making the most of them. He who did not take his chances was lost.

There is a harrowing report in the *Gentleman's Magazine* for 1748:

At a Christening at Beddington in Surrey the nurse was so intoxicated that after she had undressed the child, instead of laying it in the cradle she put it behind a large fire, which burnt it to death in a few minutes. She was examined before a magistrate, and said she was quite stupid and senseless, so that she took the child for a log of wood; on which she was discharged.

In J. H. Plumb's words, in Georgian society, 'without protection, the poor and the weak and the sick went under; the rich and the strong prospered'.

Slightly over half the nation was female. Yet, compared with men, we know little about what women felt, thought, and did.

It was men who left most records behind – a fact that speaks all too eloquently of how muted women were. Public life was a men-only club (as were almost all clubs themselves). There were no female parliamentarians, explorers, lawyers, magistrates, or factory entrepreneurs, and almost no women voters. For Dr Johnson, the idea of a woman preacher was 'like a dog walking on his hind legs'. A woman hoping to be accepted intellectually had to run an obstacle race. Catherine Macaulay, the republican writer, one of the few women to do so, was jeered off the track (she had also committed the heinous _faux pas_ of marrying a man half her age). In the public eye, women were laced tightly into constrictive roles: wives, mothers, house-keepers, domestic servants, maiden aunts. Few escaped. The commonness of the stereotyping created a kind of invisibility: women were to be men's shadows.

Much of our evidence about what women were like, and what they thought or were expected to think, comes from men – from sermons, courtesy manuals, and essays written by male authors, from male diarists and letter writers, from male painters and doctors. We know little about 'Tetty' Johnson or Margaret Boswell except through their husbands. Women who wrote about themselves – such as Lady Mary Wortley Montagu, or the 'bluestockings' in the salon 'petticoateries' which surrounded Mrs Delaney, Mrs Chapone, and Mrs Vesey – lamented their circumstances: the pains of pregnancy, the odiousness of suitors, the vapid tedium of polite society. But at bottom many shared men's views about women's place and the relations between the sexes. Sometimes the tone was high-minded propriety: some 'bluestockings' no less than men expected female chastity and submission. When she became pregnant out of wedlock, Mary Wollstonecraft was cold-shouldered by female friends such as the author Mrs Inchbald and the actress Mrs Siddons (were they shocked, or did they have their own reputations to think about?). 'Wit in women is apt to have bad consequences,' adjudged Elizabeth Montagu icily in 1750; 'like a sword without a scabbard, it wounds the wearer and provokes assailants. I am sorry to say the generality of women who have excelled in wit have failed in chastity.' Mrs Chapone, a fellow bluestocking, could defend a husband's 'divine right to obedience', while paradoxically asserting 'the general truth, that women as rational and accountable beings, are free agents, as well as men'. Sometimes, however, women's tone in accepting their place was cynical or resigned: self-censorship became second nature. So Lady Mary Wortley Montagu advised her daughter to 'conceal whatever learning she attains, with as much solicitude as she would hide crookedness or lameness'. This dumbness was exactly what men prescribed. Dr Gregory advised a young woman: 'If you happen to have any learning, keep it a profound secret, especially from the men.' In Samuel Richardson's influential novel, it was virtue (crudely, virginity) that got the servant Pamela her husband.

In a man's world it is not surprising that a woman parroted her master's voice. Many languished, repressed and ill, but few positively rebelled against their fate, despite its mortal dangers (tens of thousands died in childbed). Indeed, it was easier to renounce male–female intercourse than to find ways to reform it. Thus Mary Astell, the early eighteenth-century Greek scholar, dreamed of college retreats ('nunneries') where spinster academics could pursue religion and scholarship. But there was no organized 'feminist' movement campaigning for women's rights in public life – just brave individuals, misfits, victims, and rebels, from the satirical playwright Mrs Mary Manley at the beginning of the century to Mary Wollstonecraft at the end.

The basic assumption which governed relations between the sexes and underlay attitudes and institutions, backed ultimately by law, was that men and women were indelibly different in nature and capacity and so ought to play quite distinct social roles. Anatomy determined one's destiny, and men were designed to be on top. Men were intended (said men) to excel in reason, business, action, decision; women's forte was to be passive, maternal, submissive, modest, docile, and virtuous (reality, however, was not so simple: men were terrified of 'shrewishness'; husbands who capitulated to 'petticoat government' were laughing-stocks). High public office, the professions, the universities, and the Church were closed to women (many, however, such as Sarah Churchill and the Duchess of Devonshire, exercised immense behind-the-scenes power, because of their high rank, breeding, and force of personality). Throughout their lives they were as far as possible to depend on men – as daughters, on their fathers, and, once wives, on the 'masculine dominion' of their husbands. At the beginning of the century it was still usual amongst the landed classes for a father to arrange his daughter's marriage: she would at best have the right to veto his choice. In common law, wives had no rights over their children or to matrimonial property (though land could be held in trust for wives). This was because, in Blackstone's words, 'In marriage husband and wife are one person, and that person is the husband': 'the very being, or legal existence, of the woman is suspended during marriage.' 'Women in England,' an early eighteenth-century book put it, 'with all their moveable goods so soon as they are married are wholly *in potestate viri*, at will and disposition of the husband'; even a woman's 'very necessary apparel, by the law, is not hers, in property'. A husband had the right to beat his wife, ruled a judge, so long as the stick was no thicker than a man's thumb. A married woman could make a will only with her husband's consent, and after her death he could have it set aside. Whereas men could be themselves, women had to think of how they would appear in men's eyes and how they could conform to the sort of expectations men had of them: for instance, in Samuel Richardson's novel, *Pamela*, Mr B. set out some forty rules for what he expected in a wife.

Many men judged women to be simply inferior, the weaker vessel. 'There is inequality in the sexes,' thought Lord Halifax. For Lord Chesterfield, 'women are children of a larger growth' – 'a man of sense only trifles with them'. And so in polite society the sexes were segregated – more than they were, say, in France. Frenchwomen could preside over the salons of the *philosophes*: English ladies were encouraged to conserve their strength by indulging only in tea-table gossip and ornamental pastimes such as embroidery. As for talk, a lady's was assumed to be small, tittle-tattle in fact: society ladies withdrew after dinner, leaving the heroes to settle the nation's destiny, toast their mistresses with bumpers, and drink themselves under the table. 'Imbecility in females is a great enhancement of their personal charms,' observed the acid Jane Austen.

Obedient females were type-cast as the guardian angels of family and virtue, as James Thomson's unctuous verses show:

> Well-ordered Home Man's best delight to make;
> And by submissive wisdom, modest skill,
> With every gentle care-eluding art,
> To raise the virtues, animate the bliss,
> And sweeten all the toils of human life:
> This be the female dignity and praise.

In polite society a lady's chastity before marriage, and fidelity after, were crucial for gentlemen. Men generously conceded that they themselves could not match such Alps of sexual purity, but as Dr Johnson explained, 'If we require more perfection from women than from ourselves it is doing them honour.' Aside from the yellow-eyed monster of male jealousy, this double standard expressed a practical fear. No husband could contemplate a cuckoo in his nest, nor would he wish to bequeath his property to a son unless he was sure of paternity. Dr Johnson did not beat about the bush: 'The chastity of women is of all importance, as all property depends on it.' By contrast, 'between a man and his wife, a husband's infidelity is nothing . . . Wise married women don't trouble themselves about infidelity in their husbands . . . The man imposes no bastards upon his wife.' (The fates of serving-wenches, milliners, and mistresses did not even get into that Christian's reckoning.) A wife's adultery was ground enough in law for a husband to obtain a divorce, but not *vice versa* (although divorces were very rare, since they required a private Act of Parliament). In reality, however, society ladies – especially in London – were much less submissive than these stereotypes suggest, some being happy to collude in men's clandestine games of flirtation and conquest. Moreover, force of character, charm, inherited wealth, or family backing made many ladies heiresses or matriarchs with enormous bargaining strength and a chance to influence family destinies.

In affluent society, boys and girls, even small ones, were educated separately. Girls were much more likely to be consigned to nurses, servants, and aunts, and fewer were sent away to school. They were thus 'nurs'd upon ignorance and vanity'. Lady Mary Wortley Montagu wrote of her nurse, 'She took so much pains, from my infancy, to fill my head with superstitious tales and false notions, it was none of her fault I am not at this day afraid of witches and hobgoblins or turned methodist.' Young ladies were groomed with matrimony uppermost in view, and with reason. If a daughter failed to trap a husband, she might become an 'old maid', a burden on her family, forced into a frustrating post as lady's companion or governess, with no independence and paltry wages, existing in a no-man's land between family and servants.

When a gentleman was looking round for a husband for his daughter in the early-Georgian matrimonial market, his prime considerations were security, family, title, and land. Matrimony was not narrowly about the couple's happiness, but was a matter of family policy, securing the line's honour and fortunes – and families were patrilineal. Sir William Temple had not been too cynical when he wrote, 'Our marriages are made, just like other common bargains and sales, by the mere consideration of interest or gain, without any love or esteem.' Fathers had to dangle handsome dowries as bait to catch well-connected, landed, titled husbands for their daughters. Up to £25,000 might be needed to hook a peer. Newspaper announcements made no attempt to disguise the horse-trading:

MARRIAGES

25 March 1735, John Parry, Esq. of Carmarthenshire, to a daughter of Walter Lloyd, Esq. member for that county, a fortune of £8,000.
The Lord Bishop of St Asaph to Miss Orell, with £30,000.
Married, the Rev. Mr Roger Waind, of York, about twenty six years of age, to a Lincolnshire lady, upwards of eighty, with whom he is to have £8,000 in money, £300 per annum and a coach-and-four during life only.

In good society, marriage was recommended as an alliance of sense. Sensibility – still more, sensuality – were suspect; giddy romance would wither on stony soil. A circumspect settlement might allow an everyday respect to take deep root between husband and wife; but it was the successful aggrandizement of name and acres which probably mattered most to hard-headed families, marriageable daughters (and sons) being merely strategic pawns (though as pawns they had some power). Cheapened by market-place haggling, small wonder holy matrimony was cynically viewed. As Jarrett has written, 'The world of the popular prints was one in which the marriages of labourers disintegrated into violence, while those of noblemen degenerated into vice.' Daughters loathed being served up as sacrifices to strangers 'People in my way are sold like slaves, and I cannot tell what price my masters will put on me,' wrote Mary Wortley Montagu, who, detesting her father's choice of mate, eloped. Yet if matrimony had many pains, spinsterhood had no pleasures (in any case, as the witticism went, it was worth enduring marriage for the benefits of widowhood), and, unlike men, few women remained single by choice. A wife might at least have the run of a house and financial security.

Once married, a lady in polite society had four cardinal functions. The first duty was to obey her husband. Second, she was an heir-producing machine. Women's letters harrowingly chronicle the fatigue, ill-health, and premature ageing they suffered as time after time they grew full-bellied. Lady Bristol, who married at the age of nineteen in 1695, bore a son in 1696, a daughter in 1697, a son in January 1699 and another in December in the same year, and yet another in 1701. She miscarried of triplets in the same year, produced a son and a daughter in April 1703 and a stillborn son in 1704. Between 1706 and 1710 she bore three more sons and two daughters, and she had sons in 1712 and 1713, and daughters in 1715 and 1716. At thirty-nine she had had her last pregnancy, having produced twenty children, few of whom lived to grow up. Lady Bristol's fertility was exceptional, but there was, in general, a deep dread of the childbirth treadmill. 'I am in a great fright,' wrote Lady Caroline Fox to her husband on first indications of pregnancy, 'and if my fears prove true, I shall be vastly angry with you . . . for 'twould be very hard for me as I have not yet recovered my strength from the last lying-in.' Many tried to space their confinements, by delaying weaning their previous infant, by coitus interruptus, or simply by denying their husband access to bed, perhaps pleading illness. Patent abortifacients were advertised in newspapers. But there is little sign that women used mechanical contraceptive appliances (though French ladies had sponges and douches). Condoms (called by Casanova 'English overcoats' and by Boswell 'armour') were on sale in London, but were used to ward off venereal disease by men dallying with whores rather than as contraceptives.

Having brought an infant into the world, the early-eighteenth-century lady's duty to it was largely discharged, for affluent families hired attendants, wet-nurses and nurse-maids, and later governesses, tutors, singing teachers, and dancing masters. Ladies of breeding traditionally had little to do with the routine upbringing of their infants, for parents were not encouraged to be interested in childish things. Relations between parents and children were meant to be formal, and often distant; even in happy and succcessful families respect was more visible than affection. With child mortality high, not becoming too attached to one's children was possibly a useful defence mechanism.

The third duty of the married lady was to run the household. This involved providing food, drink, and comforts; commanding domestic servants, especially personal maids and kitchen staff; supervising accounts; and arranging entertainment. Her fourth duty was to be ladylike, an ambassadress of grace. Ladies' polite accomplishments included the arts of dressing, conversing agreeably (but not fishing in male ponds such as politics or religion), singing, or playing a delicate instrument (spinets were ideal), and cultivating taste in decoration, furnishing, and the arts – sewing, lace-making, painting with water colours.

During the century, the roles of wife and mother within the professional and landed classes began to evolve. Not that the ultimate male–female power imbalance was redressed: in 1800 women were still totally disadvantaged in law and locked out of public office. But attitudes towards marriage were changing in ways which curbed the power of parents over their offspring's choice and gave a more positive role to wives as mothers within the domestic family. Moralists and churchmen had always deplored the *mariage de convenance*, and gradually more people began to accept the superior claims of personal choice of mate, affection, and even romance. Increasingly, prospective partners were allowed to explore love (though, in polite society, not sex) before marriage. This involved giving daughters a greater say in the choice of a potential husband (with parents settling only for the right of veto, and the eloquence of the purse). A season of balls, family parties, and visits to resorts such as Bath had to be invented to give Miss more chance to sound out eligible suitors. The *quid pro quo* for this restraint on parent power was Hardwicke's Marriage Act (1753), which forbade the marriage of those under the age of twenty-one without parental consent and requiring the publishing of banns, thereby aiming to end the much-used lovers' loophole of elopements and instant, legally binding weddings performed by sympathetic or mercenary parsons (though dashing runaways could still gallop towards a matrimonial paradise in Scotland). Marrying for love became respectable. 'Anything is to be preferred or endured,' advised Jane Austen, early in the next century, 'rather than marrying without affection . . . Nothing can be compared to the misery of being bound without love.'

Warmth, and even desire, stole across the public face of married life. 'Husband and wife are always together,' wrote the Duc de La Rochefoucauld of polite society in the 1780s (he exaggerated, but hit upon the essential modulation), 'and share the same society . . . They pay all their visits together. It would be more ridiculous to do otherwise in England than it would be to go everywhere with your wife in Paris.' Spouses began treating each other less formally. Couples whose parents or grandparents had 'Sir'd or 'Madam'd each other now used familiar terms of endearment. Children were now allowed to address their parents as 'mama' and 'papa'.

Above all, the wife's domestic situation changed. As living grew more refined and the inner emotions of wifehood were cultivated, the lady's role as quartermistress of the house, as commissar of the laundry and maker of cheese, preserves, and poultices, developed upon the shoulders of the fierce, key-jangling housekeeper. (During the century, more and more household items such as soap and starch were purchased rather than home-made, in any case.) The lady became freed to culti-vate the more 'feminine' graces: her toilet, the arts of tea, shopping, spending pin-money, paying and receiving calls, philanthropy, the vapours, scents and sensibility, all encouraged and mirrored by that recent invention, the novel. Chic learn-ing, including Newtonian science, was presented palatably pre-digested in books specially written for ladies, and women's magazines such as the *Ladies' Diary* appeared, including mathematical problems, history, and geography. Spending too much time on household management, ambiguously warned a magazine in the 1740s, might win a lady 'the reputation of a notable housewife, but not of a woman of fine taste'.

Ladies made more time for the children, too. From about mid-century it became the done thing for well-bred ladies to interest themselves with nursing their babies and training toddlers – more with the delight of discovering a new pet under one's nose than the dutiful devotion of the stern Victorian matriarch – though Queen Charlotte was a foretaste of Queen Victoria. For some, maternal breast-feeding replaced hired wet-nurses; swaddling went out of fashion, partly because of mothers' new-found desire to fondle, dandle, and dress their infants. Mothers began to take their children out of servants' hands, for (as William Darrell wrote) 'peasantry is a disease (like the plague) easily caught'. Mothering and domesticity came into vogue, faithfully mirrored in the novels of Jane Austen. Joseph Addison had planted the nursery seed early in the century: 'Female virtues are of a domestic turn.' The bluestocking Mrs Chapone watered it: 'The principal virtues ... of a woman must be of a private and domestic kind.'

Becoming the angel in the house promised fulfilment to many ladies whose talents and emotions were otherwise offered no outlets whatever. Enhanced maternal affection may have provided long-overdue attention and warmth for the children too (possibly one factor in checking infant mortality, thus explaining the increasing size of grandee families). But ultimately the cult of the family merely created dolls' houses for women to live in within a man's world, underlining men's grip on the rest of society. And ladies grew doll-like, ornamental, flirtatious, delicate, helpless. As Mary Wollstonecraft remarked,

Ladies spend many of the first years of their lives in acquiring a smattering of accomplishments; meanwhile strength of body and mind are sacrificed to libertine notions of beauty, to the desire of establishing themselves – the only way women can rise in the world – by marriage. And this desire making mere animals of them, when they marry they act as such children may be expected to act, they dress, they paint, and nickname God's creatures. Surely these weak beings are only fit for a seraglio. Can they be expected to govern a family with judgment, or take care of the poor babes whom they bring into the world?

Lower down the social scale, women were spared the option of retreating into the world of mere domesticity. Among working people, marriage had always meant – alongside affection – making an astute bargain in order to set up working household partnerships. For most, marriage alone established their independence as a producer or proprietor. Through marriage, women gained the strength, protection, status, and earning power of husbands; men got the domestic management and labour of a wife (and the savings nest-egg she might bring with her). Together, men and women needed the labour and earning power of children around farmyards, in domestic industries such as textiles, and in running shops. Children were also expected to support their parents in old age. Independent women with some property (for example, widows) sometimes refused a church wedding, however, for if they married their property would pass in law to their spouse. They might prefer a 'common law' community ceremony, sanctified by such symbolic actions as jumping backwards over a broom.

We know little about what working women felt about their lives and their mates. Autobiographical writings of working *men*, such as Daniel Defoe or Francis Place, suggest that sturdy and comely housewives were often preferred as marriage partners to flighty girls. Married women might easily be reduced to the level of drudges and chattels. Indeed, highly ritualized wife sales were sometimes set up by working men – with the wife's consent – seeking to escape the 'wed-lock' (these sales being the only practical – though not legally binding – divorce ceremonies available to any but the very rich). A wife would fetch a few guineas, or might be traded in for an ox. Yet, through controlling the household, the children, the farmyard or kitchen garden, working women must often, in fact, have ruled the roost, especially those whose husbands were away as migrant workers, soldiers, or seamen. However, men avenged themselves on women who too openly wore the breeches by caricaturing them as scolds.

Particularly at the beginning of the century, it was customary for women to work alongside men. Women traditionally did heavy 'men's' work, in the fields or in industry (for example, carrying baskets of coal on their backs up mineshafts), and were commonly apprenticed to trades (there were, for instance, female barbers). And though most women worked in subordinate positions, as domestic servants, or alongside their husbands on the family smallholding or in a cottage industry, there were also independent women who tended their own flocks, or ran millinery shops, chop-houses, taverns, brothels, or even lunatic asylums. Many of these small businesswomen were daughters who had taken over from their fathers or widows who had kept on the family concern after their husbands' deaths (as, for instance, the widow of John Baskerville, the noted Birmingham typefounder). This situation was quite common as women tended to outlive men, and moreover businessmen generally took younger wives. Occasionally, a very exceptional woman smuggled herself, disguised, into the army, as did Hannah Snell, or followed a profession (Mrs Lydia Walliss became a valuer).

The coming of factories offered certain new openings for female labour, while closing others, above all dramatically curtailing domestic spinning. The textile factories of the late eighteenth century (though as yet few in number) introduced for the first time a hungry demand for concentrated female labour outside the face-to-face world of the farm, domestic service, and cottage industry. Factory work reduced the operative to a robot, and the hours were extremely taxing, but it was better paid than domestic service (though women got less than men), and not living under a master's roof probably gave single women a whiff of independence. Factory girls began to marry younger: they were freer than domestic servants, they reached their earnings peak early, and their cash savings attracted husbands.

Factory work perhaps extended the options open to young working women; but these options certainly contracted in a numerically more telling field: agriculture. Early in the century women performed largely similar tasks to men in the fields. But gradually women were made more marginal to such employment (and reduced to poorly paid tasks such as weeding), especially in the great corn belt of central and southern England. This was perhaps partly due to the growing use of heavier tools, such as the scythe, but it was mainly because of the growing surplus of male labourers. As population outstripped jobs, men commandeered the work and kept their womenfolk at home. Farmers preferred to employ men, rather than pay them poor relief. The same situation affected crafts, where it became rare for women to be apprenticed. Squeezed out of the labour market, women looked to early matrimony as their safest career bet. The eighteenth century developed the pattern of the man at work and the woman at home.

As critics pointed out at the time, most women lived in a 'Hobson's choice' world. In some ways their sights became *lowered*, as men moved into traditional female vocations such as midwifery and hair-dressing, and witches were hounded. As married lady or spinster, domestic servant or factory girl, mother or 'old maid' – with, in all cases, what Mrs Chapone called devotion to 'religion ... discretion, good sense ... good temper' – virtuous women had been placed on a pedestal which gave them little room to move, except to fall. It led to minia-tured lives of dependence, frustrations, and waste, ashes which occasionally flashed diamonds in pens such as Fanny Burney's. Of course, one option *was* to fall. In a man's world there was a honeycomb of openings for women in the sex trades, and by the standards of other centuries Georgian actresses, dancers, coquettes, courtesans, and *demi-mondaines* – women such as Kitty Fisher and Kitty Kennedy – were respected and even socially fêted. Lavinia Fenton, an ale-house keeper's daughter, went on the stage, became the mistress of the Duke of Bolton on '£400 during pleasure and £200 p.a. for life', gave him three sons, and married him on the death of his Duchess. It was easier for a woman to achieve notoriety than power.

But the great majority of women who obediently and hon-ourably did what they were told were condemned to a second-class life hedged with briars. The autobiography of Elizabeth Ham is a rare record of such a bleak existence. Born in 1783 of a Dorset yeoman family which gave her cold baths but denied her affection, Elizabeth was brought up by a cousin, offered a cheap, broken schooling in petty accomplishments,

and driven by parental hardship into a spinster existence as a
governess. Trapped between the servants and family, her work
was humiliating, empty, and bitterly lonely. Religion alone
gave her solace (though her Unitarianism itself lost her jobs).
Such was the pathetic life of a 'career girl'. But the cult of
motherhood, sensibility, and the home could also be a cage.
Every door opened on to a blank wall.

The life and death of Mary Wollstonecraft form a tragic coda
to these dilemmas. She was one of very few women who
attempted to walk clean out of the male-allotted range of female
parts, asserting *The Rights of Woman* in her book of 1792 which
complemented and challenged Tom Paine's *Rights of Man*. She
wanted women to be free to carve out careers, and proclaimed
free love to end the sexual double standard, denouncing marriage as 'legalized prostitution'. She envisaged women as independent and whole, uniting the qualities traditionally parcelled
out between Adam and Eve: rationality *and* feeling, career *and*
motherhood. Yet even in her ideas, she could not escape her
times, her autobiographical novels *Mary* and *Maria* succumbing
to modish, morbid sensibility, her concept of female fulfilment
glorying in the domestic mother, her vision of women seeing
them as born victims. And her life enacted but did not solve
these contradictions: high-minded and cerebral radicalism in
London gave way to passionate sexual involvement with an
American in Paris during the Revolution, followed by suicide
attempts when he asserted *his* freedom.

She remained utterly ambivalent about marriage and mono-
gamy. Her liaison with the philosopher William Godwin, and
marriage to him on becoming pregnant (both had denounced
matrimony), were tragically followed by death in childbed.
Her courage in the face of vilification is undeniable – Horace
Walpole dubbed her a 'hyena'. But her truncated life echoed
her fictions with novelettish doom, as she failed successively to
transcend contrarieties. Biology and society baulked escape.

Great Britain was not the least important eighteenth-century
invention. The Act of Union (1707) abolished the Scottish
Parliament by agreement, united the governments of England

and Scotland at Westminster, and established the Union Jack. In Georgian parliamentary politics, Caledonia was to lead the field in corruption. The century closed with the end of short-lived Irish parliamentary self-government, by the inclusion of Ireland in the Union in 1801. Great Britain, however, was a euphemism for greater England. No eighteenth-century monarch visited Wales, Scotland, or Ireland (though George I and George II frequently went home to Hanover).

Though some regions (Dublin and the midland valley of Scotland, for example) became anglicized, the Celtic fringes retained their identity (as did off-shore islands such as Guernsey and Man, both in effect smugglers' lairs). They stayed distinct partly because they were increasingly made to be primary producers for England's economic needs. In their contrasting ways, the Scottish and Irish economies were drastically reshaped by Westminster. John Bull's other island, anglicized Ireland, was the most colonial part of Britain, being bullied and bled by a frequently absentee Protestant landlord class. Landlords' incomes trebled during the century, largely at the expense of the indigenous Catholic peasantry, and by 1750 three quarters of a million pounds in rent was leaving Ireland annually. Bishop Berkeley thought London was the Irish metropolis, though Dublin itself was English enough. In peacetime the largest concentration of the British army had to be stationed in Ireland. Catholics, though the vast majority, suffered legal disabilities, including disfranchisement. Furthermore Irish industry was sacrificed to English manufacturers, export of Irish wool and cloth being banned from 1698, except to England. By mid-century, Ulster was already showing its industrial edge over the pastoral South, which was suffering worsening subsistence crises. Famine struck, particularly in 1726-9 and 1739-41, the latter killing 400,000. Even so, aided by potatoes and the parcellization of holdings, population climbed ominously, outpacing the English. There were over two Irish mouths to feed in 1800 for every one in 1700.

Scotland lacerated itself, becoming increasingly torn between the Jacobite-sympathizing, Gaelic-speaking Highland clans, which were proscribed after the quietus at Culloden of the Young Pretender's 1745 rebellion (40,000 Highlanders emigrated to America), and the Edinburgh–Glasgow axis of capitalist landlords, merchants, graduate lawyers, and clergy, who believed that Scotsmen's economic, cultural, and even religious future lay in throwing in their lot with England. In a sense they were right. Under post-Union free-trade, Scottish cattle-droving, linens, mining, and metal trades thrived. Agriculture and industry were modernized. Yet the sacrifice was high. Ambitious Scots anglicized their voices (the Irishman Thomas Sheridan gave them elocution lessons), disguised their names (the founder of Almack's smart London club was baptized John McCall), and took the high road south: Macs not Micks were the most resented immigrants in Hanoverian England – because of their success: they were the top engineers, surgeons, and philandering biographers.

Wales remained a backwater lacking even a capital; with fewer than 400,000 people in 1700 – not many more than Devon – it was a pastoral economy, freckled with sleepy market towns (Wrexham, the largest, had a bare 4,000 inhabitants, Cardiff just over a thousand), and mining, smelting, and quarrying villages. The province was in the hands of a native hayseed squirearchy and was left to itself: some of its Anglican bishops never set foot within the principality. Not until the 1770s did tourists swarm to the mountains, though the London-based Society for the Propagation of Christian Knowledge inspired a circulating school movement from the 1730s, printing Welsh Bibles. And where industry developed it depended upon English enterprise. The South Wales copper, iron, and coal industries, centred on Swansea and Neath, big business by the close of the century, were primed with Bristol and West Midlands capital.

Obviously, English possessions overseas also had lives of their own, aided by 'salutary neglect' (that is, a licence to the mercantile community to pillage as they chose). The Thirteen Colonies of North America were an Arcadian, open-society England without the presence of king and nobility, prelates and paupers, but with unlimited land, Indians to expropriate, and black slaves; or perhaps less 'England' than Britain, as waves of dispossessed Scots and Irish flooded in. The Thirteen Colonies expanded rapidly, a population of 340,000 in 1700 becoming 1,200,000 by 1760. By contrast, the Caribbean colonies, and, in the second half of the century, British India, offered a *pukka* England where nabobs – officials of the East India Company – could enact their plundering fantasies before a captive audience of natives: young William Hickey, in London a ne'er-do-well, had sixty-three servants as an East India Company clerk in Calcutta. Successful nabobs could hope to bring back a couple of hundred thousand pounds with them (though up to two thirds perished through tropical diseases).

When Edmund Burke indicted Warren Hastings for misrule in India in 1783, he complained: 'England has erected no churches, no hospitals, no palaces, no schools, England has built no bridges, made no highways, cut no navigations, dug out no reservoirs.' But native society was not spared much longer. By the early nineteenth century it was succumbing to the white man's mission, to Evangelicals and Utilitarians. 'Europeans lord it over the natives with a high hand,' wrote Byron's friend Edward Trelawney about India; 'every outrage may be committed with impunity.' Slaves were the precious life-blood of the West Indian economy, where King Sugar reigned, and in which £70 million had been invested by 1790. Under the *asiento* British slave-traders transported a million and a half Africans during the century: 'All this great increase in our treasure,' wrote Joshua Gee in 1729, 'proceeds chiefly from the labour of negroes in the plantations.' West African gold gave England the guinea. In 1787, Sierra Leone in West Africa was set up as a trial settlement of free blacks, as was New South Wales from 1788 for transported criminal whites. English society was irreversibly being skewed by her imperial wealth.

What was the anatomy of England itself? England was quilted out of myriad particularist, insular, chauvinistic communities. Everywhere there were hidden local economies and secret worlds. Yet by continental standards, it was a united kingdom. Unlike France, Poland, and Spain, not to mention such patchwork fantasies as the Habsburg empire, only one national group occupied the land, the writ of one law ran into all pockets, and only one language was spoken and written (Cornish became extinct about 1780). English-speakers from places as far apart as Truro and Berwick would certainly have blinked at each other's intonation and idiom, but contemporary Frenchmen were speaking languages as distinct as Basque and German, and numberless patois. Unlike their English counterparts, the noblemen of many other nations declined to speak the same tongue as their peasants. Russian counts spoke French, Danish lords German. England in 1700 was of course a society in which communications were sluggish and often arduous. The haul by road from Newcastle to London was ('God willing', as advertisements said) nine days; from Chester six days. Defoe thought a tree trunk might take three years to be dragged from Sussex to the dockyard at Chatham (it seasoned itself *en routè*). Ox waggons were common. Celia Fiennes, riding sidesaddle along the Great North Road, simply lost it. The mail was costly. All such obstacles reinforced insularity and a geography of cultural difference. Wayfarers and 'foreigners' were treated with suspicion. For their part, fenland settlements and mining encampments seemed forbidding to travellers, like tribal no-go areas. Northerners – custom had it – tucked in to potatoes and oatcakes and made their own clothes; southerners did none of these. Catholic recusancy was encrusted in old enclaves such as South Lancashire. Weights, measures, prices, wage-rates, the length of a mile, and even the time of day varied regionally.

Yet by continental standards England was highly integrated even in 1700. There were no provincial assemblies in the style of the French *parlements*. Even before newspapers became widespread, country people were remarkably *au courant* with St James and Westminster politics – partly through handwritten 'intelligences' which rattled down with stage-coaches. Already people were travelling not just on business or for health but for pleasure; and the brisk seasonal labour market ensured a high mobility of working people, townsfolk for example flocking out into the country for the harvest. Nostalgia's picture of a stable village England where the rude forefathers of the hamlet slept, where time stood still and generations of Hodges ploughed the patriarchal furrows, is – below the proprietorial classes – a myth. The turnover of families was rapid: there were more 'movers' than 'stayers'. Between 1676 and 1688, 40 per cent of the inhabitants of Clayworth in Nottinghamshire changed parish. In the late eighteenth century, 70 per cent of the population of Cardington in Bedfordshire had been born elsewhere. Boys, and to a lesser extent girls, were regularly apprenticed to tradesmen and farmers or sent into service in neighbouring villages. Most migration was local and caterpillar-like, towards the larger towns. But the brave went over the hills and far away, to London, to sea, into the army, or to the colonies (fewer English families emigrated, however, than in the seventeenth or nineteenth centuries). Unmarried farm servants and many journeymen expected to change jobs each year, offering themselves at district hiring fairs ('mops'), held in pastoral areas after lambing and in corn areas after harvest. Seasonal migratory labour (for harvesting, for instance) was vital to the economy and was not impeded by the Laws of Settlement. From the 1760s armies of navvies appeared like ants on the landscape, digging canals. And London was an irresistible honeypot for the young, offering employment, money, and excitement, or anonymity and escape. England's roads were trudged by men, sometimes families, tramping for work, their money sewn into the linings of their coats as protection against footpads. 'We daily see manufacturers [artisans] leaving the places where wages are low and removing to others where they can get more money,' observed one writer in 1752. And as roads and transport improved, mobility and interpenetration accelerated in proportion. Louis Simond, a French–American visitor during the Regency, hit on a truth when he wrote:

Nobody is provincial in this country. You meet nowhere with those persons who never were out of their native place, and whose habits are wholly local – nobody above poverty who has not visited London once in his life; and most of those who can, visit it once a year. To go up to town from 100 or 200 miles distance, is a thing done on a sudden, and without any previous deliberation. In France the people of the provinces used to make their will before they undertook such an expedition.

England was a close-knit country above all because its economy was interlocking, and at the centre London was a bottomless pit of consumption. London was England's one conurbation (even if sturgeon could still be caught at Stepney). It was the power-house of politics, law, the Court, fashion, and the arts and sciences (the Royal Society of London dated from 1660); the forge of luxury industry; the capital of finance (the Bank of England had been founded in 1694); the greatest port for overseas trade. The metropolis rubbed people up differently. Dr Johnson thought 'the full tide of human existence is at Charing Cross'. 'When a man is tired of London, he is tired of life.' For the bucolic William Cobbett, by contrast, it was 'the Great Wen', mere wastefulness. Yet all agreed that by its sheer size and wealth it dominated England. In 1700 London had approaching 700,000 inhabitants – about one in eight Englishmen, or close on half the town dwellers in the country. The next largest – toytown by contrast – was Norwich, with nearly 30,000 people. Of the rest, only Bristol, Exeter, (probably) York, Newcastle, Colchester, and Yarmouth topped 10,000. Most of the other 800 towns had just a thousand or two.

London integrated much of the kingdom, primarily by means of its economic tentacles. Foodstuffs trundled in from all quarters for London's maw. 'The neighbourhood of London sucks the vitals of trade in this island to itself,' punned Defoe. Corn floated down the Thames valley in barges from Oxfordshire; vegetables came up from Kentish market gardens; cattle and sheep were driven on the hoof from Wales, Scotland, and Leicestershire for fattening on the Thames marshes; cheese and salt came from Cheshire, fish from the Devon and Sussex coasts, poultry from Suffolk, potted chars from Lake Windermere. Early in the century 80,000 cattle and 610,000 sheep reached Smithfield a year. And non-edibles were drawn in too, above all coal, brought by coaster from Newcastle (70 per cent of Tyneside coal was destined for London). London's cash spurred fiercely competitive, go-ahead market agriculture and advanced commercial practices – long-distance credit, bills of exchange, and a commissariat of middle men: corn-badgers, chapmen, wholesale butchers, graziers and drovers, cattle-fatteners, and the like. The purveyance of London ran smoothly: Londoners did not fear the provinces would cause them to starve.

London lorded it over the kingdom in other ways as well. It became the cynosure for all other cities. In Tudor and Stuart times provincial towns had felt the pinch, in some cases suffering economic decline (itself largely due to metropolitan competi-

tion), in others erosion of political autonomy to grafting grandees and to Court. Partly because of the Reformation, civic life
had become comatose. In 1700 Birmingham had no bookshop
or assembly rooms. Tourists to the provinces viewed country
seats, not the towns. But from the late seventeenth century they
revived. Population grew, outports (especially those on the
west coast, such as Bristol, Liverpool, and Whitehaven) flourished. And, not least, provincial towns gained stature as foci of
polite society, consumption, communications, and the arts. In
search of cultural identity, the burghers of outlying towns did
not trumpet their 'provinciality' (in contrast to the Victorians,
who boasted of grassroots honesty and homespun values).
Rather they self-consciously mimicked the capital. London
town set the *ton*. Provincial fashion impresarios cloned London's
pleasure gardens, walks, assembly rooms, theatres, and concert
halls, and tradesmen flocked to hear London actors, such as
James Quin, Kitty Clive, and Mrs Siddons, and London scientific lecturers, such as Benjamin Martin. They bought London
newspapers, patent medicines, and couture. Bath and rival resorts tempted London visitors for the season. William Wilberforce thought Brighton was like 'Piccadilly by the sea-side'.

Yet England was a mosaic in which regional contrasts remained ineradicable. These were partly because of the hetero-
geneous demands of London food consumption and, more
generally, because England was a market economy with each
region specializing in particular commodities. Differences were
also environmental responses to variations of latitude, altitude,
soil, and climate. Local economies were epicycles in the orbit of
the national (partly because some were illicit – for instance the
underground distributive networks that poaching, coining, and
smuggling boosted).

For some there was the world of difference between London's
madding crowd and the immemorial litany of rural life, a
contrast evoked by Alexander Pope writing about Martha
Blount leaving Town:

> She went, to plain-work and to purling brooks,
> Old-fashion'd halls, dull aunts, and croaking rooks,
> She went from op'ra, park, assembly, play,

> To morning walks, and pray'rs three hours a day;
> To pass her time 'twixt reading and Bohea,
> To muse, and spill her solitary Tea,
> Or o'er cold coffee trifle with the spoon,
> Count the slow clock, and dine exact at noon;
> Divert her eyes with pictures in the fire,
> Hum half a tune, tell stories to the squire;
> Up to her godly garret after sev'n,
> There stare and pray, for that's the way to heav'n.

Yet the town and the country were not stark opposites but, rather, complementary. Most towns – places on the scale of Hertford, Stratford-upon-Avon, or Guildford – were markets of a thousand or two souls, servicing their rural hinterlands: centres for dealing in grain, livestock and provisions, for horse-trading, for making and mending tools, and for such professional agents of gentlefolk as attorneys, surveyors, and doctors. Towns offered diversions for countrymen, from taverns to theatres. Urban industry relied upon the produce of the countryside: brewers, tanners, shoemakers, carpenters, masons, and textile workers made up the backbone of their manufacturing trades. Moreover, in contrast to the French courtier's proverbial terror of catching rusticity, the English liked to think of themselves as wedding civic to country tastes. *Rus in urbe* and *urbs in rure* were cherished ideals. Edward Cave, the founder of the *Gentleman's Magazine*, astutely christened himself 'Sylvanus Urban'. Townsmen enjoyed their gardens and kept pigs (brewers fattened pigs on their spent mash). There was less in England of the continental peasants' accusation that towns were bleeding the country white, or amongst famished townsmen that growers were holding them to ransom.

Just as town and countryside were not at odds, so it would be misleading to carve up the early-eighteenth-century economy rigidly into industrial and agricultural sectors. England's economy functioned precisely because the two were so utterly hand-in-glove. Skilled workers and their families could achieve modest comfort through dual occupations by combining a smallholding or kitchen garden with spinning, glove-making, straw-plaiting, lace-making, or framework-knitting. Cornishmen combined mining with autumn pilchard-fishing. Where summer and winter, outdoor and indoor jobs were dovetailed, the chronic seasonal and climatic under-employment which hamstrung pre-industrial economies was overcome. By-employments and home-grown or home-collected food enabled craftsmen to tide themselves over periodic fluctuations of prices and demand. For its part, large-scale agriculture was increasingly run as an industry, with sophisticated estate-management, division of labour, and cost-cutting.

Yet certain regional contrasts *were* profoundly important. One was the axial divide between the South-East and the North-West. South-east of a swathe roughly from the Severn estuary to the Humber lay the best arable land. It housed the wealthiest counties, such as Middlesex, Surrey, Buckinghamshire, Hertfordshire, Bedfordshire, Northamptonshire, and Oxfordshire. Counties in this band were also traditionally the most densely populated: in 1700 Northamptonshire, Bedfordshire, Wiltshire, Buckinghamshire, and Suffolk were all more thickly peopled than Lancashire, Cheshire, Derbyshire, Leicestershire, and Nottinghamshire, not to mention the Lake Counties and the borderlands. Wages were higher in the South. Around 1700 a labourer who earned about £25 a year in London might have got about £15 10s. in the West Country in the same job, and in the North about £11 5s. Furthermore, the southern and eastern half of England housed most of the largest settlements. London aside, towns such as Tiverton, Colchester, Ipswich, Bury St Edmunds, and Cambridge were bigger in 1700 than places such as Sheffield, Bradford, Preston, Wolverhampton, or Derby, which outstripped them by the end of the century. This simply reflects the fact that around 1700 the triangle inscribed by Bristol, London, and Norwich was heavily industrialized and contained the prosperous corn-belt as well. Iron-founding, boosted by military contracts, still concentrated heavily on the woodlands of the Weald and the Forest of Dean; naval dockyards – the largest hives of workers in the realm – clustered around the Thames, Medway, and Solent; the kernels of cloth manufacture were Devon, Norfolk (chiefly around Norwich), the Essex-Suffolk border, and the Cotswolds, though the West Riding was fast emerging. Luxury trades such as coach-building, watch-making, silk-weaving, and couture, were concentrated on London. The dawning century was about to witness an unparalleled revolution in the location of industry, towns, population, and wealth.

A second basic division around 1700 lay between coastal and inland areas, or, more precisely, between places near navigable water and those not. Before canals or railways, and while roads remained a disgrace, coastal shipping and river navigation – improved in Stuart times – remained far the cheapest, safest, and often the speediest means of conveying freight. Hence ports were vital, not just as nodes of long-haul trade (for the colonies, Ireland, and Europe) and nurseries of the Royal Navy, the fisheries, and the whaling fleets but as the points where internal traffic criss-crossed. London included, all the front-rank towns in the kingdom were either ports or had easy river access to the sea. To this fact Bristol, Exeter, Lowestoft, Great Yarmouth, Boston, King's Lynn, Newcastle, and Whitby owed their eminence. At first it was still North Sea ports that predominated: they were convenient for Europe, they straddled the grain trade which flowed up and down the Trent, the Fenland rivers, and the Thames, and they were vital for the coastal traffic in Newcastle sea-coal, which was taken by water into the heart of the South and East. Areas with poor water communications, such as the West Midlands around Birmingham, were hampered until the canal age.

A third contrast is between 'lowland' and 'upland', which this time was often also the distinction between open and wooded country, between arable and pastoral, between nucleated villages and scattered settlements, between densely and thinly populated parts. English prosperity had originally been lowland, the great settlements being crossings in broad-bottomed river valleys. The grain-belt, the heartland of national wealth and health, traditionally lay on the low-lying vales of the Midlands and central southern England. Celia Fiennes, Daniel Defoe, and other contemporary travellers still saw highlands as waste-lands and found them disagreeable. 'Forest' regions were bywords for lawlessness. Arthur Young commented on the inhabitants of Wychwood Forest in Oxfordshire: 'The vicinity is filled with poachers, deer-stealers, thieves, and pilferers of every kind: offences of almost every description abound so much that the offenders are a terror to all quiet and well-disposed persons.'

All this was, however, in flux. As wood for building and firing grew scarcer, timbered areas increased in economic attractiveness. With the expansion of worsted, calicoes, and cottons, the fast-flowing streams of the West Riding Pennine slopes proved important assets. As Defoe described the textile manufacturing settlements around Halifax:

... wherever we pass'd any house we found a little rill or gutter of running water, if the house was above the road, it came from it, and cross'd the way to run to another; if the house was below it, it cross'd us from some other distant house above it and at every considerable house a manufactory or work-house, and as they could not do their business without water, the little streams were so parted and guided by gutters or pipes, and by turning and dividing the streams, that none of those houses were without a river, if I may call it so, running into and through their work-houses.

The foothills of the Pennines and the Peak and the scrubby undulating grasslands of counties such as Staffordshire and Shropshire were developing a versatile mixed economy. Grazing and herding left labour time free for domestic industry. Under-employed families holding settlements on heath and moorlands flexibly adapted themselves to new economic openings as smiths, wheelwrights, nailers, cloggers, or weavers. Upland areas were the nodal points of growth in manufacturing and extractive industries as the century progressed.

Lastly, how far was there a segregative geography of social rank? Obviously, metropolitans tended to be rich and 'posh' compared with provincials; and townspeople more so than country 'bumpkins'. The barrel-scraping playwright could always wring laughs out of his audience by juxtaposing urbanity and rusticity (though fops as well as hicks came in for stick). But the distinctions can be overplayed. An Englishman's castle was his home. Unlike their French counterparts, English lords revelled on their estates, building, landscaping, and so creating in the heart of the country a sanctum of civilization. Yet the rural great were even so intent on a disappearing act, secluding themselves from the neighbouring commonalty. Mansions were now being built back off the road, away from the gaze of the vulgar (a few lords moved whole villages to ensure privacy). Plantations, walls, and gates raised a *cordon sanitaire*, as did travelling in coaches (rather than on horseback) and in sedan chairs (rather than walking). In the same spirit from 1712 the Lord Mayor of London rode in a coach instead of on horseback for his installation parade.

Early in the century provincial towns were still too small to have elaborate spatial apartheid. Most people lived where they worked. Domestic servants, apprentices, and journeymen lived in with their employers, often in attics (though living-in was discouraged from mid-century). Class-segregated suburbs had not yet developed (Birmingham's 'aristocratic' suburb of Edgbaston was beginning to be built by the Calthorpe family at the end of the century). London was the sole exception, because of its sheer size (and it just kept on growing). In the 1720s Defoe was impressed to find 'Great Russell Street is a fair way to shake hands' with Tottenham Court. What would he have felt near the end of the century when Horace Walpole reckoned 'there will soon be one street from London to Brentford'?

The Thames was London's great artery, pulsing with shipping, wharves lining its banks. The contrast between north and south banks was absolute. South of the Thames in about 1700 there was only stinking industry – distilleries, rope-works, tanneries, shambles, shipyards, punctuated with bear-baiting and bawds, hogs and fogs. Fashionable gardens, such as Vauxhall, and up-market suburbs, such as Camberwell or Streatham, where Henry Thrale the brewer was to live, came later. The West End/East End divide was just as striking. On the Thames-side, within and east of the business headquarters of the City of London, there were sooty shanties, shipping, crime, and hordes of common people, adjacent to City counting-houses. West of the City elegance was spreading its golden grids. Bloomsbury Square was built in 1680. It was followed by Grosvenor Street (1695), Red Lion Square (1698), Golden Square (1699), Queen Square (1704), Hanover Square (1713), Cavendish Square (1717), Portman Square (1764), Bedford Square (1769), Portland Place (1778), and Russell Square (1805) – all developed not by the Crown or Government but by titled investors and speculative builders. This development of an elegant, leisured, purely residential quarter culminated during the Regency in John Nash's sinuous stuccoed swathe from Piccadilly, via Regent Street, to Marylebone and Regent's Park. And yet the dregs still festered too near the dukes for comfort. Piccadilly was just a stone's throw from the thieves' kitchen of Seven Dials. Bloomsbury bigwigs battled to boot Welsh cattle drovers, destined for Smithfield, off their elegant, wide, straight thoroughfares. Everywhere the contrasts were stark. As the Prussian von Archenholz noted in 1780:

> The east end, especially along the shores of the Thames, consists of old houses, the streets there were narrow, dark and ill-paved, inhabited by sailors and other workmen who are employed in the construction of ships and by a great part of the Jews. The contrast between this and the West End is astonishing; the houses here are mostly new and elegant; the squares are superb, the streets straight and open – If all London were as well built, there would be nothing in the world to compare with it.

(There would also, one might add, have been no tradesmen to supply it, no urchins to sweep the crossings.) Furthermore, London's fashionable contrasts were not just between residential and working quarters, for the City was itself undergoing segregation and secession. Tycoons were moving domicile from their City premises to become a pseudo-landowning pseudo-gentry, with leafy villas in the new commuterlands of Twickenham, Richmond, Kensington, and Primrose Hill. Within the City, divisions between workshops and offices, between finance and crafts, were widening all the time.

At the dawn of the eighteenth century, English society was highly differentiated. In matters such as region, occupation, gender role, and legal status, contrasts were strong, niches were legion, and inequalities vast. Yet even the discontented and the oppressed often felt passionate loyalty to their place in the order of things. Despite elements of geographical and social mobility, inheritance of stations in life reinforced jealously guarded territoriality. The social fabric was intricate, and its complexity was mirrored by a deep-rooted economic division of labour and by the moral force of custom and precedent. Diversity and localism, entrenched rights and customs, were to stymie attempts by England's rulers to streamline and steamroller their rule, as they also forestalled the formation of nationally effective resistance amongst the ruled. And, complex and interlocking though the society was, one thing was clear: the gulfs between ruler and ruled, rich and poor, propertied and unpropertied, dominated life.

2. *The Social Order*

An eighteenth-century Englishman got his public identity in relation to his birth, his property, his occupation, and his rank in the social order. Most women were defined by the honour of their presiding male. The power brought by wealth, rank, office, and status obscured equality under common law and within the family of man. English society was a pyramid, with few at the top and many at the bottom. Towards the end of the seventeenth century, Gregory King estimated that society was divided as follows (the percentages include families and dependants):

1.2%	– landowners
24.3%	– farmers and freeholders
3.4%	– professionals, including clergy
3.7%	– merchants and shopkeepers
4.4%	– artisans and handicraftsmen
26.8%	– labouring people and out-servants
29.4%	– cottagers and paupers
6.8%	– the armed forces

These figures are clearly defective: there must have been far more merchants, shopkeepers, artisans, and craftsmen than that, and domestic servants – a large proportion – do not appear as a separate category; but the general profile is suggestive. The distinctions in wealth between top and bottom were vast. Poorer labourers were receiving about £10 a year; a great peer would be getting over £10,000. Even a prosperous knight, on £800, could spend in a year as much as his threshers or mowers might earn in a lifetime. Sometimes these extreme distinctions in wealth were sealed by attitudes which almost denied that rich and poor were of the same species. Thus the Duchess of Buckingham loathed Methodists because 'it is monstrous to be told that you have a heart as sinful as the common wretches that crawl on the earth. This is highly offensive and insulting and at variance with high rank and good breeding.'

Yet the gaps between adjacent links on the chain of income and status were microscopic, and this gave great strength. Examining the gradient of English society early in the nineteenth century, David Robinson found it a cause for eulogy:

> In most other societies, society presents hardly anything but a void between an ignorant labouring population and a needy and profligate nobility ... But with us the space between the ploughman and the peer is crammed with circle after circle, fitted in the most admirable manner for sitting upon each other, for connecting the former with the latter, and for rendering the whole perfect in cohesion, strength and beauty.

The English social order was indeed finely graded. The distinctions between being a servant in or out of livery, a kitchen maid or a lady's maid, below or above the salt, lower deck or quarter deck, between being called Mrs or Madam, were fine, but they mattered in creating status differentiation at their own levels as much as the pecking-order between baronets and earls, marquises and dukes. The Leveson-Gowers clawed their way up from being barons (1703), to becoming earls (1746), and finally dukes (1833). Likewise in the professions. Physicians looked down on surgeons, but surgeons were a cut above apothecaries (who were snooty about druggists). All these nice distinctions, and the supercharged snobbery they provoked and which sustained them, shaped a social order whose gross inequalities were landscaped in a gentle slope rather than in steps. There was no iron curtain of law or blood between bondman and freeman, trade and land, commoner and noble, as there was in some parts of Europe. Mobility was considerable, eroding traditional ideas of deference, as Dr Johnson lamented: 'Subordination is sadly broken down in this age ... there are many causes, the chief of which is the great increase of money ... The shoe-black at the entry of my court does not depend on me.' What it took to be reckoned a gentleman was not legally fixed but negotiable, for by long tradition gentility in England was but ancient riches. When Defoe jauntily rhymed,

> Wealth however got in England makes
> Lords of mechanics, gentlemen of rakes

he broadly described what happened. People made bold to style themselves 'gentlemen merchants', 'gentlemen clothiers', 'gentlemen of the road' – and of course there was 'Gentleman' John Jackson, prize-fighter. 'An English tradesman is a new species of gentleman,' opined Dr Johnson. Wealth that dressed itself up in liberal behaviour and gave itself airs could pass muster for gentility, Guy Miège thinking 'the title of gentleman is commonly given in England to all that distinguish themselves from the common sort of people by a good garb, genteel air or good education, wealth or learning'.

Furthermore, partly because the crevasses between the ranks were at least in theory bridgeable, personal mobility upwards and downwards acted as a safety valve, preserving the overall profile of society. England did not seem – as, say, Spain did – to comprise a number of mutually exclusive estates. The English clergy, for example, were not an estate apart in a way comparable to their celibate continental Catholic counterparts (English Dissenting clergy often doubled up occupations). Similarly, no English Sieyès would identify the Commons as a third estate, who by their exclusion were a 'nothing', capable of becoming 'everything'. Yet it would be equally wrong to suggest that the Establishment gave a hero's welcome to intrepid social climbers. For the vast majority Dr Johnson's words were true: 'Slow rises worth by poverty deprest.' People could quite easily rise *towards* the portal of the next status group. Crossing the threshold was more difficult and required special visas. Tradesmen, however rich, were debarred from becoming magistrates unless they first bought estates. Similarly, a common sailor could rise to become lieutenant, but hardly ever to command. Perhaps ninety-nine in a hundred Negroes never escaped being slaves, servants, or seamen (though the exceptional black became a gigolo, like Soubise, or a prize-fighter, like Tom Molineux or Bill Richmond). Yet common cinders occasionally burst into glorious fire. 'Men are every day starting up from obscurity to wealth,' wrote Defoe. A few rocketed to riches: lottery winners, or the crews of warships which captured Spanish argosies (prize money was shared out disproportionately, but even an able seaman might get a couple of hundred pounds). Others shot up society. Captain Cook, who entered the navy as an able seaman, was the son of a day labourer; Henry Thrale, who became a great London brewer and an MP, was a farm worker's son; John Baskerville, the printer, started life as a footman, as did Robert Dodsley, the publisher. William Wordsworth was the son of a yeoman. One of his two brothers became Master of Trinity College, Cambridge, the other a sea captain. Archbishop Potter's father was a draper, Bishop Thomas's a drayman. Charles Hutton, the mathematician, was the son of a coal-miner. Lancelot (Capability) Brown, the landscape gardener, was the son of a small tradesman. By the age of twenty-four he was gardener at Stowe, and his son in turn became an admiral. Englishmen were not short of dreams of destiny. 'In my mind's eye,' wrote Nelson, 'I ever saw a radiant orb suspended which beckoned me onwards to renown.' But such rags to riches stories were highly exceptional, some involving a stroke of fate. Thrale had a rich childless uncle who set him up; Cook had the good fortune to be apprenticed to a Whitby coaster-owner. Spectacular ascent was often due to the magic wand of patronage, a fortunate marriage, or a chance inheritance. Stephen Duck, a Wiltshire thresher and poet, was discovered by gentlemen and patronized right up to Court (where he was made a yeoman of the guard, before drowning himself in a trout stream).

Many people made money; but it was hard to buy your way into high society. It was easier to marry a peer than obtain a peerage. The ascent towards the Lords was normally slow, arduous, and costly, though a few lawyers could take a faster route and become Lord Chancellor – as did Macclesfield, Hardwicke, Camden, Thurlow, and Eldon. National heroes such as Clive got their coronet reward. But *nouveaux riches*, however *riches*, did not easily become ennobled. They could not buy a peerage – peerages were just about the one thing not for sale in Georgian England. Nor could they themselves count on marrying peers' daughters,* though, perhaps, in the second generation they might net a younger son of a needy peer as a match for their daughter, if she had a ripe dowry. The alliance of a gentleman's son with a merchant's daughter, the landed em-

---

* De Quincey wrote that John Palmer had 'accomplished two things very hard to do in our little planet. He had invented mail-coaches, and he had married the daughter of a duke.'

bracing the loaded, was *mariage à la mode*. Peerage-ogling pluto-crats had to play a waiting game. First they had to buy rolling acres – and ready-made consolidated prestige estates were hard to come by – establish a county family and political pull, and then assiduously cultivate friends in high places. Even then, there were obstacles. The fabulously rich Jewish financier and government contractor Sampson Gideon converted to Angli-canism, but it was his son who became a baronet.

What's more, in some ways social fluidity was silting up. True, as many foreigners noted, England was exceptional in that peers' younger sons entered trade (only the eldest son inherited title and usually land); caste was not thereby lost. Lord Townshend's younger brother Horatio was a City merchant: the Earl of Oxford's brother was an agent in Aleppo. Yet only certain forms of money-making were honourable, principally large-scale overseas trade or finance (unlike domestic wholesale or retail business). In any case, the tradition of Septimus or Decimus being at the counting-house tailed off during the century, as political patronage hauled more aristocratic younger sons up in the army, Church, and diplomatic office. It got harder for *parvenus* to break into front-bench politics, high office, and high society.

Almost everyone believed there should be a graded status hierarchy. People studied precisely how their superiors lived and behaved, and then aped them ('plain' Quakers were among the few who resisted). Henry Thrale, the self-made brewer, sent his son to Eton and Oxford – a predictable catastrophe for the future management of the brewery. The same happened when his rival Samuel Whitbread sent his son to Eton and Cambridge, and on the Grand Tour. The son became a politician, near-bankrupt and eventual suicide. But though all knew the steps above and beneath them and experienced familiar social fric-tions, few would have felt able to sketch the entire structure of social relations. Daniel Defoe suggested a sevenfold division, based on wealth and consumption:

1. The great, who live profusely
2. The rich, who live plentifully
3. The middle sort, who live well
4. The working trades, who labour hard, but feel no want
5. The country people, farmers etc. who fare indifferently

6. The poor, who fare hard
7. The miserable, that really pinch and suffer want

Probing deeper, historians have debated whether Georgian England was a 'class' society (though snobbish, it certainly was not a 'caste' society – one in which people are riveted in place by blood, pedigree, and birth). Of course contemporaries had concepts such as the 'upper orders', the 'middling ranks', and 'labouring men'. Yet – as Defoe's scheme suggests – they did not think of their society as turning upon struggle between *three* distinct classes, defined as in the Marxist analysis essentially in relation to ownership and deployment of capital: aristocracy, bourgeoisie, and proletariat. People tended to lump and split groups more in terms of clutches of interests – wealth, occupation, region, religion, family, political loyalty, and connexion. In practice, when social conflict and political disturbances flared up, lines were drawn between different faiths, or between Government and a particular trade (such as cider-making), or between rival trades themselves, at least as often as between capital and labour. Struggles were less between 'class' and 'class' than between 'ins' and 'outs'. In any case, smallholders, yeomen, and self-employing tradesmen and craftsmen still comprised much of the population. Early in the century, apprentices could expect to hatch into small masters in their turn. Social position upon a person's stage in the life-cycle. Much work was still family-based (what *is* the class position of women?), or sub-contracted out to teams of independent workers. A society with such characteristics does not readily fit into a three-class model. The trawl nets of terms such as 'nobility', 'bourgeoisie', and 'proletariat', or upper, middle, and lower class, let too many fish through, and over-concentration on them always risks obscuring the vast differences in wealth and status which individual health, luck (especially that of being first-born), effort, or success could make, even within one family. Amongst the Hales family, for instance, one brother became a baronet, one, Stephen, entered the Church and remained curate of Teddington, though becoming a distinguished scientist, but another died in Newgate, a convicted forger. Every Quality family was forever keeping poor relations at bay. Richard Gough's survey in 1700 of all the inhabitants of the Shropshire parish of Myddle shows a remarkably fluid community, with rapidly fluctuating prosperity and improverishment depending on application, astuteness, and the luck of marriages and health.

People saw their standing in the world in concrete terms. 'I welcomed a friend with a shake of the hand', the bookseller James Lackington remembered about his early business days,

> but a year later I beckoned across the way for a pot of good porter. A few years after that I invited my friends to dinner, and provided them with a roasted fillet of veal, in a progressive course, the ham was introduced and a pudding made the next addition to the feast. For some time a glass of brandy and water was a luxury; raisin wine succeeded, and as soon as two thirds of my profits allowed me to afford good red port, it appeared on my table, nor was sherry long behind.

England's elite was a tight, privileged ring of landowners. Of course, European societies from feudal times down to the First World War were ruled by privileged landowners, but the titled proprietors of Georgian England were rather exceptional.

In part this was because the stranglehold of the landed nobility was something newly re-established. Dukes and earls had been axed by Henry VII's and Henry VIII's drive to secure the Tudor dynasty. New Tudor creations had not kept pace with natural wastage, and the early Stuarts then diluted the Lords by elevating favourites, many of them needy Irish and Scots adventurers, lacking local power-bases. The bills of luxuriant living outstripped incomes. The result was what Stone has called a 'crisis of the aristocracy', in which the peerage was ground, politically and economically, between the upper and nether millstones of the Crown and a confident gentry.

As an order magnates probably did not fare much better in the post-Restoration political cockpit; rather a succession of individual careerist peers such as Clarendon and Danby, Sunderland and Oxford, climbed the greasy pole. The empire of even the greatest politicians at the turn of the century – Somers, Godolphin, Wharton, Montagu – was essentially self-made. Nevertheless, the purposeful solidarity of propertied interests in rejecting James II heralded greater cohesion to come, and the

pursuit of capitalist High Farming and High Finance was beginning to pay new dividends for great landowners. Firmer control
over elections and new game laws were already signalling oligarchic tendencies in politics. Thus, by early in the new century,
the tide was flowing in favour of the magnates. They were to
become for the next two centuries easily the most confident,
powerful, and resilient aristocracy in Europe.

Being small and stable in size was a boon. By European
standards the English second estate was minuscule partly because
– unlike elsewhere – only eldest sons inherited titles. In 1688
there were just 160 lords temporal and twenty-six lords spiritual
(elsewhere they ran into tens of thousands, about half a million
claiming nobility in Spain). There were perhaps another eighty
to a hundred non-noble families of great leverage, owning
10,000 acres or more – men such as the agricultural improver
Thomas Coke of Holkham in Norfolk (who eventually con-
sented to become Earl of Leicester). The size of the Lords
remained steady until the 1780s, when Pitt became more
open-handed with ermine. There was however no rash of
Lilliput titles, or ennobling of small fry. The English peerage
(unlike the Scottish) carried few passengers; the great landowners had a chance to breathe.

In contrast to their continental cousins, English grandees were
not eaten up by legalistic jealousies over rivals' privileges – old,
indigenous titles squabbling against new royal creations, 'sword'
against 'robe', landholders against administrators, courtiers
against provincials, or money-bags against the impoverished.
Almost no English peers were down at heel. The grandees'
world was a charmed family circle radiating from great houses
such as Stowe, Bowood, and Chatsworth. Everyone knew
everyone else, and the interlocking threads of marriage-ties
were closely woven. In five successive generations of the Earl of
Guilford's family the eldest son married an heiress; Lord North's
father, in fact, married three, Lucy, the daughter of Lord Halifax, Elizabeth, widow of Viscount Lewisham, and Catherine,
widow of the Earl of Rockingham. From the late seventeenth
century, four of five successors of the Grafton estates married
heiresses. The Earl of Nottingham married six out of his seven
daughters to peers. Thus were estates, fabulous riches, and pol-

itical connexions strung together. Yet marrying a millionaire commoner's daughter could be equally advantageous. The Bedfords' fortunes were made by the marriage arranged in 1695 between the young Marquis of Tavistock and Elizabeth Howland, a London merchant's daughter. The second Viscount Palmerston married a wealthy City merchant's daughter. Peers, on the other hand, did not want to marry their *daughters* into trade, lest estates fell into mucky hands.

Family continuity was the keynote of magnate success; the individual title-holder was the ancestral baton-carrier in the relay race of family destiny. Inheritance was everything. Male primogeniture ensured that estates were not broken up. The eldest son came into the lands *en bloc*; younger sons got a consolation prize of money and a leg-up into a profession. Thus the Duke of Devonshire gave two younger sons £1,000 each to dabble in politics, and Ralph Sneyd, a substantial Staffordshire gentleman, gave his six younger sons £1,000 each: two went into the Church, two into the army, one into the navy, one into the East India Company.

Contemporaries were right to believe that grandees drew their strength and resilience not primarily from pedigree but by being 'an open aristocracy based on property and patronage', as Perkin has described it. 'What distinguishes it from all others is the ease with which it has opened its ranks,' noted Tocqueville, looking back from the vantage of post-Revolutionary France. Yet to stress this openness could be misleading, for the towering strength of the magnates lay in their coming to comprise a tight, self-reproducing oligarchy of the extraordinarily wealthy and influential, a club exceedingly difficult to join. As Speck observes, 'If anything, the English aristocracy was more of a closed circle in the eighteenth century than at any other time in history.'

They lorded it over every corner of life. Economic trends smiled on them. Landownership and agriculture were admittedly not money-spinners through the whole of the century, but land values and rents were buoyant at the beginning and rose ever more steeply from the 1760s, as did profits from the produce and materials they marketed. Overall, between 1690 and 1790, in what was increasingly a sellers' market, land values about doubled. Most important, the economics of agrarian management meant that great landowners geographically consolidated their estates and cut labour costs on their own home farms. The age of low grain prices between about 1710 and 1750 squeezed them less than small owners, who lacked capital to fund cost-cutting improvement or to see bad times through, and whose midget estates impeded diversification of techniques and crops. Better prices after about 1760 prompted a surge of magnate-led enclosure and cemented the partnership between great landowner and the go-ahead farmer to whom he rented out his lands, a partnership which promoted so much innovation in estate management, stock-breeding, and rotations. Between 1776 and 1816 Thomas Coke of Holkham doubled his estate's rental.

The profits of landowning were not the only arena in which the aristocracy prospered (no peer had all his eggs in one basket). Many grandee families were 'amphibious', having for generations also owned urban estates, especially in and around London. In the Georgian building booms, land values and rentals soared as peers laid out fashionable metropolitan sites. The Bedfords developed Bloomsbury, collecting £2,000 from their London properties in 1700, £3,700 in 1732, and £8,000 in 1771. The Grosvenors' London properties yielded £2,000 in 1772, £7,000 by 1779, and £12,000 by 1802.

Magnates also became what Cobbett termed 'fundlords', investing deeply in Government stock, the Bank of England, and the great trading companies. The Earl of Sunderland, for example, had £75,000 in stocks and shares in 1722. And not least they gained hand-over-fist from industrialization. The greatest landowners were predictably sitting on the richest mines, including the Dukes of Argyll, Hamilton, and Devonshire, Earls Gower and Fitzwilliam, Lords Middleton, Mostyn, Egerton, Dalaval, and Lowther, and the Bishop of Durham. Lord Foley had mines worth £7,000 a year on top of an estate worth £21,000 and £500,000 in the funds. Great estates yielded building stone, slates, sand, brick-clay, and timber. Peers developed ports and backed transport improvements such as turnpike trusts. It was the Duke of Bridgewater's desire to sell more of his Worsley coal in Manchester which launched the canal age. And some peers involved themselves directly in industrial ventures. James Brydges, Duke of Chandos, undertook mining projects, huge building enterprises in Bath, pearl-fishing off Anglesey, and mineral-prospecting in New York (most of these failed); he took shares in the Covent Garden playhouse, was a leading figure in the York Building Company, and equipped his own personal laboratory. The peerage made money enthusiastically and without shame (on the Continent, nobles engaging in trade jeopardized their legal caste).

Vital to their success, grandees had their jaws locked upon the profits and perquisites of the state. Peers monopolized Walpole's, Pelham's, and subsequent cabinets, appropriating office positions, patronage, and revenues. By 1720 one quarter of the peerage held Government or Court office. Places at Court (such as gentleman of the bedchamber), pensions, and sinecures were glittering prizes for titled families. Horace Walpole, the Prime Minister's son, was granted a Tellership of the Exchequer alone worth £1,200 a year, and two other sinecures besides, the Clerkship of the Escheats and the Comptrollership of the Pipe. Under Pitt the Younger, George Rose had sinecures which brought him £11,602 a year. Lord Irwin was made Governor of Barbados and allowed to keep his regiment, which, his wife wrote, 'will be a great advantage to him in paying off his debts'. Offices could be traded, fees collected: deputies did the work. In mid-century a Secretaryship of State yielded about £6,000–9,000 a year in clear profit. Many offices further allowed the incumbent to take commission from contractors, to accept *douceurs*, and handle astronomical sums of public money, with which they would play the Exchange privately for the duration. The Paymaster Generalship made the fortunes of Marlborough, Cadogan, Amherst, Sir Robert Walpole, Bubb Dodington, Henry Fox, James Brydges, and others. Brydges cleared £600,000 from his tenure of office between 1705 and 1713. Top men might simply put their hand in the till. Lord Chancellor Macclesfield was unfortunate enough to be caught and was impeached for mishandling £100,000. He was fined £30,000, which he paid off within six weeks. Not all enrichment, however, was narrowly personal; family, friends, neighbours, and even plagues of strangers clamoured for crumbs. Prime Minister

Lord North showered his stripling half-brother, Brownlow North, with ecclesiastical offices, explaining that if Brownlow had to wait till he was older he might no longer have a Prime Minister for his brother. Brownlow became Dean of Canterbury at twenty-nine, Bishop of Lichfield at thirty, Bishop of Worcester at thirty-three, and Bishop of Winchester at forty. Taught by experience that charity began at home, Brownlow in turn made his own elder son Master of St Cross Hospital, his younger son Prebendary of Winchester, and a grandson Registrar of Winchester diocese (at the age of seven), and spent £6,000 on his own residence.

In short, peers were collectively fabulously wealthy. In 1700 their average wealth may have been between £5,000 and £8,000 a year. During the century several had annual incomes topping £20,000. In 1715 the Duke of Newcastle, whose lands straddled thirteen counties, grossed £32,000.

This tide of wealth, however, flowed out almost as fast. Newcastle dissipated his fortune on Whig politics. Sir Robert Walpole's private expenditure between 1714 and 1718 totalled £90,000. Walpole and his guests at Houghton Hall downed about £1,500 a year in wine, the income of a flush gentleman. The Duke of Chandos got through as much. Just lighting Houghton cost Walpole £15 a night in candles. In 1771 Bedford House had forty-two servants who cost £859 a year. Political and electoral expenses ran into thousands, and tens of thousands changed hands in gambling. Marriage settlements – portions, jointures – became heavier drains on fortunes. And vast capital fortunes were sunk in building. Holkham Hall cost the Earl of Leicester £90,000 to put up, altering Audley End cost the Nevilles £100,000. Woburn was rebuilt between 1747 and 1763 for £84,000. The Marquis of Rockingham spent £83,000 on Wentworth Woodhouse (running it cost him another £5,000 a year). The Duke of Buccleuch kept two London houses for when he was weary of his eight country residences. The Duke of Devonshire owned Hardwick Hall, Chatsworth, Bolton Abbey, Lismore Castle, and Compton Place and in London, Burlington and Devonshire Houses. Prodigal peers and their heirs ran up astronomical debts – mortgages allowed them to do this without imperilling their estates.

Their life-style was pure eye-catching grandeur. Magnates ransacked Europe – and the globe itself – for paintings, sculpture, furniture, jewellery. They patronized artists and poets, and collected antiques, scientific instruments, and books by the roomful. The second Viscount Palmerston snapped up 300 old masters for a bargain £8,000. Flanked by landscapers such as William Kent, Capability Brown, and Humphrey Repton, they redesigned Nature, on occasion flattening entire settlements which spoilt the view. In landscaping Castle Howard, Vanbrugh drowned the village of Hilderskelfe. That champion of political liberty, Viscount Cobham, razed the village of Stowe, shunting its rustics off to Dadford. Thomas Coke re-sited the hamlet of Holkham – though perhaps later regretting it: 'It is a melancholy thing to stand alone in one's own country. I look around, not a house to be seen but for my own. I am Giant, of Giant's Castle, and have ate up all my neighbours.'

The Duke of Chandos kept ninety-three household servants at Canons and his own private twenty-seven-piece orchestra under *Kapellmeister* Pepusch. Peers introduced tropical plants, bred livestock and bloodstock. They were dictators of fashion and taste (explaining Henry Fielding's sardonic definition of 'Nobody' as 'All the people in Great Britain except about 1,200'). Towards the end of the century many invested in kennels of pedigree hounds to woo connexions down for hunting parties. This orgy of consumption was partly for personal pleasure, partly with an eye to publicity (extravagant levées would be glitteringly gossiped about down to the last diamond), but, perhaps above all, to consolidate personal stature within the political snake-pit.

For the great landlords maintained their pre-eminence by means of an unshakeable grip on political power: 'dominion follows property', as Mandeville wrote. Because none could rival their property, the magnate class basked in a long hot summer of unthreatened political superiority, treating the state as a kind of trust devised on their behalf. On the one hand, the soaring price of politics in an age dominated by management, patronage, and the spoils system raised the mace of parliamentary power beyond the clutches of mere squires (and in any case, the first two Georges were in no position to dish the Whig

'Venetian' oligarchy). On the other, with fleeting exceptions such as John Wilkes's thunderclap, the bark of radical opposition politics was worse than its bite.

In the power-seat, peers dribbled out offices of state to reward the loyalty of friends, family, and clients, and buy off the disaffected. The superior posts at Court, and in the Church, bureaucracy, consular service, administration, and, more obliquely, the armed forces, became marked in the patronage lists of party managers such as the Duke of Newcastle. In 1762 John Boscowen Savage was made an ensign in the 91st Foot Regiment at the age of two. 'Patronage was a social nexus,' writes Perkin, 'less formal and inescapable than feudal homage, more personal and comprehensive than the contractual relationships of capitalist cash-payment.' The state at their disposal, grandees pioneered the art of political asset-stripping.

The Church of England's pickings in particular were once more gobbled up by peers and their minions. In Stuart times it had not been honourable for men of noble family to take the cloth. This changed. As William Warburton observed in 1752, 'Our *Grandees* have at last found their way back into the Church. I only wonder they have been so long about it . . . The Church has been of old the cradle and the throne of the younger nobility.' Under the early Stuarts, up to 25 per cent of bishops had been non-genteel in origin; by the time of George III only about 4 per cent were. The change came about partly because competition intensified for eligible openings in other liberal walks of life, the Church being a refuge for the staider sort (Lord Chesterfield thought it ideal for a 'good, dull and decent' young man). But the return to the Church was speeded partly because the emoluments and tithes of rectors and the higher clergy were becoming more attractive. The Archbishop of Canterbury could reckon on £7,000 a year, the Bishop of Durham £6,000, the Bishop of Winchester £5,000. A cathedral stall-holder would receive a comfortable £350; and 'the life of a prebendary,' as Edmund Pyle reflected from personal experience, 'is a pretty easy way of dawdling away one's time: praying, walking, visiting – and as little study as your heart would wish.' Many took a second – or third – helping by pluralism. Bishop Richard Watson's bag of some £2,200 a year was made up from tithes of two churches in Shropshire, two in Leicestershire, two in Llandaff, three in Huntingdonshire, five other impropriations to the Bishopric of Llandaff, and two to the Archdeacon of Ely. Above all, clergy were advanced to sees to act as dependable pro-ministerial voting fodder in the House of Lords. Certain prelates, such as Bishop Hoadly, were rewarded for being indefatigable government pamphleteers; others rose by connexion, family, and sheer importunacy.

The state underwrote magnate parasitism upon society in another crucial way: through the law. Unlike in continental regimes legal privileges *per se* for lords (such as the right to trial by one's peers) were paltry; nor were English peers exempt from taxation. But the law and its devices were tireless allies in maintaining grandees' estates, in sanctioning primogeniture, and also in backing the instruments of mortgage, strict settlement, and entail, all of which put in stalwart service from the Restoration. Mortgaging estates enabled landowners to raise capital to make improvements, settle offspring, or pay off debts, without having to shed acres. Entail blocked occupants of estates from selling them; the inheritor became in effect a life tenant on behalf of his family line. Recent research suggests that these devices probably did not result – as was once thought – in vast further agglomerations of estates: the biological and psychological fortunes of families were too up-and-down for that. Too many grandees died without male heirs, too many sons prematurely, too many wayward sons were disinherited; counterclaimants always had to be satisfied – the centrifugal forces were clamorous and constant. Yet these legal arrangements did help to stabilize estates, which was vital at a time of rising claims on property, such as jointures (an annual income provided for a wife), portions (a lump sum paid to a daughter), and cash settlements to younger sons – all drastic drains on an estate's annual yield. The net result was that Georgian landlords were spending more, and piling up vast debts, yet few estates were being liquidated and dispersed.

In other ways, the law secured the great landowner, not only against the masses, but even against other men of property. The classic instance is the game laws. Under an Act of 1671 the right to take game, even on one's own land, was restricted to proprietors of estates worth more than £100 a year: even substantial farmer-tenants and freeholders were disqualified. The game laws were thus remarkable in privileging grandees even against other members of the landed orders.

But this is not surprising. For magnates were laws unto themselves in their own shires. One of the most profound consequences of the Civil War (1642–6), the Restoration (1660), and the Glorious Revolution (1688) was the establishment of more or less autonomous magnates as satraps of local communities, scarcely checked by Crown, Church, or *intendants* of a kind who emerged in France. Magnates monopolized high local office, active and honorific, from the Lords Lieutenancies to the Chancellorships of the universities – all carrying authority and patronage. They pulled strings at the hustings, and carved up electoral contests through chicanery, bully-boys, interest, and the creation of votes. They headed charities and acted as trustees for canal projects. Their home-based power as consumers, employers, and fountains of favour – though bitterly resented – almost defied challenge, except by rival peers. 'The idea I gave Lord Rockingham of this county,' wrote a Nottinghamshire correspondent in 1769, 'was four Dukes, two Lords, and three rabbit warrens, which I believe, in fact, takes in half the county in point of space.' (Not all counties, however, were like this: Kent had few peers.) England rather resembled a 'federal republic of country houses'. The lion's share of parliamentary legislation comprised magnate-sponsored local, private bills – for enclosure, canals, imparking, regulating trade. Parliament, wrote Trevelyan, was a kind of Grand National Consolidated Quarter Sessions. The Great House was the power-house, avatar of dominion.

The aristocracy's prepossessing role as rural patriarchs had conviction because they revelled in country life on their property. As Arthur Young observed, 'Banishment alone will force the French to execute what the English do for pleasure – reside upon and adorn their estates.' 'The multitude of gentlemen's houses, scattered over the country, is a feature quite peculiar to English landscape,' observed Louis Simond – 'the thing is unknown in France.' Magnates threw themselves into blood sports – 'they are all quite mad about them,' wrote La Rochefoucauld: 'A-hunting we will go!' They patronized agricultural improvement and cultivated their tenantry. Deep in the French countryside, Arthur Young noted:

At an English nobleman's there would have been three or four farmers asked to meet me, who would have dined with the family amongst the ladies of the first rank. I do not exaggerate when I say that I have had this at least a hundred times in the first houses of our islands. It is however a thing that in the present manners in France would never be met with from Calais to Bayonne.

Young was right about England. Lord Hervey recorded that Walpole invited friends down to Houghton in Norfolk 'to hunt, be noisy, jolly, drunk, comical, and pure merry during the recess', detailing a typical Walpolean dinner:

We used to sit down to dinner a little snug party of about thirty odd, up to the chin in beef, venison, geese, turkeys, etc.; and generally over the chin in claret, strong beer, and punch. We have Lords Spiritual and Temporal, besides commoners, parsons, and freeholders innumerable.

Lower down, the Duke of Norfolk gave a supper to 350 of his labourers in 1764. It was with fraternizings such as these in mind that Trevelyan remarked that 'if the French noblesse had been capable of playing cricket with their peasants their chateaux would never have been burnt'.

And yet this charade of 'paternalism' was wearing thin. Doubtless complacent magnates liked to regard themselves as – in Burke's words – the 'great oaks that shade a country', but the veneer of patriarchalism was time and again corroded by the brutality with which great landowners emparked, enclosed, exploited the game laws, and rode roughshod over customary tenant and villager rights. Contemporaries were not fooled. Rural violence, the crescendo of poaching, and the snarl of anonymous threatening letters all testify to the sporadic and defensive bush-war which communities were waging against rapacious landlords. 'If every man who wears a lace coat was extirpated,' asked no less an idolator of rank than Dr Johnson, 'who would miss them?'

Magnates were on the horns of a self-created dilemma. Greed urged them to maximize agrarian profit, pride to bask in undisturbed private grandeur – both alienating the community. The richer they got, the more they cultivated tastes – Palladianism, French fashions, fine manners, and connoisseurship of the arts – which elevated them above their natural right-hand men, homespun squires and freeholders. Patricians grew more snooty about the vulgar world, many itching to suppress popular festivities, wakes, church-ales, and fairs as being silly and troublesome. And yet popularity was the kiss of life. Lacking private armies, in the end they had to rule by bluster and swank. Authority could be upheld only by consent, through tricky reciprocal negotiations of will and interests, give and take. As political bosses and parliamentary candidates, grandees wooed and cajoled tenants and ratepayers for their votes before they bullied them. As Josiah Tucker wrote, 'without the assistance or approbation of the people, they cannot be considerable either in the Senate or out of it'. The fraternizing game, however nauseating, however phoney, had to be played. At election time, according to the Earl of Cork,

our doors are open to every dirty fellow in the county that is worth forty shillings a year; all my best floors are spoiled by the hobnails of farmers stamping about them; every room is a pig-stye, and the Chinese paper in the drawing room stinks so abominably of punch and tobacco that it would strike you down to come into it.

Horace Walpole was amused by the palaver of being a candidate at King's Lynn in 1761:

Think of me, the subject of a mob, who was scarce ever before in a mob! addressing them in the town-hall, riding at the head of two thousand people through such a town as Lynn, dining with above two hundred of them, amid bumpers, huzzas, songs, and tobacco, and finishing with country dancing at a ball and sixpenny whist! I have borne it all cheerfully; nay, have sat hours in *conversation*, the thing upon earth that I hate, have been to hear misses play on the harpsichord, and to see an alderman's copies of Rubens.

Even in his own sanctum, no less, the lord knew at bottom he needed to buy the good-will of wheedling tradesmen (he lived on credit) and of his own domestic servants ('the greatest plagues on earth'), ever troublesome behind the mask of deference. The miasmatic plebs were threatening to pollute everything and undermine the age of elegance. ' 'Tis not my dairy maid that is with child,' spat Elizabeth Purefoy in 1738, 'but my cookmaid, and it is reported that our parson's maid is also with child by the same person who has gone off and showed them a clean pair of heels for it. If you could help me to a cookmaid as I may be delivered from this, it will much oblige.'

So, to cope with self-created rural polarization, which reached its peak in the game war and the blighted pauperism of Cobbett's countryside, grandees stage-managed a more studied theatre of power: conspicuous menace (and mercy) from the Judge's Bench; exemplary punishment tempered with silver linings of philanthropy, largesse, and selective patronage; a grudging and calculating display of *noblesse oblige*: 'This is the day of our fair,' sulked Sir Joseph Banks in 1753, 'when according to immemorial custom I am to feed and make drunk everyone who chooses to come, which will cost me in beef and ale near £20.'

This was the sly magic of authority. But the underlying power was real. By 1800, the notables were absolutely and relatively wealthier and more united than their grandfathers. In 1700 peers had owned about 15–20 per cent of England's landed wealth; by 1800 the figure was probably between 20 and 25 per cent, and a score of peers owned more than 100,000 acres each. Rent-rolls were rising from mid-century, in many cases doubling between 1790 and 1815, and peers were sitting beneficiaries of industrialization. And the French revolutionary wars underscored their virility as warrior champions of Church, State, and Britannia. It was indeed a good time to be a lord.

Beneath the magnates stretched down some 15,000 further landed families. These 'gentry' (owners who did not personally have to do hard labour on their land) were lordlings combining local clout and office with – for some at least – national stature as the backbone of the backbenchers. They ranged from baronets, who in 1700 might have over £1,500 a year (by 1800 perhaps £4,000), down to the squire feeling the pinch on as little as £300. In England, however, there were no endemically threadbare gentry, like the Spanish hidalgo who 'ate black bread under the genealogical tree'. But these were times when the economics of consolidated capitalized agriculture and the nip of the land tax helped big gentlemen to get fatter and sped smaller ones, alongside spendthrifts, towards bankruptcy and even the debtors' gaol. By 1800, £300 would no longer support a squire. On the other hand, especially where they had commercial interests alongside agriculture, gentlemen could live snug. Early in the century the Archers of Warwickshire, topping up their landed income with the profits of forestry and iron forges, were netting close on £3,000 a year. The Whitbreads began the century as small Bedfordshire squires; by the end, they had £8,000 a year from their London brewery as well as £22,000 from land. The coal trade was the road to gentrification for northern families such as the Cooksons, the Liddells, and the Curwens. By contrast, other gentry lines – such as Sir Watkin Williams Wynn's in Denbighshire – were ruined by the rocketing bill of politics; the Verneys of Buckinghamshire were shipwrecked by their unsuccessful bid to wrest the county's political primacy from the Grenvilles. To Gibbon's intense annoyance, gracious living burned a hole in his father's pocket. And many a small Tory squire – especially crypto-Jacobites – skulked biliously or went broke under the early Georges, following ejection from local office and favour.

Squires did not come in one standard type. Booted, bloated, and bigoted Squire Westerns were real enough. Horace Walpole called their Norfolk counterparts 'mountains of roast beef'; 'their mornings are spent among the hounds,' wrote Lady Mary Wortley Montagu, 'and their nights with as beastly companions – with what liquor they can get.' Hannah More confirmed this image of the squire as purblind traditionalist:

> He dreaded nought like alteration
> Improvement still was innovation.

Yet these were easily counterbalanced by plenty of astute businesslike figures such as Colonel Walpole, JP and MP in North Norfolk, father of Sir Robert. As J. H. Plumb has observed:

The two Walpoles, father and son, illustrate some of the more interesting aspects of English social and political life from 1660–1760; the prudent, intelligent, but essentially homespun father, with his ambition adjusted to those ends that were well within his reach – an increased estate and the leadership of his county – was so typical of all that was best in the gentry of his day: whereas the brilliant son, greedy for power, greedy for riches, yet creative in all that he did, was limitless in his ambition; in the brilliance of his taste and the grandeur of his opulence, he outshone the aristocratic world in which his ambitions lay.

The squire's spiritual half-brother was the parson (lean-shanked curates are another matter): men such as James Wood-forde, who as a bachelor was comfortable on £400 per annum. Most rectors, farming the glebe and harvesting tithes, lived well. Anglican clergy politicked, tally-ho'ed, farmed, and guzzled with the squires. Many were hardly distinguishable. 'His size, and figure, and countenance and manner,' Boswell wrote of the Rev. Dr Taylor, 'were that of a hearty English Squire, with the parson super-induced.' Some 'squarsons' were probably no more sober than mere squires. Yet there were learned and scholarly clerics, antiquarians, naturalists such as the Rev. Gilbert White of Selborne, and hosts of other sober, decent men. Towards the end of the century incumbents were increasingly in demand as Justices of the Peace, as they were thought to discharge their office with more punctilio than their lay counterparts.

Below the gentry, English landed society forked: there was a line of owner-occupiers reaching down through yeomen freeholders to copyholding smallholders; and a breed of tenant-farmers also consolidated itself. At the turn of the century Gregory King thought freeholders, numbering some 100,000 and making £50-100 per annum, were better off than farmers; Patrick Colquhoun at the end thought the reverse. Farmers probably did overtake freeholders in fortune during the century (though many individual yeomen rose into the gentry). As a breed freeholders lacked investable funds to compete with capital-intensive progressive agriculture. The modest owner-occupier did not of course disappear. Indeed in some areas, such as the Lake District, sturdy yeomen remained thick on the ground, and contrary to the opinion of some historians, small-holders normally had their rights confirmed in enclosure awards. But except in unusual boom conditions (for instance at the time of shortage during the French revolutionary wars) the lives of petty owner-occupying families got tougher. 'I regard these small occupiers as a set of very miserable men', wrote Arthur Young. 'They fare extremely hard, work without intermission like a horse ... and practise every lesson of diligence and frugality without being able to soften their present lot.' Tenants of tiny farms did little better. As the Rev. John Howlett put it,

The small farmer is forced to be laborious to an extreme degree; he works harder and fares harder than the common labourer; and yet with all his labour and with all his fatiguing incessant exertions, seldom can he at all improve his condition or even with any degree of regularity pay his rent and preserve his present situation. He is confined to perpetual drudgery, which is the source of profound ignorance, the parent of obstinacy and blind perseverance in old modes and old practices, however absurd and pernicious.

By contrast, substantial tenant-farmers prospered. For instance George Culley, a Northumberland stock-breeder who had learnt his trade with Robert Bakewell, had an income of £4,000 a year by 1801 and bought up Fowberry Tower. He wrote in 1810, 'Whenever I am at Fowberry, I am struck with astonishment when I reflect on our beginning in Northumberland forty three years ago. To think of my son, now inhabiting a *palace*! although his father in less than fifty years since worked harder than any servant we now have and even drove a coal cart.' Farmers succeeded partly because prudent landowners valued businesslike tenants and were prepared to rent them attractively large holdings (200–600 acres), grant long leases, and underwrite capital improvements. Farmers slip-streamed magnates along the turnpike road of improvement.

By 1790 about three quarters of England's soil was cultivated by tenants. The tenant-farmer – a species rare elsewhere in Europe – was for many commentators the epitome of English agriculture. Farmers did well, their rising wealth and importance reflected in the barrage of moralizing envy they increasingly drew as they 'gentrified' themselves, rebuilding farmsteads and investing in fine china and furniture, silver plate, sprung carriages, and vintage cellars. As Arthur Young put it:

... sometimes I see a piano forte in a farmer's parlour, which I always wish was burnt; a livery servant is sometimes found, and a post chaise to carry their daughters to assemblies; these ladies are sometimes educated at expensive boarding-schools, and the sons often at the University, to be made parsons. But all these things imply a departure from that line which separates these different orders of being [gentlemen and farmers]. Let these things, and all the folly, foppery, expense, and anxiety, that belong to them, remain among gentlemen: a wise farmer will not envy them.

A pair of rhymes satirizes the social pretensions of the farmers:

1722	1822
Man to the plough;	Man tally-ho;
Wife to the cow;	Miss piano;
Girl to the sow;	Wife silk and satin;
Boy to the mow;	Boy Greek and Latin;
And your rents will be netted.	And you'll all be gazetted.

Cobbett warned of the wider effects: 'When farmers become *gentlemen* their labourers become *slaves*.'

Down a peg from the landowning Quality, England could boast more prosperous folk than almost any other nation: self-employed men and masters of movable property, men of money. Sandwiched between the 'rise of the bourgeoisie' which Marxist historians have traditionally located in Tudor and Stuart times, and the steam-powered advance of business wealth in the age of the Great Exhibition, the fortunes of these middle men in Georgian England have remained in historical limbo – oddly, since the age was one of accelerating urban growth and advance in trade and manufactures.

One difficulty is that we don't accurately know what portion of the community the moneyed made up. Gregory King thought that around the end of the seventeenth century their numbers and yearly family incomes were as follows:

1,500 persons in liberal arts and sciences	£60
5,000 shopkeepers	£45
5,000 big office-holders	£240
5,000 lesser office-holders	£120
2,000 big merchants	£400
8,000 lesser traders	£198
10,000 men in law	£154
2,000 higher clergy	£72
8,000 lower clergy	£50

But these figures – both aggregate numbers and incomes – seem to be underestimates, spectacularly so in some cases. Granted that few men of liquid wealth could match substantial landowners in assets, a recent calculation shows that at the end of the seventeenth century 22 per cent of London freemen had estates of between £1,000 and £5,000, and 5 per cent had ones of £5,000.

Before the days of the great entrepreneurs, when Manchester became Cottonopolis, the middle orders were indeed chameleon-like. There were no armed 'bourgeois' or 'Jacobin' insurrections in England against the old regime as there were in some parts of Europe and of course in the American colonies: they were unnecessary – such men already had their fingers in established society. Yet this dearth of organized, articulate bourgeois revolutionaries has left men of business and trade rather well camouflaged. Certain historians, notably E. P. Thompson, have discussed Georgian social distinctions mainly in terms of 'patricians' and 'plebeians', and in this polarizing scenario middle men remain largely behind the scenes, operating a client economy servicing the Great. Of course, this is just what very many did. Thousands of master-craftsmen and small manufacturers made their living primarily out of the Quality market: jewellers, tailors, carriage-builders, perruquiers and milliners, the blind musicians who fiddled at aristocratic orgies, and even top portrait painters such as Joshua Reynolds. Landed estates yielded bumper crops of litigation for lawyers to reap, and physicians made their greatest profits from gouty peers, especially in spa towns such as Bath. Every gentleman needed the services of a penumbra of bailiffs, attorneys, clergy, surveyors, stewards, mortgage-brokers, and horticulturalists. Directly and indirectly, the livelihoods of artists, poets, architects, designers, and tutors lay in the palms of the Great.

Many middling men hated thus being superior flunkeys, for clientage required sycophancy's mask. Economic dependency was humiliating and nerve-racking, especially because the nobs expected boundless and eternal credit from their suppliers (who in turn made them pay through the nose). Even if all bills were finally honoured, the system meant that tradesmen were being forced to invest in their betters, like the National Debt. Those who could tried to cut the strings of clientship. 'A patron is a man who looks on with unconcern at a man struggling for life in the water, and when he reaches the bank, encumbers him with help': Dr Johnson's exposure of Lord Chesterfield's uselessness as the patron of his dictionary expressed the silent gall of many. Johnson was one of the fortunate who became able to swim for himself.

Few were as successful as Johnson, and throughout the century tradesmen and artists fawned. Yet imitation was also the sincerest form of flattery. What did envious bourgeois want more than to be welcomed into genteel society? (As Cannadine has written, 'The ultimate proof of success in business was the ability to leave it.') 'Merchants are commonly ambitious of becoming country gentlemen': Adam Smith's observation was a platitude. In moneyed men's attempts to become gentlefolks, a good marriage could often do the trick. Sir James Bateman, governor of the Bank of England and director of the East India Company, saw his son marry the daughter of the Earl of Sunderland and become Viscount Bateman. Land could do the same. City plutocrats had traditionally bought up acres in the Home Counties (Defoe had his fictional Robinson Crusoe buy land in Bedfordshire on his return to England) – though a token estate, such as a gardened villa at Chiswick, would increasingly do. In Leeds, merchants tended to be Tory and Anglican, aligning not down with textile manufacturers but up with the outlying gentry. The town's merchant princes, such as the Gotts, Milneses, and Denisons, realized their dreams by purchasing estates and hiring prestige architects and artists such as Benjamin Wilson and Romney. But upstart entrepreneurs of the Industrial Revolution equally aspired to gentility. It was, apart from anything else, good business sense. Jedediah Strutt the hosier informed his son about ingratiation:

You are not to be a nobleman or prime minister but you may possibly be a tradesman of some eminence and as such you will necessarily have connexions with mankind and the world; and that will make it absolutely necessary to know them both: you may be armed if you add to the little learning and improvement you have hitherto had, the manners, the air, the genteel address and polite behaviour of a gentleman, you will absolutely find your act in it every transaction of your future life – when you come to do business in the world.

But it was also vanity and emulation. Manufacturers rushed pell-mell into land: Marshall of Leeds, Arkwright, Strutt, Horrocks, and Peel all bought estates, and thus status. Land was at least a secure investment, though yielding meagre profit – but it wasn't bought for profit. With the estate went its accoutrements: 'The merchant,' wrote Soame Jenyns, 'vies all the while with the first of our nobility in his houses, table, furniture, and equipage.' Nor could genteel bearing be neglected. Strutt rushed his son Billy a copy of Lord Chesterfield's *Letters to His Son*, advising, 'It is almost as necessary to learn a genteel behaviour and polite manners as it is to learn to speak or read or write' (though Dr Johnson thought the *Letters* taught 'the morals of a whore and the manners of a dancing master').

In all ways 'the middle class of people in this country', as Chesterfield himself put it, were 'straining to imitate their betters'; to turn, if not into landed gentlemen, at least into a para-gentry who could put 'Esq.' after their names without blushing. When Josiah Wedgwood started to design fashionable pottery, he looked first to conquer the Quality market, coining brand names like Queensware, partly with the aim of later appealing to the much larger market of the middle-class snobs.

English moneyed society wanted to cover its tracks; to show it was no vulgar 'shopocracy', but rather a rightful guest at the Quality ball. One sign of this is that it did not unite to form its own exclusive political ideology, party, or machine. The multifarious interests of the mercantile community never saw eye-to-eye with each other on war and foreign policy. Explicitly middle-class political activism was as yet fleeting (the middle class by contrast could parade as the rock of political wisdom by the Reform years of the next century). But it was not entirely absent: City radicals were rehearsing the refrains, as did William Beckford, the London alderman, in 1761: 'When I talk of the sense of the people, I mean the middling people of England . . . the manufacturer, the yeoman, the merchant, the country gentleman, they who bear the heat of the day' (though the social fricassee in Beckford's list is itself revealing).

Political causes which rallied tradesmen and masters, though frequent and boisterous, were usually triggered by very particular grievances, especially trade downswings; they were now pro-war, now anti-war, but generally anti-Spanish, anti-Court, and anti-excise. Alignments were formed not on class lines, but by a sense of Them and Us, Ins and Outs. Deep resentments and anxieties about the arbitrary power and privileges of the Great became vocal in popular Toryism and then in the pro-Wilkes agitations in London and the provinces in the 1760s, but the adventures of this gadfly in the Establishment ointment were a *détour de force*: they gelled into an ideology of the defence of rights but did not give rise to a sustained programme of middle-class political emancipation. Similarly, radical movements such as the Society for Constitutional Information, snapping at the heels of a corrupt legislature, won urban support; yet they had aristo-cratic leaders and their demands were couched in the traditional constitutional rhetoric of the redemption of the ancient Consti-tution. Business leaders in the mushrooming industrial com-munities of the Midlands and North were in two minds about parliamentary reform. They resented their own lack of repre-sentation, yet neither did they want their pitches queered by the debauched aristocratic carpet-bagging · candidates and the mobs' para-political disturbances that Eatanswill elections being a moneyed man and backing radicalism. For every bour-geois Friend of the People, there were a dozen friends of prop-erty, and a score more who just raised their goblets to trade. Middling men were not dyed-in-the-wool Whigs or Tories (though most Dissenters were Whiggish). Classic bourgeois shibboleths such as the career open to talent still lay in the future.

Rather in political matters the mercantile classes chose to operate a system which, though not theirs, could provide them with leverage at strategic points. In Parliament neither nabobs and businessmen - such as Henry Thrale the Southwark brewer - nor MPs for mercantile constituencies such as Bristol tried to develop middle-class alliances. Instead they shepherded the in-terests of particular trades, either through pledging their services with ministries as place-men or contractors, or, through back-bench lobbying, currying the favour of ministers. Even when they set up the (soon abortive) General Chamber of Manufac-turers in 1785, master manufacturers such as Samuel Garbett, Wedgwood, and Boulton argued for their commercial goals in the snuff-filled ante-rooms of Westminster, not on the streets, or at the hustings.

Another way in which these middling men are protean is in their vocational aspirations, which defy modern stereotypes. Professional pride of the kind later prominent in the Victorian civil service code of 'duty' meant little. In liberal callings such as medicine and the law, there was scant idealistic *esprit de corps* policing lofty standards of training and responsibility. Chartered professional corporations such as the College of Physicians or the Inns of Court operated as closed, oligarchic monopolies jealously guarding their privileges. There were only forty-five Fellows of the College of Physicians in 1745, and fewer than 400 practising barristers. Entry into the higher echelons was not by proven merit but by completing courses of social rituals: one qualified for the Bar by eating dinners at the Inns of Court. Though the professions were monopolistic – all barristers had to be called to the Bar – most workaday practitioners of medicine and law were excluded from their governing bodies and privileges. Thus by statute, only doctors licensed by the Royal College of Physicians could practise as physicians in and around London. Surgeons were licensed only to operate (and only surgeons could operate), apothecaries only to dispense drugs. An Oxford, Cambridge, or Dublin degree was necessary for becoming a Fellow of the Royal College of Physicians (although the top medical schools were Leiden in Holland, Edinburgh, and Glasgow). Apothecaries, of vast importance as general practitioners, and attorneys (solicitors) were trained, like craftsmen, on the job by apprenticeship. Though many attorneys were the younger sons of gentlemen, the occupation had little éclat. Dr Johnson once remarked that 'he did not care to speak ill of any man behind his back, but he believed the gentleman was an *attorney*'. Yet attorneys, their fingers in every pie, fixing mortgages and acting as bankers and political agents as well as handling litigation, were indispensable to local communities. Outside the courts, they were much in demand as informal arbitrators, conciliators, and honest brokers. Their numbers expanded and many got rich. By the end of the century Bristol and Liverpool both had over seventy attorneys. The Sheffield attorney Joseph Banks, who acted as a moneylender, put £40,000 into land between 1705 and 1727. A successful provincial doctor such as Erasmus Darwin at Derby could net over £1,000 a year in fees.

Few occupations were anxious to elevate themselves into formally chartered, liberal professions. Tooth-drawers, mill-wrights, schoolteachers, valuers, architects, land-agents, and civil servants – all groups which became haunted in the nineteenth century by the quest for professional security and status – remained unincorporated; without academic training, exams and paper qualifications, without codified professional ethics, without a closed shop. No surgeon was knighted until 1778; no engineer until 1841. Though surgeons left the barbers' company in 1745, they did not get a royal charter until 1800.

Outside holy orders and the medical and legal top brass middle-class occupations were fluid and personal. This is partly because many remained small in absolute numbers. There was only a score of professors. In Georgian times, most 'white-collar' work was done by unpaid amateurs and part-timers, from MPs, JPs and overseers of the poor to philanthropists. The tally of Whitehall civil servants wielding quills in fusty offices was tiny (as distinct from the hated revenue officers, who had shot up to about 20,000 by the end of the century). In 1743 the Treasury staff was twenty-three; eight clerks manned the Admiralty. (France by contrast had tens of thousands of heredi-tary bureaucrats whose families had invested in office.) Entry was essentially personal through recommendation, patronage, or nepotism. Many 'service' employments also remained low in status. It was a vicious circle. Nurses in the London hospitals were low-paid and untrained, and were regularly dismissed for tipsiness, schoolmasters often young unbeneficed clergy click-ing their heels. Both lived down to expectations. Walter Gale, failed fabric-designer, sign-painter, and hop-farmer, was taken on at £12 a year by Mayfield parish in Sussex to run the village school. Tom Paine, stay-maker by training (and later revolu-tionary), had spells as schoolmaster and excise-man. Next to nothing was done for threadbare curates on £10 or £15 a year. (Queen Anne's Bounty helped a little.) No one thought a job such as prison warder could be a social-service vocation; it was treated as a licence to milk inmates of fees.

White-collar occupations did not tend to breed binding corporate professionalism: why should they? Their practitioners were content to be men of business, guineas jingling in their purses, rather than public servants. Upward mobility was individual rather than collective. It was no-holds-barred in the clamour for advancement. Competition was fierce amongst doctors for patients and for fees (medical ethics were as yet ill-formulated through Thomas Percival published some in 1803). Thus it was a source of gossip rather than professional ignominy when two leading London physicians, Richard Mead and John Woodward, duelled. Rewards could be high. A successful London physician, such as the Quaker John Lettsom, could pocket up to £12,000 a year in fees. Lord Kenyon, who began his career as an attorney, earned £80,000 in twelve years as Master of the Rolls. Lord Chancellor Eldon's fees in 1810 amounted to £22,730 (he died worth £700,000, with land on top).

If professionals had an ambiguous identity, businessmen and tradesmen, however, presented a much more solid front. In many continental monarchies most bourgeois comprised bureaucrats, from mandarin crown servants down to clergy and schoolmaster's. England by contrast had a swelling and confident middle rank dedicated to making money: manufacturers (from the ubiquitous workshop master to the brand-new factory owner), wholesale and retail tradesmen, speculators, investors, and scriveners, down to master-butchers, bakers, and candlestick-makers. Many had scrappy academic education and none paper qualifications, but they knew how to seal a deal. Though lacking national political power, they had a nose for business. Making money needed no excuse: 'I soon came to a resolution of making this launch into the wide world, repairing to *London*, in order to SEEK MY FORTUNE', said John Cleland's heroine, Fanny Hill. Except in the social stratosphere, trade was respectable. 'Our tradesmen are not as in other countries,' explained Daniel Defoe, 'the meanest of our people. Some of the greatest and best and most flourishing families, among not the gentry only but even the nobility have been raised from trade.' No one denied this, from haughty scholars such as Edward Gibbon ('Our most respectable families have not disdained the counting house or even the shop') to the Birmingham jack-of-all-trades, Dissenter William Hutton ('the man of business is the man of liberal sentiment; a barbarous and commercial people is a contradiction').

Middle-class wealth stretched from the cols of the money mountain down to the foothills. In 1750 it was reckoned one needed a capital of £20,000 to set up as a banker, £2,000–10,000 to be a brewer and £1,000–5,000 to be a woollen draper; £10–100 would start you off as a butcher. At the top, the pick of the plutocrats lived in London, quite a few of them Huguenots or Sephardic Jews – Janssens, Lamberts, Da Costas, Medinas, Salvadors, Pereiras. Sampson Gideon subscribed £300,000 to the Government loan of 1744, bequeathing a fortune of over £500,000. The Lord Mayor of London in 1724, Sir Peter Delmé, held £122,000 in South Sea stock and £118,000 in Bank stock. Insurers, brokers, discounters, jobbers, contractors – men who got richer in their sleep – crowded into Wren's City. Over 90 per cent of those holding more than £5,000 Bank of England stock at the beginning of the century lived in London and the Home Counties. Aside from the boom world of the money market, fortunes grew vast most easily in overseas trade. John Pinney, born into a family of West India merchants, started with £70,000 and turned it into £340,000. 'Some merchants,' wrote César de Saussure in 1727, 'are certainly far wealthier than many sovereign princes of Germany or Italy.'

But merchant princes – 'the life, spring and motion of the trading world', according to Addison – also flourished outside the metropolis. Indian nabobs turned themselves into country gentry, buying parliamentary seats to forestall investigations of their business skulduggery. Bristol had tobacco barons and slave-traders such as the Colstons, Yateses, and Youngs; Liverpool had its Rathbones and Gladstones. The Liddells, Blacketts, and Ridleys were the kings of the coal vent in Newcastle. King's Lynn trade was controlled by the Turner family, relatives of the Walpoles. These cohorts of the upper-middle class – perhaps 2,000 in 1700, rising to 3,500 in 1800 – intermarried, pooled capital as partners, and passed their businesses on, especially when religious scruples, as with the Quakers, foreclosed the stampede into land. The fashionable roads to ruin being shut off, parsimonious friends such as the Lloyds, the Gurneys and the Darbys, lasted for generations, accumulating all the time. On their fringes were fast-increasing numbers of men and women of some capital – many of them retired – who lived off annuities and investments.

Beneath the plutocrats was an anthill of petty traders, horse-dealers, builders, inn-keepers, and manufacturers who excelled in turning a penny for themselves: men prepared to work hard, adapt to the ups and downs of the market, put their irons in many fires and drive hard bargains. As one of the leaders of the cut-throat Newcastle coal trade put it, it was 'every man for himself and God for us all'. In Newcastle competition often erupted into gang violence between the agents and the hired thugs of the top merchants.

Prospects were particularly good for wholesalers as markets widened, fairs declined, and haulage improved. There were good pickings in transport itself. William Chaplin's coaching service in Regency London employed 2,000 men and used 1,800 horses. Pickford's ran ten canal boats and fifty waggons in the 1790s. The opportunities were there for those who could take them. 'Each man has his fortune in his own hands,' intoned the Birmingham businessman, William Hutton, quoting Francis Bacon. He knew from experience. Born in 1723, son of a Dissenting wool-comber, and apprenticed at seven, Hutton came to Birmingham in 1741 as a stockinger seeking work. Whereas his father 'had no ideas of business or economy', the son was ambitious. He set up a small bookshop and circulating library; on the profits he tried bookbinding, paper-making and then land-dealing. By 1768 he was worth £2,000; he had property worth over £8,000 destroyed in the Birmingham Riots of 1791. Similarly Francis Place, son of a dissolute but energetic baker, began work as a breeches-maker. Through thrift, self-control, and entrepreneurial talent, he rose to be one of the top manufacturing tailors in London, earning £3,000 a year. Parallel success stories are legion. William Strahan, apprenticed to an Edinburgh printer, came to London in 1738 to try his fortune. He made friends with the literati, published Hume, Johnson, Gibbon, and Adam Smith, became the king's printer, and died worth £95,000. Another who learned the lessons of the industrious apprentice was the Newcastle merchant William

Cotesworth. Starting out as a tallow-chandler's apprentice, at his height he traded 'for upwards of £30,000 a year in anything he could gain by'.

Others did well at more modest levels. Abraham Dent of Kirkby Stephen in Westmorland was primarily a grocer, and had a turnover of £1,000 a year from his shop. But – a pluralist like so many others – he also made money as a brewer, bill-broker, small landowner and wholesale hosier, supplying locally woven stockings to Government contractors in London (slipping in juicy *douceurs* of Westmorland hams).

Furthermore, even before the advent of the entrepreneurial moguls, tradesmen who could blaze a trail got even fatter pickings. In 1774 James Lackington, self-educated ex-cobbler and Methodist, set up in business at Finsbury Circus as a second-hand bookseller aided by a loan of £5 from his co-religionists. He modernized bookselling by standardizing prices, pricing each item, pioneering remainder-selling and issuing catalogues. Unusually for a tradesman, he gave no credit. By 1791 he was selling 100,000 volumes a year, and with slim margins and giant turnover was making a profit of about £5,000 through being 'the cheapest bookseller in the world'. 'Small profits, bound by industry, and clasped by economy' was his motto; his boast: 'Small profits do great things.'

England teemed with practical men of enterprise, weather-eye open, from tycoons to humble master-craftsmen. Richard Savage, wrote Dr Johnson, 'having no profession became by necessity an author'. In the 1740s the poor curate at Broughton in Yorkshire kept a pub. Some, especially Dissenters, were dour, penny-pinching and cheap-living, pursuing the moral rules for business probity spelt out by Hogarth's prints, and Defoe's and Franklin's writings ('Early to bed, early to rise'). But many breezed along in a more free-and-easy way, improvisers, convivial, living from day to day. They liked their leisure and pleasure – Defoe was worried about shopkeepers' 'ostentation of plate'. Few had very strict accounting methods (there were exceptions, such as Josiah Wedgwood). With labyrinthine credit networks, speculative investments, coin shortages, irregular cash-flow, and large outgoings on property and family, traders often had little control over the wheel of their fortunes. Taking profits and losses as they came, great businessmen such as Henry Thrale occasionally had to go round cap-in-hand to their friends. And bank crashes and credit collapses meant that even sound businessmen were always at risk of finding themselves bankrupt, or whisked off to the debtors' gaol.

What characterized the trading classes was the itch to make money and make a name for themselves. 'Oh, what pleasure is business,' exclaimed Thomas Turner, the Sussex shopkeeper. 'Here lies Jedediah Strutt' – the industrialist ordered to be chiselled on his gravestone – 'who, without Fortune, Family or friends raised himself to a fortune, family and name in the world.' As he himself acknowledged, money was at the root. 'I was this day through Cheapside, the Change, etc.,' he wrote in 1767,

and could not help immediately reflecting that the sole cause of that vast concourse of people, of the hurry and bustle they were in, and the eagerness that appeared in their countenances, was the getting of Money, and whatever some divines would teach to the contrary, this is true that it is the main business of the life of man.

They put great trust in industry and success. 'The orders I have made,' insisted the iron-founder Ambrose Crowley, 'are built upon such a rock that while I have my understanding it shall be out of the power of Satan and all his disciples to destroy them.' Beneath big fish such as Strutt and Crowley were shoals of small businessmen and master-craftsmen who played a vital role in the economy. Not least in importance were shopkeepers. Long before Napoleon, Adam Smith had called England 'a nation of shopkeepers' – by late in the century there were upwards of 170,000.

Shops and small manufactories were everywhere. Petworth was a Sussex town of about 1,000 inhabitants, serving the local farming community, and provisioning the house and estate of the Earls of Egremont. About 5 per cent of its population consisted of professionals – clergy, doctors, lawyers. A further 20 per cent were of the commercial middle class – merchants, shopkeepers, inn-keepers, retailers, millers, maltsters, peruke-makers, vintners, tanners, butchers, surgeons, barbers, school-teachers. The inventories of Petworth tradesmen show about 30 per cent leaving goods and property worth between £100 and £500. Birmingham directories list the following tradesmen in the 1770s:

248 Innkeepers	46 Brassfounders
129 Buttonmakers	39 Shopkeepers
99 Shoemakers	39 Bucklemasters
77 Merchants	36 Gunmakers
74 Tailors	35 Jewellers
64 Bakers	26 Maltsters
56 Toymakers	24 Drapers
52 Platers	23 Gardeners
49 Butchers	21 Plumbers/Glaziers
48 Carpenters	21 Ironmongers
46 Barbers	

It was these swarms of the petty bourgeoisie who helped make the English economy special. For, antedating and quite independently of the Industrial Revolution, England had a lively economy in which plenty of enterprising masters and dealers were successful, while home consumption amongst middling families proved a bellows for workshop-based manufacturing capitalism – as Patrick Colquhoun indicated:

> It is not ... an excess of property to the few, but the extension of it among the mass of the community, which appears most likely to prove beneficial with respect to national wealth and national happiness. Perhaps no other country in the world possesses greater advantages in this respect than Great Britain, and hence that spirit of enterprise and that profitable employment of diffused capitals which has created so many resources for productive labour beyond any other country in Europe.

As Giuseppe Baretti noted, 'The English do their utmost to make money: but once they have made it, they spend it freely.'

As the century wore on, new occupations wedged themselves between the plutocrat and the humble shopkeeper. Whereas Gregory King had not thought it necessary to list 'manufacturers' as a separate occupational group, later social statisticians such as Joseph Massie and Patrick Colquhoun registered their growing numbers: Colquhoun thought there were 25,000. The term 'manufacturer' itself began to shed its traditional generalized meaning of 'craftsman', becoming increasingly restricted to large-scale owners of plant and employers of labour. Greater numbers carved out careers as technical specialists. Agricultural experts such as Arthur Young, guidebook writers, and handbook compilers emerged, making their living by the pen. Surveyors, technicians, civil engineers, instrument-makers, cartographers, mill-wrights, turnpike-builders (such as Thomas Telford, the 'Colossus of Roads') swelled in number as the economy became more technologically orientated. Samuel Bentham, brother of the Utilitarian Jeremy, set the manufacture of ships' biscuits for the navy on a production-line basis. Whereas abroad technologists generally formed a state salariat or held military rank, in England most were self-employed entrepreneurs of expertise. For instance William Smith, England's pioneer geologist, was a self-educated land surveyor, canal engineer and mines prospector. And more openings were continually appearing for writers, commercial artists, industrial designers, and impresarios of the arts. Bewick, the Newcastle engraver, bird painter, and writer, was the son of a small farmer.

Finally, towards the end of the century, something like a self-conscious Enlightenment intelligentsia was coming into being: writers such as Joseph Priestley, Richard Price, James Burgh, William Godwin, Thomas Beddoes, Mary Wollstonecraft, William Hazlitt, and Arthur Aikin, making a living by teaching, journalism, lecturing, editing, publishing, reviewing, and translating; mostly young, astringent in tone, temperament, and belief, many of them lapsed Dissenters. Clustering round radical publishers such as Joseph Johnson and the Dissenting academies in villages such as Hackney and Newington Green, abutting London to the north-east, they were associated with budding Romanticism, heterodox religion, and philosophical radicalism. This *avant garde* (and similar coteries elsewhere, such as the Dissenting communities in Warrington and Manchester) was only obliquely a political force: they were concerned more with ideals and exposing the privilege of the mighty and the corruption of the state than with wresting power. Yet they formed the nerve centre of a new cadre of professional thinkers and communicators (Coleridge's clerisy), experimenting in alternative life-styles – earnest rather than Bohemian – from vegetarianism to Coleridge's golden-age dream of Pantisocracy on the banks of the Susqueshanna.

In the nation moneyed men enjoyed economic sway rather than political clout at Westminster, though many commanded great local influence within corporations and vestries. Banding themselves together in clubs, masonic lodges, and tavern free-and-easys, celebrating conviviality, their social aspect and living habits endorsed the values vital to commercial success: confidence, good credit, connexion, fellowship, and consumption. They exuded self-respect (respectability came later), typified by the rubicund tradesmen who swaggered down Beer Street in Hogarth's etchings cheering for Pitt the Elder. Many would have encored Joseph Priestley's sunny view that 'there appears to be much more happiness in the middle classes of life who are above the fear of want, and yet have a sufficient motive for a constant exertion of their faculties'.

Their clubs, toasts, songs, and slogans made trade, freedom, patriotism, and credit (financial and moral) all link arms. Their constitutional and debating societies, their experience of service on corporations, vestries, and parishes, served as auditions for the national theatre of politics to come. They howled against interference and taxation (though because capital and movable property were almost untaxed they actually came off lightly), and thereby served notice to their betters that their prosperity must not be jeopardized.

Beneath the moneyed men, were the craftsmen and artisans, the labourers and the poor. There was nothing homogeneous about the lower orders, who ranged from weavers to watermen, from ostlers to shepherds, from ploughmen to piemen, from crossing-sweepers to coal-miners. Women traditionally did similar jobs to men's; they also washed clothes, sold milk and greens, stitched gowns, and were wet-nurses and prostitutes. Above all, women span, kept house, and raised children. Working families very commonly won a living by piecing together a variety of seasonal, part-time, and casual employments: the land and the loom, hop-picking, spinning, fishing, barking timber, weeding, etc. And there were vagrants, paupers, the old, the sick, the unemployed, and society's flotsam and jetsam – and their young. Labouring people's strength was sapped for little reward and no thanks. In most other countries the bulk of them were serfs or peasants: in England, they were largely wage-labourers (though still insistently called 'servants' by their masters). Although there were droves of self-employed workers, such as thatchers, woodcutters, tinkers, and knife-grinders, by mid-century between 40 and 50 per cent of all English families were wage-earning. Those who did not control their own labour but worked for others included farmhands, a growing body; journeymen in manufactures and building; and spinners, carders, rovers, weavers, and stocking-knitters in large-scale putting-out industry run by capitalist clothiers and later on in factories. They included most women and children, who worked in subtle or direct dependency on husbands, fathers, and masters; servants in husbandry, and domestic servants – predominantly young and single and easily the largest occupational group, numbering some 600,000–700,000. England was traditionally 'the purgatory of servants', and the jurist Blackstone called master and servant – meaning employees in general – one of the three great relations of private life. And they included apprentices, living in, who received board but scant wages.

Within the traditional handicraft economy the standing of many workers rose with their age and point in the life-cycle. The teenager was put into service or apprenticed for seven years to a trade. In their twenties they would become journeymen and marry; some would in time become small masters. Yet, with growing capitalization, in many industries the gap between owners and labourers was widening. In mining for example, where shafts became deeper and more costly to sink, self-employing gangs of workers gave way to capitalist owners of winding and pumping gear, employing labourers. In the second half of the century, moreover, the rising numbers seeking work tipped the balance of economic power in favour of employers. Guild restrictions on entry into trades were smashed, the pool of day labourers swelled, and a greater proportion of working people spent their whole working lives as mere labourers, becoming a real proletariat.

Such polarizing effects caused concern. Working men's 'motives to industry, frugality and sobriety are all subverted by this one consideration,' wrote Dean Tucker, of the highly capitalized Gloucestershire cloth trade, 'that they shall always be chained to the same oar, and never be but journeymen'. Furthermore, apprentices might be little better off than slaves. Maltreatment of child apprentices was not infrequent; especially vulnerable were the London waifs and orphans farmed out to contractors and manufacturers. In 1764 a farmer from near Malmesbury was committed for trial for maiming and castrating two apprentices. It was alleged that having received the premium for them, he tried to kill the boys off by giving them smallpox.

Duty hours – especially for servants-of-all-work – were gruellingly long. Dawn to dusk was a common span, though in certain trades journeymen's combinations had secured a ten-hour day. Household servants were hardly allowed lives of their own. Working conditions were often hellish – the flames and sulphureous fumes of vats and furnaces, the lethal damps and gases of the coal-face, the perils of the sea, doubled by under-manned, waterlogged, but well-insured vessels. Workmen in physical trades such as sawyers became prematurely wizened, succumbing to ghastly industrial diseases; fumes and dust brought on lung and bronchial conditions, many lead-miners for example contracting plumbism and no new legislation protecting against occupational diseases and hazards was introduced. Around ports, common seamen were never safe from the shanghai'ing press-gangs. Women's earnings in particular were derisory; they got only about two thirds the wages of men. Workers had no compensation against slumps or seasonal under-employment, when snow, floods, or drought halted trade (the well-off working man was the one in employment twelve months in the year). Men were subjected to brutality from their masters (soldiers and sailors were flogged as matters of routine), women, especially servants, were prey to sexual exploitation. Further hardships were piled on, for instance payment by truck rather than in coin, or long in arrears (though this did enforce a form of savings). Even Dean Tucker, a friend of capitalism, admitted that in some industries the relationship between master and worker 'approached much nearer to that of a planter and slaves in our American colonies than might be expected of such a country as England'.

The well-to-do feared the labouring poor, yet many also acknowledged their skills and steadfastness and counted themselves fortunate that England was not infested with beggars and bandits as other places were. The American traveller Louis Simond offered a crumb of comfort: 'the poor do not look so poor here as in other countries,' yet humanitarians could see that many of the labouring classes did not receive a subsistence wage, John Wesley being scandalized by what he saw. 'I found some in their cells, others in their garrets,' he wrote in his diary in 1753, 'half starved with cold and hunger, added to weakness and pain. But I found not one of them unemployed who was able to crawl about the room. So wickedly, so devilishly false, is that common objection, "They are poor because they are idle."'

People admitted that the working masses bore the luxury of the well-to-do on their shoulders. 'I never see lace and embroidery upon the back of a beau,' wrote a correspondent to the *Northampton Mercury* in 1739, 'but my thoughts descend to the poor fingers that have wrought it ... What would avail our large estates and great tracts of land without their labours?' Or, as the pope of capitalism, Adam Smith, disarmingly phrased it, 'In a civilized society the poor provide both for themselves and for the enormous luxury of their superiors.' Under these circumstances, although the polite upbraided the insolence of what Horace Walpole dubbed 'our supreme governors, the mob', the wonder was they were so tractable. 'The sufferings of the poor are indeed less observed than their misdeeds,' wrote Henry Fielding. 'They starve and freeze and rot among themselves, but they beg and steal and rob among their betters.' The humanity of labourers was sacrificed on the treadmill of work. Many hardly lived outside work (miners often slept down the pit). As a haberdasher's assistant Robert Owen often worked till two in the morning. Abigails and apprentices were expected to be chaste; their private lives were under surveillance. Servants might even lose their own names, being dubbed (like pets) 'Betty' or 'John Thomas'. They received most of their remuneration indirectly, not in money wages, but in bed and board, cast-offs, shelter, perks, tips. A maid-of-all-work might be paid a princely £3 a year.

The workplace was often exhausting; there was as yet little labour-saving machinery. Yet it could also have its compensations – often more so than home life. In long-established urban trades such as tanning or tailoring, covered by the Elizabethan Statute of Artificers, guilds and companies were still strong. Their rules and traditions restricted entry and upheld apprenticeship (enforcing the seven-year term and limiting the number of apprentices per master), and by-laws made established rates of pay and terms of work enforceable by magistrates. Indentured apprenticeship requirements gave qualified journeymen in effect a closed shop, a property in their skill. The presence of statutes gave muscle to collective bargaining: workers were demanding only their legal due. Thus freemen of London companies often applied to the Lord Mayor's court – a kind of industrial tribunal – for relief against masters who introduced blacklegs.

In workshop teams skilled journeymen enjoyed their own time-hallowed rituals of collective strength and conviviality, with their ribald work-songs and traditional horse-play. Trades had their own coats of arms, regalia, slang, anniversary parades, and licensed fooleries, competing against each other in sports and setting up benefit and friendly societies in taverns. For particularly gruelling work, such as sheep-shearing, workers would be rewarded with cakes, ale, and jollification. In town, events such as executions or mayors' parades were cues for time-off, dressing-up, and revels. In many trades ancient usage protected the rate for the job and fringe benefits, and journeymen dug in their heels against encroachments – often with success. Strikes, though localized, were part of the fabric of industrial relations and could be backed up by intimidation – anonymous threatening letters, effigy-burning, or machine-smashing. John Kay's home was attacked in 1753 by workers protesting against his 'flying shuttle'. A few years later Blackburn spinners destroyed Hargreaves's spinning jennies. Nottinghamshire hosiers smashed hundreds of Arkwright's stocking frames in 1779 after failing to secure a minimum wage (significantly the workers won their point, and there were no successful prosecutions against the wreckers). As the century wore on, combinations (trade unions), mostly clandestine and masked by 'box-clubs', increased. Journeymen tailors and stay-makers were the most powerful London combinations, but they were strong amongst carpenters, joiners, bricklayers, masons, shipwrights, lightermen, wool-combers, and in many other trades.

Protection of work within a 'moral economy' worked well enough for craftsmen in the first half of the century when labour was in relatively short supply. Later, things got more difficult. With inflation climbing from the 1760s, workers increasingly needed to press to raise wages. Thus, in 1775, Islington hay-makers, customarily on 1s. 4d. a day, struck for 1s. 6d.: they got it. But the flooding of the labour market as population rose, and owners' introduction of new technology requiring less skilled operatives, put craftsmen's backs against the wall. For example, late in the century in the Cotswold cloth industry, capitalists were introducing mechanical gig mills to replace properly apprenticed skilled labour. The workers resisted fiercely but lost. Strikes against innovations in machinery and the undermining of apprenticeship regulations grew more frequent. Government responded by repealing legislation protecting apprenticeship and terms of work (statutory apprenticeship was abolished in 1814). In any case, the Elizabethan protective legislation had never applied to 'new' trades, such as cotton-spinning and calico-printing. Under the 1799 and 1800 (anti-)Combination Acts, workers forming illegal combinations could be summarily gaoled for three months, after appearing before only one magistrate.

Working people won some control over their lives – and some relief – in two ways. First, many of them took advantage of working under the noses of their betters, domestic servants above all. Appreciating what Gibbon called 'the indispensable comfort of a servant', no gentleman wanted to be surrounded by lousy, stinking ragamuffins. It was in masters' interests to supply wigs and bodices, medical treatment, and even some education for those who served and waited. Though deploring their impertinence, many wished to use such upper servants as footmen and lady's maids as confidantes, accomplices, go-betweens, and pets. William Hogarth painted his. Perhaps particularly early in the century, servants might be regarded as part of the family. A few eccentric families, most notably the Yorkes at Erddig in North Wales, took loving care of their staff, writing verses about them and having their portraits painted (though they still paid them badly). Gentlemen's gentlemen such as John Macdonald might be choosy about their employers – he got through twenty-seven masters. Service for him was an opportunity for foreign travel and raffish sexual adventure, leaving him savings enough to establish a hotel. Ex-butlers often set up inns. Charles Fortnum, once a footman of George III, founded the later illustrious provision shop. Servants were not slow to exploit their immense blackmailing potential. What the butler saw frequently came out in testimony against their masters in court, especially in adultery cases, and sometimes their silence had to be bought. They scrutinized low life above stairs, and mimicked high life below stairs.

In any case custom gave servants many perks. Cooks were allowed to sell off dripping and cinders, and they expected commission from shopkeepers; maids inherited clothes when their mistress died. Servants who lived in ate well. So thumping were the tips (called 'vails') which servants expected from house-guests (some would take only silver) that a campaign to abolish 'taking the vail' went as far as the Commons – provoking servants to riot in 1764. What is more, there were endless openings for tipplers and the light-fingered. In the intricate hierarchy of servants' hall, upper servants assumed airs, wielding their own authority. Not least, the exceptional maid might – like Pamela in Richardson's novel – marry her master. Boswell records an attorney who wed his cookmaid 'because she dressed a lovely bit of collop'.

Servants' lives might be degrading; they were always on call, their personal life was stifled, and jeopardizing their good character could spell ruin. Yet masters' complaints about pert servants (where could trusty ones be found?), and servants' own high mobility from post to post, proves they had real bargaining power. Many undoubtedly used service as an entrée into a superior world.

The other respite for the lower orders was that they did not worship the idol of work. They knew labour did not ennoble *them*. Few possessed the 'bourgeois' spirit of thrifty accumulation (not too many of the bourgeoisie did, either). This was quite rational: with wages low and labour long, increasing earnings significantly would have been a pipedream for most. They preferred leisure to working harder and saving, and spent what they had (again rational: possessing savings was likely to disqualify a family from poor relief). Because out-work paid by the piece, many artisans could work their own hours. They commonly took Monday off (St Monday) – the devout honoured St Tuesday too – and then they worked like maniacs through to Saturday, when pay-day brought a binge. Also – as Benjamin Franklin and Francis Place bemoaned – Englishmen downed quarts while they worked.

Because of their irregular work habits, labouring men were always being cursed as feckless. 'When wages are good,' prated Defoe, 'they won't work any more than from hand to mouth; or if they do work they spend it in riot or luxury.' He concluded, 'we are the most lazy-diligent nation in the world'. J. Powell echoed this complaint fifty years later in 1772: 'If a person can get sufficient in four days, to support himself for seven days, he will keep holiday the other three, that is he will live in riot and debauchery.' Labourers fretted the employing classes, because they kicked against their allotted life of drudgery, preferring addiction to ale and letting off steam. As Dr George Fordyce put it, workmen earn large sums,

which they spend in drinking ... always idle when they have any money left, so that their life is spent between labour ... and perfect idleness and drunkenness. Their women also, passing from affluence to distress almost every week, are forced, though soberly inclined, to lead very disorderly lives.

But, as with the problem of pauperdom, punitive solutions only bred fresh problems. Whereas Adam Smith advocated a high-wage economy, to give labourers inducements to work and save, the cautious believed Dr Johnson's retort: 'Raising the wages of day labourers is wrong for it does not make them live better, but only makes them idler.' Yet reducing wages sapped incentives, hit consumption, and threw more on the parish.

Anxiety over the lower orders' improvidence was greater with those least dependent upon regular pay packets: seasonal and casual workers, self-employed pedlars, wild-fowlers,

mole-catchers, charcoal-burners, and hurdle-makers; the secret
people who lived on the waste or in coppice-clearings, getting
a living out of the commons in a 'scratch-as-scratch-can' way.
A hundred thousand cottagers' families subsisted chiefly in
scrubby woodland areas and were widely believed to top up with
petty crime – sheep-stealing, poaching, receiving, coining. Living outside villages, they escaped more than most the discipli-
nary eye of magistrate, neighbours, or the Church (not that
Anglicanism or Old Dissent restrained the lives of many of the
lower orders). Colliers formed another group who, huddled
around isolated pits, were reckoned unusually wild and lawless.
In some of these communities – for instance amongst the tinners
of Cornwall and the colliers of Kingswood Forest just outside
Bristol, thought 'an ungovernable people' – popular Methodism began to exercise a sobering influence in the latter half of
the century.

Collectively at the workplace, labouring men could give a
show of independence. Males in particular could spend their
wages in the dram-shop buying oblivion. Spirits were always
cheap. Early in the nineteenth century Francis Place recalled,
'Until lately, all the amusements of the working people of the
metropolis were immediately concerned with drinking –
choir-clubs, chanting clubs, lottery clubs, and every variety of
club, intended for amusement, were always held at public
houses.' By contrast, plebeian home life must generally have
been pinched. The professional and landed orders may have
cultivated domesticity and improved their décor, but the lower
orders' harassed domestic economy left little room for the
graces. In fact, home life for many grew even starker. As more
country workers lost common rights and became proletarianized fewer had wood for firing, a cow for milk, or hens for
eggs. Fewer brewed and baked for themselves: even country
folk were buying bread in shops. Checking the diets and living
standards of the poor became an improving pastime for their
voyeuristic betters (as did collecting their ballads and folklore).
Without exception philanthropic snoopers found country
workers – especially in the great arable belt of central southern
England – reduced to a cheerless breadline: bread, cheese, cold
fare: Lent all the year round. Better off than many – note the

princely outlay on tea and sugar – was an Oxfordshire rural labourer, near the end of the century, who laid out each year for himself and three children:

4½ peck loaves a week at 1s. 2d. each	£13 13s.
Tea and sugar	£2 10s.
Butter and lard	£1 10s.
Beer and milk	£1
Bacon and other meat	£1 10s.
Soap, candles, etc.	about 15s.
House rent	£3
Coats	£2 10s.
Shoes and shirts	£3
Other clothes	£2
Total expenses	£31 8s.

As a carter and digger he earned a beggarly 8s. or 9s. a week. His expenses thus exceeded his income by over £5 a year. The parish partly made this up; but he was £5 in debt.

How did the lot of the labouring poor change during the century? The horrors of a peasantry multiplying while food production and job openings remained static were gripping much of rural Europe in the late eighteenth century, leading to serf revolts, mass vagrancy, beggary, and a flood of the starving into towns such as Naples. England avoided the worst of this. The expansion of manufactures and marketing opened new employment. Many more families found full-time or part-time work spinning, weaving, and stocking-knitting, dotted through the countryside and concentrated in sprawling industrial villages. A loom of one's own promised independence and self-respect. In the Black Country and south Yorkshire the metal trades forged ahead. Where relatively unskilled work (for example weaving) was plentiful, couples tended to court seriously and marry earlier, producing more children. In such areas the steep population rise of the last third of the century was a response to the tonic of job openings. Elsewhere, in less prosperous areas, unemployment and parochial dependence were probably what precipitated earlier marriage and larger families. There was a steady, creeping migration from rural hinterlands towards the manufacturing districts. The move to the towns, however, was not a direct consequence of husbandmen being turfed off the land by enclosure. In fact, enclosure for pasturage, so common in the Midlands from the 1750s to about 1780, created both short-term and long-term employment. Industrial areas, rather, were magnets offering better employment prospects, and the demand for labour in manufactures forced up wage-rates in the Midlands and North. These gains were wiped out, however, by inflation and taxation in the 1790s, when wartime disruption of export trades also created crippling unemployment. Women and children were in great demand for factory work, and wage levels were attractive (though of course entrepreneurs went for female and child labour partly because it was cheaper than male). Technologically sophisticated textile factories in turn created demands for ancillary labour. Spinning factories thus multiplied the need for home-loom weavers, whose wages were reaching short-lived halcyon levels (sometimes over £3 a week) at the end of the century.

Were industrial working conditions deteriorating? The new factories were steamy, full of unguarded machinery and disciplined by martinets and the ceaseless throb of the engine. Yet they accounted for a tiny fraction of the labour force, and workshop or home labour was often performed in cramped, dusty, dingy conditions, under a tyrant master or husband. Certainly industrialization multiplied crippling occupational diseases, and deeper mine shafts spelt more colliers' widows. Yet the new villages such as Cromford and Styal planted by textile magnates in the rural valleys of Derbyshire, Cheshire, and Lancashire in the early days of industrialization were garden-town models of enlightened planning, with stone houses, shops, and allotments. However we assess urban conditions in industrializing areas, the flow of labour was all in their direction.

It was workers on the land whose situation was unambiguously eroded as the century progressed. In the seventeenth and through much of the eighteenth century farm labour was chiefly performed by 'servants in husbandry', young, unmarried workers who lived in with the farmers, usually on an annual contract. In time, however, farmers reduced this practice, not wanting their 'improved' farmsteads polluted by labourers, and finding it cheaper to hire labour only when the occasion arose, at harvest for instance, by the day or task. The decline of living-in made farm labourers more dependent on money wages yet also left many without employment for much of the year. These pressures were exaggerated where enclosure reduced independence by depriving labourers of customary access to common land, which had helped them eke out a living with firing, grazing, nuts and berries, and the odd rabbit. The Rev. Richard Warner, touring the southern counties, mused, 'Time was when these commons enabled the poor man to support his family, and bring up his children. Here he could turn out his cow and pony, feed his flock of geese, and keep his pig. But the enclosures have deprived him of these advantages.' Furthermore, in the rural southern counties, only the more poorly paid forms of by-employment (such as sock-knitting in Hampshire) tended to be available, and the lack of large industrial towns nearby meant it was harder for families to migrate in search of work (surrounding parishes would boot them back to their place of settlement, fearing a charge on the rates). The underemployed became more dependent upon outdoor relief. Its cost soared (but it was still cheaper for farmers than paying wages all the year round). By 1800, 28 per cent of the population was in receipt of poor relief; £532,000 had been paid out per year in 1680; by 1780 the figure was almost £2 million. As Cobbett vividly described, the southern rural proletariat was becoming demoralized. Not only were they afflicted in the midst of plenty, but even when they were in employment they could not command a living wage. 'In visiting the labouring families of my parish ... I could not but observe with concern their mean and distressed condition ... Yet I could not impute the wretchedness I saw either to sloth or wastefulness', wrote the Rev. David Davies in 1795. Arthur Young, once a supporter of enclosure, by 1801 characterized the fatalism of the rural displaced:

Go to an ale-house of an old enclosed country, and there you will see the origin of poverty and poor-rates. For whom are they to be sober? For whom are they to save? (Such are their questions.) For the parish? If I am diligent, shall I have leave to build a cottage? If I am sober, shall I have land for a cow? If I am frugal, shall I have half an acre for potatoes? You offer no motives: you have nothing but a parish officer and a work-house! – Bring me another pot!

The biggest labour problem of the next century was staring people in the face: rural pauperism.

Georgian England had its underground people, its concealed world of beggars, small-time thieves, gipsies, dossers and vagrants, sharpers, cheats, who got by on practically nothing. The German traveller Lichtenberg described the destitute, dangerous shanty-town people:

... persons born in the fields, generally near the brick-kilns round London ... They grow up without learning to read or write, and never hear the words 'Religion' or 'Belief', and not even the word 'God', excepting in the phrase 'God damn it'. They gain their livelihood by all kinds of work in the brick-kilns, helping the drivers of hackney coaches, and so forth, until the old Adam in them is aroused: then they take to stealing and are generally hanged between the ages of 18 and 26. A short life and a merry one is their motto, which they do not hesitate to proclaim in court.

Outside London, however, professional criminals were few. Many of the men who took to petty theft (few women did) were labourers who stole to get over hard times.

But, alongside, a permanent body of proletarianized paupers was gathering: proletarians in that they possessed no source of income save their labour, no customary rights over the land, no roots; paupers in that they had no work (often through old age, illness, disease, or infirmity) or only casual work, or – very often – because wages would not support a household. Particularly in the last years of the century price inflation was outstripping wages. Wheat had cost 34s. a quarter in 1780; it was up to 58s. in 1790 and 128s. by 1800. Although Adam Smith and his acolytes sanguinely prophesied that the march of capitalism would eradicate poverty, the reverse was happening. To the trapped poor, Burke offered cheerless, though realistic, belt-tightening advice: 'Patience, labour, sobriety, frugality, and religion, should be recommended to them: all the rest is down-right fraud.'

Did it suit the propertied to be lapped by the choppy sea of the lumpenproletariat? In some ways, not at all: they proved a bottomless pit into which poor rates were poured; they created crime and disorder; they did not pull their weight as consumers; they were the tinder of disaffection waiting for a spark. That is why Malthus advised the poor to breed less. Marx argued that expansive, profit-hungry, free-market capitalism needed such people as a plentiful reserve army of labour, to plug gaps in the work-force and depress wage levels. In a sense the proletarianized poor did constitute such a reserve army: industrial capitalism was not strangled at birth by labour shortage. Yet what use were the urban riff-raff and country yokels to employers? Outside the work-force they were not serviceable; they were merely a residue, the left-overs of economic change such as enclosure, the cast-offs of a cut-throat society in which local and myopic administration adopted not very humane protocols and no one shouldered ultimate responsibility. As Frederick Eden observed, 'It is one of the natural consequences of freedom that those who are left to shift for themselves must sometimes be reduced to want.'

The century did not witness any dramatic transformation of the social structure, rather a gradual change. Several groups swelled out – especially the capital-deploying trading classes and the proletarianized poor – but the league table of wealth and esteem (headed by great landowners) was much the same in 1800 as a century earlier. The complex fabric, in which social power was compounded of many factors, including family, clientage, privilege, inheritance, status, occupation, and regional, political, and religious connexions, had by no means boiled down by 1800 into a society where clear-cut class armies glowered at each other across industrial battlefields. So long as landowning remained profitable as well as prestigious, there was no prospect of upset at the top; below, so long as mass concentrations of workers remained highly exceptional and the poor law regulated rural society, there was no imminent threat to stability. Limited access to upward mobility and the rise in tandem of aggregate wealth and social pretensions ensured that the social order neither collapsed nor was overthrown.

3. Power, Politics, and the Law

Georgian England is sometimes pictured as an Eden of ease, elegance, and equipoise; George Saintsbury coined the phrase 'the peace of the Augustans' to evoke its majestic imperial calm. *'Quieta non movere'* was after all the key to Robert Walpole's statecraft, and a lifetime later Jane Austen could write of Regency England without a lurid background of insurrection, Luddism, radicalism, and repression. Such a pastoral viewpoint sees England as a happy hierarchical hunting ground of Toby-jug squires and their dogs, paternalist grandees flanked by deferential retainers, the great aristocratic oaks sheltering the bumpkin multitude. It was - one historian tells us - 'an age when the less fortunate classes still meekly accepted their lot in life ... there was none to challenge the squire's monopoly of power and few to question it'. 'The early part of the eighteenth century has something of the glamour of Arcadia,' wrote Dorothy George. 'We think of it as the last age of old England, of solid, stable, rural England.' In particular, Sir Lewis Namier and his followers have portrayed mid-Georgian politics as the apogee of oligarchy, when public affairs became handled as the family business of a closed clique of clans. High politics were mature and stable, the argument runs, because bigwigs made no bones about concentrating on the nitty-gritty of power, intrigue, manipulation, and machination. As R. J. White observed, Namierite history has patience only for the 'politics of manoeuvre' in which 'the stage' is reserved for 'the great actors', 'although a People doubtless exists offstage, supernumeraries who are doubtless to be occasionally addressed, and relied upon for shouts and choruses'. In this scenario, the people are passive beneficiaries of the gentry's 'astonishing record of service to the community'.

More recent historians, however, have dynamited this idyll

of Georgian harmony. Within the velvet glove, they show, an iron fist was clenched. At all levels chaos was threatening to restore her dread empire. Beneath the powdered wig, emotional and psychological disorder seethed: this was after all the century when Lemuel Gulliver saw men as monkeys and wished to be a horse. In one of his gloomy and drunken fits James Boswell hurled a lighted candelabra at his dear wife. Clive of India, an opium addict, was one of many who despaired and took his own life (England became notorious for suicides). Dr Johnson went in fear of losing his wits, and the poet William Cowper charted his own psychological shipwreck:

> No voice divine the storm allay'd
> No light propitious shone
> When, snatch'd from all effectual aid
> We perish'd, each alone
> But I beneath a rougher sea
> And 'whelm'd in deeper gulfs than he.

Out of doors, crime was rife and could be bloody: smugglers had little compunction about murdering excise officers. And the watermark of direct, physical action stained the pages of public and political life. From the rough-house of the crowd to the dragoons' musket volley, violence was as English as plum pudding. Force was used not just criminally, but as a matter of routine to achieve social and political goals, smudging hard-and-fast distinctions between the worlds of criminality and politics. Thus, while thieves as such got little sympathy, the gangland leader Jonathan Wild achieved sardonic glory as the minnow who got caught, while the pestiferous sharks of high society, such as Prime Minister Walpole, were let off the hook: the theme of *The Beggar's Opera* and countless satires. An 'Advertisement Extraordinary' in the Wilkite *Middlesex Journal* for 1769 harped on the same theme:

Whereas a gang of notorious robbers have for some years past infested the neighbourhood of St James and the Treasury, and have in a daring manner, and in open defiance of the laws of the land, plundered the public of several millions sterling, to the great loss of his majesty's liege subjects; and have lately absconded loaded with their plunder. These are therefore to require all good and well disposed people, born on this side of the Tweed, to apprehend such traitors and robbers, and bring them to justice, and in so doing, shall on conviction and execution, receive the reward due to the distinguished Patriots of Old England and be recorded in history for future generations.

Highwaymen were romanticized, with a hidden irony, as 'gentlemen of the road', smugglers fêted because excise-men were hated (why should free trade in imports be a crime, especially when everyone, from Walpole to Parson Woodforde, bought up contraband, Walpole using an Admiralty barge to run his smuggled wine up the Thames?).

Upright citizens – not just blackguards and bravoes but the village Hampden too – did not shrink from force to get their dues. There was a continual hubbub of verbal violence: newspapers, cartoons, and street ballads attacked their targets with scabrous insults and Billingsgate scurrility; political sermons thundered from pulpits. And frequently just the whiff of rough stuff was sufficient. Casanova was astonished when Drury Lane patrons, finding a different play performed from the one billed, threatened to wreck the theatre unless the manager, David Garrick, abjectly apologized: 'On your knees,' they yelled; Garrick knelt. Even so Drury Lane was wrecked by riots in 1743, 1750, 1755, 1763, 1770, and 1776. To celebrate popular causes such as a triumph for John Wilkes, London mobs would order householders to light up their windows under threat of pulling the frontage down. And crowds often took the law into their own hands. Brothels were rifled by disgruntled punters, homosexuals stoned to death in the pillory. Corpses were sometimes hacked down from the gibbet and snatched away by friends and family in hope of revival and to prevent anatomical dissection by surgeons (itself another form of violence, and one of Hogarth's Four Stages of Cruelty). Crowds, often led by women, would break in to stop farmers and dealers selling corn above fixed prices or contrary to market regulations, or would attack mills and granaries, sometimes wielding firearms, to prevent grain being bulk-shipped elsewhere in times of local shortage. Bread and food riots were endemic, not least because they were successful. In 1740 disturbances paralysed Norwich for five days over the price of mackerel. Bloody food riots in Somerset and Wiltshire in 1766-7 involved attacks on stores and looting: 3,000 troops were sent in. Turnpike gates, hated as a new concealed tax, were rooted up. Severe turnpike rioting occurred in Gloucestershire, Yorkshire, and Nottinghamshire (in one at Beeston ten people were killed by the military). In 1749 the *Gentleman's Magazine* reported,

about 400 Somersetshire people cut down a third time the turnpike gates on the Ashton Road ... then afterwards destroyed the Dundry Turnpike, and thence went to Bedminster headed by two chiefs on horseback ... the rest were on foot, armed with rusty swords, pitch-forks, axes, pistols, clubs.

Strikes for higher wages and machine-breaking to halt the installation of new technology were commonplace. The entre-preneur Matthew Boulton was laid about by Cornish tin-miners in 1787, buying them off with 20 guineas for drink. Over 400 labour disputes have been recorded during the century.

The river of violence and its threat ran through the political landscape, sometimes underground, sometimes on the surface. Unpopular politicians were often ragged, peers' carriages pelted and rocked as they left Westminster, their windows smashed, whereas heroes such as Sacheverell or Charles James Fox were cheered and chaired. Minorities were tempting targets. Meth-odists were shied at (though Wesley saw it as proof of Divine favour that no brick hit him personally), as were homosexuals, witches, bawds, and Frenchmen. The Act to allow the natural-ization of Jews in 1753 brought baying anti-Semitic mobs on to the streets: it was immediately repealed. Anti-Irish and Anti-Scots outbursts were national sports. Fear of popery sparked the Gordon Riots in London in 1780, though targets broadened to include the rich, Lord Mansfield, breweries, and Newgate gaol. The City lay paralysed in the hands of the crowd for a week; £100,000 of damage was done to property (ten times as much as in Paris throughout the French Revolution) before troops restored order at the cost of 290 citizens' lives: twenty-five looters were later executed. Prejudices against Dissenters, especially Unitarians, led to insults against them and attacks on their property, particularly in the 1790s, when Tom Paine was also often burnt in effigy by loyalist crowds, supervised by constables. When John Wilkes presented himself in the 1760s as

St George rescuing fair English liberties from the dragons of general warrants, Lord Bute, George III, and Parliament, crowds flocked on to the streets, marched, cheered, badgered the support of bystanders – for instance, forcing publicans to stand toasts – and intimidated opponents. During the explosive 1790s, ministers quaked, terrified that violence might erupt just about anywhere.

Alarm was well founded, partly because the fabric of law enforcement was patchy. Most parishes boasted only an amateur constable or two: aided by community vigilance these could cope with petty crime but not with disturbances. Faced with disaffection, mayors and JPs sometimes trembled to act: their own sympathies often lay with the anti-government or anti-middle-men rioters. They themselves risked prosecution if they overstepped the law. In any case they lacked disciplined, readily mobilized forces, for there was no national police to summon. Magistrates were unwilling to call upon the Home Secretary to send in troops: it was an admission of defeat, invited centralism, and in any case they quickly learnt that a platoon of soldiers billeted on their borough created more disruption than it quelled. Bristol Corporation sought troops from the Secretary of State to deal with labour disputes in 1791. By 1794 it had found it could deal with rioters better itself.

Disturbances were alarming because they were so often lightning forays. Black-faced nocturnal bands ripping up fences or burning ricks were hard to catch or convict. They also rattled the guardians of order because most rioters were not earmarked as hardened criminals, agitprop demonstrators, looters, or the scum of society. Even rock-solid citizens resorted at times to militancy as a means of collective bargaining by direct action: artisans, master-craftsmen, yeomen, stevedores, smallholders, ex-soldiers, sedan chairmen, often led by someone of higher standing, a publican or a maverick gentleman for instance. It was the English at large who were an ungovernable people. Nor were riots just hunger-spasms. Demotic disturbances were political acts, howling down corruption and the abuse of power and championing traditional values: No General Warrants! Wilkes and Liberty! 1688! No Scots! Old Prices! The blasphemous anonymous letters flung at the doors of bailiffs, millers, and magistrates threatened blood, but threatened it in the name of Freedom, the British Constitution, or Christian Justice, as this one from Rossendale in 1762, addressed to James Bailey, a JP:

> This his to asquaint you that We poor of Rosendale Rochdale Oldham Saddleworth Ashton have all mutaly and firmly agreed by Word and Covinent and Oath to Fight and Stand by Each Other as long as Life doth last for We may as well be all hanged as starved to Death and to see ower Children weep for Bread and none to give Them nor no liklyness of ever mending wile You all take Part with Brommal and Markits drops at all the principle Markits elceware but take This for a shure Maxon, That if You dont put those good Laws in Execution against all Those Canables or Men Slayers That have the Curse of God and all honest Men both by Gods Laws and Mens Laws so take Notice Bradshaw Bailey and Lloyd the biggest Rogue of all Three I know You all have Power to stop such vilonas Proceedings if You please and if You dont amaidatley put a Stopp and let hus feel it the next Saturday We will murder You all that We have down in Ower List and Wee will all bring a Faggot and burn down Your Houses and Wait Houses and make Your Wifes Widdows and Your Children Fatherless for the Blood of Shul de hill lyes cloose at Ower Harts and Blood for Blood We Require.
>
> Take Care. Middleton.

Rioters thus saw themselves as avenging angels of equity and redress, as Robin Hoods. Their political intelligence was high and often expressed in Biblical cadences. Their allegiance was to an Old England of popular rights, customary law, neighbourliness, and roast beef. The *vox populi* chanted out its demands through the sympathetic magic of slogans, riddles, graffiti, effigies, songs, and caricature. Excluded from Westminster by the ramparts of oligarchy, the blood of popular politics coursed through the propaganda media of newspapers, handbills, ballads, posters, and cartoons, through tavern and coffee-house debate.

Georgian England was pockmarked with disorder – foreigners were astonished at the licence permitted to the common people. They found the English extraordinarily politically well informed and assertive, from peers down to shoe-blacks and the millions in between, clamouring around the outworks of the official political nation. 'There is scarce any man in England,' wrote Joseph Addison early in the century, 'of what Denomination soever, that is not a free-thinker in politics, and hath not some particular notions of his own ... Our nation, which was formerly called a nation of saints, may now be called a nation of statesmen.' Continentals found the people's participation in political debate without parallel at home. The German Moritz commented in the 1780s:

When one sees how the lowliest carter shows an interest in public affairs; how the smallest children enter into the spirit of the nation; how everyone feels himself to be a man and an Englishman ... as good as his kind and his king's minister ... it brings to the mind thoughts very different from those we know when we watch the soldiers drilling in Berlin.

Yet the political fabric – much abused, pulled, torn, tattered, and patched – was never ripped up. If the socio-political nation really had been verging on anarchy or revolution, the Jacobite rebellions of 1715 and 1745, or the Gordon Riots, would have sparked explosion. But crypto-Jacobite sympathies – though widespread – did not lead to people taking up arms in England; the Gordon Riots did not spread beyond London or become a general cause, and most radical bodies of the 1790s such as the Friends of the People (1791) and the London Corresponding Society (1792) expected to carry the day through Reason – by education, pamphlets, and petitioning. Piecemeal violence never turned into general insurrection.

Why? One reason for this was the particular protocol of rioting. Protesters' aims were usually concrete, defensive, and limited, such as the restoration of long-standing wage-rates or rights of way. Their appeal was to a traditional order, to be restored by society's traditional leaders. The crowd did not want to direct the grain market itself, still less abolish private property in grain; it wanted magistrates to enforce the regulatory statutes. In place of Lord Bute, Wilkite crowds did not demand popular assemblies, but English liberties. And once a mob had aired its grievances – uprooted a toll gate, destroyed a recruiting office – it dispersed. Crowds had no programme of socialist revolution, no manifesto of modernity. Riots were dramatic enactments like theatre, and similarly cathartic. They were demonstrative, almost liturgical, aiming to lance the festering body politic, exposing corruption, venality, toadyism, and tyranny. The crowd had its icons to remind the nation of equity: the Liberty Cap, the scales of Justice, the cuckold's horns, a loaf of bread wrapped in mourning crêpe. John, Earl of Bute, was demonized into a Jack Boot. This expressive but circumscribed role for disturbances made good sense in a society where people experienced grievances nearest the bone in local contexts and where – alongside violence – the surest hope for redress was by appeal to law, customs, and magistrates.

The ruling oligarchy soaked up a lot of punishment from disturbances, generally used a kid-glove approach, and emerged essentially unscathed. It did so partly because of its own resilient union of social, economic, and political strength, and partly because political leaders remembered the lessons of 1642 and did not again commit suicide by warring against each other. The alliance of monarchy and magnates which successfully managed the ungovernable people was in many respects nothing strange, being paralleled throughout *ancien régime* Europe. The Tudor and Stuart eras had seen the Crown elevate itself against rival princelings, and the Reformation had made the monarch Supreme Head of the Church. Meanwhile deep socio-economic trends had also been consolidating an effective landed class. The early disappearance of serfdom and the brisk land market from the sixteenth century had encouraged agrarian capitalism. Land, profits, and power became plaited together. The political broils of the Stuarts checked threats from divine-right monarchy to autonomy in the county community, and left property absolutely secure. Yet the Hanoverian state had two special strengths. First, the partnership between Crown and grandees was exceptionally harmonious. Second, between them they exercised a stranglehold upon an expanding state apparatus which paid big dividends even while securing property and personal influence.

The marriage was partly one of necessity. By the seventeenth century, the nobility no longer possessed assured private *military* strength – armies, retainers, the skills of command. The king, served by the flower of the nobility, had lost the Civil War on the battlefield; in no other state were rebels so successful in arms. Furthermore, to counterbalance military decline, by mid-Stuart times the leading proprietors had not yet evolved new instruments of political control. Squabbles with the Crown (for instance with Charles II in the Exclusion Crisis) had split the magnates, leaving them *as a body* without automatic access to the corridors of power (though many used the back door and winding stair to Court). Especially over Puritanism and Catholicism, deep rifts had opened between the great nobles and the solid gentry.

Magnates needed the protective armour of state power. Yet even under William and Mary and then Anne, the struggle for mastery in high politics produced such turbulent and sectarian conflict as to imperil the ship of state. The generation straddling the new century was irremediably strife-torn. Both William III and Anne had regal wills of their own. The prospect of disputed succession after Anne loomed as a Doomsday, polarizing and paralysing the nation. Would Anne ever produce an heir who outlived her? If not, would the Hanoverians be toppled? Would the Stuarts return? In religion, how exclusive, privileged, and autonomous was the Anglican Church to be? How much toleration would be granted to Dissenters and Catholics? These issues splintered the loyalties of the ruling order at the turn of the new century, creating rabid infighting and schism. Gambling on the political future was make-or-break for politicians such as St John, Harley, Stanhope, and Walpole. Whig and Tory, Low and High Church, landed and moneyed property, pro- and anti-war, pro- and anti-Hanoverian factions tore at each other's throats like fighting cocks. Factions factionalized, and affected all arenas of life within the political nation. In London newspapers, coffee houses, and theatres became sucked into party whirlpools. Tory theatre-goers patronized Drury Lane, Whigs the Haymarket; Tories went to the Cocoa-Tree coffee house, Whigs joined the Kit-Kat Club. The commission of the peace was dramatically purged for political reasons in 1696, 1700, and 1710. Political dissension *within* the ruling order – 'the rage of party' – had not been so cut-throat since the Civil War. Moreover elections held every three years or more (an unprecedented ten elections were called between 1695 and 1715), vitriolic propaganda, and street mobs meant that the fight within the ruling order for power and its spoils spread to embroil – and divide – the localities. This was especially because the electorate had expanded up to about 300,000 (maybe one in six adult males), and a large portion of constituencies were being contested: twenty-six counties went to the polls in 1705, twenty-three in 1710.

When the new century dawned the pattern of future relations between the Crown and the political nation was hence an open issue. Stuarts and Hanoverians were both waiting in the wings, and many hedged their bets. Whoever became king, he would not be very English, in birth, religion, or policy. The monarch could still make a crucial difference. After all, William of Orange had distrusted English politicians, followed a continental strategy, Dutch rather than English in orientation, and had succeeded in making the monarchy more commanding than any Stuart had. Relations between state and society hung in the balance. Another century of prolonged Stuart constitutional conflicts might have polarized and impoverished English landed society or castrated the Crown, turning England into a Poland.

And yet control of power was promising more than ever, as the spoils were greater. For governments' disposable revenue was soaring, partly through the rise of customs receipts following commercial expansion and increasingly through the easing of borrowing. The Charter of the newly founded Bank of England (1694) authorized the Bank to advance £1,200,000 to the Government, increased in 1709 by a further £2,900,000. Between 1690 and 1700 total Government borrowing amounted to £11.7 million. Government income also rose through the leaping direct and indirect taxes levied to finance continental war. In the 1690s alone, some £45 million were collected. Spoonfuls of this rich gravy were to be ladled back through Court and ministers to their henchmen and supporters. Indeed, the Government establishment itself was snowballing. Warfare created more army and navy commissions, more contracts and concessions. Commercial and imperial growth meant new openings in the colonies and the excise, the expansion of Treasury clerkships, cashierships, and controllerships, and the setting-up of the Board of Trade – all carrying jobs in the Government's pocket: by 1718 there were 561 full-time and another 1,000 part-time customs officers in the Port of London alone. Every post's official salary could be doubled by fees and perks; and most office-holders had their deputies. Not least, the mushrooming of sophisticated credit finance associated with the National Debt gave the backroom boys of the Government, those fingering the bills and calculating percentages – men such as John Aislabie and James Cragg – plenty of scope, above and below board, for manipulation and pickings.

But if the plums of office were becoming so much choicer, so were the costs of winning and holding them. Fierce competition, frequent elections, the need to win voters over, the strain of making friends and influencing people, all gobbled up money. Party vendettas grew more bitter and vindictive. In 1710, the Whig Government put the High Churchman Henry Sacheverell on trial. Succeeding Tory Governments met spite with spite by axing the civil liberties of Dissenters with the Occasional Conformity (1710) and Schism Acts (1714). Political costs and struggles for power were threatening to get out of hand: the Sacheverell crisis alone produced over 1,000 controversial salvoes. Yet in fact the early years of the century proved to be the *molto agitato* overture to the period of greatest political stability ever known in England. For slowly the executive was beginning to tighten its python grip over the political nation. The once populist Whigs, seated in power, began to perfect the techniques of oligarchy. The Tory Stamp Act of 1712 had dampened publications. The Whig Riot Act of 1715 was meant to clamp down on street politics. Power became concentrated in varied ways. For example, new legislation of 1710 had already imposed a land qualification of £6,000 for county MPs and £300 for borough MPs. And soaring electoral costs began to restrict politics to the wealthy. In 1689 Pepys had spent £8 5s. 6d. on an election at Harwich, but by 1727 Viscount Percival needed £900 for the same constituency. Electioneering was to become a rich man's sport. Many independent gentry families of long political standing got squeezed out of participation by the cost. Sir William Fostwick, MP for Bedfordshire from 1698 to 1713, ran up £26,000 in political debts: he had to sell up and leave the country.

Furthermore, as the costs of politics rose, there was a greater premium upon not wasting money, but shepherding political investments better. The Septennial Act (1716) gave MPs seven years' tenure on a seat, not three as before, and with elections only every seven years the bubbling political stew began to cool. But less frequent polls in turn put up the price of a seat still further (at the Oxfordshire election of 1754 the Tories spent no less than £40,000 to unseat the Whigs – and failed). With electoral costs threatening to go sky-high, it increasingly made sense to avoid a contest wherever possible, especially in county seats, where electorates were large and freeholder voters often truculent. So advance deals were struck to secure candidates' election unopposed; two-member constituencies were often carved up by agreement between Whig and Tory. At the same time borough-mongers tightened their grip on small constituencies. Political management grew in sophistication. With costs and rewards so high, the arts of fixing seats, bribing voters, placing supporters, cultivating influential interests, and not least resorting to gerrymandering, graft, and legal chicanery became a major part of the Hanoverian statesman's accomplishments. By mid-century, the hyperkinetic political nation had been tranquillized. In 1761 only eighteen out of 201 borough constituencies with fewer than 500 voters actually polled. Between 1754 and 1790 twelve counties never went to the polls at all.

The politics of oligarchic control had been growing since the Restoration, with grandees steadily getting their tentacles around boroughs and corporations. But management came into its own with Walpole, who steered the political nation out of the South Sea Bubble crisis. Walpole and the Duke of Newcastle doubled as the Machiavellis of the age, recognizing that every man craved his place and had his price. Their task was simplified partly because of the unexpected ease of the Hanoverian succession. Because Tories dithered over giving the Hanoverians firm support, the Whigs – a vociferous, ambitious minority desperate for political survival – grabbed the Crown and exploited the Jacobite rising of 1715 to launch a calumnious witch-hunt against the Tories. Under the first two Georges, Tory diehards came to be permanently proscribed from political office, central and local – Tory squires for example were purged from the Commission of the Peace, officers from the army. Tories continued to have deep grassroots political support, yet the costs of permanent exclusion from office were so damaging that from the

late 1720s some Tories cut their losses and came in from the
cold, deserting to the Whig and Court party in an abject trickle,
their sons seeking preferment in the post office and the excise.
The result was the consolidation of a broad-bottom coalition
of pro-government politicians, proprietors, and their clients
(nominally Whigs), united above all by their desire to be where
the power and rewards were.

Walpole's overbearing ministries, muzzling critics with spies,
informers, and propagandists financed by secret service funds,
were extraordinarily unpopular with backwoods squires and
vocal opinion at large – those who thought that 1688 had
been the revolution to purge centralism and corruption, not to
reinforce it. And throughout the century, bitter populist hatred
of ministries and monarchs forced its way to the surface. Yet
low food prices and the expansion of job opportunities helped
to head off any coalescence of plebeian and gentry disaffection,
and the importunities of power-seekers and the servility of
office-holders made oligarchic one-party government not
just possible but ultimately – though great tact and acrobatics
were required – plain-sailing. 'The rage of party gave way to
the pursuit of place,' as Plumb put it. 'Place was power;
patronage was power,' and patronage 'scarcely bothered to wear
a fig leaf'.

Georgian ministerial politics concentrated on managing and
milking society at large. This was done partly through control
of elections. Ministerialists needed to cushion themselves against
the occasional jolt of the hustings. In some boroughs (for instance naval dockyard towns such as Chatham) the Court itself
could pressurize electors, since voters were Government employees and voting was in public, not secret. In others, candidates (and their ventriloquists, the borough-monger patrons)
cajoled voters by bribes and threats or bought up properties
carrying the franchise. In 1768 Marlborough obtained a seat at
Oxford after helping to pay off the corporation debt of £5,676.
The Last Determinations Acts (1696, 1729) aided corporations
and borough-mongers, who wanted to limit the size of electorates, by deeming that, in cases of dispute, the most recent
electoral roll should stand (notwithstanding claims that it was
by custom broader).

Management and manipulation brought a political cynicism into the open, which defused tensions amongst the elite by focusing attention on the division of spoils. Many candidates were opportunist carpet-baggers. Bubb Dodington thus recorded in his diary his contest of the Bridgwater election in April 1754:

April 11. Dr Sharpe and I set out from Eastbury, at four o'clock in the morning, for Bridgewater, where, as I expected, I found things very disagreeably framed.

12. Lord Egmont came, with trumpets, noise, etc.

13. He and we walked the town; we found nothing unexpected, as far as we went.

14., 15., 16. Spent in the infamous and disreputable compliance with the low habits of venal wretches.

17. Came on the election, which I lost by the injustice of the Returning Officer. The numbers were for Lord Egmont 119, for Mr Balch 114, for me 105. Of my good votes 15 were rejected: 8 bad votes for Lord Egmont were received.

18. Left Bridgewater – for ever.

Especially in boroughs, the typical franchise holder, exercising his dwindling opportunities to vote, could be relied on to plump for Mr Most. The Duke of Richmond called the constituency of New Shoreham a 'new whore that is anybody's for their money'. Not all seats could be controlled, however – some boroughs such as Westminster, and many counties, had electorates of several thousands. Bath had just thirty-two voters – the corporation – yet they were notoriously obstreperous. But most boroughs with electorates of a few hundred or less were safely in the pockets of patrons. In mid-century about 255 out of 405 borough seats were under oligarchic control. The Walpoles had Castle Rising in Norfolk as their pocket borough, and substantial interests in King's Lynn and Yarmouth; the Lowthers controlled about seven seats in Cumbria; the Duke of Newcastle disposed of up to twelve. Electoral management was child's play in Scotland, where electorates were tiny. In 1788 Scottish counties had a combined electorate of 2,662. But management was usually successful, pre-empting any real choice and power amongst voters. Shropshire had no contest between 1722 and 1831, Wiltshire only one poll between 1713 and 1818.

In 1780 only two English county seats actually polled. In short, Georgian governments became exceptionally secure against the electorate. A diminishing number of seats actually came up for contest, and of those that did, the smaller boroughs could usually be fixed in advance.

The other arm of management lay within Parliament itself. There, judicious dispensing of Court patronage and pensions, and the cultivation of clients' interests and family alliances, were increasingly skilfully used to build up safe ministerial majorities. Sinecurists might not have much official business to do, but they were expected to be loyal and politically active to earn their keep. In 1742 the Commons contained 139 placemen; by 1780 the number was up to 180. The top politicians clustered into family cabals, in 1761 the Commons boasting five Townshends, five Mannerses, four Cavendishes, and four Yorkes. Behind such big guns the Whigs marshalled great landlords, with their immense local influence, but also contractors, civil servants, City financiers, Low Churchmen, and Dissenters.

Even though the Whig Old Corps was derailed in the early years of George III's reign, nothing shook the continuity of magnate government. The soft furnishings of the house of oligarchy were shifted around, but the foundations hardly trembled. Though an interregnum of ministerial reshuffles perplexed the 1760s, the regimes of North, Pitt the Younger, and Liverpool piloted what was effectively a one-party state safely into the 1820s. Of course ministries and oppositions, 'ins' and 'outs', roused themselves to oratorical paroxysms about despotism, demagogy, nepotism, anarchy, or the Church in danger. But it was all ultimately shadow-boxing, because no inside political connexion poised on the threshold of power wanted to kill the goose that laid the golden eggs.

Prudent ministries patched up family alliances and applied balm which healed rifts and mollified malcontents: a sinecure here, a pension or a promise there. John Gay the writer became Commissioner of the State Lottery; Edward Gibbon was made a Lord of Trade on £800 a year. Even if the cornucopia of state was usually three quarters empty, men great and small begged for tempting scraps of offices and perks. Being a Trimmer, a vicar of Bray, a political yes-man, was no disgrace; such conduct

was not merely worldly wise, but perhaps even family duty.★
Politics were mercenary, and though moralists on the by-lines
huffed and puffed about 'corruption', few had qualms about
feathering their own nests. For the state was their life-line,
providing those who clung on with security and prospects in the
forms of favour and pensions (defined by Dr Johnson – soon to
accept one himself – as 'pay given to a state hireling for treason
to his country'). Office was especially welcome to younger
sons, who, because of primogeniture, had to wave goodbye
to the family estates. Furthermore, the ties of importunity and
gratitude, of begging and granting, the queue which political
patronage created all the way down the scale, satisfied honour
and civilized hungry ambition. 'I think it my duty,' wheedled
Thomas Newton to the Duke of Newcastle, 'to acquaint your
grace that the Archbishop of York lies a-dying and, as all here
think, cannot possibly live beyond tomorrow morning if so
long; upon the occasion of two vacancies, I beg, I hope, I trust
your Grace's kindness and goodness will be shown to one who
has long solicited your favour.' There was of course endless
disappointment and petulance, but this was individual and it
neither killed hope nor threatened to dash the system.

Despite endless bickering over jurisdictions and spoils, the
different limbs of the state worked harmoniously together.
Limited, constitutional monarchy was an important unifying
force, powerful enough to calm great proprietors' fears of any
resurgence of Cromwellian republicanism, but not so powerful
as to threaten magnate property or independence itself. True,
the Hanoverian kings hardly warmed the nation's heart. George
I and II were graceless domestic tyrants, addicted more to
Hanover than to England (people thought it fitting when
George II died in the privy). George III, who at least was
English, gained some dignity by losing his wits, and some popularity as Farmer George. Their courts were mean, their taste
was drab, their family feuds vindictive. Yet they were active
and determined rulers, anxious to keep the Court the centre of
politics, and – their trump card – they were indelibly Protestant.

★ The epitaph of Mrs Bates stated that 'by means of her alliance with the illustrious
family of Stanhope, she had the merit to obtain for her husband and children twelve several
appointments in church and state'.

Maintaining the Protestant succession was one of two things all Englishmen could agree on in politics (the other was that, in the last resort, kings were more trustworthy than politicians). The Crown, as head of the executive, still appointed the leading ministers and courtiers, and directly shaped policy, especially foreign and religious affairs. George II personally led his troops into battle, if only once. The king's wider family held key appointments, particularly in the armed forces. The king disposed of a privy purse and immense powers of patronage at Court and through the civil list (there were over 1,000 appointees connected with the royal household). Only diehards prepared to risk being permanent castaways (crypto-Jacobite squires in the 1720s or a sprinkling of reforming Whigs in the 1790s) dared forsake currying royal favour. With the possible exception of young George III in the 1760s, the Georges did not make the Stuart mistake of neglecting politicians' good-will; they did not seek to construct a Versailles or rule through mere creatures. The first two Georges accepted Whig dominion: George III clung to Bute, North, and Pitt the Younger. The Crown was not dramatically weaker or its scope for political manoeuvre more eroded in 1800 than in 1700.

During the century, the grandees tightened their hold on the headquarters of state. By 1800, 11 per cent of navy officers came from titled families and a further 27 per cent from landed families; the army similarly recruited its officers from the sons and friends of the ruling elite. Above all the Church of England was increasingly annexed to the state, its prize livings occupied by numinous families. Clerics were advanced to prelacies because they would loyally vote with the Government in the Lords. 'No man,' lamented Dr Johnson, 'can now be made a bishop for his learning and piety; his own chance of promotion is his being connected with someone who has parliamentary interest.' It had fleetingly seemed possible under Queen Anne that clerical high-flyers would resist the absorption of the Church within the state. The Whigs, however, by proroguing Convocation and advancing their minions, nipped serious Church-state conflict and ecclesiastical independence in the bud until the Oxford Movement.

The blueprint for this snug fit between the proprietorial

classes and their protective, insulating shell of state (symbolized
by the Crown) was the Constitution. The governing classes
were proud of the British Constitution (which supposedly had
existed 'time out of mind') as 'the most beautiful combination
ever framed' (the phrase is George III's), glorying in the time-
hallowed distinctions in jurisdictions between Crown, Lords,
and Commons, between executive, legislature, and judiciary,
between Church and state ('Herein consists the excellence of the
English government,' asserted Blackstone in 1765, 'that all parts
of it form a mutual check upon each other'). They emphasized
that MPs were independent representatives, not delegates. All
of these constitutional finesses they vaunted as freeborn Englishmen's guarantees against despotism. The conservative revolution of 1688 had rescued liberty from danger: in turn its
settlement must now be preserved. Even anomalies – rotten
boroughs almost bereft of voters such as Old Sarum and Gatton
– were properties making for diversity, which could not be
invaded without risking wholesale erosion of ancient rights.
Traditional liberties – politicians argued – were best protected
by traditional grandees, who, because they owned freehold
estates, were not creatures of the Court. 'I cannot help feeling,'
argued that stalwart friend of the people Charles James Fox,
'that in this country at least, an aristocratic party is absolutely
necessary to the preservation of liberty.'

Of course, this sedative rhetoric of constitutional liberty (with
its polite fictions such as 'virtual representation' 'proving' that
the disqualified were just as properly politically represented as
the enfranchised) rationalized the regime of the great proprietors. Within this mythology, it was their guardianship of
property rights that was in turn every Englishman's security
against despotism or mob demagogy.

> The nations, not so blest as thee,
> Must, in their turns, to tyrants fall,

chorused magnates who were sultans in their own shires. Or, as
Arthur Young expressed it, 'The principle of our constitution
is the representation of property, imperfectly in theory, but
efficiently in practice ... the great mass of property both landed
and moneyed and commercial finds itself represented.' In other

words the landed classes did not just commandeer political
power. Rather the constitution was the idealized veneer which
glossed their own essence (that is, property), as *rights*. Realist as
ever, however, Adam Smith blew the gaff: 'Civil government
... so far as it is instituted for the security of property, is in
reality instituted for the defence of the rich against the poor.'

Of course, despite the vaunted checks and balances and
separations of power which allegedly forestalled tyranny, all
branches of effective power sprang from one single trunk.
Crown, ministries, and Commons were in league, intermin-
gled, and it was the executive that pulled the legislature's strings.
The king's choice as first minister could expect to piece together
a parliamentary majority. Management in the shires and boroughs meant that no ministry lost a general election for over a
century after the Hanoverian succession, and the Commons was
kept obedient partly by subaltern ministerial placemen, and
partly from the Lords via the plethora of sons and relatives of
peers sitting in the Lower House.

What impact did the organs of the Georgian state have on
society at large? To twentieth-century eyes the things it didn't
do are very conspicuous. Kings and their ministers did not set
out to implement manifestoes of social justice or interest themselves in reform. They didn't pursue comprehensive and long-
term industrial and agrarian policies or promote programmes
of education and welfare. 'Providence has so organized the
world,' said Lord Shelburne, 'that very little government is
necessary.' But the lens of the state did magnify social trends
already at work, not least by acting as an undercover income
redistributor. Stuart government had been very cheap. It had
to be, because the Commons had fought tooth and nail even
the shoestring taxes the Stuarts had demanded. Eighteenth-
century rule by contrast became immensely costly. In 1700 the
Government had raised £4.3 million in revenue; by 1800 it
levied £31.6 million. Put another way, central Government
public spending was about 7 per cent of the Gross National
Product in 1715, about 16 per cent in 1783, and about 27 per
cent in 1801. But Parliament came to vote taxes more readily.
This was partly because the political nation now controlled
spending and was the major beneficiary from taxation. Taxes

financed profitable wars, officers, sinecures, and pensions, and above all underwrote Government credit, guaranteeing the National Debt, keeping the growing army of rentiers content. With sound credit, ministries could embark on imperial conquest and borrow almost limitless sums (Britannia's wars were won on credit). Between 1688 and 1697 governments had raised £16 million by loans; between 1793 and 1815, £440 million. Taxes were increasingly earmarked for servicing the National Debt, the shareholders of this gilt-edged security ranging from great proprietors and plutocrats down to the spinster with a few hundred pounds in the Funds. The Debt, standing at £14.2 million in 1700, had rocketed to £130 million in 1763 and to £456 million in 1800. By 1784 the cost of debt-servicing alone was £9 million a year, by 1801, £20 million (Charles II's entire Restoration state had had to run on just over £1 million a year). Parliament thus now had a cardinal stake in maintaining public credit, for finance had become the soul of the enterprise of England, and no government could survive without the City's support. 'The stability of the Bank of England,' wrote Adam Smith, 'is equal to that of the British government ... It acts not only as an ordinary bank, but as a great engine of state.'

Proprietors could thus contemplate higher taxation with some equanimity, partly because their own contributions came back to them in the form of office and interest, but also because their own share of the load was diminishing. In 1700 the chief direct tax was the land tax, which could be as high as 20 per cent. Because assessed valuations were not indexed to actual values, the land tax actually bit less hard as time went on, except against freeholders and minor gentry without alternative sources of revenue.

Per capita taxation more than doubled between 1715 and 1803. Yet liquid capital as such escaped, and investment incomes of financiers and industrialists got off scot-free. Income taxes had long been deemed inquisitorial (though finally raised by Pitt the Younger in 1797 in wartime emergency), and most new levies were indirect taxes on consumption. Thus in the late seventeenth century 35 per cent of taxation had been direct: by 1790 only 18 per cent was. Indirect taxes fell on luxuries such as carriages but they also hit the people. Heavier excises were laid even on certain basic commodities. In 1769 a foreigner remarked that the English

> are taxed in the morning for the soap that washes their hands; at 9 for the coffee, the tea and the sugar they use at breakfast; at noon for the starch that powders their hair; at dinner for the salt that savours their meat; in the evening for the porter that cheers their spirits; all day long for the light that enters their windows, and at night for the candles that light them to bed.

He unaccountably omitted bricks, coal, leather, and glass. William Blake raged: 'Lawful Bread, Bought with Lawful Money, & a Lawful Heaven, seen thro' a Lawful Telescope, by means of Lawful Window Light! The Holy Ghost, & whatever cannot be Taxed, is Unlawful & Witchcraft.' Contrary to the patriotic stereotype, the common people of free, representatively governed England were surrendering more in taxes than their French *ancien régime* counterparts.

The state could function as the private patrimony of grandees and their clients, both as a protective shell and as a carcase ripe for parasites to gorge off. It was riddled with fiscal opportunism – everyone was on the make, demanding his fee, his cut. A new Knight of the Garter had to pay £400 1s. 7d. in fees. Even George I discovered he had to slip 5 guineas to the man who fished his carp out of St James's pond. This translation of politics into jobbery, though not universal, was ingrained and unashamed. At the turn of the nineteenth century Louis Simond wrote:

> If I were asked, at this moment, for a summary opinion of what I have seen in England, I might probably say that its political institutions present a detail of corrupt practice – of profusion – and of personal ambition under the mask of public spirit, very carelessly put on, more disgusting than I should have imagined.

Exposure of 'corruption' was, of course, often oratorical rant, moved by sour grapes, yet it highlights the fact that the system was oiled by venality, and chiefly benefited those at the top and on the inside, and all their hangers-on.

Besides being the heirloom of the powerful, the state sometimes also looked after their private wishes. When a nobleman wished to enclose a common, divert a watercourse, develop a harbour, or – more difficult – divorce his wife, a private Act of Parliament legitimized what might be seen as an act of robbery or injustice. Parliament operated largely to do private and sectional business – 'a mere quarter session,' declared Horace Walpole, 'where nothing is transacted but turnpikes and poor rates.' Parliament protected established rights and defended the shores, but beyond that its responsibilities to its citizens were few, practically all matters of social policy devolving upon local government. Indeed, with the rise of a laissez-faire lobby, Westminster sloughed its long-standing mercantilist paternalism, one by one repealing laws regulating wage-rates, employment conditions, and markets, contrary to the free play of capital. Perhaps it was fortunate that the Government was so lackadaisical, for, in Arthur Young's words, 'everything is well done in England, except what is done with public money' (much of which ended up in private pockets). The Georgian state was thus personal, venal, and nepotistic in its administration; yet this was in many ways appropriate to a relatively face-to-face society, of immense local diversity, where familiarity and 'pull' really did count for more than abstract expertise. Moreover the root-and-branch denunciations of 'corruption' by back-bench politicians and by Utilitarians were in their own ways self-serving (Utilitarians wanted to substitute a corps of professional bureaucrats). The penalty of venality, however, was that abuses remained deeply entrenched. There was concerted resistance to reform, orchestrated by landed proprietors themselves, and to any encroachments by centralized government upon time-honoured jurisdictions or vested interests. Thus standing armies were despised because they involved mercenaries and barracks, and despite rising fear of crime and disorder there was immense resistance to the idea of professional police and salaried magistrates, for those stank of jobbery and tyranny. Even in the wake of the Gordon Riots, a Government proposal in 1785 to set up a London police of 225 men was defeated. In 1753 Thomas Thornton, MP, helped to defeat the Bill to conduct a national census, saying, 'I hold the prospect to be totally subversive of the last remains of English liberty.' Responsibilities remained individual, local, private. It was for generals to dredge up soldiers for their own regiments. They employed recruiting officers, themselves small businessmen, often pocketing £5 for every soldier who took the king's shilling. Generals clothed and fed their own regiments, profiteering on the side. Naval commanders were laws unto themselves on board their own men-of-war (crews took captured prize money, not the state). Paying rewards to individuals who brought criminal prosecutions commended itself as the cheapest and least tyrannical way of catching offenders (it was also perhaps quite efficient). Criminal informers got a 'Tyburn ticket' which excused them from the burdens of civil office – these tickets themselves becoming transferable pieces of property with a market price. Parish officers got 5s. for every vagrant arrested. In the clampdown against 'Jacobin' radicalism in the 1790s, a motley crew of dregs and zealots received under-the-counter funds to serve as spies, informers, and *agents provocateurs*.

The agencies of state were patchy and often bungling, partly because – despite vast expansion in departments such as the Revenue – key areas such as the embryonic Home Office remained skeleton-staffed. In 1792 the Home and Foreign Offices each had staffs of nineteen. Incompetence and delays were sometimes exposed to devastating effect, as in the War of American Independence, yet reformist demands to separate career bureaucrats from party influence (for instance by excluding civil servants from the Commons) made scant headway before the 1780s. Bentham's Utilitarian aim of reforming administration on rational, centralized lines smacked of continental absolutism. Admittedly, overbearing oligarchy and the tyrannies of tax collectors and press-gangs were hated by the people at large. The 'despotism' of Walpole and Bute and the maladroit handling of the American crisis in the 1770s drew furious protest. But parliamentary reform movements received only fitful and opportunist backing from within Parliament itself, and pressure out of doors was neither organized, continuous, nor influential enough to succeed. Wilkes's whirlwind movement sought to reinstate certain fundamental freedoms (such as his own right to his parliamentary seat) *within* the existing scheme of government. In his motion Dunning noted – rightly – that 'the power of the Crown has increased and is increasing', arguing it ought to be diminished, and the Yorkshire Association hoped to achieve this through some redistribution of parliamentary seats, mainly to raise the leverage of county gentry. But no excluded rival bloc, no 'alternative government' – as manufacturers were eventually to become – was as yet breathing down the necks of the magnates. In any case, no one challenged the power-house, the Lords, lair of the real dynasts. Moreover, it was far from reformers' minds to make government stronger and more centralized. Most, like Tom Paine and William Godwin, thought there was a surfeit of government already and aimed to fumigate the state of its leeches.

Reform was in the air by the 1780s, in part because the old generation of politicians – Newcastle, Chatham, North – had finally been replaced by their juniors, such as Charles James Fox and the younger Pitt. Paltry reforms were brought in. Burke's Act abolished 134 offices, Shelburne's Act 144. In 1789 Pitt abolished 765 jobs. Revenue officers were disfranchised and royal household expenditure brought under control. In 1780 the Commissioners for Examining the Public Accounts were set up. But though sinecures subsided, there was no electoral reform, no shift of power. The machinery of placemen and patronage, factions and juntos at Westminster, and borough-mongering in the localities, steamrollered on into the nineteenth century with what Plumb has called 'adamantine strength and profound inertia'. And all the time Parliament was becoming even more unrepresentative: by 1801 four out of the seven largest towns in England had no MP. The apparatus of state reinforced and exacerbated the social division of power. Why was it not challenged more effectively?

In part, it was because the state was ramshackle enough not to be consistently oppressive. Oppression checked oppression, and most interests could find a protector. So long as England was for many a land of economic opportunity, in which the state did not blight enterprise and prosperity, pressures for reform from moneyed men were piecemeal and intermittent. Above all the long arm of patronage offered loaves and fishes to enough people right down the social scale, and crumbs of comfort kept others' hopes alive. Sycophantically the poet Edward Young salaamed before Walpole:

My breast, O Walpole, glows with grateful fire.
The streams of royal bounty, turn'd by thee,
Refresh the dry domains of poesy.

It was the very pervasiveness of patronage and dependence that
gave the system its strength and durability.

Unlike France or Prussia, eighteenth-century England was a
polity in which grandee power flowed down to the capital from
the shires. The Revolutionary Settlement had guaranteed
landed proprietors a lot of rope for running local affairs, and
lesser people probably preferred it that way as well. Smallholders, traders, and cottagers might have little love for the carriage
folk, but closed ranks with them in reflex action against such
central interference as the imposition of a new cider tax, higher
militia levies, or threats to tamper with the corn bounty.
Atomistic decentralization and rabid regional chauvinism
were recipes for administrative pluralism. Local government
units formed a jungle whose only rationale lay in history.
Beccles in Suffolk for instance was governed by the owners of
its fen; Haverfordwest in Pembrokeshire enjoyed the same
privileges as the City of London, with its own Lord Lieutenant
and Keeper of the Rolls. In the Palatine County of Durham the
Bishop had powers resembling a German ecclesiastical prince.
Moreover, as population expanded and migrated, the skin of
legal authority was being stretched out of shape and split by
growing communities. Mushroom towns were still being run
by manorial courts which had once served feudal manors. By
1750 Halifax parish had 50,000 inhabitants yet still no acting JP.
In Manchester administration was still by court leet bearing the
vestiges of baronial jurisdiction. In the interstices of higher jurisdictions, private manorial and hundred courts survived, dealing
with infractions of by-laws, nuisances, and tenure disputes.
Furthermore, when reforms *were* brought in, to improve
street lighting, scavenging, or policing, these too sprang from
local initiatives, piloted by private self-help rather than by
central direction. This was both a boon and a bane. Local
legislation generally met local needs well, but could not solve
problems that were fundamentally regional or national. The

upshot was a crazy patchwork of new administration stitched piecemeal over the threadbare fabric of the old. There was no national rhyme or reason in the siting of new turnpike roads or poor law unions: such things were never decided nationally (except for roads of military importance: the London to Holyhead road was improved as it was the highway to Ireland).

Great landowners, and in towns merchant oligarchs, possessed vast fields of force because of their pull as employers, consumers, and dispensers of favour and patronage. Those who were also politically strong-armed, such as peers, MPs, and their henchmen, could exercise further authority, acting as ears and mouthpieces between the local community and Westminster, as protectors, supplicants, negotiators. But above all it was the local offices, hogged by the regional elite and backed by law, which dictated the destinies of communities.

The top tier of county office was the Lord Lieutenancy. The post was largely honorific, with few day-to-day chores, yet the Lord Lieutenant recommended JPs for appointment and commanded the militia (sometimes called out to enforce civil order). Carrying great prestige, the Lord Lieutenant had powers of patronage, appointing to such offices as the Clerkship of the Peace (especially prized as it was tenured for life). Ministerial and Court directives filtered down through him into his shire. The lieutenancy was an office vital for party management, increasingly coveted by national political bosses. For instance, the Duke of Bolton was Lord Lieutenant for Hampshire, Dorset, and Carmarthen, the Duke of Newcastle for Sussex, Nottingham, and Middlesex. Beneath him, the sheriff, and their respective deputies, carried out similar functions on a lower level. Sheriffs had real political sway, being responsible for the protocol of electoral polls, their siting, timing, conduct, and supervision.

The workhorse of everyday magistrate power was the Justice of the Peace, who combined his own clout as a landed gentleman (from 1732 JPs had to have an estate of £100 yearly) with extraordinarily wide and unsupervised judicial and administrative powers. Acting summarily on their own, JPs issued warrants for arrest and punished offenders for scores of misdemeanours such as drunkenness, vagrancy, or profanity.

Scapegrace poachers came up before them. Magistrates had petty offenders publicly whipped, fined, or put in a house of correction; for more serious crimes – such as simple larceny and assault – they committed miscreants for trial at quarter sessions. Typical were two cases eventually handled by Wiltshire quarter sessions at Devizes in 1746:

> Hannah Carrington of Corsham, spinster, for stealing one shift value 5s., the goods of John Pearce – pleads not guilty, jury guilty, whipt and imprisoned for 3 months.

> Benjamin Winter of Devizes, weaver, stealing 2 hens and a cock value 2s. 6 of the goods of James Buckley – pleads not guilty, jury guilty, whipt and 3 months imprisonment.

A brace of justices could exercise summary jurisdiction over alehouses, bastardy suits, runaway servants, and apprentices. A JP also had the power to commit suspects for trial by judge and jury at the county assize courts, which circuited the country twice a year and which had the power of life and death in criminal cases. In addition to their role in bringing offenders to justice, JPs also fixed wages and prices, regulated apprenticeships, swore in constables, ordered highway maintenance, suppressed nuisances, oversaw markets, assessed county rates, and licensed – or banned – fairs and amusements. In executing the poor law, JPs made settlements, heard depositions, conducted examinations, ordered removals, and assessed ratings.

JPs were unpaid, and their duties were onerous and Sisyphean, though some were more zealous than others. Henry Purefoy, a Buckinghamshire JP, found he had his time cut out attending to the nerve-fraying housewifery of his community: disputed wills, settlements, appointments to vestry offices, obstructions to highways, the destruction of woods, runaway servants, etc. Yet many relished their standing as village Solomons. After all, they were bastioning their own interests with legal sanctions: a justice might well be punishing poachers of his own game. Hardly supervised from above, their discretionary powers were enormous. As Plumb has pointed out, 'They played ducks and drakes with the law when it suited them, breaking with impunity what they were supposed to maintain'

– though suits could always be taken out against them by a plaintiff at the King's Bench.

In the countryside, the JP and an oligarchical parish vestry of property-owners; in the borough, the corporation. Most great towns of early Georgian England – places such as York, Exeter, and Coventry – were incorporated (though many unincorporated townships raced past them during the century, Birmingham being a prime example). Corporations exercised wide regulatory powers over residents, owning property, levying rates and rents, managing town lands, licensing trades and markets, and administering charities. As magistrates they passed by-laws. They also manipulated borough politics and patronage (frequently the aldermanic bench held all the parliamentary franchises). By the eighteenth century most corporations were co-opting, self-perpetuating, and intent on taking advantage of their good fortune. Yet in certain places, elections to local offices, such as the mayoralty, were open and split the community right down the middle on party-political and religious grounds.

The prince of corporations was of course the City of London. Government of the City was shared between an upper court of twenty-six aldermen (elected for life) and a lower (the Court of Common Council) made up of 234 freemen elected annually from the various ancient livery companies. Against central government the City corporation jealously guarded its own jurisdictions and privileges, including those of electing its own sheriffs and commanding its own private militia, and championed the cause of commerce and finance. No ministry dared alienate the City. Yet disputes between the two chambers were endemic, partly because freeman radicalism was on the boil. Up to 12,000 Londoners voted in elections for their aldermen and councillors.

The bedrock unit of local administration was the parish (or, in the North of England, the township), of which there were about 10,000. It was at parish level that community feeling had to be harmonized with directives from above. Parishes were run by officers appointed annually by JPs or elected by ratepayers: churchwardens, constables, the surveyor of the highways, and overseers of the poor (and humbler figures such as the pinder, who kept the cattle pound). Being unpaid and often unwilling, some officers recouped their lost time in reclaiming 'expenses' and in junketings. The overseers of the poor at St Martin-in-the-Fields once laid out £49 13s. 9d. on a dinner ('Every parish officer,' complained Francis Grose, 'thinks he has a right to make a round bill on the Parish during his year of power'). Most parish business was indeed parochial, part of the perennial negotiation of domestic interests, settling of grudges, and restoring of neighbourliness, which were the everyday stories of countryfolk (and townsfolk too). In addition to apprehending offenders, constables had to ensure their parish's militia quotas were met (ballots were held, and those chosen might serve in person or find substitutes). Surveyors of the highway had a right to six days' unpaid labour from parishioners for road-mending.

The age saw counterpointed trends in local government. First, established institutions grew more exclusive, oligarchic, and unrepresentative. Certain vestries ceased to be open and became 'select' (or co-opting) – for example in 'select' parts of London such as the West End. Closed institutions were not always, however, corrupt: the select vestry of St George's, Hanover Square, was energetic and public-spirited, whereas the open vestry at Bethnal Green, with 2,000 voters, was a veritable Tammany Hall. More corporations became self-perpetuating, with aldermen nominating their successors. To restrict entry, levies for becoming a freeman were raised. Within corporations there were the fiercest personal and factional rivalries for office and reward, but, legally secured from challenge from without, torpid corporations became oblivious to public duty, basking in their privileges, fingering fees, eating dinners, and exploiting the economic windfalls offered by their rights to build, regulate markets, administer land and property, and admit freemen. Thus when public-spirited citizens of Leicester set about founding a hospital, the corporation merely stared. Yet some corporations *were* active in developing public utilities: knowing which side its bread was buttered, Liverpool Corporation built fine docks. There was no popular agitation for a clean-sweep central reform of corporations or of JPs' powers. Suggestions for the appointment of more stipendiary magistrates (there were a few in London) were denounced as arrant jobbery. Roach has dubbed it an age of 'collective inertia' in local administration.

Meantime, the needs of localities were becoming ever more complex and pressing. As population and industrial plant grew, new public utilities became priorities. Outlying fields circling towns had to be enclosed to allow expansion for new housing (where they weren't – as at Nottingham – warrens of slums resulted). Towns had to be cleansed and drained, markets expanded, roads widened, and crumbling city walls removed. Human excreta and industrial waste and effluent were becoming festering nuisances. Parish constables could no longer cope with offences where communities grew larger and anonymous, criminals more mobile, and 'capitalist crime' – property theft – increased. Six days' shirking labour on the highways could not keep the commercial arteries of the nation in trim. But many vestries and corporations bumbled on, and no reforming *Diktat* came from St James's. Hence interested parties acted to set up private utilities in the interstices between existing authorities, coexisting with them rather than replacing or reforming them. Private Acts were piloted through Parliament sanctioning the setting-up of panels of commissioners or trustees for particular towns, empowered to raise a rate to finance services such as sewerage and water. Between 1761 and 1765 the City of Westminster secured private Acts for paving and lighting. In 1769 an Act licensed the Birmingham Street Commissioners, a board of fifty – the property qualification for trustees was £1,000 – with power to levy a rate of up to 8d. in the pound, charged to regulate building. Here, as elsewhere, commissioners expanded the scope of their activities as time went on. Manchester obtained a Cleaning and Lighting Act in 1765, an Improvement Act in 1776, and a Police Act in 1792. Between 1785 and 1800, 211 such private Acts were passed. Private initiative also founded dispensaries, hospitals, and other charities. In commercial centres such as Birmingham small-debt and conciliation courts were set up to give summary, cheap, and quick justice in money disputes.

The migraine of local government were the poor. On the one hand England possessed a *national*, statutory poor law (unlike most Catholic nations, where relief was left to alms distributed by the Church: Ireland also had no poor law; in Eastern Europe relief of poverty was generally left to the extended family). On the other hand, as the Law of Settlement and Removal of 1662 confirmed, responsibility for relieving poverty was given to the smallest unit of *local* administration, the parish. The 1662 poor law, conceived with surveillance uppermost in mind, defined responsibilities with regard to each pauper. Every native was deemed to possess a 'settlement' in one parish, and in one parish only. Such a settlement – a typical English property right – could be established most commonly by (a) birth in a parish if a bastard, (b) having a father settled there, (c) marrying a husband there, (d) being hired as a covenant servant for a year there, (e) being apprenticed there, or (f) renting a house there. A person requiring relief on account of destitution, sickness, incapacity to work, etc. had the right to relief in that parish and no other.

This policy had the merit of providing relief and identifying responsibility for it. It also served to immobilize the poor and forestall droves of vagrant beggars, by encouraging residence in or near their parish of settlement. In law a person needed a certificate before leaving his parish of settlement to seek work (in buoyant times this was often waived, especially for healthy males, who were least liable to become a charge). Paupers in receipt of relief were to wear a 'P' badge on their clothes. But the right to a settlement was also an entitlement to remove. Officers had power to drive back to their native parish vagrants and all those without a settlement who might become a burden on the rates.

Entitling each person to a right in a stipulated parish (frequently, of course, the place of residence) had its virtues. Personal acquaintance could excite compassion for the unfortunate. Overseers were often sympathetic towards familiar faces, for whom dribbling payments of a shilling or two were made for house repairs, funerals, clothes, tools, or medicines, or for tiding them over hard times. In 1788 the Oswestry overseers paid Mary, widow of Richard Francis, three years' rent and allowed her 3s. a week. She was also granted 1s. to have her garden hedged, 3s. to buy seed potatoes for the garden, and £1 for straw to thatch her cottage. Her family needing clothes, widow

Francis received doles for shoes and stockings for her children, as well as for shoe repairs, and so forth. At Leytonstone in 1740 an understanding overseer gave Beck Mitton money 'to fetch her stays out of pawn'. In a multitude of small ways, the poor law served as a thorough-going system of support for and control over parishioners, complementing the family as the main regulator of life. In the first half of the century in particular, poor law overseers seem to have been quite generous in their paternalistic supplements to domestic income. As long as labour remained in relatively short supply, it made good sense to husband the local work-force.

But there was a black side, too. Parishes would accept no responsibility for people without a settlement, and never hesitated to pass the buck. The poor, old, and sick were ruthlessly driven on (or sometimes even bribed to leave). Unmarried pregnant women were treated particularly barbarously: no parish wished to have a bastard 'dropped' on its doorstep, since thereby the baby gained a settlement. Women big with child were sometimes bullied into shot-gun weddings with bridegrooms from other parishes, for the baby would take its settlement from its father's parish. Performing such ceremonies distressed Parson Woodforde: 'It is a cruel thing that any person should be compelled by law to marry.' Yet he complied. Other women were hounded out of the parish even when in labour, in order to 'pass the baby'. The brutality could be reptilian, as parish accounts witness:

1722 To a big bellyd woman several days and nights at Nursing at Robinson, & conveying her to Chigwell after she had gathered strength to prevent her lying in here, she fell to pieces in two or three days there 17/7d.

The terror of incurring liabilities produced bundles of costly litigation and even black comedy on occasion. East Hoathley in Sussex spent no less than £80 in settling one Thomas Daw in another parish – 'Yet I believe,' wrote pennywise ratepayer Thomas Turner, 'it is a very prudent step', for Daw was one-legged and had a blind wife. Overseers perfected petty bullying and developed ruses for profiteering and evading responsibility. One common device was to farm out pauper infants to minders or masters for a small premium. No one asked questions if the children then died.

Enormous energies were expended in grappling with the problem of the poor, against the pressure of soaring rates. In 1700 the cost was about £600,000–700,000 and was even then thought to be a disgrace. By 1776 it had shot up to £1,500,000, and then went through the roof: £2 million in 1786, £4.2 million in 1803. Part of this went on relieving the sick, the ancient, the unemployed, but more and more went on 'topping up' the income of workers who couldn't support their families on skinflint wages or who could find only seasonal employment. Following the Speenhamland ruling (1795), 'topping-up' was index-linked to keep pace with inflation. Scandalized magistrates fumbled for answers.

Every fresh 'solution' got tied in knots because of contradictory attitudes towards the poor. The masses – ratepayers believed – were feckless; naturally idle, they would work no more than they had to. The moment they had spare cash they would squander it, turning to drink, debauchery, and crime. As Frederick Morton Eden primly put it: 'the miseries of the labouring poor arise, less from the scantiness of their income (however much the philanthropist might wish it to be increased) than from their own improvidence and unthriftiness'. What exasperated the authorities was their own well-meaning impotence. They could hold no effective sticks or carrots over the poor. Defoe complained:

> When wages are good they won't work any more than from hand to mouth; or if they do work they spend it in riot or luxury, so that it turns to no account to them. Again as soon as trade receives a check, what follows? Why then they grow clamorous and noisy, mutinous and saucy another way, and in the meantime they disperse, run away, and leave their families upon the parishes, and wander about in beggary and distress.

Under these circumstances, magistrates believed that wages should be pared down to keep labourers at work longest (this suited employers). 'The only way to make the poor industrious,' thought William Temple, 'is to lay them under the necessity of labouring all the time they can spare from rest and sleep, in order to procure the common necessities of life.' 'Everyone but an idiot,' echoed Arthur Young, 'knows that the lower class must be kept poor or they will never be industrious' (though he recognized that the poor also needed incentives to be industrious, for: 'The great engine wherewith the poor may be governed and provided for the most easily and the most cheaply is property'). But the problem with 'low-wage' solutions was that they kept labourers only a farthing away from destitution's door: the slightest accident or trade downswing would turn a sturdy family into instant beggars, chargeable to the parish. Furthermore if the wages of the employed were at starvation level, the parish pauper's lot seemed hardly less eligible. Why should anyone work for just a shaving more than he would be given? Observers noted that institutionalized paupers generally ate better than independent labourers' families.

These were intractable problems, but sanguine schemers always thought they had the answer. One much-canvassed, though long-term, solution was to recondition minds: 'to train up the lower classes in habits of industry and piety,' as Hannah More phrased it; to break them in to work, and make them thrifty and frugal. Charity schools, sermons, titbit rewards for labourers who served the same master for forty or fifty years – all hoped to teach that labour was a blessing. But this would take time.

One instant and radical way to keep people off poor relief was to abolish it. This modest proposal, popularized by Joseph Townsend, Frederick Morton Eden, and perhaps Thomas Malthus, argued that relief, far from relieving it, stoked poverty, because it robbed recipients of motives for self-respect, responsibility, and providence. Remove the safety net and people *would* provide for themselves (with perhaps charity as a long-stop in cases of real misfortune, though no doles as of right). As Townsend put it: 'Hunger will tame the fiercest animals, it will teach decency and civility, obedience and subjection to the most perverse ... In general, it is only hunger which can spur and goad the poor on to labour; yet our laws have said they shall never hunger.' This audacious stroke was never tried. Georgian statesmen, flattering themselves on their humanity and paternalism, shrank from it. Anyway, dispensing relief by the spoonful was a useful technique of control. The hand that fed would not be bitten, and the poor law served the important functions of regulating where labourers lived, and immobilizing a work-force which was little charge to employers when there was no call to hire labour.

A favourite nostrum was that hand-outs should have strings attached; notably, that to accept relief should mean loss of liberty. The *deus ex machina* was to be the workhouse – called by Jeremy Bentham 'a mill to grind rogues honest, and idle men industrious'. There the poor would earn their keep (thus sparing the ratepayers) and be taught skills, discipline, and piety. All birds would be killed with one elegant stone. A seventeenth-century development, large-scale workhouses were first tried in Bristol from 1697, and in a couple of hundred other places subsequently, endorsed by the Knatchbull Act (1723), which gave discretion to curb the right to outdoor relief for any refusing to enter a house of industry. Workhouse management was often farmed out to contractors whose chief interest was profit, for example Matthew Marryott, who was running thirty houses of maintenance in Buckinghamshire in the 1730s. The philanthropist Jonas Hanway had a black view of farming the poor: 'Parish officers never intend that parish infants should live.' He believed that an infant of one to three years might on average survive a month in a London workhouse. The death-rate in the workhouse of St George's, Middlesex, was 100 per cent. Out of 2,339 children received into London work-houses in the five years after 1750, only 168 were alive in 1755.

> Is it a holy thing to see
> In a rich and fruitful land
> Babes reduc'd to misery
> Fed with a cold and usurous hand?

No one answered Blake's charge of the slaughter of the inno-cents.

As economical cures for poverty, workhouses proved duds. One problem was that the inmates were – by definition – the nation's most unpromising work-force: a rubbish tip including the very young and the aged, the chronic sick and infirm, rogues, vagrants, and village simpletons. Many were unem-ployed and on the parish because of trade slumps: the hope that

self-financing workhouses could somehow buck the economic
trend was moonshine. In any case workhouses readily became
nests of jobbery, run by contractors who pocketed allowances
and provisioned them in their private capacity as tradesmen.
Many thought workhouses were failing because the individual
parish was too tiny a unit, so parishes banded together, particularly in East Anglia, to set up poor law unions, with joint
houses of industry, a movement encouraged by the Gilbert Act
(1782). But bigger workhouses just ran at bigger losses. Only a
few hundred were founded. Their main 'success' was custodial
– they shunted paupers out of sight (for this reason locking
people up was a solution which went from strength to strength).
Parson Woodforde visited a Norfolk workhouse in 1781:

> We dined at 3 o'clock and after we had smoked a Pipe etc., we took
> a ride to the House of Industry about 2 miles West of Dereham, and a
> very large building at present tho' there wants another Wing. About
> 380 Poor in it now, but they don't look either healthy or cheerful, a
> great Number die there, 27 have died since Christmas last.

Parishes floundered from expedient to expedient. Supplemen-
tary relief would be tried and then abandoned for a spell in
favour of a house of correction or an experimental workhouse,
followed by contracting out to entrepreneurs, and then back to
botched-up outdoor relief.

All these responses to poverty – both off-the-cuff and program-
matic – fell short because they were treating surface symptoms,
not root economic causes. What is more, they were treating the
symptoms locally, when the problems were national. Society
itself, with its exploitative system of inversely sharing out work
and rewards, was producing a pauper residuum (a process economists thought vital for the nation's well-being: 'Poverty is …
a most necessary and indispensable ingredient in society, without which nations and communities could not exist in a state of
civilization,' argued Patrick Colquhoun). At the same time,
through the spreading laissez-faire ideology which fetishized
competitive individualism, the political nation was washing its
hands of responsibility or resorting to punitive expedients such
as the workhouse. At the end of the century Malthus told the
indigent that poverty was their own fault: they bred too fast.

Endemic pauperism was one of the nightmare monsters spawned by the eighteenth century.

Elsewhere there might be the sultan's caprice, the *lit de justice*, judicial torture, the slow-grinding mills of the canon law's bureaucracy, and the *auto-da-fé* of the Inquisition. In England, by contrast, king and magistrates were beneath the law, which was the even-handed guardian of every Englishman's life, liberties, and property. Blindfolded Justice weighed all equitably in her scales. The courts were open, and worked by known and due process. Eupeptic fanfares such as those on the unique blessings of being a free-born Englishman under the Anglo-Saxon-derived common law were omnipresent background music. Anyone, from Lord Chancellors to rioters, could be heard piping them (though for very different purposes).

Subjects at large, and vulnerable minorities in particular, looked to the law for protection against the mighty – as well of course as being anxious to have their own limbs and property secured against cutpurses, sharpers, debtors, and footpads. As formulated on the statute book and established by judicial precedent and time-honoured custom, the legal process did actually offer redress to many plaintiffs (married women and children came off worst). Even the poor initiated civil litigation (often the aim was not a court ruling but to encourage out-of-court settlement of a long-running dispute). Wilkite radicals dazzlingly exploited the courts on points of law to trip up the executive. Even magistrates who ordered troops to fire on rioters were liable to find themselves prosecuted. In 1765 a soldier sued his colonel at the Court of Common Pleas for reducing him from a sergeant to a private, winning £70 damages. Mercantilist legislation had long regulated wages and prices, terms of apprenticeship, and the like. Habeas Corpus guaranteed protection to the person. Freedom of worship (albeit incomplete) was enshrined in the Toleration Act (1690).

In England, ministries could not even count on judges to be time-serving reserve arms of executive power, as they could on much of the Continent. Following publication of the supposedly libellous issue number 45 of the *North Briton*, John Wilkes was arrested on a Government general warrant. Chief Justice Pratt had him released on grounds of his privilege as an MP and cast doubt upon the legality of such warrants. Thomas Hardy and other radicals, tried for sedition in the 1790s, were acquitted. Cases against many a thief and murderer had to be discharged through loopholes and procedural defects in the prosecution – such as misspelling of names in indictments. In felony cases Englishmen had the reassurance of being arraigned by their countrymen. Almost all prosecutions were privately laid; in court a defendant's family and friends could vouch for his character, and it was his peers serving as jurymen who reached the verdict (going before a jury was called 'putting yourself on your country'). Magistrates themselves constantly played roles as arbitrators in trade disputes. In short, from the hue-and-cry to the macabre carnival of the public hanging, the law and its execution were not just Government fiats or ruling-class weapons but an intimate part of community life.

Nevertheless the law was at bottom framed and enforced by those with power to cajole and coerce the rest, as Goldsmith's laconic monosyllables state: 'Laws grind the poor, and rich men rule the law.' There was clearly one law for the rich, another for the poor. 'Tippling in an ale-house may be punished,' wrote a 'gentleman' in 1753, 'but not drinking in a tavern; bawdy houses may be searched but not bagnios; and in every other instance the laws themselves vindicate our tyranny over the poor.' One way the law was increasingly nipping the common people was the encroachment of statute upon areas hitherto regulated by custom alone. In many crafts, it had been customary for workers to keep scrap or sell left-overs, such as wood chips, of materials supplied by their employers. At the instigation of employers, new embezzlement and theft laws were passed, turning these massive, annoying but hitherto winked-at fringe benefits into offences. An act of 1740 made it criminal for a worker to purloin materials entrusted to him; by 1773 this offence carried three months' gaol. Rights to search workers' premises were granted, and the burden of proving innocent possession placed upon them. Between 1726 and 1800 eleven new embezzlement statutes were passed in the woollen, fustian, and worsted trades (though they proved almost impossible to enforce). Breach of contract was turned in some instances from a civil into a criminal offence. Similarly, many cottagers without legal title had customarily occupied common and waste land. In enclosure settlements, such squatters received no rights or compensation, and in issues of grazing, gleaning, or of rights of way, the complex bundle of users' rights (usufruct) tended to be simplified into absolute property right, to the benefit of the ultimate landowner. Customary tenures were also assailed. The law was being brought increasingly into line with the needs of new forms of property and securities in a sophisticated capitalist economy. The law of false pretences was introduced in 1757. Much case law on credit, contracts, paper money debts, bills, and other vital commercial issues dates from the judicial decisions of Lord Mansfield at the King's Bench between 1760 and 1788. Fresh forgery and counterfeiting statutes were brought in to protect the currency and credit (thus in 1771 the misdemeanour of coining copper coin was made a felony). Two thirds of those found guilty of forgery were actually executed.

Two other developments gave savage twists to statute law's class screw. First, legislation made the penal code more ferocious. There had been fifty capital offences in 1689; by 1800 there were four times that number. Many specified death for small-scale theft such as pick-pocketing goods valued more than 1s., or shoplifting items worth more than 5s. New capital offences included such heinous activities as being out at night with one's face blackened, breaking down fish-ponds, cutting hop-binds, destroying turnpikes, sending threatening letters, and destroying silk on the loom. The Waltham Black Act (1724) created fifty new capital offences at a stroke. Successive tightenings of the game laws meant that by the early nineteenth century offenders caught poaching were frequently transported; the poacher who fired a gun at a keeper committed a capital offence.

Second, the protection of property loomed larger in legislators' minds. Property was of course the soul of eighteenth-century society, residing in anything from mere goods to rights (a vote or an apprenticeship was a property) or persons. Thus Negro slaves were openly sold as chattels – witness the *London Advertiser* (1756):

To be sold, a Negro boy age about fourteen years old, warranted free from any distemper, and has had those fatal to that colour; has been used two years to all kinds of household work, and to wait at table; his price is £25, and would not be sold but the person he belongs to is leaving off business.

There was a thriving trade in making ornamental collars and padlocks for slaves. But prestige commissions were bought and sold as well. The *Morning Post* advertised

An Ensigncy in an Old Regiment returned from Egypt and now at Malta to be sold, £60 under the regulated price. There are several vacancies in that regiment which makes it an eligible purchase.

In mid-century an ensigncy cost about £400, a lieutenant-colonelcy about £3,500.

Locke had written, 'The great and chief end, therefore, of men's uniting into commonwealth and putting themselves under government is the preservation of their property'; and the governing classes went about doing this with a will, for 'economic crime' was on the increase. By 1736 servants who pilfered from their masters were liable to hanging; in 1741 sheep-stealing was made a capital offence (this became a much-used statute). Homicides might very often be given nominal sentences, or acquitted (the great actor Charles Macklin slew a colleague in a temper and walked out of the Old Bailey free, convicted of manslaughter, 'to be branded on the hand and discharged'). But thieves found guilty of felony were generally sentenced to hanging. The great majority of men and women 'turned off' were hanged for theft. In London and Middlesex between 1749 and 1771 only seventy-two out of 678 people executed were murderers. Crimes especially damaging to capitalism were punished with exemplary severity. Coiners and forgers were shown no mercy, for they betrayed the system of credit from top to toe. In 1789 a woman was burned at Tyburn for coining (yet such was the shortage of legal tender that coiners – especially minters of copper money – helped to make the economy go round).

The law was capital's bulldog in other ways. From the 1720s statutes were passed restricting trade unions. Combinations were outlawed amongst tailors in 1721 and 1767, in the woollen trade in 1726, amongst hatters in 1777, in 1797 amongst paper-makers. By the time of the general (anti-)Combination Acts (1799 and 1800) over forty Acts were already on the statute book forbidding combinations to raise wages. Above all, the game laws were made ever more savage. From 1671 no one without an estate of £100 a year was allowed to kill game (not even on his own land), but it was from about the mid eighteenth century that game preserves were set up in large numbers and poachers cracked down upon, possibly because they were starting to use guns. Under an Act of 1770 nocturnal poachers were liable to six months' imprisonment. A further Act of 1803 prescribed death for poachers resisting arrest with arms and an 1816 Act, transportation even for an unarmed man caught with a net. From mid-century gentlemen set up Game Associations, to expedite prosecutions. By 1827 poaching crimes were accounting for one seventh of all criminal convictions in England. Even the panegyrist Blackstone believed that the game laws showed ideas about property run riot, being founded on 'the ... unreasonable notion of a permanent property in wild creatures ... productive of ... tyranny to the Commons ... The game laws have raised a little Nimrod in every manor.' Whether or not the propertied grew more heartless, protection of property certainly became more urgent, for as material goods multiplied, employers and property holders became more vulnerable. In certain putting-out trades, up to a twelfth of employers' materials were disappearing into workers' pockets. As communities grew and, like London, became more mobile and anonymous, it was easier for thieves to melt into the crowd. (Yet other developments made criminals' lives harder. For example, listings of stolen property and highway robberies in newspapers facilitated detection.) All species of property found champions in the courts, from deer to votes, from army commissions to chattel slaves. Despite the much trumpeted Somersett ruling of 1774, even the rights to own Negro slaves in England remained stubbornly secure through the whole of the century.

Yet the proliferating terrors of the criminal code probably had very little deterrent effect, just as the poor law did not prevent poverty. Many felons could not afford to contemplate the scaffold or didn't give a damn about it. There were few professional criminals: most took to theft only when bad times had shut off other courses. Trade slumps made crime rocket: craftsmen in the metal trades took to coin-clipping, and de-mobilized soldiers, finding no work, slithered into lawlessness. Children were inducted into prostitution and pocket-picking by their elders. Abandoned girls became street-walkers (many prostitutes were not full-time 'professionals', but women who went on the streets when times were difficult). In 1741 a nineteen-year-old, Elizabeth Hardy, was sentenced to hang for theft of goods worth 13s. 6d. Forsaken by her husband, she was a stranger in London who had stolen out of desperation. She got a last-minute reprieve and was transported.

The penal system was known to be ineffectual. At the end of the century the London magistrate Patrick Colquhoun summarized what reformers thought was wrong:

1. The Imperfection of the Criminal Code.
2. The Want of a proper System of Police.
3. The Want of a Public Prosecutor for the Crown.
4. The Unnecessary Severity of Many Punishments.
5. The Abuses of the System of Granting Pardons.
6. The Entire System of Imprisonment in Hulks.
7. The Want of a proper Penitentiary House for the Employment and Reformation of Criminals.

As legal reformers such as Jeremy Bentham insisted, laws which prescribed execution indiscriminately for murder *and* for lifting handkerchiefs were unlikely to restrain from heinous crime. Some magistrates were corrupt. In the London area so-called 'trading justices', having bought their offices, were eager to milk them through fees and bribes: Horace Walpole was not the only one to believe 'the greatest criminals of this town are the officers of justice'. Punishments neither deterred nor re-formed. The hangman's victim had his inebriate moment of celebrity. Instead of being pelted, those clapped in the pillory might be lionized by the crowd – as was Daniel Defoe. And before the 1780s few expected prisons to reform miscreants – 'prison,' thought a writer in 1726, 'is a place fitter to make a rogue than reform him. Bolts and chains are used as bugbears to extort money from those who are supposed to have it, while such as pay readily are indulged in the greatest freedom, and excess, be their crimes of what nature so ever.'

Prisons were laws unto themselves, run on private-enterprise sub-contracting systems through which the governor and his underlings hoped to make tidy profits, for instance by selling liquor to inmates or renting out superior accommodation to those who could pay. Lord Derby owned Macclesfield gaol and made £13 a year from it. Many gaols were small and ruinous – even ale-houses might be used as lock-ups – and there was only fitful inspection from sheriffs. Gaols aimed to do little more with their inmates than confine them, and internal discipline was often exercised by groups of prisoners themselves (the King's Bench had its 'college'). Prisoners were a mishmash of humanity, most awaiting trial or transportation, with no segregation of the sexes. William Smith described some occupants of Middlesex prisons in 1776 as 'vagrants and disorderly women of the very lowest and most wretched class of human beings, almost naked, with only a few filthy rags almost alive with vermin, their bodies rotting with distemper, and covered with itch, scorbutic and venereal ulcers'. Extortion, prostitution, and drunkenness were routine. Many rotted and died in the feculent conditions – gaol fever took more victims than did justice. Yet many prisoners brazened it out. Racketeers found the inside of a gaol fertile soil for their dealings. Prisoners could bring their families in and even keep pets (though pigs were banned from Newgate after 1714).

In any case, the law and the courts worked in mysterious ways. Thousands of debtors were clapped without trial into King's Bench gaol by creditors. In the 1770s almost half the total prison population were debtors. But they were confined at the creditors' expense – and by gaoling debtors, creditors might wreck their chances of repayment. Many debtors cannot have minded being gaoled, for they could carry on their trade from prison (they were let out of King's Bench prison during the daytime) and while they were confined, their property was legally safeguarded.

The law, moreover, remained ineffective because catching lawbreakers was a hit-and-miss affair. England's police was unpaid, part-time, and parochial, concerned with visible street offences rather than with detection work. Petty thefts committed by neighbours or servants in a hamlet were relatively easily sniffed out (few amateurs were good at covering their tracks). But wheezing watchmen and constables had a harder time in London and other great cities. In the late eighteenth century, the metropolis, its population nearing one million, had no more than 1,000 officers and 2,000 watchmen. (Paris, by contrast, had 7,000 officers and 6,000 Swiss guards, under greater central control.) The authorities relied heavily on private initiative. Citizens were encouraged to set themselves up as thief-takers by the offer of a £40 reward for every highwayman turned in, the respectable front of the gang-boss and fence Jonathan Wild being as a thief-taker and restorer of stolen property.

Exceptional London magistrates, such as Thomas de Veil, Henry Fielding, and his blind half-brother John, took steps to establish a more effective police force, Henry Fielding securing secret service funds to set up the Bow Street Runners in 1749. Runners were paid a guinea a week plus a share of the parliamentary reward for each criminal successfully prosecuted. Patrick Colquhoun's Thames Police dated from 1798. But parliamentary funding was sporadic, because of disquiet lest a paid central police became an executive tool. Hence citizens formed vigilante groups to plug the gap. Large numbers of Societies for the Prosecution of Felons were formed in the second half of the century, particularly amongst urban employers. Similarly in 1792 the inhabitants of Hoxton, just outside the City of London, formed a 'military association for the protection of their persons and properties against the attacks of ruffians'. Desperate for remedy against body-snatchers, mourners set spring-guns around graves.

Finally, the law and the penal system had only oblique impact because of the hiatus between crime and punishment, what statutes prescribed and what courts did. Magistrates, judges, and juries hesitated to enforce the full terror of the law, believing that atrocious penalties should be earmarked for vicious blackguards and in occasional exemplary circumstances. The bench winked at undervaluing stolen goods so as to slim down grand larceny – a hanging offence – into petty theft. Masters would

often plead successfully in court for clemency towards servants
or poor relations. Overkill would erode respect for the law.
Theatrical use was made of mercy and pardons to set off social
superiors in a better light. Hence the paradox that in Georgian
England capital statutes and, probably, crime grew, but hangings steadily decreased from their Stuart peaks. In the late
eighteenth century only about twenty people were being
hanged a year in London and Middlesex, compared with about
140 early in the seventeenth century. Though there were 200
capital statutes, no more than about 200 people a year were
hanged in England and Wales. Similarly, many of the new
statutes against labour were little used in the event: employers
found it preferable to settle by negotiation. And reprieves were
common (especially in cases of theft). In late-eighteenth-century
London, only about one in three people sentenced to death
were actually hanged.

   Agitation mounted about the supposed cascading of crime,
and in particular about the emergence (alongside shoals of
small-fry swindlers, fences, con-men and their trollops, molls,
and jades) of organized big-time racketeering in London. Yet
through most of the country professional crime remained rare,
banditry was almost unknown, and premeditated assaults
against the person uncommon. The moral supervision exercised
by communities preserved high levels of law-abidingness. And
compared with the legalized violence, exploitation, and extortion carried out by society (in the form of press-gangs, military
discipline, taxation, enclosures, whippings at home, workhouses
and workshops, and unchecked looting and rape in the expanding empire), the social impact of criminal activities just scratched
the surface. As the rhyme asked,

> A sin it is in man or woman
> To steal goose from off the common
> But what, then, is his excuse
> Who steals the common from the goose?

Nevertheless, society became more anonymous, and the security of capital and goods more critical, fears of crime grew, and
toleration of disorder – both criminal and plebeian – diminished.
Towards the end of the century, reformers were blueprinting
social machinery to police society, to clamp down on crime and

degenerate rogues. The emphasis tilted from prosecution to prevention, from punishment towards reform, from instant physical terror to long-term institutional management. The age in which the prisons would be the portals to social discipline was just around the corner.

To say English political and legal institutions worked in favour of the propertied and privileged is truistic. More significantly they formed a suit of legal armour snugly protecting the independently powerful body of the socially eminent, particularly in the localities. There was no autonomous absolutist centralized 'state', staffed by a distinct rank of bureaucrats, cutting across their interests – that was exactly what the landed orders had quashed in the previous century. Yet precisely because central powers had been attenuated, it was possible for divers groups to use public institutions such as the law for their own ends; and also for new bodies (as in local government) to spring up between the cracks. Social conflict remained piecemeal, dispersed, allegiances in flux. While parish control could be oppressive, the eighteenth-century central state was lax, a beanfeast to those in power rather than a tyrant lash on the backs of the ruled. Its most grievous exaction was taxation, and since England's productive classes were multiplying and wealth was increasing, this was a burden the grumbling hive could bear.

4. *Keeping Life Going*

Two mirages float up before unwary eyes attempting to picture everyday life in eighteenth-century England. Both must be dispelled. One is the image of some wholesome 'community', engaged on satisfying creative craft-work, each 'peasant' snug within the bosom of the extended family. Recent researches, such as those of Laslett and fellow 'family reconstructors', have buried many fathoms deep the myth of the extended peasant family – and even of a peasantry itself – at least for Georgian England. Certainly, the *family* was a key institution,* the elemental unit of living and dying, reproduction and socialization, education and business, love and hate. Gregory King tabulated the English population not by individuals but by families. But the typical family was simple.

The basic and most common household arrangement amongst the working population was for the house to be occupied by a single married couple. Their young children would live with them, though sons, and slightly less so, daughters, were likely to move out as soon as they were apprenticed to a trade or sent into service in their early teens. But a married couple did not normally have their parents living with them (if they were still alive – and very many would be dead – they would continue to live in their own dwelling), and it was most exceptional for a married pair to be living under the roof of their parents. Courting couples did not generally marry until the man could support his wife and set up home. For in-laws or members of the wider family to be living in, except temporarily, was unusual. By contrast it was normal for domestic servants, apprentices, unmarried farm servants, and lodgers to live in with the family. Even quite poor tradesmen and small-

---

* Though in England, as in much of north-western Europe, family loyalties were sharply circumscribed. Even brothers might feel little obligation to get each other out of a financial scrape. And not all families were happy families.

holders would have young household servants, for they were plentiful and cheap, and houses ate up labour. For teenagers, going into service was the normal thing. Husbands ruled families, and family decisions were made by the breadwinner, not by the wider family in conference, unlike in some continental peasant societies.

The second and contrasting mirage is that of an England akin to a present-day, under-developed, 'third world' country, at least before the Industrial Revolution. It is sometimes assumed that before heavy industrialization, the primitiveness of technology, hygiene, and medicine, together with illiteracy and population pressure, meant lives verging permanently on the dunghill for the masses. But this was not so. Life was certainly gruelling, and upwards of one family in five received poor relief. Yet there is plenty of evidence that even needy labourers had some disposable income, participated in the money economy, and exercised some say in the patterning of their lives. They possessed a few heirlooms and went in for the odd luxury: tea-drinking was to spread right down the social scale. Labouring men possessed skills, initiative, and their own 'appropriate technology', and were mobile in their jobs and domicile. Theirs was not the expropriated hopeless begging-bowl destitution of parts of the present-day third world. The ordinary Georgian working family did not bask in a folksy golden age, but neither did it have one foot inside the refugee-camp.

Life within the household and the community followed tightly organized, highly regulated, businesslike rounds of routine drills, plotted from the cradle to the grave. Prudent performance of what was allotted and expected made all the difference between merely surviving and living well, between failing and thriving according to one's lights. Through moral precepts, authority figures, family demands, and work-routines, communities applied continual physical, moral, and emotional pressure upon their members. Each life involved harmonizing regulations imposed from above (such as the law or the employer's command) with peer group pressure and with personal hopes and ambitions. Sometimes the adjustment was easy, sometimes agonizing. What youth would not leap at the chance of marrying his master's daughter, or widow, as did Robert

Owen's brother, William, but how many daughters wanted to stay at home and nurse crotchety parents? The community's wishes were often accepted, internalized, and put into practice, because they were the tried and tested ways of getting on. Sons, if dutiful, would eventually inherit; runaway apprentices, by contrast, would lose their 'character'. Debating matrimony and eventually declining it, Edward Gibbon experienced just these pressures: 'I sighed as a lover; I obeyed as a son.' Quakers who married out risked being expelled from the meeting; unneighbourly old women were branded as witches.

Creating cohesion was vital where people had to operate in harmony. Husbandmen tilling open fields had to agree on crop rotations, or on when to allow post-harvest stubble-grazing. Ploughs and ox-teams were shared, as were wells and pumps. Millers', farmers', and bargees' claims on running water had to be reconciled. Many jobs involved cooperative physical labour, pulling in unison: sawyers, for example, worked in teams of two. Work songs such as shanties kept team efforts in time.

Codes of basic values distilled in proverbs and wise sayings aimed to make vital interests converge. Families needed to win for themselves and their dependants a livelihood, struggling against nature and economic rivals. But they also needed ways of negotiating personal relations so that mutual rights and duties could be allocated and disputes settled (from tiffs to feuds), and these made solemnly binding on future generations. The warp of self-preservation had to be interwoven with the weft of neighbourliness. Circumscribed by need, villagers abided by the time-honoured proprieties, and heads often had to rule hearts. Thus working mothers swaddled their babies or farmed them out to wet-nurses because they couldn't afford their work to be interrupted by toddlers' demands. You had to be coolheaded when it came to choosing company, a spouse, a trade.

Two activities particularly tightly regulated were work and sex. Production and reproduction had to be kept in fine balance. Too few able bodies and the depleted work-force would not sustain well-being. Too many mouths and pauperism would edge in. Below leisured society, everybody could expect to be put to work, and few retired, until forced by incapacity. Infants might tread washing; from the age of four or five some would scare crows or keep cows from the corn, or would be doing domestic work in textiles. Defoe admired the economy of the West Riding of Yorkshire because he found 'hardly any thing above four years old, but its hands are sufficient to itself'. Around the age of ten boys might well be apprenticed – to shopkeepers, craftsmen, or, more appallingly, to chimney-sweeps. Once in his twenties, a journeyman would begin serious courting with a view to setting up on his own, using his wife's labour and that of the anticipated children.

Within the working family, the quality of life had to be practical. Our glimpses of petty bourgeois and artisan domestic life reveal level-headed relationships, in which adults took priority over children and men over women in meeting the needs of production. William Hutton, who was to become a flinty Birmingham businessman, records that he was never hugged or kissed by his Nonconformist mother: this is probably not untypical. When his mother died, his nanny upbraided his tears: 'Don't cry, you will soon go yourself.' Hutton wrote, 'I was an economist from my cradle.'

Few craftsmen or professional men were so impetuous as to marry until they had saved enough to set up home or had inherited their father's tools or holding (mere labourers had less reason to wait). Many married women older than themselves, often widows. Widows were proven mothers and housewives and were likely to have a nest egg put by (marrying an older woman was also a hedge against having too many children). Matthew Boulton advised, 'Don't marry for money, but marry where money is.' Men above all needed wives to be what Richard Gough called 'prudent, provident and discreet', Defoe speaking of how in seeking a bride a man might well choose 'the homeliest and eldest' out of a bunch, for 'it was application and business they were to expect assistance in'. And men themselves married quite late. Salad-days marriages were uncommon. Early in the century, journeymen generally wed after apprenticeship in their mid to late twenties; professional men often later. Their brides were a little younger. This pattern of late marriage special to north-western Europe, meant that about half of all parents never lived to see their children grown up. Overall it was a society in which economic prudence strongly regulated family formation (especially early in the century many never married at all). Though contraceptive appliances were hardly used, family size was purposely kept in check partly by delayed marriage and perhaps by sexual restraint within marriage. A marriage bond, once formed, generally held together until the death of one of the partners. Few widowers remained unattached for long: they needed a spouse to look after the home and children.

If amongst ordinary folk matrimony was postponed until starting a household and family became prudent, pre-marital sexual experience itself was very commonly forgone, particularly amongst women. Of course, many dashing young men sowed their wild oats, actors and soldiers being notorious for loving and leaving, and every village had its molls who were known to go with men. But most young maids probably went without. Considering there was a decade or so between puberty and matrimony, there were few bastards (through most of the century they amounted to about 2 per cent of recorded births). Of course, recorded bastards may tell us little about pre-nuptial sex. Many illegitimate births went unrecorded (stillbirths, early mortality, and infanticide silenced plenty), and in any case, in an age when fertility was low, sex did not often result in conception. Bastardy, however, went up in the second half of the century. The prudence and prohibitions which in late Stuart times had dictated delayed marriage and curtailed pre-marital sexual activity, and had meant that many remained single, all loosened in line with eath other. As a rising proportion of the population married, and married younger, so the disadvantages and stigmas of bearing bastards were also reduced. A swelling percentage of marriages became contracted after pregnancy.

Rising bastardy may also indicate enhanced fertility accompanying better health and nutrition, sex inside and outside marriage more often leading to pregnancy. It may be evidence of anticipated marriages falling through. Couples frequently began having sex once they were courting in earnest, intending marriage when circumstances were right:

> Bobby Shafto's gone to sea
> Silver buckles on his knee
> When he comes back he'll marry me.

But if an accident such as a war or unemployment put obstacles in the way of marriage the woman might be left holding the baby. Bastards were thus frequently the wages not of casual sex but of serious courtship not resulting in marriage. The rising bastardy figures are also possibly a consequence of the stricter definition of legitimacy following Hardwicke's Marriage Act (1753). Upon pregnancy, it had been customary in many communities to recognize established couples as *de facto* man and wife ('consensual marriage'); even many clergymen had looked upon the offspring of such unions as legitimate. The 1753 Act, however, made a properly conducted church wedding the test of marriage. Henceforth, parish clerks were much less likely to regard children of 'consensual marriages' as legitimate.

All in all, the low bastardy rate and the desire of many cohabiting couples not legally married to have some public recognition of their union are indicative of a society where individuals marched to the strict drum-beat of the community's values. Except in big towns or right off the beaten track, people were continually in the public eye, and censure was shameful and disabling. Shorter is probably right to suggest that 'Sexuality in traditional society may be thought of as a great iceberg, frozen by the command of custom, by the need of the surrounding community for stability at the cost of individuality, and by the dismal grind of daily life.'

People certainly trimmed their wills to their ways and means. Trade downswings meant postponed marriages. By contrast, in the Midlands and North economic effervescence in the last third of the century encouraged faith in the future and thereby boosted population. In the framework-knitting centres of Leicestershire and Nottinghamshire for example, couples began to marry earlier, confident of work and anticipating that with the growth of manufacturing large families would be a boon rather than a bind. As Arthur Young expressed it, 'It is employment that creates population: marriages are early and numerous in proportion to the amount of employment.'

Parents, kin, masters, friends, and communities all expected to have their say over private lives. Many people never escaped direct dependency (marriage would bring a man full membership of society, but his wife only switched superiors). The private lives of domestic servants were supervised and often exploited. Servant girls who bore a bastard – often their master's – might have their name besmirched and hopes of respectable marriage dashed, for once dismissed as an outcast such a girl's life easily became a harlot's progress. Mothers and nurses, no less than fathers and masters, habitually inflicted physical punishment. Young Francis Place was frequently beaten by his father until the stick broke: 'a word and a blow, but the blow always came first'. John Wesley's mother, Susanna, said of her babies, 'when turned a year old (and sons before) they were taught to fear the rod, and to cry softly'. Autobiographies show that children from the lower orders in particular experienced parents as figures of direct power. In many families, youngsters were often still expected to stand silently in their parents' presence, and obedience was the child's golden rule. Many children had been constrained from birth by months of swaddling. 'I lay very quiet,' Richard Steele imagined a newborn babe thinking, 'but the witch [i.e. the mother] . . . takes me, and binds my head as hard as possibly she could; then ties up both my legs, and makes me swallow down an horrid mixture. I thought it an harsh entrance into life, to begin with taking physic; but I was forced to it.' John Locke, philosopher and tutor, was as concerned to drill children to go to stool as go to school, and alongside rigorous toilet-training, cold baths came into vogue to harden the fibres. Girls of genteel family were fastened into backboards, corsets, and stays to improve posture. For being naughty, Fanny Kemble was imprisoned for a week in a toolshed, Charlotte Charke was tied to a table leg.

By virtue of their seniority parents compelled submission, but did age command respect, or even love? Gibbon frankly thought the young were relieved when their parents died. 'Few, perhaps, are the children who, after the expiration of some months or years, would sincerely rejoice in the resurrection of their parents, and it is a melancholy truth that my father's death . . . was the only event that could save me from an hopeless life of obscurity and indigence.' For, with long apprenticeship, professional training, and late marriage, young men were financially insecure and could be kept under their elders' thumb for half their days. For tedious years the future Lord Kenyon, training in the law, languished on £50 a year from his father. The old could be irksome because they didn't retire (most could not afford to, having no insurance for old age: Tom Paine was an early advocate of old age pensions). Overall, it was not an era which revered grey hairs. Ageing Georgians did not try to impersonate long-bearded patriarchs: wigs and cosmetics, used even by men, were to keep an appearance of youth. The outlook of the Age of Reason led Henry Fox to bring up his son, Charles James, to believe that 'the young are always right, the old are always wrong'.

Impatience with the old was not surprising in a society where most people were young and clamouring to get on. Over 45 per cent of the population was under twenty: there were juveniles galore. Yet there was an extra-fast lane to power for the privileged young: Pitt (the 'Younger') could rise to be Prime Minister at twenty-four; Brownlow North was a bishop at thirty; Wolfe got his army commission at fourteen and was a major at twenty.

Ceremony and show regulated life more than now: witness the complex degrees of formal mourning attire. Distinctions in dress were cameos of status and occupation. Thus physicians had distinctive wigs and carried gold-headed canes, wearing swords to show that they were gentlemen. But clothes also signalled much other private and public information, from the schoolmaster's gown of authority to the cap worn by the ageing spinster to show she had withdrawn from the marriage market. Charity school uniforms, provided free, were badges of poverty. In days before savings-banks, people invested more of their wealth in fine and formal clothes. Even wigs, accessories, and stuccoed cosmetics, modes of dress and undress, could reveal rank, age, and even politics (where ladies stuck their face patches was a clue to their party allegiances). The lace tongue of the fan could scandal-monger, or it could seduce. Up to the 1770s it was unfashionable for men not to wear a wig; then suddenly even a tonish servant such as Fag in Sheridan's *Rivals* would not have been seen dead wearing one. As a peer, Lord Ferrers, who had murdered his steward, went to his execution in his wedding suit embroidered with silver, begging to be hanged with a rope of silk.

Life was animated and punctuated by the festive calendar, many days having their own distinct rituals. Hair was still cut at full moon, blood was let in the spring. Feeling continued to run strong against marrying in Lent, traditionally forbidden by the Church, and parishes seem to have had their own preferred months for weddings and baptisms. Birthdays were times of private jollification but also reminders about one's body. Thus Thomas Turner, schoolmaster, recorded in his diary in 1755: 'This day being my birthday, I treated my scholars with about five quarts of strong beer and had an issue cut in my leg': beer and blood flowed together. Festivities marked off the stages of the farming year – Plough Monday, sheep-shearing, rush-bearing, harvest home. Trades had annual processions – weavers on St Blaise's Day, for instance – giving licence for apprentice high-jinks. In boroughs mayoral processions, like mini-coronations, signalled a change of authority. César de Saussure noted:

> The Lord Mayor's day is a great holiday in the City. The populace on that great day is particularly insolent and rowdy, turning into lawless freedom the great liberty it enjoys. At these times it is almost dangerous for an honest man, and particularly for a foreigner, if at all well dressed, to walk in the streets, for he runs a great risk of being insulted by the vulgar populace, which is the most cursed brood in existence.

Some holidays were holy days – although Christmas, Twelfth Night, and Shrove Tuesday were plaited with pagan good cheer, eating, merriment, and wassailing. On Shrove Tuesday men played football, youngsters shied at cocks. Whitsun over-lapped with the summer wakes and was the season of well-dressing. 'On Good Friday,' wrote Samuel Bamford about his native late-eighteenth-century Lancashire, 'children took little baskets neatly trimmed with moss, and went "a pace-egging", and received at some places eggs, at some places spiced loaf, and at others half-pennies, which they carried home to their mothers.' Other rural festivals enacted pagan and magical lore, such as the Helston Furry (or Flora) Dances or the horn dance at Abbots Bromley in Staffordshire, palimpsests of Christianity and nature worship. A puppet, Jack O'Lantern, was tossed around on Ash Wednesday, celebrating the death of Winter. Christening was a sacrament but it was also believed to ward off sickness. Folk wisdom held that Christian confirmation was a specific against rheumatism (nothing doctors gave you did any good). Good Friday bread was preserved for months to be used as a remedy.

Customs, feasts, and mummers' pageants kept traditional beliefs alive and kicking. People danced round maypoles, and morris men jangled their bells, rode hobby horses, hoisted corn dollies, and sang refrains about 'the Green Man' and other fertility and virility symbols. 'Tom Poker', 'Old Shock', 'Will o' the Wisp' – such ancestral bogeys and ghosts thread in and out of popular stories, frightening children on dark nights. Games such as barley-break and the nine-men's morris were full of legend. Rituals such as those of St Valentine's day and Mayday gave personal emotional release and perhaps helped tongue-tied young people to initiate courting. Thus Henri Misson described St Valentine's day:

On the eve of the 14th of February, St Valentine's Day, a time when all living nature inclines to couple, the young folks in England, and Scotland too, by a very ancient custom, celebrate a little festival that tends to the same end. An equal number of maids and bachelors get together; each writes his or her true or some feigned name upon separate billets, which they roll up and draw by way of lots, the maids taking the men's billets, and the men the maids'; so that each of the young men lights upon a girl that he calls his Valentine, and each of the girls upon a young man which she calls hers. By this means, each has two Valentines; but the man sticks faster to the Valentine that is fallen to him, than to the Valentine to whom he is fallen. Fortune having thus divided the company into so many couples, the Valentines give balls and treats to their fair mistresses, wear their billets several days upon their bosoms and sleeves, and this little sport often ends in love.

Mayday gave a maid a chance to pay her addresses to a youth, but it was also when Shropshire colliers battled with farm labourers for possession of the summit of the Wrekin and London chimney-sweeps went on parade. Elsewhere others danced round maypoles and girls were crowned Queen of the May. Most festivals allowed children to scrounge cakes and half-pennies, and let off steam for once in a while.

In Georgian England, the holiday calendar was heavily political or dynastic. There were fireworks for the king's birthday and bonfires for Guy Fawkes' day (5 November was also providentially the anniversary of William of Orange's landing at Torbay); 23 April was St George's Day, 28 May the birthday of George I (for Jacobites, 10 June was the birthday of the Old Pretender). These rituals, with their parades and bonfires, stoked up the fires of patriotism. Rites of inversion – such as pupils locking masters out of school – allowed authority to be mocked with impunity one day a year, serving to reinforce authority itself. MPs' footmen held their own mirror Parliament, prisoners their own mock assizes.

Customs gave chances for release – for tipsiness, or paying off old scores – and ritual play put a smile on the back-breaking drudgery which was the curse of working lives. Fasts were epilogued with feasts, solemnities with sport. As Samuel Bamford recollected his late-eighteenth-century childhood:

Some two or three weeks before Christmas it was the custom in families to apportion to each boy or girl weaver a certain quantity of work, which was to be done ere his or her holidays commenced. An extra quantity was generally undertaken to be performed, and the conditions of the performance were such indulgences and gratuities as were agreeable to the working parties. In most families a peck or a strike of malt would be brewed; spiced bread or potato custard would be made, and probably an extra piece of beef, and some good old cheese would be laid in store, not to be touched until the work was done. The work then went on merrily. Play hours were nearly given up, and whole nights would be spent at the loom, the weavers occasionally striking up a hymn or Christmas carol in chorus ... Before Christmas we frequently sang to keep ourselves from sleep, and we chorused 'Christians, awake' when we ourselves were almost gone to sleep ... Christmas holidays always commenced on the first Monday after New Year's Day. By that day every one was expected to have his work finished.

Sunday was a day apart. A vestige of the Puritan day of enforced godliness, it was still a time of enforced inactivity. Even before the Evangelical sabbatarian crusade late in the century, most trading, work, and entertainment were banned. As Dr Johnson put it, Sunday 'should be different from another day. People may walk, but not throw stones at birds.' Yet he himself had suffered 'heavy' Sundays as a child, when his mother droned to him *The Whole Duty of Man*. 'Nothing is more wearisome, more silent, more gloomy than an English Sunday,' concluded the Swedish historian Erik Gustaf Geijer.

The formalities and transitions of life were acted out ceremoniously to emboss them on the public memory, the times for living, loving, and dying. Rites of passage marked the openings and closures of chapters in individual lives – vital in a society which set less store by calendar age than by stage of development. Boys for example would be publicly 'breeched'. When in Laurence Sterne's novel Tristram's father declared, 'We should begin to think, Mrs Shandy, of putting this boy into breeches,' he created a domestic furore, because the transition from skirts to breeches signalled the close of a mother's reign over her son. The induction of new apprentices would be marked with elaborate and often barbaric pranks. Weddings involved customs such as kissing the bride, bedding the couple, and a battle over the bride's garter. Many couples who did not want to go through a regular church marriage (perhaps because a partner previously married whose spouse had disappeared feared bigamy) wanted community recognition to mark their union, and there was always a sympathetic – or unscrupulous – cleric to be found to give his blessing to popular moral feelings. How a man departed this life was a matter of public example. 'See in what peace a Christian can die,' boasted Joseph Addison to his stepson, while James Boswell haunted the death-bed of the sceptic David Hume hoping to find recantation or terror. Imposing death-bed scenes, last words, and stately and lavish funerals aimed to fix an indelible last image of the departed and to forestall the family rifts that the will might create (burials were more formal than weddings).

Particularly in the countryside, where so many of the vital arrangements of life were not written down but guaranteed by long-standing, the solemn, conspicuous, and symbolic reiteration of rights of way, boundaries, terms of work, and mutual rights and responsibilities was paramount. For example, parishioners annually 'beat the bounds' around the perimeter of the village to assert their territory. When the rules of this 'moral economy' were broken, the community stepped in to restore propriety. 'Rough music' – raising a din and parading indecent effigies – was the neighbours' way of shaming shrewish wives or cuckold husbands into putting their houses in order. By contrast, at Great Dunmow, a flitch of bacon was awarded yearly to the happiest married couple. Acts of communal defiance greeted tradesmen, bailiffs, and gamekeepers, who infringed traditional rights and customs: they might be tarred and feathered or receive threats in riddles; farmers might have their ricks burned and cattle maimed. And with its mimic street theatre, the people's culture mercilessly deflated the *poseur* pomp of the mighty. For instance the mock election of the 'mayor' of Garrett in Surrey (where men qualified for the broad franchise if they had 'enjoyed a woman in the open air in the district') burlesqued the corrupt farce of parliamentary hustings and the bare-faced lies of politicians.

Overall, community wisdom felt the need for peace, neighbourliness, and harmony deep in its bones (it had to, for communities were highly disputatious). Ringing through popular feeling was the chorus of Hospitality. The flowing bowl, the pipe of tobacco, the songs of 'Begone dull care' and John Barleycorn, processions, oaths, healths, toasts, pledging – these were the ways people sought to patch quarrels and keep neighbours sweet, or hoped to sugar the bitter pills of life.

The people of this neighbourhood are much attached to the celebration of wakes [wrote the Rev. A. Macaulay about Claybrook, near the end of the century]; and on the annual returns of these festivals, the cousins assemble from all quarters, fill the church on Sunday, and celebrate Monday with feasting, with musick, and with dancing. The spirit of old English hospitality is conspicuous among the farmers on these occasions.

In the tone of extreme unction, however, which was being rehearsed amongst paragons of respectability, he wanted to suppress this communal release from care:

But with the lower sort of people, especially in the manufacturing villages, the return of the wake never fails to produce a week, at least, of idleness, intoxication and riot; these, and other abuses, by which these festivals are so grossly perverted from the original end of their institution, render it highly desirable to all the friends of order, of decency, and of religion, that they were totally suppressed.

English *bonhomie* gelled into the distinct form of the club. 'Man is a sociable animal and we take all occasions and pretences of forming overselves into those little nocturnal assemblies which are commonly known as *clubs*,' wrote Joseph Addison. These ranged from august bodies such as the Whig Kit-Kat Club and Dr Johnson's Literary Club (Johnson deemed the mark of a gentleman lay in being 'clubbable'), down to the Ugly Clubs, the Tall Clubs, Farters' Clubs, Surly Clubs, burial societies and tippling clubs of ordinary men. Lancashire weavers won fame for their musical societies, and gardening clubs flourished. Quint-essentially English was the Sublime Society of Beefsteaks, founded in 1735. Anticipating the Lunar Society of Birmingham, the farmers of Aveley in Essex set up a 'Lunatick Club' in 1763 to meet monthly at full moon (riding home merry was safer then). Some were orgiastic, from the Hell-Fire Club of the rakes down to a London club which the German Lichtenberg described in 1770:

it consisted of servants, journeymen, and apprentices. On these evenings every member laid down fourpence, for which he had music and a female gratis; anything else had to be paid for separately. Twenty of the girls were brought before Sir John Fielding; the beauty of some of them aroused general admiration [Sir John, alas, was blind].

The rise of private aristocratic clubs, like White's and Almack's, whose gaming tables were the sepulchres of fortunes, tolled the knell of coffee houses. Fashionable 'speculative' free-masonry also took root, combining the all-male cheer of the club, the fraternity of trade, and non-denominational lay piety (English lodges were not politically radical, as they were on the Continent). Secret signs and mumbo-jumbo bound masons together – chiefly men in trade, hoping to find a degree of commercial stability in unity. Other clubs, such as the Spitalfields Mathe-matical Club, were more intellectual and educational. Trade guilds provided conviviality in health and benefits in sickness. Their freemen were bonded together by their initiation rites and oaths of secrecy and by trade cant for materials, tools, and processes (preventing outsiders from breaking in and industrial spies from understanding the 'mystery'). And friendly societies ('box clubs') mushroomed amongst the lower orders, offering mutuality and rudimentary social insurance, and serving as a front for trade-union activities. By 1800 friendly societies had well over 600,000 members.

Clubs created identity and partisanship. Political clubs (like the Calves Head) cheered either the Whigs or Tories, Hanoverians or Jacobites, rowdies carrying these allegiances out on to the streets with their flags, cockades, sashes, colours, and chants. More than most, minorities banded together to safeguard their identity. Expatriate Welshmen and Cornishmen in London, for instance, were already forming exiles' associations. Particularly in London, fringe religious communities gathered and dissolved like clouds – Sandemanians, Swedenborgians, Muggletonians, Moravians. The London Negro population (numbering up to 14,000; mostly slaves, personal servants, and sailors) had its own musical bands, taverns, and meeting places, and London's Germans had their own churches. Ghetto areas formed. Thus immigrant Huguenot silk-weavers cocooned themselves in Spitalfields.

All in all, the make-or-break of working people's lives lay in their success in adjusting to the day-to-day routines of earning a living, maintaining a family, and coping with the occasional but critical watersheds of existence. Ordinary people were accustomed to adjusting their individual lives through community expectations (enforced in the end through the parish poor law). Much of the custom of everyday life was traditional; some (like friendly societies) was new and adapted to new needs. In pacing their life and work rhythms, common people did not jump to attention by reflex at orders barked directly from above (for instance from Anglican pulpits): the metabolism of communities was more self-regulating. Popular wisdom, a living manual for maintaining life's fabric and reproducing it for the generations to come, kept going strong.

Unlike today, perhaps, most eighteenth-century learning went on outside officially designated systems of instruction. Education was not organized by the state, compulsory, or geared to precise age groups. There were hardly any exams or paper qualifications: finding a good patron and being able to pen begging letters were far more useful. Few jobs were won by open public competition. Most education was learning for living, in particular for earning a living. For the elite, Greek and Latin Classics inculcated politeness, style, the graces, and a habit of superiority. At humbler levels, nursery rhymes spelt out body language, and counting on your mother's knee; decks of cards taught the ABC and numbers, and shop and tavern signs and church interiors familiarized people with words and their associations: scraps of history, morality, mythology, and the Commandments. Mothers, aunts, nurses, and friends explained the arcana of baby care to brides; masters imparted know-how to apprentices, elder children taught younger. Sayings, lullabies, songs, and riddles parroted all you needed to know about the weather, money, omens, charms, home cures, cooking, and courting:

> If you marry in Lent
> You'll live to repent.

Crossing knives on the table, killing crickets or money spiders, chopping down holly trees, putting anything other than a prayer book on top of a Bible, passing someone on the stairs – all these, this hand-me-down wisdom told you, were unlucky. It was bad luck to say your prayers at the foot of the bed, but (who would believe it?) lucky to fall downstairs. Put milk on the fire and the cows will go dry. Proverbial wisdom invested everything with significance, inevitable in a society in which accident and disaster struck often without warning or explanation.

Sewing samplers taught girls how to be good even as they stitched the letters:

> Patience is a virtue
> Virtue is a grace
> Both put together
> Make a very pretty face.

Elizabeth, daughter of the Kirkby Stephen shopkeeper Abraham Dent, copied into her handwriting book stern but improving sentiments such as 'Knowledge procedures general esteem', 'Labour improves wealth', 'Misfortunes are a kind of discipline', 'Quarrelsome people are dangerous', and 'Youth is the best time for learning'. During the century more and more of this traditional lore was also being circulated in cheap teach-yourself books – though, alongside these, the old favourites – chapbooks such as *Jack and the Beanstalk*, *Guy of Warwick*, and *Tom Thumb* – remained well thumbed.

Countless people – and not just the poor – picked up their book-learning not in school, but by finding out for themselves as children or adults, browsing through the family bookshelf, or being taught by kin and friends. There were proud auto-didacts galore, such as the mathematician Charles Hutton and the novelist Thomas Holcroft. The pioneer canal engineer James Brindley was taught by his mother and worked out many of his designs in his head, lying in bed. Lack of nice accomplishment did not necessarily hold men back. 'Give me leave my lord,' Admiral Pye begged Lord Sandwich,

to make one Observation more and I have done – that is When you peruse Admiral Pye's letter you would please not to scrutinize too close either to the speling or to the Grammatical Part as I allow my self to be no proficient in either. I had the Mortification to be neglected in my education, went to sea at 14 without any & a Man of War was my University.

In any case, schooling itself was no guarantee of an education. Many parents sent their children from pillar to post. Poet-laureate-to-be Robert Southey attended six different schools. Other literati such as Coleridge delved into books to *escape* their schooling. After an unhappy home upbringing where Molly, the family servant, 'hated me' and his brother Frank 'had a violent love of beating me', he went to Christ's Hospital where 'the school boys drove me from play and were always tormenting me – and hence I took no pleasure in boyish sports but read incessantly'.

The trade in cheap editions – teach-yourself books, pocket imprints of the classics, instruction manuals, dictionaries, primers for handwriting, accounts, and foreign languages (books like *Reading Made Quite Easy*) expanded beyond recognition. When young William Cobbett left home to tramp to London for work, he spent his last threepence on Swift's *A Tale of a Tub* and read it from cover to cover, entranced. Cobbett, to become the greatest journalist in England, seems never to have gone to school. It was easier to be an autodidact than ever before. But people didn't need to be. For the century also saw a huge expansion in school places. This was no thanks to central or local government, which acknowledged no brief for teaching. Moreover, many old endowed academic institutions atrophied. 'Whoever will examine the state of the grammar schools in different parts of the kingdom,' wrote Lord Kenyon in 1795, 'will see to what a lamentable condition most of them are reduced. If all persons had equally done their duty, we should not find, as is now the case, empty walls without scholars, and everything neglected but the receipt of salaries and emoluments.'

Some of these grammar schools decayed because they were myopically bound by statute to a Classical curriculum in waning demand, for parents in trade increasingly wanted an education including 'modern' and 'useful' studies, such as arithmetic, accounts, French, handwriting, navigation, shorthand, commercial methods, and maybe a little science. Other grammar schools, however, did move with the times, teaching more mathematics and practical subjects; still others moved up-market, taking fewer parish boys but converting themselves into fee-paying boarding schools for sons of the genteel and the would-be genteel. The public school super-league – Westminster, Eton, Harrow, Charterhouse, Rugby, Winchester – consolidated itself, enhancing its reputation partly by self-perpetuating sleight-of-hand: classy people attended such schools because other classy people had: old school ties were already strong. But they did actually offer the intimate liberal and Classical grounding patricians valued, their cadets being 'lashed into Latin by the tingling rod'. Life in the Georgian public school, as in its gaols, was regulated not from above but from within by a senate of senior boys who tyrannized over the younger. Vicesimus Knox, headmaster at Sevenoaks, wrote that while a pupil at Merchant Taylors he had 'lived as a fag under a state of oppression from my schoolfellows unknown to any slave in the plantations'. Beyond flogging, the masters did not interfere much in boarders' lives; outside lessons the young gentlemen were left to themselves. (The idea that every second of schooldays should be timetabled with improving activities such as 'sporting' team games was not invented until the next century.) Public-school culture was that of their fathers in embryo; boys drank, gambled, rode, fought, and gained precocious bi-sexual experience. They frequently rebelled: the militia had to be called in to storm Eton (battles of all kinds were won and lost on its playing fields).

Public schools were, wrote Henry Fielding, 'the nurseries of all vice and immorality'. Yet this kind of schooling was reckoned a good baptism in English freedom for the nation's junior rulers. As Gibbon, who attended Westminster, thought:

> I shall always be ready to joyn in the common opinion, that our public schools, which have produced so many eminent characters are the best adapted to the Genius and constitution of the English people. A boy of spirit may acquire a praevious and practical experience of the World, and his playfellows may be the future friends of his heart or his interest. In a free intercourse with his equals the habits of truth, fortitude and prudence will insensibly be matured: birth and riches are measured by the standard of personal merits; and the mimic scene of a rebellion has displayed in their true colours the ministers and patriots of the rising generation.

Like grammar schools, the two English universities (Blake's 'dark satanic mills'?) still all-male, celibate, and Anglican – also declined in matriculants. Christ's College, Cambridge, had just three freshmen in 1733. By mid-century Oxford's intake had fallen to fewer than 200 freshmen a year. Oxford and Cambridge came to be attended principally by sauntering young gentlemen filling in time with bagatelles (few troubled to graduate) and by penurious sorts on scholarships, many the sons of curates, seeking ordination into the Church. It was grinding tutors and slumbrous pedants who made an academic career in the colleges: the great scholars of Georgian England – the law reformer Jeremy Bentham, historians such as Edward Gibbon, Archdeacon Coxe, and Charles Burney, and scientists such as Joseph Priestley and Henry Cavendish – were not dons. Oxford dons, in Gibbon's vignette, were steeped in port and privilege:

'decent easy men', who supinely enjoyed the gifts of the founder; their days were filled by a series of uniform employment; the chapel & the hall, the coffeehouse & the common room, till they retired weary and well-satisfied, to a long slumber. From the toil of reading, or thinking, or writing they had absolved their conscience. Their conversation stagnated in a round of college business, Tory politics, personal anecdotes & private scandal: their dull & deep potations excused the brisk intemperance of youth.

Oxford ('that nursery of nonsense and bigotry' according to Horace Walpole) and Cambridge (which Lord Chesterfield called 'an illiberal seminary') became more genteel, luxurious, and costly, and so deterred poorer students, except those who gained scholarships. Oxford's crypto-Jacobite politics repelled some, as did the ultra-modern curriculum based on geometry, mathematics, and Newtonian science which Cambridge evolved in its sleep. The torpid universities hardly transformed themselves (though Cambridge was introducing written exams at the end of the century), and no reform was imposed from outside. Ministries let sleeping dons lie.

   Those who needed higher education for a profession such as medicine usually went elsewhere. Early on medical students flocked to the Dutch universities; later Edinburgh and Glasgow were popular. As centres of literary and intellectual ferment Oxford and Cambridge were eclipsed by the metropolis (significantly, Richard Porson, the great Cambridge professor of Greek, chose to live in London). The universities became rather pocketfuls of patronage and the starting line in the race for Church livings. Fellowships were prized as short-term but remunerative pieces of property, generally free of teaching responsibilities and handy to be going on with for a fledgling clergyman who was eyeing a choice parsonage, many of which were in the colleges' gift. Yet in the long term they might prove a life sentence. 'A fellowship is an excellent breakfast,' wrote George Faber, 'an indifferent dinner, and a most miserable supper.'

   A new skyline of learning was shooting up which suited the times better. Many liberal families mistrusted the public school and university diet of birch, boorishness, buggery, and the bottle, and put their trust in private tutors (flanked by music teachers and dancing masters), with a European Grand Tour thrown in as icing on the cake. Lady Leicester of Holkham obligingly bribed her great-nephew with £500 a year if he would take a Grand Tour rather than be ruined at one of 'those schools of vice', the universities. Grand Tours of France, Italy, Germany, and Holland gobbled up money, costing up to £5,000 for three years.

Protestant boys from the trading classes, excluded by religious tests from Anglican grammar schools and universities, generally went to Dissenting Academies. Many of these – such as Kibworth, Taunton, Daventry, Kendal, Warrington, and Mile End – presided over by such distinguished scholars as Philip Doddridge and Joseph Priestley, became justly known, by sheer quality even attracting Anglican students. Mainstream Old Dissenters, and in particular Presbyterians, weren't too precise to appreciate polite learning (though 'plain' Quakers were), and they set out to blend canonical Classical studies with 'useful' subjects such as geography, shorthand, arithmetic, and science (bound by no charters, they could be flexible). The long-term social importance of the Academies was that, ironically, they became fifth columns, undermining orthodox Dissent. They were privately run by the schoolmasters themselves, without statutes or day-to-day supervision from Nonconformist church elders. These schoolmasters often had leanings towards the more heterodox tenets of Dissent, rejecting Calvinism, and used open and 'rational' ways of teaching which encouraged doubt and question. The upshot was a revolt of Dissenting youth against orthodoxy. Hackney and Hoxton schools in particular became hotbeds of theological ferment; Calvinism was undermined, Socinianism taking its place. Thus, though a youth of Sandemanian learning, William Godwin was admitted to Hoxton Academy, proceeding to become a pantheist and anarchist. Burke dubbed Hackney Academy 'the new arsenal in which subversive doctrines and arguments were forged'. Prestige academies such as Hackney, Warrington, and Hoxton were forced to close when church elders could no longer stomach theological anarchy. By the end of the century, Dissenting schoolmasters and their ex-pupils were floating away from orthodoxy, buoyed up by the hot air of free-thought.

'It is here not uncommon,' wrote Pastor Moritz, 'to see on doors in one continued succession "Children educated here", "Shoes mended here", "Foreign spiritous liquors sold here", "Funerals furnished here".' Moritz's acid *in memoriam* on the 'pupils' progress' spotlights the forest of private-enterprise commercial schools shooting up all over England. These catered to the same social ranks as Dissenting Academies – business-minded families – but lacked their religious commitment. Hundreds of younger sons, beneficeless clergy, and penurious writers set up day schools and boarding schools, teaching anything from the Classics to gunnery and navigation, with a heavy emphasis on the drills of spelling, handwriting, mathematics, and casting accounts, their wives and sisters acting as matrons. Such schools were frequently short-lived, and many mercifully so, yet they met a need in giving boys from craftsmen and petty bourgeois backgrounds the practical skills needed for earning a living or entering an apprenticeship: bookkeeping, a little law, commercial practice, writing business letters, arithmetic. Not least, such schools were cheap. A sound boarding education could be had in the North of England for as little as £10 a year. Boys from the middling orders were getting a more down-to-earth and applicable education than at any previous time. When they were a little older, it was just these people who formed the audiences for another major new venture in free-market instruction: popular lectures. For a few shillings young men could enrol in the larger towns for evening courses, both in vocational subjects like navigation and in cultural pursuits such as natural history and antiquities. Sometimes women were admitted.

The number of schools for girls as well went up by leaps and bounds, though many, such as the one set up at Newington Green by Mary Wollstonecraft, taught little more than some reading, sewing, and drawing, being glorified childminding establishments. Jane Austen for example attended three boarding schools, starting at the unusually early age of seven, but picked up most of her education from her clergyman father. Polite society did not take girls' minds very seriously. 'I don't think so much larning becomes a young woman,' said Sheridan's Mrs Malaprop; and she wasn't alone. The more refined girls' schools aimed to groom girls for their future compliant and decorative role in fashionable society, teaching manners, deportment, religion, French, arts and graces and even cards.

Lower down the social scale, parents were perhaps less eager to send their children to school: they could ill afford to forgo their labour or meet fees. But more schools were being provided for them, free or at nominal cost, by philanthropists. Not that everybody agreed that the poor ought to receive schooling. Some feared they would get ideas above their station, become idle, and be seduced into radicalism. For Bernard de Mandeville, 'The more a shepherd, a ploughman . . . know of the World, the less fitted he'll be to go through the 'fatigue and hardship of it with cheerfulness and content.' Soame Jenyns judged ignorance 'the opiate of the poor, a cordial administered by the gracious hand of providence', or as Davies Giddy put it in 1807,

Giving education to the labouring classes or the poor would be prejudicial to their morals and happiness; it would teach them to despise their lot in life, instead of making them good servants in agriculture and other laborious employment. Instead of teaching them subordination, it would render them fractious and refractory.

But promoters of schooling for the masses gave reassurances that the education offered would be cheap, wholesome, and indoctrinating, and countered the Jeremiahs with the expected benefits. Schooling the poor would teach godliness and subordination, drill them for work, impart craft skills, and ensure that the masses would not be a drain on or threat to society. 'It is through education,' assured John Evans, 'that the poor become acquainted with the duties they owe to society.'

One spur to setting up charitable schools for the poor came from religious bodies such as the Society for the Promotion of Christian Knowledge (SPCK), founded in 1699. Such charity schools were generally financed by subscribers, mostly laymen, and run by shareholders on joint-stock principles. Some were inter-denominational within Protestantism. Other schools had sprung from bequests. Thus at Hallaton in Leicestershire early in the century there was a school for poor children, financed out of a bequest, where a master taught twenty children the catechism and led them to church on Sundays. The town also had a small Dissenting school. Later the scheme of holding school on Sunday won favour (in 1787 one estimate put the number of children at Sunday school at 250,000). Sunday school did not interfere with the working week and would keep children out of mischief on their free day.

Methodists also set up schools for labourers' children, principally giving religious instruction. Mary Fletcher, a Methodist schoolmistress, explained in 1764, 'Our method of educating our children is this: As our design is to fit them for good servants, we endeavour as early as possible to inure them to labour, early rising, and cleanliness.' She let pupils have fifteen minutes a day recreation in the garden but ensured 'they do so with a degree of seriousness and they know it is for their health'. 'We never use the term play, nor suffer any to give those toys or playthings, which children are usually brought up to spend half their time in.'

Charity schools for the lower orders became part of a tissue of conspicuous philanthropy. Upwards of 1,700 were actually set up. Many clothed their pupils, free or cheaply, in a distinctive uniform, and there were annual church services to praise God and the subscribers (including a mammoth congregation at St Paul's). They taught (boys and girls together) a straight and narrow curriculum, principally reading and Scripture. Catechizing was staple fare. Some taught writing as well, though others forbade it as prejudicial. The emphasis was above all on discipline: pupils chanted rhymes like

> It is a sin
> To steal a pin.

Mechanical methods of instruction and repetitive drill were taken up, partly to simulate workshop discipline and partly for economy. In the last years of the century Andrew Bell's system of rote teaching using pupil monitors offered itself as 'the Steam Engine of the Moral World'.

What was the impact of education? Neither the state nor the Church buttoned the nation into a uniform suit of indoctrination; educational licensing had effectively broken down. The result was a bran tub of distinct schoolings, from dame schools to Eton or fashionable Rousseauism, pioneered by Thomas Day and Richard Edgeworth. In this educational free market, the instruction children got, determined by parental choice and pocket, tended to *reinforce* existing social, cultural, and gender distinctions rather than break them down and make new ones. There were no hordes of idealistic lower-class scholarship boys trying to storm the citadels of state, to become over-qualified unemployed graduates. Literacy was gently rising (though it slumped again among the masses in the years of rampant population increase and mobility during the early Industrial Revolution). Almost all males from the middle class and above were literate, but only something like half of labouring men (women were proportionally less literate). Literacy was counting for more: with the emergence of newspapers and magazines there was more to read. The ploughboy could still rap on the farmhouse door asking for work, but skilled operatives might now scan the 'situations vacant' section of the newspaper. Increased reading made the culture more metropolitan, more immediate, uniform, and modern. Yet literacy was certainly not indispensable. 'Bridging' processes, such as reading out loud to others, brought the written word to the illiterate. It was a century in which rising demand for education and awareness of its manipulative uses called new schools into being; but the schooled were far from the sum of the educated. The broad basis of literacy and learning came not from school but from self-help, the family, or the community.

It is hard to judge the impact of the more blatantly directive charity schools. Their managers were themselves in a cleft stick: should they emphasize literacy, numeracy, and Scripture? Or should they chiefly run schools of industry, where children would repay expenses by spinning, picking oakum, beating hemp, knitting, or performing similar menial chores? Schools of industry failed to pay for themselves. Furthermore, there was the dilemma of how schools could teach subordination while whetting ambition. Did charity and Sunday schools teach the poor respect? The labouring classes did not become much more disciplined (and when they did it was probably more in response to the demands of the work-face). Above all charity schools won the loyalties of few of the lower orders to Anglicanism. And the hand of instruction always risked sowing dragons' teeth. It was far easier to teach people to read than subsequently to direct their reading.

Like family discipline and schooling, religion indoctrinated people for life. It gave divine reasons for social relations, spelling out mutual responsibilities, the bonds between the dead and the living, the duties of the present to the unborn. Divinity explained the riddles of existence and taught salvation through Christ crucified, but the Georgians knew it was also social medicine – or at least a placebo. Marx's 'discovery' that worship was an opiate would have been greeted with barely stifled yawns. 'It is certain', wrote Addison,

the Country-people would soon degenerate into a land of Savages and Barbarians were there not such frequent returns of a stated time, in which the whole village meet together in Church with their best faces, and in their cleanest habits, to converse with one another upon indifferent subjects, hear their duties explained to them, and join together in Adoration of the Supreme Being.

Many people rarely went through a church porch between being christened and being buried. Yet practically everyone, in his own fashion, had faith. Much of it was a fig leaf of Christianity covering a body of inherited magic and superstition, little more than Nature worship (the polite, doctrinally correct form of this was natural theology). But everyone had his own vision of a Creator, of a 'place' in Heaven, and convictions of Good and Evil, reward and punishment. Though many were careless about their devotions, Dr Johnson was right to say 'there are in reality very few infidels'. Deism – belief in a nonpersonal Deity, lacking Christianity's historical Incarnation – made headway amongst intellectuals early in the century, sickened by sectarian fanatics, Popery, and clericalism. But as Christians allowed their sword of persecution to sleep in their hands, elite enthusiasm for Deism and free-thought waned. The most prickly intellectual challenges were to come not from atheists but from heretics on the inside. The most notorious Georgian materialist was not some flash *philosophe* but the Bible fundamentalist and millennialist Joseph Priestley. Debate *within* theology remained heated, Anglican theology oscillating between rationalism and obscurantism, Dissenters divided over free-grace and Calvinist predestination. This was because it was hard to adjust literalist dogma to a new world of material prosperity, science, and freedom of inquiry. Religious divides went deep – this is evident from the reams of sermons and theological polemics published and avidly read – and only bashing the old bogey of Popery could unite Protestants.

Contemporaries voiced fears that the age was mumbling Christianity's *nunc dimittis*: worship had diminished, but ought to have been increasing. At the dawn of the century Joseph Addison bemoaned, 'There is less appearance of religion in England than in any neighbouring state.' Visiting England Montesquieu enlarged this view: religion in England 'excites nothing but laughter'. Devotions withered. 'I was at home all day,' Thomas Turner confessed to his diary one Sunday, 'but not at church. O fye! No just reason for not being there.' Whereas in 1714 seventy-two churches in the metropolis had offered daily services, in 1728 there were fifty-two, and by 1732 but forty-four. The liturgical temperature sank. Parson Woodforde almost never held a service except on Sunday. Amongst Anglicans, family prayers became uncommon. 'Oh! may religion once more rear up her head in this wicked and impious nation,' beseeched Thomas Turner.

Yet beneath all the rationalism, worldliness, and indifference, religious urges remained ingrained. Samuel Johnson was terrified of damnation (by which he meant being 'sent to Hell, Sir, and punished everlastingly'). Searching for identity in his teens, Gibbon fleetingly became a Catholic convert, as did Boswell. Many instinctively believed in special providences and omens. When his razor snapped while shaving one Sunday, James Woodforde confided to his diary, 'May it be a warning to me not to shave on the Lord's Day, or to do any other work to profane it, *pro futuro*.' Even people who had no intention of allowing Christ to transform their lives nevertheless knew religion was a charm to ward off ills and a social glue, rather as Lord Chesterfield commended at least lip-service to his son:

Depend upon this truth, that every man is the worse looked upon & the less trusted, for being thought to have no religion, in spite of all the pompous & specious epithets he may assume, of esprit fort, free thinker or moral philosopher; a wise atheist (if such a thing there is) would, for his own interest, & character in the world, pretend to some religion.

Mainstream Dissenters no less than Anglicans thought godliness should complement virtue and prudence, rather than demanding abandonment of this world as a vale of tears. Even the sincerely pious were sure that religion tripped hand-in-hand with mundane values ('whatever is, is right,' concluded Alexander Pope). Sin and saintliness were both soft-pedalled. Piety was to be natural, common-sense, easy, the workaday world in Sunday suits. Near the close of the seventeenth century, the influential Archbishop Tillotson set the tone for Georgian Anglicanism by thus characterizing Christ: 'His Virtues were shining without Vanity, Heroical without anything of Transport, and very extraordinary without being in the least extravagant.' Spellbinders who preached demonic possession and ecstasy, devils and spirits, the new birth, grace abounding, or even the transforming power of the Cross were now treated with great suspicion as 'fanatics' by new 'Latitudinarian' Churchmen and laymen alike. 'Enthusiasm,' concluded Joseph Butler, Bishop of Durham, 'is a very horrid thing.'

Opinion-makers complimented themselves on their religious moderation: there had been much, they believed, in religion in need of being moderated. Religion ought to be a force for restraint and civilization. Desperate for security after generations of blistering sectarian strife, Georgians saw meekness as the Gospel's first commandment. In a sermon in 1715 the Bishop of Gloucester accused zealots of wreaking 'more cruelty, wars, massacres, burnings, more hatred, animosity, perverseness, and peevishness' than almost anyone else. Fanatic Puritans had fomented civil war a century earlier, making a mockery of Christ's ministry of peace. And Papist Jacobites were still plotting to topple the state. By contrast, 'His commandments are not grievous' and 'Be not righteous overmuch' became favourite texts for the Latitudinarian 'Christianity without tears' sermons read from Anglican pulpits throughout the century, syncopated (so Hogarth depicted) to the snores of slumbering congregations.

Georgians could urge that the spirit of religion was peace, not the crusading sword, partly because the epoch of persecution was indeed ceasing. Though animosities continued, the Act of Toleration (1690) had guaranteed religious freedom with strings. Admittedly the Anglican Church was established by law (bulging tithe barns were its witness). Anglicans were privileged: choice areas of the state, such as the universities and civil office, were out of bounds to those beyond the Anglican communion, and Catholic recusants still paid mulcts. In reality, however, Protestant Dissenters who could stomach the farce of occasionally taking Anglican communion need not have their ambition thwarted. Nearly forty 'occasionally conforming' Dissenters became MPs during the century, many others becoming London aldermen; for sixty years the mayors of Nottingham were Dissenters, and in London even a number of Jews held local government office. And if the front door of the state was still only just ajar to non-Anglicans, less stigma was now attached to those who sported their minority religion like gentlemen. Witness the Catholic Lord Petre, an aristocrat of easy spirituality, who, though of Jacobite descent, entertained George III at Thorndon in 1779, and confirmed his influence as a borough-monger. 'I have lived here above thirty years,' the Catholic Sir Henry Arundel pointed out to his friend, Lord Hardwicke, 'and thanks to the lenity of ye government, without ever having had the least molestation given me.' Nonconformists and Anglicans cooperated on philanthropic and missionary endeavours.

True, stiff-necked sectaries were liable to be vilified and – like Defoe – occasionally set in the pillory. But by contrast the entire Protestant population was expelled from France in 1685, and heretics were still being burnt throughout the century in Catholic Europe, Pietists in Calvinist Switzerland.

In England private faiths were tolerated: in Defoe's words, 'each man goes his own byway to heaven'. It was a land of a hundred sects (even if – as the quip went – there was only one sauce). And since, as Voltaire also observed, a single religion in a country spelt tyranny, and two, civil war, but a multitude meant peace, England's was a highly enviable situation:

Enter the London stock exchange [wrote Voltaire], that place more respectable than many a court. You will see the deputies of all nations

gathered there for the service of mankind. There a Jew, a Mohamme-
dan, and the Christian deal with each other as if they were of the same
religion, and give the name of infidel only to those who go bankrupt;
here the Presbyterian trusts the Anabaptist, and the Anglican honours
the Quaker promise. On leaving these free and peaceful assemblies,
some go to the synagogue, others to drink; this one goes to have
himself baptized in the name of the Father, the Son and the Holy
Ghost; that one has his son's foreskin cut off and Hebrew words
mumbled over the child which he does not understand; others go to
church to await the inspiration of God, their hats on their heads; and
all are content.

Toleration was not just good for religion: it was good for
commerce as well.

The Anglican Church was the nation's largest and wealthiest
institution, spear-headed by twenty-six bishops, each occupying
a cathedral in which deans, canons, and prebends officiated
(about 1,000 in all). Beneath these higher clergy, there were
some 10,000 parishes – the whole of England was emparished.
The Church's local pull was enhanced, since the ecclesiastical
parish also doubled as the cell of local government (parsons
were appointed as JPs in increasing numbers).* Rectors and
vicars – now almost all graduates – were presented to livings
by ecclesiastical and lay patrons (in mid-eighteenth-century
Oxfordshire only 11 per cent of advowsons lay in the Church's
gift), getting their income out of tithes and by farming the
glebe. Many parsons were non-resident and pluralist, having
installed cut-price curates to perform their ministry (these got
'leavings' not 'livings'). About a quarter of parishes did not have
a resident minister, and this worsened. In Devon in the 1740s
just over half the rectors were non-resident; by 1780 nearly
70 per cent were. The Church maintained its own system of
spiritual courts, though these were waning, and also a monopoly
grip on English universities. Only subscribing Anglicans could
graduate, and almost all dons were in holy orders, as were most
grammar school masters. Yet if the Church had a strong grip
on society, government had a stronger grip upon the Church.
From 1717 central Church government (Convocation) was
prorogued by the Whigs, fearing the rabid Toryism of its lower

*It is revealing that when Richard Gough set out to survey all the inhabitants of Myddle
in 1700, he described the people pew by pew.

house. Thereafter the Church had no spiritual leadership of its own, for prelates were generally thick as thieves with the politicians who were their nursing fathers.

As an institution, the Church kept its books in comfortable balance through the century. Input was adequate: there was no shortage of ordinands. The Church syphoned off a tenth of prosperity in tithes, in kind or cash. By mid-century a few episcopal incomes were topping £5,000 a year (Archbishop Hutton made a clear £50,000 out of twelve years' tenure at York). Output was also maintained. Few Anglican clergy failed scandalously to perform their undemanding duties. Parsons may have been, as Crabbe styled them, 'cassock'd huntsmen and fiddling priests' ('ropes of sand' in Wesley's words). But they intoned their weekly sermons with correct diction, married couples, baptized their children, and buried the dead (occasionally even saying prayers on saints' days). This may have been all they did, but few parishioners expected them to be evangelists, or even very saintly shepherds of their flocks (though they should be blameless and make up a rubber at whist with the squire). They were thought none the worse for not believing that faith was something you wrestled with. George Pryme wrote that in his youth in the 1780s, 'if a rector performed the service on a sunday, and visited the sick *when sent for*, it was thought quite sufficient'. At Weston Longueville it was an innovation in 1777 when Woodforde said prayers on Good Friday.

Most bishops were businesslike diocesan managers, efficient at conducting visitations and mass confirmations. Above all, the higher clergy served their political masters well. Thus Viscount Percival vignetted Bishop Willcock of Gloucester in 1730:

> He resides as much as any bishop in his diocese, at least four months in the year, and keeps a very generous and hospitable table, which makes amends for the learning he is deficient in. Though no great scholar nor a deep man, he is a very frequent preacher and this with his zeal for the government, good humour and regular life, makes him very well liked by the government and all that know him.

Few parsons were criminal or sexual scandals, even if few were saints. Church fabric was often allowed to fall into

picturesque disrepair, but parsonages were improved. Gentlemen of the cloth kept their genteel patrons happy, comfortable
in their private, curtained, upholstered box pews, heated if not
with spirit at least with their own stoves. They preached deference and obedience not just to God. Because preachers readily
supposed that virtue, temporal success, and heavenly prospects
formed a Trinity – the politically or socially radical parson was
a rare bird indeed – very few of the pedigree flock deserted the
fold to browse in strange pastures.

Yet the Church did not have much of a hold on the hearts
and hopes of plebeian parishioners, many of whom were at best
a surly captive congregation (under the squire's eye, in the lady's
retinue) or were absentees (in some cases worshipping elsewhere). Masterless men – many of the urban tradesmen class
for example – leant towards Protestant Dissent. The gentry
fretted at the heathenism of the common people (and specifically
their non-Anglicanism). Even in the countryside, most were
not church-goers (many loathed parsons as gentrified tithe-
gatherers). Slapton in Devon had only thirty-two communicants out of 200 families. Near-by Churchstow had forty-three
families, just four of whom were communicants. In mid-
century Oxfordshire, only about one person took communion
for every three families. Moreover, things were getting worse.
Thirty Oxford parishes which between them had 911 communicants in 1738 had just 685 in 1802. Only about one in ten
English people took Easter Communion in Anglican churches
in 1801. But little was done. Parishioners could no longer be
prosecuted for not going to church, and curates, some paid less
than £10 a year by absentee rectors, frequently could not afford
to reside in their parishes, riding over every few weeks to take
a service.

The spectre of lower-class irreligion worsened with population rise and redistribution. As Midland and Northern hamlets
mushroomed into industrial centres and ribbon developments
spread up valleys, the old jigsaw of parishes bore ever less
resemblance to actual settlements. Industrializing Lancashire
and Cheshire had only 156 parishes; Essex, Suffolk, and Norfolk,
1,634. Concentrations of population were left with grotesquely
inadequate church seating. Manchester, with some 20,000
people in 1750, had one parish church. In 1800 Marylebone

had a population of 40,000 but a sole Anglican church seating 200. By 1812 there were just 186 Anglican places of worship in London, compared to 256 Dissenting. And within churches, space-eating box pews could not be replaced by benches, for they were sacred private property.

It was easy for Dissenting congregations to move in. Their form of church government was devolved, voluntaristic, and flexible, their ministers maintained by the worshippers, though they might have to top up their income by schoolmastering. Red tape and property rights made it so much more difficult for the Church of England to adapt. Building new churches meant endowing new parishes to support incumbents, thereby reducing others, robbing St Peter's to pay St Paul's. Plans drawn up by reformers such as Edmund Gibson, Bishop of London, for major equalization of church income met entrenched resistance. The London Churches Act of 1711 set money aside to erect churches, but only ten out of a projected fifty were actually constructed, largely because the trustees opted for a small number of architectural jewels rather than many functional ones. The year 1800 dawned with the Anglican Church ill-equipped to serve the nation which had sprung up over the previous century.

But who missed it? Some Dissenting ministers spoke to common people's hearts, and certain Anglicans had long been alert to this need. Anglican voluntary societies (such as the Society for the Propagation of the Gospel and the Society for the Promotion of Christian Knowledge) sought the ear of ordinary people, through charity schools, tracts and, later, Sunday schools. Cascades of cheap Anglican literature, from the *New Whole Duty of Man* to Hannah More's uplifting tracts, peddled religion to the poor. But was this fare palatable? Did the poor really take to heart prayers like this one from the *New Whole Duty of Man*?

Oh God, I believe that for just & wise reasons thou hast allotted to mankind very different states & circumstances of life, & that all the temporal evils which have at any time happened unto me, are designed by thee for my benefit: therefore, though thou hast thought fit to place me in a mean condition, to deprive me of many conveniences of life, & to exercise me in a state of poverty, yet thou hast hitherto preserved & supported me by thy good providence, & blessed me with advantages above many others . . .

One movement within Anglicanism undoubtedly had the common touch. That was Methodism. Wesley was far from the only evangelist in the eighteenth-century Church, the religion of the heart having many independent tongues. There was Wesley's silver-voiced co-worker George Whitefield (who thought Archbishop Tillotson had known no more about religion than Mahomet), and John Law in Oxford; there were field preachers such as Samuel Walker of Truro, John Berridge of Everton, the Yorkshireman William Darney, Hywel Davies, Daniel Rowland, and Howell Harris in Wales; and from the 1770s a coherent Evangelical revival got under way. But Wesley was unique as an Anglican evangelist in preaching to the savage 'pagans' of society ('poor almost to a man' as he described his congregations), while organizing his ministry as a national missionary movement. 'I love the poor. In many of them I find pure genuine grace, unmixed with paint, folly & affectation.' As his brother Charles's hymn put it,

> The rich and great in every age
> Conspire to persecute their God.
> Our Saviour by the rich unknown
> Is worshipped by the poor alone.

John Wesley was a true-blue Anglican. He was Arminian in his theology, believing in salvation for all; High Church and High Tory in his politics, a paladin of the Crown and the law; and loyal to the Church of England to his dying day (he detested Dissent and stood out against Methodists separating, wanting at most to institute a church within a church). But his religious practice was everything the Church's wasn't. An itinerant preacher who saw the whole world as his parish, Wesley put England's new turnpikes to the test, riding 25,000 miles and preaching 40,000 sermons, many in the open air. A fanatic 'brand plucked from the burning', he was an arch-critic of Mammon's profligates. 'To speak the rough truth,' he wrote, 'I do not desire any discourse with any person of quality in England.' His 'vital religion', finding tongue in mesmerizing sermons and passionate hymns, melted the hearts of scoffers and the indifferent. Hardbitten frontier mining communities and fishing ports immune to charity schools, tracts, and other forms of soup-kitchen religion from above embraced Wesley's heart-cleansing salvationism.

Of course, Wesley taught resignation, obedience, and subordination. 'He who plays when he is a child, will play when he is a man'; 'avoid all lightness as you would avoid hell-fire.' His way with children was short: 'Break his will now, and his soul shall live, and he will probably bless you to all eternity.' He was haunted by anarchy: 'Mend your clothes, or I shall never expect you to mend your lives.' Yet he was also self-critical, seeing how easily, how inevitably, Methodist spiritual living might fossilize into numb, worldly respectability:

For the Methodists in every place grow diligent and frugal; consequently they increase in goods. Hence, they proportionally increase in pride, in anger, in the desire of the flesh, the desire of the eyes, and the pride of life. So, although the form of religion remains, the spirit is swiftly vanishing away.

Methodism's importance must not be pre-dated. There were only 24,000 Methodists in 1767 and 77,000 by 1796. It is an optical illusion of some historians to see Methodism as having 'saved' England from a 'French Revolution', or indeed as having almost caused one. Neither did it remain a unity. By the end of the century, Wesleyanism was recruiting in more presentable quarters, speeding its own rupture into authoritarian and populist elements ('Primitive Methodists'). Yet Methodism became the century's most fertile new national organization, sustained from the grassroots if inspired, commanded, and dogmatized over from the centre, for each congregation had its own governing cell sending delegates to an annual conference, where Wesley passed down the tablets of the law. It challenged the Establishment more than any contemporary political movement, because it had the richness to generate enduring self-respect and self-government amongst its converts, and because Methodist ministers escaped the obloquy of being parasitic tithe-gatherers. The Wesleyan connexion proved capable of sprouting in many directions, including the political radicalism of many Primitive Methodists and the sturdy self-help culture of the artisan lay preacher.

Those who attacked Wesley – many with stones – were

correct to see his 'inner light' teachings, his hysteria-raising sermonizing, his passionate eucharistic love feasts, his lay preachers – practices, said Dr Johnson, 'utterly incompatible with social or civil society' – as a time bomb under the complacent Latitudinarianism. And Methodism of course suffered inner contradictions: a populist movement led from above by an egomaniacal authoritarian prophet; a spiritual and transcendental faith which insisted on worldly discipline and industry. Yet the ostrich scions of the Church believed they did not even need to grapple with these paradoxes, thinking they could just anathematize Wesleyanism and ignore what it stood for. Thus Augustus Toplady (Evangelical author of the hymn 'Rock of Ages') condemned Wesley's views as 'an equal portion of gross heathenism, Pelagianism, Mahometanism, popery, Manichaeism, ranterism, and antinomianism'. Squires and parsons incited mobs to pelt 'Pope John' – Wesley noted how the gentry often 'headed the mob in person'. Ladies such as Elizabeth Prowse dismissed servants who attended meetings. Methodism was a challenge to the bishops to come to terms with the independent religious witness at the grassroots. Their response was to drive it out of the Church. Thereafter the national church bade popular religion adieu.

Many denominations carved niches for themselves in Georgian England. Because religion was as concerned with orderly conduct as with faith or theology, confessional allegiances reinforced, rather than cut across, social boundaries. Thus, for example, on top of its old recusant communities, English Catholicism was increasingly identified with immigrant Irish labourers. The numbers of gentry who were Catholic fell, as many made the pilgrimage to Canterbury. It was a strain to be a gentleman without being an Anglican. Once-Catholic lords such as Sefton, Molyneux, Gascoyne, and Montague were unwilling to remain on the social margins and converted, and with them went their flocks. The 115,000 Catholics of 1720 had shrunk to 69,000 by 1780. Even gentry who remained Catholic reintegrated themselves into the community; fewer sent their daughters abroad for a nunnery education. Nicholas Blundell, impenitent head of a prominent family of Lancashire Catholics, actually served on the Anglican vestry.

Similarly, the old Puritan gentry trickled over to Anglicanism. Dissenters being second-class citizens, the cream were under pressure to convert: 'The Dissenter's second horse carried him to Church.' Wealth and status seduced even some of the normally stiff Quakers. The Gurney family, for instance, gave up being 'plain' and became 'gay' (worldly), and successful Quaker businessmen such as Ambrose Crowley and the Barclays went over to Anglicanism. Dissenters faced the dilemma of being neither persecuted nor privileged. The letter of the Corporation and Test Acts disqualified them from the trophies of office; yet, in the absence of persecution, Old Dissent lost zeal and minded its own business, and the grandchildren of revolutionary Puritans became quietist, inward-looking, and even lukewarm, as worldly in their own prim way as Anglicans. Early in the century there were about 179,000 Presbyterians, 59,000 Independents (or Congregationalists), 58,000 Baptists, and 38,000 Quakers. Many sidled over to conformity or just became indifferent. The total of Dissenters may have fallen by up to 40 per cent between 1700 and 1740.

Dissenters tended to be a good deal more sober than their Anglican brethren, but their worship – especially Presbyterians' – became as moderate, anti-enthusiastic, and moral-minded. Their church government, giving prominence to lay 'elders', was hierarchical. As with Anglicans, wealthy Dissenters had their own pews or raised seats (servants sat at the back) and exercised patronage. Many meetings required a guinea a year subscription to qualify for a say. Since elders and their friends were paying for their ministers, they called the tune even more directly than rich Anglican parishioners usually could. Old Dissent was essentially bourgeois. As John White put it in 1746:

The main body of Dissenters are mostly found in cities & great towns among the trading part of the people & their ministers are chiefly of the middle rank of men, having neither poverty nor riches ... If I had a son brought up in any trade & had no consideration either for him or myself in another world, I should be ready to say to him at setting up, — *my son, get Money & in order to do that, be a Dissenter.*

In 1730 the Dissenting leader, Philip Doddridge, candidly admitted that Nonconformity was not catering for 'the plain

people of low education and vulgar taste'. His own very correct
meeting-house expelled members for 'failing in the world'
through bad debts or extravagance.

Bourgeois Nonconformity contributed something unique to
English culture: scruple. Theirs was an earnest, conscientious
desire to exercise control – over self and others – for righteousness's sake. To a liberal conscience they added a demure
seriousness that could teeter towards self-righteousness and
casuistry. They discovered 'deserving causes'. The prominent
Dissenting writer Mrs Barbauld thus gave up sugar in protest
against slavery. They stood out as educators of youth, reformers,
and doctors, Dissenting practitioners being conspicuous in
towns such as Liverpool, Manchester, and Chester in campaigning for better public health, hospitals, and morals. Quakers in
particular mobilized opinion against the slave trade, before its
abolition was piloted through Parliament by Wilberforce, the
Anglican Evangelical leader.

Most Protestant Dissenters, from skilled artisans up to the
most opulent merchants, professional men, and manufacturers,
were townsfolk. Nearly a third of the populations of Bristol
and Norwich were Nonconformist. Country areas noted for
weaving, especially in the West Country, also had high Nonconformist concentrations. In certain parliamentary constituencies, for instance Tiverton, Dissent formed an electoral lobby
with real leverage. In politics Dissent, with its own pressure
group, the Dissenting Deputies, was happy to trail the coats of
Whiggery even though Walpole had failed to repeal the Test
and Corporation Acts (Tories were implacably hostile to Dissent). Walpole placated Dissenters with money out of the privy
purse for ministers' widows. Dissenters wanted civil equality
and redress but their zeal for socio-political reform should not
be exaggerated. The prominent Nonconformist John Aikin
characteristically dismissed Tom Paine: 'he is not like a gentleman'. Not till the 1780s, and then only amongst a hothead
minority, did Nonconformity show a potential for political
radicalism.

Escape from the harassment suffered under the later Stuarts
took the millennialist strain out of other Dissenting groups such
as Baptists and Congregationalists (though they remained be-

lievers in a Calvinist elect), and overall numbers of all Dissenting sects dropped. Rural districts were worst hit. Hampshire had forty Presbyterian chapels in 1729, two in 1812. Unlike Anglicanism, however, Dissent was always in ferment. Its fabric was open-textured. Dissent had early spawned a plethora of sects and anarchistic schisms, and (though each group had its own 'tests') there was no single test of orthodoxy, unlike the Thirty-nine Articles within the Anglican Communion. Dissenting conventicles were at bottom self-governing. Hence Nonconformist fission constantly produced its own dissidents, a very diverse brood. At one extreme there sprang up Antinomians and Millennialists, Moravians and Sandemanians, and other tiny, exclusive pentecostal cells, emphasizing scriptural literalism, personal conversion, and emotional, participatory worship. At the other end of the spectrum some became more rational and liberal, gravitating towards Arianism, Socinianism, and Unitarianism – all more or less repudiating the divinity of Christ, the Trinity, and the miracles and mysteries of Christianity. Joseph Johnson, the radical Unitarian publisher, had been brought up as a Particular Baptist: Joseph Priestley, the leading Unitarian, was of a Calvinist Independent background. William Godwin, son of a Dissenting minister, moved via Sandemanianism to pantheism. (Though most Unitarians had journeyed through Dissent some, however, had started off Anglicans, such as Theophilus Lindsey and Gilbert Wakefield.) By the close of the century Unitarians were an articulate minority seeking to resuscitate religion by purging it of all but liberal politics and middle-class morality. Whether seen as Protestant radicalism (fidelity to one's intellect and scruples) or as what Erasmus Darwin called a 'feather bed to catch a falling Christian', Unitarianism, which early in the eighteenth century had been a clerical fringe, drew a growing lay following, especially amongst such expanding professional groups as scientists, publishers, writers, reformers, campaigners, and educators – the grandfathers of the Victorian honest doubters.

Because Dissent had not sunk into a morass of livings, rights to present, tithes, and patronage squabbles, it was flexible and could adapt and expand. In the last third of the century a 'New Dissent' gained ground, recruiting down the social order, wooing and winning artisans in fast-growing industrial areas. The 15,000 Congregationalists of 1750 had swollen to 35,000 by 1800; the Particular (that is Calvinist) Baptists went up from 10,000 to 24,000. The race for the souls of the emergent labour aristocracy finished in a dead-heat between Dissent and Methodism. Evangelical missions of New Dissent had success in the countryside too. 'Almost the whole country is open for village preaching,' proclaimed the Baptist John Rippon in 1798.

In Georgian much more than Stuart times, religious communion generally cemented pre-existing social bonds. Anglicanism was polite society, or the squire-dominated village, at prayer; Old Dissent the meeting of craftsmen and solid provincial traders in their Sunday best; Methodism became the faith of isolated work-forces such as colliers. Rarely did religious affiliation *create* independent social adhesion where none had existed before. Fringe sects, however, promised just this. Cellular congregations of the 'perfect', led by born-again prophets, attracted urban lost souls. New Worlders of the 1790s such as the disciples of Joanna Southcott (who claimed she was to give birth to Shiloh, to 'rule all nations with a rod of iron') and Richard Brothers (self-styled nephew to the Almighty) remind us that many Georgians, castaways on the anonymous lonely seas of megalopolis, found hope in rebirth and religious utopias. Capturing a common disgust with the Babylonical times, their leaders drew out to lengths of logic and literalness that few would follow. Sectaries saw visions of a New Jerusalem, even a green and pleasant Albion. Lord George Gordon, one-time fanatic anti-papist, became a long-bearded convert to Judaism. James Graham, former pedlar of health through sex-therapy and mudbaths, later founded the 'New and True Christian Church', practised Adamic nakedness, and died insane. Prophetic anger flamed into art in the pen and brush of William Blake, baptized in the streams of mystical underground religion.

The most stable group whose religious protocols created a tight community set apart were the Quakers. Rather like the Jews (of whom there were about 10,000), Friends segregated themselves by their distinctive, aggressively humble manners, antiquated sombre dress and plain speech ('theeing'), and above all by the expectation of marrying in. Those who married out were thrown out, as were culpable bankrupts. Quakers were not proselytizers; they became closed and quietist and declined in numbers from about 38,000 in 1700 to about 20,000 in 1800. But this evaporation left them socially more select: the proportion of merchants and professional men rose and of artisans declined. Friends were in a quandary. Their origins lay in persecution and in George Fox's noble egalitarianism: they rejected war and despised the insolence of rank and the idiocies of Vanity Fair. There were no Friends in high places. Yet in the workaday world many were bankers, corn-dealers, brewers, and arms-manufacturing iron-masters, with money coming out of their ears: the Peases, Barclays, Frys, Reynoldses, Perkinses. They contained these contradictions by scrupulous plain dealing (Quakers pioneered fixed-price retailing), industriousness, loyal support of other Friends, family solidarity, philanthropy, and blamelessness. Firms such as the Quaker London Lead Company championed industrial welfare for their employees. Quaker meeting-houses were 'schools for the inculcation of business and clubs for encouraging the practice of them'. The long-lasting family firms of the Gurneys, Lloyds, Wilkinsons, Darbys, Backhouses, and others form a muster of undissipated industrial talent unmatched elsewhere in the eighteenth-century world.

Religion in Georgian England rubber-stamped social, power and property relations, generally ingrained already. Denominational boundaries sanctified social divides more than they cut across them. Stuart religious fervour had sowed dragons' teeth, producing sectarian strife, civil war, and visionaries awaiting the Second Coming. Georgian piety by contrast ambled along with society. Yet this detracts neither from religion's sincerity nor its importance. Religion was still the language people spoke in earnest, on oath. For all the self-congratulatory rationalism of the Enlightenment, it was Christian zealots who were the selfless reformers of abuses: John Howard, Captain Cook of the prison world, Thomas Clarkson and Granville Sharp, campaigners against the slave trade. What first galvanized large sections of the work-force into self-help and self-respect were not polite letters, Enlightenment rationalism, or Deism, but Methodism and New Dissent. And when polite society itself felt the earthquake tremors of revolution at the end of the century, it was to religious scourging and revival – to God – that it turned. Religion was still the idiom of the people, though its accents and dialects were many. By 1800 English piety was decisively shaped by social rank. Denomination itself had become a litmus of social position.

5. Getting and Spending

Every country and every age has dominant terms, which seem to obsess men's thoughts. Those of eighteenth century England were property, contract, trade and profits. [Sir Lewis Namier]

Ages before the eighteenth century the English economy had ceased to supply mere subsistence. Their ability to harness the surplus wealth-creating labour of wage-earners had long consolidated a propertied ruling elite dominating productive relations. The business of family formation, and of instilling values through education and religion, the interlocking of family with labour, production with reproduction, individual with community – all these ensured regular inheritance of capital goods, skills, drills, and know-how from generation to generation. These self-adjusting mechanisms were buffers against catastrophe. But on top of all this there was a new buzz of activity in the eighteenth century. The market economy expanded and accelerated, especially from mid-century, creating an effervescent atmosphere where individuals could try their fortunes and prosper. There were fresh openings for men (and it was chiefly *males*) who were competitive, mobile, ambitious, or lucky enough to possess some capital or skills in demand. Subterranean tensions and hardships of course resulted. The centrifugal effects of individualistic multiplication of wealth threatened traditional order. The enrichment of farmers and manufacturers often involved the impoverishment and displacement of the labouring poor. But a panoramic view showed prosperity smiling over the fast-changing landscape. 'You would not know your country again,' Horace Walpole told his friend, Horace Mann, late in the century. 'You left it as a private island living upon its means. You would find it the capital of the world.' Especially after industrialization got up steam from the 1780s, the wealth of England admitted no doubters. As the republican French traveller Meister wrote at the close of the century:

> Why is the soil of England so well cultivated? It is because England is rich. Why is England the seat of liberty? It is because England is rich. Why does England at present pay so little regard to the attainments of art and literature? It is because England is too rich ... Why is England not more peaceable and happy? It is because England is too rich. Gold is the sun of the nation.

But long before, it had become a platitude that England was an unusually prosperous island, her trade robust, bustling, and successful. 'The great British Empire, the most flourishing and opulent country in the world,' trumpeted Defoe: 'no clothes can be made to fit a growing child.' He was informed by two foreigners at Bushey Heath, 'England was not like the other countries, but it was all a planted garden.' In the 1760s Smollett could write, 'I see the country of England smiling with cultivation: the grounds exhibiting all the perfection of agriculture, parcelled out into beautiful enclosures, corn fields, hay pasture, woodland and commons.' Henry Homer agreed: 'Everything wears the face of dispatch; every article of our produce becomes more valuable.' In the business community, confidence mounted.

The English supplanted the Dutch as the commercial top-dogs who scurried around trading and money-making. 'There was never from the earliest ages,' thought Dr Johnson, 'a time in which trade so much engaged the attention of mankind, or commercial gain was sought with such general emulation.' The new discipline of political economy blessed the pursuit of profit, above all in Adam Smith's *Wealth of Nations* (1776), which celebrated a high-production, high-wage economy. Anything that would turn a penny was tried. In London you could hire spy-glasses for $\frac{1}{2}$d. to view the Jacobite heads on Temple Bar, and souvenir Tyburn rope fetched 6d. an inch. Getting and spending was everyone's business – at least everyone who could afford it. 'So great is the hurry in the spirit of the world,' lamented the Quaker John Woolman – Quakers were certainly no exceptions – 'that in aiming to do business quickly and to gain wealth the Creation at this day doth groan.'

More than potential rivals such as Holland, England had the right catalysts for sustained economic improvements. Vital raw materials were to hand, most on England's own doorstep, some from the colonies. Extractive industries flourished, coal (for heating, power, and smelting in the non-ferrous metal trades) being especially plentiful, and in some places dug open-cast. In 1700 London used 800,000 tons of coal, in 1750, 1,500,000 tons, and by 1790, 2,500,000 tons, mainly for domestic and industrial burning.

Furthermore, England had a favourable political and legal infrastructure. With the fleeting exceptions of the '15 and the '45, English soil was not a battleground. There were no swingeing internal customs duties, as there were among the German states or in France (though of course turnpikes and later canals took their toll). Great Britain was Europe's biggest common market. Adam Smith highlighted the absolute protection that English law gave to private property:

> That security which the laws in Great Britain give to every man that he shall enjoy the fruits of his own labour, is alone sufficient to make any country flourish ... In Great Britain industry is perfectly secure, and though it is far from being free, it is as free or freer than in any other part of Europe.

The state wasn't a clog to trade, as it was elsewhere, though grumbling commercial lobbies were perennially up in arms. There was no profits tax, no capital gains tax. Successive ministries' economic policies switched tariffs to protect home manufactures and cheapen exports. Thus in 1700 import of silks and printed calicoes was banned, and Combination Acts forbade skilled craftsmen from emigrating. Most wars were waged in pursuit of trade. A smaller proportion of national wealth was being poured down the drain on a dropsical bureaucracy, a giant permanent standing army, or a pyrotechnical court than in most states. In 1783 Berlin housed 57,000 officials and soldiers amongst a total population of 141,000: its commercial and industrial bourgeoisie was insignificant. By contrast, in the boom towns of England, few people were not directly involved in the cash economy.

The economic infrastructure also met the needs of business

well. It was, above all, the age of *commercial* capitalism. The techniques of exchange became faster, cheaper, more reliable. The potential had long been there; for centuries nowhere had been very far from a market, a fair, even a crossroads. Thus Northampton had long been a thriving market for horses (as was Barnet fair), Uttoxeter for cheese, and Guildford for the bark used in tanning. But the Georgian century saw exchange quicken. 'An estate is but a pond,' wrote Defoe, 'but trade is a spring.' Quietly and piecemeal a wide-ranging and flexible credit network took shape. The stability of the Bank of England (*parliamentary* not *Crown* credit) gave confidence to the fast-growing section of the public investing in the Funds or the Chartered Companies. Authorized to receive deposits and lend them out at interest, especially to the Government, the Bank became so secure that it was able to draw large funds from abroad, particularly Holland. City banks – there were about twenty early in the century – accepted deposits, issued notes ('promises to pay'), and discounted bills. They specialized in dealings with the aristocracy, especially in raising mortgages and handling Government securities. The paper-money economy grew. Bills of exchange passed into circulation from clients to shopkeepers, from retailers to wholesalers, from manufacturers to their raw-material suppliers. All forms of credit-worthy paper – even lottery tickets – tended to become negotiable and pass into circulation. In the provinces, merchants, goldsmiths, and attorneys inevitably but eagerly became bill-brokers and discounters.

Credit transactions were vital, not least because England was endemically short of circulating coin (entrepreneurs resorted to issuing trade tokens which passed as money: the iron-master John Wilkinson's tokens were so valuable as to be forged). But credit enabled business to expand by trading upon expectations, even if collapses often landed unfortunate parties in the debtors' gaol. Interest rates, moreover, remained low – fluctuating just above 3 per cent – because capital was plentiful. Whatever the project – land improvement, turnpikes, canals, building, or colonial trade – there was cheap money to finance it. Most businesses were stoked up with privately raised family capital; manufacturers tapped hoarded wealth by begging their relations, entering into partnerships, or making judicious marriages. Thus Josiah Wedgwood got his initial capital through marriage to his cousin Sarah, daughter of a Cheshire cheese-dealer. Mortgaging enabled landowners to raise capital for building, enclosures, or drainage, to underwrite jointures, or to pay off gambling debts. Turnpike trusts and canals got most of their capital from local shareholders, from grandees down to the £50 shares of scores of inn-keepers and widows. For more and more moderately affluent people found it more convenient to have their wealth in securely invested capital than in pockets of land with all the attendant problems of management. In many instances, local attorneys, brewers, or merchants were catalysts in raising and releasing capital. Such men had long provided banking facilities, but in the second half of the century country banks proper emerged from them, issuing their own notes. Coutts' bank was founded by an Edinburgh corn-dealer, Gurney's by a Norwich worsted-manufacturer. In 1750 there were just twelve, by 1797, 290 (though they were not as secure as City banks, and many crashed). The development of insurance further helped to safeguard property. The Phoenix (1680) and the Sun Fire (1708) pioneered fire insurance in London; the Royal Exchange Assurance and Lloyds looked after marine insurance. Life assurance was beginning to make headway later in the century.

England's successful trafficking economy was consistently energized by highly favourable overseas trade, especially with the fast-growing empire. The merchant marine almost trebled from about 3,300 vessels (260,000 tons) in 1702 to about 9,400 ships (695,000 tons) in 1776. As Atlantic ports expanded, London's share declined from over 40 per cent to just under 30 per cent. England's grip on major primary producers – such as the Caribbean, Canada, and India – tightened, and the Navigation Acts enforced a monopoly of carrying and entrepôt trade with the colonies. At the beginning of the century England was legally importing about £6,000,000 worth of goods each year and exporting about £6,470,000. By 1770 imports had doubled to about £12,200,000 and exports increased to £14,300,000. (The clandestine ledger of contraband would further swell these figures dramatically.) Surviving records of shopkeepers, such as Abraham Dent of Kirkby Stephen, show that even in the fastnesses of rural England customers were being served with produce from the corners of the globe: ginger, molasses, cinnamon, quinine. Dent sold forty different types of cloth. In turn English goods went to distant parts: Cheshire cheese was shipped to the Falkland Islands, Burton ales to the Baltic.

A thousand other developments expedited trade. For instance, foreigners complimented the English on their retailing. 'The magnificence of the shops,' wrote Von Archenholz, 'is the most striking thing in London.' Defoe underlined the key distributive role of shops (bright, glass-fronted and bow-dowed) in enabling English householders to obtain goods from the length and breadth of the country – hangings from Kidderminster, a looking-glass from London, blankets from Witney, rugs from Westmorland. He rhapsodized over their sheer number: 'I have endeavoured to make some calculation of the number of shop-keepers in this kingdom, but I find it is not to be done – we may as well count the stars' (yet the old Puritan in him begrudged the outlay lavished on their tinsel display). Advertising swelled enormously, especially in newspapers. Between 1747 and 1750 Bottely's *Bath Journal* carried 2,740 advertisements, between 1780 and 1783, 5,805. Provincial newspapers especially sowed envy of metropolitan taste. Thus a North Walsham staymaker advertised in the *Norwich Mercury* in 1788 notifying ladies 'that he is just returned from Town with the newest Fashions of French and Italian Stays, Corsetts and Riding Stays ... their Orders will be executed in an Height of Taste not inferior to the first shops in London' (who could resist?). A Newcastle-on-Tyne lady demanded a Wedgwood dinner service with an 'Arabesque Border' before her local shopkeeper had even heard of it; she wanted that pattern having discovered it was 'much used in London at present', and refused to be fobbed off with substitutes. In 1777 Abigail Gawthern noted in her diary that she 'used a parasol for the first time ... the *first* in Nottingham'. Advertising's role in puffing demand was well understood. 'Promise, large promise, is the soul of advertisement,' wrote Dr Johnson, who believed 'the trade of advertising is now near perfection that it is not easy to propose any improvement'. Advertising's magic whipped up demand for knick-knacks, curios, and the disposable, and increased turnover in fashion. Handkerchiefs were hawked bearing Marlborough's five great victories painted on them; others celebrated Dr Sacheverell or the Peace of Utrecht. The radical John Wilkes's squinting face was plastered over mugs, jugs, tea-pots, plaques, and plates.

England teemed with middle men. Since the Tudor statutes, marketing regulations for grain had almost denied the need for middlemen (traditionally branded as parasites), producers being required to sell in small quantities directly to the consumer at market. By the eighteenth century this system was increasingly obsolescent. More merchandise was being bought and sold in bulk, through advance contract, by wholesale capitalist butchers, drovers, grain-dealers, millers, brewers, maltsters, and of course mere speculators. Though consumers, looking to the traditional 'moral economy' of the face-to-face, regulated market and the just price, decried such dealers as profiteers, in fact they were the inevitable off-shoots of concentrated production and the remorseless geographical broadening of the market. Only substantial middle men could satisfy bulk demand from buyers such as Government contractors (who required stockings for soldiers in lots of ten thousand) or the great brewers (who demanded barley of constant tip-top quality).

Lastly, communications improvements, even before the canal age, made exchange easier, widening markets and mobilizing effective demand. Early in the century engineering works extended navigable rivers from about 960 miles in 1700 to about 1,160 in 1726. The Aire and Calder navigation was improved to aid the Yorkshire woollen industry, the Weaver deepened to get Cheshire salt down to the Mersey. By 1750, the Don was made navigable up to Sheffield. But above all, the movement to turnpike roads gathered momentum. England's old roads were atrocious, largely because the bulk goods hauled in huge waggons rutted them, and livestock droves turned them into ribbon dungheaps. Foul roads long kept England a land of pedlars and packhorses.

Turnpike-building, by local private enterprise, started around London in Stuart times. Further afield it was patchier. As late as 1740, there was no turnpike on the London to Edinburgh road north of Grantham, and the journey could still take over a fortnight. By 1750, however, the trunk roads connecting London to such major cities as Manchester, Bristol, Birmingham, York, and Dover had all been turnpiked. In 1750 there were 143 turnpike trusts covering 3,400 miles, by 1770, 500 trusts administered 15,000 miles of roads.

Road improvement produced its own booming sub-economy of inns, ostlers, coachmen and coaching services, highwaymen, and illicit dealers in game. Foreigners complimented the English on their hostels (though some remained insufferable: 'God sends meat,' lamented John Byng, dining at one, 'but the Devil sends cooks'). Turnpiking also spurred horse-breeding – the eighteenth century has rightly been called the 'age of the horse'. Cleveland bays were the favoured coach horses, though Suffolk Punches and Clydesdales were preferred as shire horses. Better roads made freight quicker, safer, and easier to haul. Henry Homer estimated in 1767 that 'the carriage of grain, coal, merchandise, etc., is in general conducted with little more than half the number of horses with which it formerly was'. Regular passenger stage-coach services were established. Another spin-off was the setting-up of a reliable and swift (but not cheap) mail delivery.

'Good roads, canals and navigable rivers are the greatest of all improvements,' judged Adam Smith. Certainly visitors admired English highways. 'These roads are magnificent,' wrote César de Saussure in the 1720s, 'being wide, smooth and well kept.' Not all were, of course – some left the agricultural writer Arthur Young apoplectic: 'The country from Tetford to Oxford is extremely disagreeable, barren, wild, and almost uninhabited. The road called, by a vile prostitution of language, a turnpike, but christened, I apprehend by people who knew not what a road is.' There were 109 Turnpike Acts between 1720 and 1750, 389 from 1751 to 1772. Turnpikes were new, and supposedly better maintained, but not until late in the century did engineers like Blind John Metcalfe, Thomas Telford, and John MacAdam substantially improve surface quality, reduce gradients, and replace fords and ferries with bridges. And turnpikes certainly didn't make haulage or travelling cheap (canals did): coaches charged 2d. or 3d. a mile; in 1774 it cost Parson Woodforde £4 8s. to cover the 100 miles from Oxford down to

Castle Cary in Somerset by post-chaise. Yet road improvement axed travelling times, as the following list of times taken (in hours) to get to London shows:

	1700	1750	1800
Norwich	50	40	19
Bath	50	40	16
Edinburgh	256	150	60
Manchester	90	65	33

Better roads encouraged more traffic, acting as a socio-economic multiplier. Thus, though an important market, up to mid-century Leicester possessed almost no scheduled links with other towns. Public passenger traffic began in 1753, when a chaise was sent up to London (as the owner put it) 'on Monday, Tuesday, Wednesday or Thursday'. In 1759, a thrice-weekly coach service from London to Leicester, Nottingham and Derby was added. From 1765 a 'flying machine' was doing the journey between Leicester and London in one day, at 25s. for an inside passenger, 12s. 6d. for an outside; this soon became a daily service. By the end of the century Leicester's communications network with other provincial towns had been etched in. A Manchester coach was set up in 1776, one to Birmingham in 1781 (it took thirteen hours), followed by others to Sheffield and Carlisle. Similarly in 1740 there had been only one stage-coach a day from Birmingham to London; by 1763 there were thirty. All in all, improvements in roads sped turnover and the pace of life and sucked more remote areas into the hectic economy of consumption and emulation. 'I wish with all my heart,' fumed John Byng, 'that half the turnpike roads of the kingdom were ploughed up, which have imported London manners and depopulated the country.' But Arthur Young saw the other side:

> The general impetus given to circulation; new people – new ideas – new exertions – fresh activity to every branch of industry; people residing among good roads, who were never seen with bad ones, and all the animation ... and industry, which flow with a full tide ... between the capital and the provinces.

Until late in the century English manufacturers were dominated by small-scale crafts, cottage and workshop industry.

Their growth did not hinge on revolutionary innovations in entrepreneurship or technology, but on the steady sucking of wealth into circulation, better use of labour reserves, and new techniques for making exchange of goods and services easier, faster, and more reliable. The heroes of this march of commercial capitalism are largely anonymous, not least the rank-and-file distributors, hauliers, shippers, transporters, and even the humble waggoner, packman, tinker, carter, or huckster. Up to 1760 there had been no decisive breakthrough in mechanization, in work organization, in the scale of the work-place, in power. The agricultural sector remained paramount, the fluctuating price of corn still largely dictating the tempo of commercial and industrial activity. Thus when agricultural profits were low in the 1730s, turnpike building tailed off. In mid-century, two thirds of British iron was still being used for agricultural purposes.

Even highly profitable expanding trades continued to organize their labour force in traditional ways, often within guild or company rules. Regulation ensured stability and was not generally a brake on expansion. Most manufacturing remained in workshops, based on the household work unit. Putting-out persisted in textiles. Master-clothiers supplied workers – carders, rovers, spinners, weavers – with materials, usually a week's supply, which they worked up on their own premises, using their own or rented wheels and looms. This system was a cost-effective use of capital. The capitalist had frozen little fixed capital in his plant and had flexibility in hiring and firing labour. Sub-contracting remained ubiquitous as a mode of employment and industrial organization, for instance in the 'butty' system in shallow Midlands coal-mining. It shared investment risks, profits, and the problems of managing the work-force. (Publishing books by subscription is a parallel case, obviating the need for the author and printer to lock up too much of their own capital in the project.) Where metal extraction was regulated by ancient laws and courts, as in Cornish tin and Peak District lead-mining, each sinking was undertaken by a gang supplying its own capital and equipment and getting its return, not in wages, but in shares of ore sales. 'Middle-management' was not a regular profession. Most intermediaries in businesses were not salaried foremen or 'executives' but were part of the family or sub-contracting small bosses in their own right. Employment was direct, responsibility personal, rewards proportionate to success.

Industry remained largely labour-intensive and skill-intensive. Weaving, smithying, hat-making, the furniture and cutlery trades, and thousands more expanded by recruiting more hands. When demand was high it was easy to take up the slack (and especially from mid-century population pressure made the labour market a buyers' market). Women and children in particular could be drafted into the labour force.

There were of course a few mammoth factories in the first half of the century. Thomas Lombe's silk-throwing mill in Derby employed 500, his twenty-three-foot water-wheel driving 26,000 spindles. But this was highly exceptional – and not very successful (nor indeed original: Lombe merely copied Italian factories). There were also a few colossal entrepreneurs. Ambrose Crowley, the iron-master, who made a mint out of navy contracts, commanded a work-force of nearly 1,000 and pioneered the techniques of shop-floor organization, discipline, and welfare taken up in later generations by industrialists such as Josiah Wedgwood (Crowley had no alternative: he directed his Tyneside works by letter from London). In his 'Law Book of the Crowley Ironworks', all instructions begin 'I DO ORDER'. Crowley knew it paid to take pains over his workers. He housed his employees on company property – but enforced a 9 p.m. curfew – and provided a doctor and poor relief, but the recipients had to wear a badge inscribed 'Crowley's Poor'. Yet such a man was utterly exceptional – a 'giant in an age of pygmies' as his biographer has called him. Only a national buyer such as the wartime navy could create such a concentrated demand: civilian consumer requirements did not support titan captains of industry so early. Indeed, only the naval dockyards themselves had a comparable scale and division of functions. As Defoe described Chatham in the 1720s:

The building-yards, docks, timber-yard, deal-yard, mast-yard, gun-yard, rope-walks; and all the other yards and places, set apart for the works belonging to the navy, are like a well-ordered city; and tho' you see the whole place as it were in the utmost hurry, yet you see no confusion, every man knows his own business.

Even in the later period of industrialization, the expansion of great iron firms such as the Carron Works, Walkers, and Wilkinsons depended largely on military contracts.

Furthermore, in the first two thirds of the century, technological innovations rarely revolutionized a trade. The development of the coke-smelting of iron by the Darbys of Coalbrookdale was of course to be vital in facilitating mass iron-casting. But, despite rising charcoal prices, this innovation made slow headway (the Darbys kept it secret). New textile machinery such as Kay's flying shuttle also came in slowly. Newcomen's steam engine was used almost solely for pumping mines, and all industrial power still came from animals, hands and feet, wind and water. The characteristic economic pattern was one of growth developing existing technologies within traditional structures of employment. And England continued to excel in high-skill industries. In mid-century she led the world in timepieces and scientific instruments; she came to dominate piano manufacture.

Typical of the piecemeal expansion of traditional industry was the increased extraction of mineral riches. English non-ferrous metal-mining reached its peak, Cornish tin and copper in particular prospering. Over 5,000 tons of Cornish copper and 3,400 of tin were being mined a year by the end of the century. Pennine lead-mining expanded from Allendale south to the Peak. Aided by Newcomen's steam pump, coal shafts around Newcastle reached depths of over 100 fathoms. Coal-mining, sometimes under the sea, brought new wealth to Cumberland. Yet on most fields pits remained shallow – in the West Midlands frequently less than 100 feet deep – and were worked in time-honoured ways by a gang of men, a few women and children, and a horse. In 1660 $2\frac{1}{4}$ million tons of coal were mined, 4.3 million in 1750, 6.4 million in 1770, and almost 14 million by 1800. The South Lancashire coalfield's output leapt from 78,000 tons in 1740 to 680,000 in 1800, using traditional methods. 'What signify all your Balls, Ridottos, etc,' demanded Sir Henry Liddell, 'unless navigation and the coal trade flourish?'

In some sectors, growth took place by streamlining, reducing waste. Many parts of rural England saw a highly effective integration of agricultural and industrial labour, families pursuing multiple trades when no one would singly win a decent living, or could be followed all the year round. Buckingham-shire attained prosperity through its integration of lace-making, felt-making, and straw-plaiting with cattle-droving and dairying. Bedfordshire families combined husbandry with lace-making, osier basket-weaving, and brick-firing. Suffolk and Norfolk villagers made sailcloth; paper was milled in the Mendips and in Kent.

Greater profits could be won by gradual expansion within existing industrial techniques, know-how, and organization. Brewing was a growth industry, not through sudden techno-logical transformation, but because it became more heavily capitalized and thus enjoyed economies of scale. This was partly because porter became a popular drink, for, being more stable than ale, it could be stored longer and transported further. Thus limits upon market size were overcome. Developments favoured big producers. In 1700 there were 174 London brew-ers; by 1799 only 127. Already by 1760 Ben Truman's plant was valued at £30,000, and he had a floating capital of over £100,000.

The success of the Black Country is a signal example of regional piecemeal growth. West Midland towns – from leaders such as Birmingham down to pint-sized Wednesbury, Darles-ton, and Bilston – were dominated by small masters in the hardware trades working their own forges and smithies, making nails, buckles, locks, hinges, pots, buttons, tools, guns, etc. Supplies of coal and iron-ore were to hand. Because there were no guilds and corporations, it was easy for masters to adjust to market openings. Growing division of labour made for effi-ciency, as was known long before Adam Smith. Dean Tucker observed in 1758:

In many provinces of the Kingdom, particularly *Staffordshire, Lan-cashire*, and certain districts of *Yorkshire*, with the Towns of *Manchester*, *Norwich*, and some others, the labour . . . is very properly proportioned . . . so that no Time shall be wasted in passing the goods to be manu-factured from Hand to Hand, and that no unnecessary Strength should be employed. For an instance of both Kinds, take one among a Thou-sand at *Birmingham*, viz. When a Man stamps on a metal Button by means of an Engine, a Child stands by him to place the Button in readiness to receive the Stamp, and to remove it when received, and then to place another. By these Means the Operator can stamp at least double the Number, which he could otherwise have done, had he been obliged to have stopped each Time to have shifted the Buttons: And as his Gettings may be from 14d to 18d and the Child's from a Penny to 2d *per* day for doing the same Quantity of Work, which must have required double the Sum, had the Man alone been employed; this single Circumstance saved alone 80, or even 100 *per cent* at the same Time that it trains up Children to an Habit of Industry, almost as soon as they can speak.

A few Midland manufacturers were becoming very big fish. Matthew Boulton – Boswell christened him 'the iron chieftain' – was employing 500 at his metal-works by the 1770s. But throughout the century, the workshop, owned by a master, with a fistful of journeymen and apprentices, remained the norm in the metal-working trades. Middling prosperity depended less on new machines than on energetic and ambitious men with a nose for gain, trying their luck in a buoyant sector of the economy. Arriving in Birmingham in 1741 looking for work, William Hutton was impressed by its beavering industry:

> I was surprised at the place but more so at the people: They were a species I had never seen: They possessed a vivacity I have never beheld: I had been among dreamers, but now I saw men awake: their very step along the street shewed alacrity. Every man seemed to know & prosecute his own affairs.

An instance of such a man was Peter Stubs. Born in 1756, Stubs was a Warrington file-maker who attained prosperity, though not because of any revolution in the techniques of file-making. Stubs benefited from a lively market: in an age before standardization, all machine parts had to be filed to size by highly skilled 'fitters': almost all trades needed files. He profited from favourable credit arrangements: he could obtain his Sheffield steel on long-term credit: his customers bought from him on tick. He took advantage of the excellent communications network already existing, winning orders from London and overseas as well as from local customers. He expanded business by taking on more skilled workers, most of whom he employed by putting work out to them. Though steady workers were hard to find, their debts and his tough bargains made them, once found, tractable: Stubs could bind them with contract indentures. Furthermore, like so many bouncy minor industrialists, Stubs had many irons in the fire. He dabbled in property, kept an inn, and was a successful brewer.

The brisk competitiveness of the market, and especially the growing surplus of labour in the second half of the century, gradually eroded economic regulation. Furthermore, new trades were not covered by the restrictions (for example on numbers of apprentices) in the Elizabethan Statute of Artificers. In these circumstances, previously backward but unrestricted regions could rise to importance at the expense of traditional ones, for it was a contemporary commonplace that where there were no guilds or corporations enterprise would flourish: 'A town without a charter is a town without a shackle.' Being free, wrote Lord Kinnoul in 1767, places such as Manchester were ones where 'genius had free scope, and industry is exerted to the utmost without control, check or interruption'. The absence of protection for labour did not hit workers badly in the developing North and Midlands, because employment prospects were good and wages competitive.

To take an example of regional growth. Before 1700, the far North-West of England, the Lake counties, was a self-contained, poor region of husbandmen which had actually suffered mortal famines in Stuart times. During the Georgian period the great natural wealth of the Cumberland coalfield was tapped by the Lowther, Senhouse, Christian, and Curwen families. The harbour of Whitehaven was built up by the Lowthers, to become for a time one of the half-dozen biggest ports in the country, largely because of coal shipping, but also because of its tobacco imports and as an embarkation point for the Isle of Man and Ireland. Walter Lutwidge, its greatest tobacco merchant, a Whig and Dissenter, tellingly called one of his vessels *The Walpole*. Along the same coast, Workington and Maryport were developed respectively by the Curwens and the Senhouses. Inland, agriculture was integrated into the wider national market, with cattle-rearing thriving. The population of Kendal, a modest 2,000 in 1700, had leapt to 8,000 by 1800, as a result of the prosperity of traditional industries such as stocking-weaving, tanning, glove-making, and gunpowder manufacture. By

1784 Kendal had at least twenty shops. It was run by an oli-garchy of Dissenting merchants (many of them Quakers) who dominated local government and gave the town a cultural gloss by its support of an illustrious Dissenting Academy (headed by Caleb Rotheram), a newspaper, a book club, a subscription library, and a theatre.

In some cases, it was geography that had the last word in thriving or failing. Salt helped Cheshire to prosper. Brewing clustered where the water was sweet, as on the Trent. Smug-gling gave moonlighting employment along the coastal strip and in distribution networks deep inland. Naval expansion was the making of Chatham, Portsmouth, and Plymouth. The most spectacular growth points early in the century were west-coast ports such as Liverpool and Bristol (not until the eighteenth century did Bristol break out of its medieval boundaries and town-plan). Both combined the advantage of being well placed for Ireland and the colonies (especially for the slave trade) with command of an industrial hinterland. Bristol was the focus for Somerset and Kingswood coal, Mendip lead, and the South Wales copper-smelting trade. It controlled the Severn and Avon and housed important potteries, glass-blowing, bottle-making, soap-boiling, zinc, and distilling industries. Horace Walpole called it 'the dirtiest great shop I ever saw' – a town where 'the very clergy talk of nothing but trade and how to turn a penny and are in a hurry, running up and down with cloudy looks and busy faces, loading, carrying and unlading goods and mer-chandizes of all sorts from place to place'.

But then Liverpool nosed ahead of Bristol. As industry tended to migrate up the Severn valley to the Midlands, Bristol's industrial pre-eminence was captured by Worcester-shire, Shropshire, and the Black Country. Abraham Darby the leading iron-smelter moved his works from Bristol to Coal-brookdale in Shropshire. Later in the century, the web of canals tended to make the natural outlet for the West Midland indus-tries the Mersey and Liverpool rather than the Severn and Bristol. Bristol delayed building docks; Liverpool seized the moment.

Though its population was under 10,000 in 1700, by 1800 Liverpool had become the second largest town in the kingdom.

It thrived on overseas merchant investment, specializing in tobacco and slaves (the painter Fuseli wrote: 'Methinks, I everywhere smell the blood of slaves'), but then its wholesale merchants cornered the expansion of Lancashire cottons. Its corporation energetically improved harbour facilities, building the first wet-dock as early as 1715 (London's main docks were not built until the close of the century). Liverpool's corporation acted like a private company. The Rathbones and other merchant oligarchs prudently funnelled some of their wealth into civil utilities such as dispensaries, theatres, pleasure gardens and libraries, alms-houses, and charity schools.

Industries were migrating all the time. High labour costs and guild restrictions pressed London manufacturers to look elsewhere: shoe-making moved out to Northamptonshire, stocking-knitting to Nottinghamshire, silk-throwing to Derbyshire (in some cases the finishing part of the trade remained in London). In 1700 the major textile centres had still been the towns of southern England: Exeter, Tiverton, Frome, Taunton, Colchester, Norwich, and clusters of villages such as Woodchester and Nailsworth nuzzling in Cotswold valleys. In these places, manufacturing was still tightly regulated by apprenticeship rules and work-place customs, and labour organization was robust. They made high-quality products, but were resistant to change. During the century rivalry increased, above all from the West Riding, where wage rates started lower and capitalists faced fewer 'restrictive practices' when trying to modify and cheapen products to suit the customer. Many markets traditionally supplied by the South-East, such as Spain and the Mediterranean, stagnated, whereas West Riding merchants won new orders, particularly in the colonies and later the United States, partly by concentrating on worsteds. The consequence was the demise of textiles in Devon and Essex (Norwich fared better, though Arthur Young in 1771 found trade there only 'neither brisk nor very dull'). The weaving trade plummeted in places such as Colchester, Braintree, and Bocking, and many once-prosperous Essex weaving areas remained ghost-towns throughout the nineteenth century. Yet so buoyant was the economy that some centres could bounce back despite the decline of their major industry, often by becoming servicing centres for gentry consumption, housing bankers, estate agents, tailors, attorneys, and gunsmiths, and sprouting assembly rooms and theatres; or by developing processing industries, such as brewing, leatherwork, and milling. Already in the 1720s Defoe noted gentrification of the economy in Bury St Edmunds in Suffolk:

> Here is no manufacturing in this town, or but very little except spinning; the chief trade of the place depending upon the gentry who live there, or near it, and who cannot fail to cause trade enough by the expense of their families and equipages among the people of a country town.

The economic infrastructure and tonic atmosphere of eighteenth-century England put prosperity within the reach of many. Obviously, growth was neither universal, uniform, nor linear. Trade operated in cycles. Capital investment, building etc. fluctuated from boom to gloom, and back again. Economic zest depended largely upon uncertain factors such as harvests and warfare, which affected prices, interest rates, and the pulse of markets. Perhaps at some point during the century, the trade cycle supplanted the harvest as the heartbeat of the economy.

In an economy as regionally diversified as England's to propose general, national trends runs the risk of masking more than it reveals. One place's meat was another's poison. Chester's decay as a port was given the *coup de grâce* by the growth of Liverpool. The Worcestershire town of Bewdley stagnated after its merchants missed the boat of canal development. Near-by Stourport became a canal junction and outstripped it. In any case, it is folly to be categorical about economic movements: our statistics will not bear it.

Nevertheless, certain patterns of long-term development are discernible. The century dawned on an expansive note. Population, which had fallen between 1650 and 1680 and remained stagnant until the end of the seventeenth century, was beginning to climb. The 5.058 million of 1700 had become 5.230 million by 1710. Commodity imports and exports were rising. The War of the Spanish Succession meant fat Government contracts on items such as weapons, ships, uniforms, and boots. Furthermore, imperial and commercial expansion was multiplying overseas trade outlets. From 1707, the Act of Union opened free trade with Scotland, providing ready markets for England's manufactures. Not least, the early century was a time of hectic activity in the City. Because the Bank of England seemed to have secured credit by linking investment with Government, speculation in shares and above all investment in Government securities soared to new peaks. More companies were floated. The many new patents taken out indicate great expectations. The rich were gambling with surplus wealth rather than leaving it idle.

In the late 1710s and 1720s, however, this movement evaporated. Not all sectors were affected. Thus exports continued to move ahead. Worth £6.4 million in 1711, they went up to £7.5 million in 1721, £8.4 million in 1731, and £9.1 million in 1741, the increase being due mainly to a steady rise in manufactures. Over 100 ships were leaving Bristol a year on the slave trade, with capacity for about 30,000 slaves. Between 1714 and 1760, imports rose 40 per cent and re-exports 50 per cent. Yet in the 1720s the rise in population shuddered to a halt – albeit temporarily – in part because of waves of lethal epidemics ravaging the country. Typhus, malaria, and other fevers struck and struck again, 1718-19, 1727-31, and 1740-42 being particularly severe spells. In a single year an epidemic could wipe out in a locality the population gains of a decade. Thus Dr Deering reported how Nottingham had been visited by a

distemperature in the air once in five years, which either brings along with it some epidemic fever (though seldom very mortal) or renders smallpox more dangerous than at other times ... but in the year 1736 the distemperature swept away a great number (but mostly children).

Contemporaries witnessed the devastating (though temporary) effects of these epidemics. Dr Hillary at Ripon saw the poor dying like flies in 1727: 'Nor did any other method which art could afford relieve them; insomuch that many of the little country towns and villages were almost stripped of their poor people.' Largely because of epidemics, there were about 100,000 fewer people in England in 1730 than in 1720.

A falling population meant checked consumer demand. Labour dearth and consequent high wage-rates meant sunny times for artisans but did not encourage capital holders to embark upon expansion. Furthermore, from 1713 the coming of peace had eased back demand for military and naval supplies. The financial boom broke. Company flotations had never been very stable: ninety-three joint-stock companies existed in 1695; in 1712 only twenty-one were left. But it was the bursting of the South Sea Bubble in 1720 which killed off investment mania. Subsequent laws restricting company formation (a royal charter was required) nipped in the bud any possible stock-market for industrial projects. Eighteenth-century industrial investments remained private, not corporate or speculative.

But arguably the greatest dampener on economic ebullience was low agricultural profitability (after all, so much of the national product and surplus capital came from the land). Improvements in agricultural technology and management, and a run of exceptionally good harvests meant that grain production was outstripping operative home demand. Corn output went up from 13.1 to 14.7 million quarters between 1700 and 1760. Much was exported – in 1750, a million quarters: as late as 1766 a Frenchman could still call England 'the granary of Europe'. More and more was distilled into spirits, especially gin (by 1743 output of spirits was six times higher than in 1700). Overproduction forced grain prices down. For consumers, this was a godsend. Cereals became cheap – prices were about 30 per cent lower than they had been in 1660, which meant that through much of the 1730s and 1740s the overall cost of living was more than 10 per cent less than in 1700. People were better nourished than for generations (though since much surplus grain was consumed as 'Mother Gin', plenty actually spelt alcoholism and death for some). But cheap food and high wage-rates depressed profits, and bumper yields meant a sticky wicket for farmers. Minor gentry and freeholders unable to diversify felt the pinch most. Many farmers went out of business, others got into debt, having to be hauled through bad times by far-sighted landlords. Rents fell into arrears, or had to be lowered, some farms became tenantless, and incomes in the landed sector stagnated or dropped. Yet necessity is the mother of invention. Tight profit margins forced the go-ahead landlord or farmer into greater cost-efficiency and productivity (by contrast yields per acre were falling in some parts of Europe, such as Brittany and Lorraine). Penny-pinching, not the expectation of large profits, spurred agricultural innovation in the first half of the century.

Of course, improvement in husbandry had been going on at least since Tudor times, and was to continue throughout the Georgian period. There were many incentives (including simply the lure of novelty and experiment). But its main dimensions are clear. Of key importance was the aim of reducing labour costs. Where possible, farmers eroded the traditional annual contract for the labourer, hiring rather by the day or week. There was also the drive to maximize land use. Fens and waterlogged lands were being drained, wastes (which Gregory King thought covered a quarter of the country) were being brought under the plough. Fertilizers such as marl, seaweed, and lime were being tested. The century's showcase estate for land reclamation was to be Thomas Coke's at Holkham, Norfolk. Over a lifetime (1752-1842) he transformed this region with the aid of his tenants and imitators, and – more importantly – gave rural improvement immense publicity. When he began farming in 1778 he found barren country, much worth only five shillings an acre. By marling the sandy top-soil he converted it within fifteen years into rich cornlands, raising the value of the estate from £5,000 to £20,000 a year. Yet Coke was by no means the earliest Norfolk improver. Since the beginning of the century, families such as the Townshends and Walpoles had been improving rotations, experimenting with marling, and sowing wheat and barley.

Stock-breeding became more systematic. Robert Bakewell of Dishley in Leicestershire, the century's most prestigious breeder, viewed a sheep as 'a machine for turning grass into mutton'. Many of the great English breeds, such as Hereford or Shorthorn cattle or Southdown sheep, date from this period. New crops were introduced to meet specific needs. Above all, crops such as legumes, sainfoin and clover and root crops such as turnips, swedes, and mangelwurzels came into use on light sandy soils, to improve the tilth and provide fodder crops for overwintering livestock. Livestock were energetically folded for their dung, regenerating the soil. In some areas water meadows were flooded in the spring to provide an earlier, lusher bite. And there was a long-term switch in the geography of production.

For, as time went on, the traditional corn-belt of the Midland clays switched to livestock pasturage, partly because of the rising demand for meat. By 1790 William Marshall could describe Leicestershire as 'a continuous sheet of greensward'. By contrast, former sheep-grazing areas such as Oxfordshire, the Wiltshire downs, the Chilterns, Norfolk, and the North and South Downs, aided by convertible husbandry, were being put to the plough, especially late in the century. According to Arthur Young 'half the county of Norfolk within the memory of man yielded nothing but sheep feed', but by the end of the century it was covered with fine barley, rye, and wheat. In 1803 Thomas Rudge reported similarly on the Gloucestershire rural economy:

The HILL DISTRICT includes the Cotswolds. Within these last hundred years a total change has taken place on these hills. Furze and some dry and scanty blades of grass were all their produce, but now with few exceptions the downs are converted into arable enclosed fields.

Begun long before, flexible agricultural improvement of this kind, sensitive to market demand and aimed at cost-effectiveness, continued during the difficult years between the 1720s and 1750s. The innovators – the great landlords, in league with big tenant farmers to whom they granted long leases – had the required capital to press ahead. Under the sharp prick of the goad it was a gamble to make farming pay.

In the short term, however, surplus production and low profits dictated a generation of circumspection from the 1720s amongst the economy's big spenders. Few major new fields of industrial investment were opened. The number of new industrial patents declined. Canal-building did not get under way until the end of the 1750s. The economy did not suffer a slump, but rather had reached a plateau.

From the mid-1740s, however, demographic and economic growth began an acceleration which, with only the occasional hiccup, carried through into the Industrial Revolution. The reasons for recovery at this time are not totally clear. The first forty years of the century saw a run of low prices – the cost of living was regularly less than in the late seventeenth century –

and buoyant incomes (rising exports and stagnant population made it a sellers' market in skills). Hence many had surplus disposable income, translated in time into higher consumer demand, stimulating growth in manufactures. Relatively abundant food, helped by measures taken in 1751 to cut gin consumption, may at last have produced a more robust and fertile population, more resistant to epidemic disease (though decreasing mortality was probably minor as a factor in demographic growth). Certainly population began to creep up again from the 1730s. The total population of 5.263 million in 1731 was about the same as in 1650. But by 1741 it had risen to 5.576, by 1751 to 5.772. The wars of the 1740s gave an artificially induced, state-centred economic injection, and the Seven Years' War (1756-63) secured new colonies (Canada, India, and Caribbean islands) which boosted trade.

From the 1750s there was no looking back (with the exception of a spell around 1780 when British losses in the War of American Independence seriously disrupted trade, panicked the money market, and led to bank crashes, eroding confidence). Even before changes specific to industrialism, England was overcoming the age-old blocks to sustained population rise and economic growth. How?

Improvement may have been somewhat fortuitous. Mortality from epidemic diseases declined, not peaking again until the emergence of festering white-man's-grave slums in London and the new industrial towns early in the next century, and the coming of cholera. This was a biological windfall, but better nutrition and environmental conditions, such as the draining of stagnant waters, the paving of towns, the enclosing of sewers, and the spread of piped water, probably helped. The enormously successful adoption of smallpox inoculation (thousands were inoculated in mass sessions) and, later, vaccination saved many lives directly and also may have resulted in a more fertile population (smallpox sometimes lowers fertility among male survivors).

Once population began to rise from the 1740s, it boosted home economic activity, increasing demand and cheapening labour. Rising demand required more wage-labour, in turn encouraging further population expansion, for, as Arthur Young put it, 'the increase of employment will be found to raise men like mushrooms'. The 5.722 million English people of 1751 became 6.147 million in 1761, 6.448 million in 1771, 7.042 million in 1781, 7.740 million in 1791, and 8.664 million in 1801. A pool of cheap labour welled up to man industrial expansion. Expansion could continue unchecked, partly because capital was there to be invested; the century saw it put to wider and more productive uses.

One channel of investment which had lasting effect was canals. In 1759 James Brindley completed for the twenty-three-year-old Duke of Bridgewater the first canal of industrial significance, carrying coal from his Worsley pits to sell in Manchester. From then on canal construction pressed ahead – both short-haul ones for single purposes (usually linking collieries to towns) and longer trunk canals linking rivers, such as the ninety-three-mile Grand Trunk which connected the Mersey to the Trent and served the Potteries. Ninety out of 165 Canal Acts passed by 1803 had been to serve collieries: 'A navigation,' said Bridgewater, 'should have coals at the heel of it.' The profits from Bridgewater's own mines shot up from £406 in 1760 to £48,000 in 1803, partly because the canal halved the price of coal in Manchester.

Canals were sanctioned by Acts of Parliament, and financed by incorporated companies issuing shares, bought mainly not by a general rentier public (as railway shares were later), but by interested local parties (shares were often £200 each). The Duke of Bridgewater estimated that a canal cost up to 10,000 guineas a mile. The Grand Trunk Canal cost £200,000. The Pennine Link was estimated at £320,000 but ate up much more. By 1795. £8 million had been invested in canals; by 1815, £20 million. Construction was undertaken by sub-contracting separate stretches – viaducts, locks, bridges, junctions – to particular builders, thus sharing the risks and avoiding the headache of centralized supervision.

Canals linked the Severn and Mersey by 1772; the Trent and Mersey by 1777; the Severn and Thames in 1789; and the Mersey, Trent, and Thames in 1790. By 1790 (the start of a decade of 'canal mania'), Liverpool, Hull, Birmingham, Bristol, and London were all linked up. Direct routes across the Pennines, however, linking industrial Lancashire and Yorkshire, were delayed. Canal-building created employment, directly for technicians and navvies, indirectly for supply industries. Above all it made inland transport cheaper and easier, especially for the bulk freight of industrial raw materials, such as coal, metals, stone, fire-clays, bricks, and grain. A horse pulling a long barge could haul 25 tons, whereas a 6-ton waggon needed eight horses. Canal freight was up to four times cheaper than road. Canals also made carriage of breakable goods such as ceramics safer, and so encouraged a national market in such wares to emerge. A town such as Reading, traditionally cut off by waterlogged roads from even the near-by Midlands, suddenly had ready access by canal. Canals provided an enormous boost to enterprise. Sometimes with profit to shareholders, sometimes not, canal construction was one of the key ways in which private initiative established the infrastructure of utilities upon which industrialization thrived.

In two other areas, basic capital investment gave the economy new momentum. The Georgian period saw unparalleled urban reconstruction. This made fat profits for property speculators and provided lasting work for builders, surveyors, designers, decorators, joiners, cabinet-makers, painters, and a host of similar craftsmen, as well as timber suppliers and builders' merchants. Urban renewal meant more inns and shops, coaching-houses, social centres such as theatres, assembly rooms and concert halls, where service employment was created, money spent, and business transacted, releasing fresh capital into circulation. Dock construction got under way. Bridges, jetties, and lighthouses were erected, and many ports developed their warehouses and harbour facilities.

By channelling resources into productive use, enclosure was likewise a shot in the arm for the economy (though a kick in the teeth for many workers on the land). Enclosure required costly surveys and parliamentary approval (involving fat lawyers' fees), and then new roads, fencing, walls, hawthorn hedges, farmhouses, barns, cottages, and perhaps drainage systems. Enclosed land yielded fatter stock and heavier crops but fringe benefits as well. For instance, grazing animals haphazardly on vast open fields probably spread livestock diseases (contemporaries frequently associated open fields with sickly stock). It was much easier to isolate infected stock on enclosed lands. Since certain animal diseases are transferable to humans – such as tuberculosis through infected milk – enclosure may even have benefited health. Open fields tended to drag everyone down to the level of the least efficient.

Enclosure had been going on in the countryside for centuries: about half the cultivable land had been enclosed by 1700. The great area of fields remaining open early in the eighteenth century was the swathe running from the southern counties up through the Central and East Midlands to Lincolnshire and the East Riding of Yorkshire, including Dorset, Wiltshire, Oxfordshire, Berkshire, Buckinghamshire, Northamptonshire, Huntingdonshire, Cambridgeshire, Leicestershire, and Nottinghamshire. Much of this was enclosed during the course of the century, as the following figures of the number of Enclosure Acts in each decade suggest:

1740–49	64	1780–89	150
1750–59	87	1790–99	398
1760–69	304	1800–09	574
1770–79	472	1810–19	422

Georgian enclosure was two-phased. First, the open-field clays of the Midland counties were enclosed, chiefly for pasturage, between about 1745 and 1780. Then from the late 1780s the open fields, wastes, and commons of the South and the East were enclosed for cereals, as population increase pushed grain prices to record levels, boosting profit margins. Between 1760 and 1799 enclosures brought between two and three million acres of waste into cultivation.

Enclosure could properly be carried out privately by 'agreement' (at the prompting of big landowners and yeomen, in Adam Smith's words 'sensibly dividing the country among opulent men'), or by Act of Parliament (usual where much common land was at stake). In fact, enclosure was sometimes bulldozed by naked act of aggrandizement. In 1716 John Warren, Lord of the Manor in Stockport, simply started selling common land on his own initiative for building and industrial purposes. The one patch of land left as common he set aside as the site for a gaol, and some of the profits of enclosure were earmarked to build a workhouse for 170 people, thus anticipating the plight of the people under enclosure.

The initiative to enclose usually came from large landowners, since they stood to gain most (and not only in husbandry: in many parts, enclosing fields was an effective way of seizing absolute control of mineral rights, quarries, or valuable building land on town perimeters). Much ink and passion have been spilt by historians debating the injustice and social consequences of enclosure, but the main lines of developments seem clear. Open-field farming was not necessarily primitive or hidebound. Nevertheless cultivating enclosed fields was generally more productively efficient. Holdings were consolidated. Less land was wasted (as on baulks and headlands), and it lay fallow for less time. Stock was healthier, for even stinted commons were frequently overgrazed. Under enclosure it was easier for the individual agriculturalist to innovate or be flexible. The muck-spreading journalist Arthur Young was right to say that farmers on enclosed land were more go-ahead ('Enclosing has changed the man as much as it has improved the country').

Not just great landowners and enterprising tenant farmers but many freeholders securely in possession of deeds to a sizeable holding were keen to enclose. Much enclosure was by agreement (though 'enclosure by agreement' in reality was often 'enclosure by pressure'), and enclosure commissioners generally acted with equity to husbandmen who could demonstrate good title. Hence, as well as setting up handsome, consolidated farms (the broad-acred tenant farms which came to typify English agriculture though almost unknown elsewhere), enclosure also planted thousands of compact holdings of perhaps 30–100 acres. Enclosure did not make the smallholder an endangered species, for their holdings were certainly viable in the boom years towards the end of the century and through the Napoleonic Wars. Many went broke in the depression after 1815, but not until the 1870s did the smallholder really go to the wall.

Three groups suffered desperately from enclosure. First, those independent cultivators whose strips on the open fields were so minute as to make access to commons and waste (for geese, for grazing the odd cow or pig, for wild food, twigs and bracken for firing) a vital supplement. On a diminutive enclosed holding, without further outlet to the soil, their livelihood became attenuated and precarious. Overheads – and often debts – were alarmingly increased by the need to fence, drain, and build a new barn, without compensating savings from economy of scale. Enclosure can rarely have brought benefit to this class of smallholder. They were the first to be forced to sell up at the slightest misfortune or economic downswing.

The second group to suffer were the many cottagers who did wage-labour on farms for part of the year while also following trades such as nail-making or hurdle-making. They had little or no holdings in the common fields, but by ancient custom kept a cow or a few hens on the common. By enclosure they lost an important economic safety-net, as well as their sense of having a stake in the land. Thomas Bewick observed that by enclosure, 'The poor man was rooted out, and the various mechanics of the villages deprived of all benefit of it.' As the Rev. David Davies, rector of Cookham in Berkshire, put it in 1795, for a dubious economic benefit, 'an amazing number of people have been reduced from a comfortable state of partial independence to the precarious condition of mere hirelings, who when out of work immediately come on the parish.'

But most calamitously hit were those who had hitherto been tolerated squatters occupying shacks on the common or waste. Without a share in the open fields, they scratched a living by seasonal agricultural wage-labour and by trapping rabbits, collecting wood, or burning charcoal, topping it up perhaps by petty theft, above all poaching. Without a 'right' to use the common (such a 'right' was not established without forty years' occupancy), such families were simply ejected (ratepayers were often glad to see them off the parish). Victims of what Arthur Young called the 'open war against cottagers', they became a landless (and even homeless) rural lumpenproletariat. For a while enclosure created job openings for such people (immediately after enclosure, there was much hedge-planting, fencing, road-construction, and barn-building to be done). But, turfed off the land and with no secure employment, many such families sank into pauperdom, drip-fed by parish doles and immobilized under the eye of the constable and the overseer of the poor. In Arthur Young's words, 'By nineteen out of twenty Enclosure Bills the poor are injured and most grossly ... The poor in these parishes may say with truth, "Parliament may be tender of property; all I know is, I had a cow, and an Act of Parliament has taken it from me."'

What did enclosure do? First, it fundamentally altered the landscape. The familiar chequer-board pattern of fields with ruler-edges, hedgerows, and wide straight roads dates from enclosure. Second, it gave proprietors further encouragement to treat agriculture as a business. It turned the land into absolute private property and abolished usufruct, customary usages, commoners' and occupants' rights; it consolidated the great landowners – that is why the Hon. John Byng could describe enclosures as 'the greedy tyrannies of the wealthy few to oppress the indigent many'. It made capitalist wage-labour paid by the day or task the norm on the land, as factories were later to do in towns.

Third, enclosure boosted rural output and profits. Despite Malthusian fears, England remained astonishingly able to support its soaring population. The land was feeding half as many people again in 1800 as in 1750, and corn production increased by about 43 per cent during the century. Perhaps three fifths of this increased production was due to higher efficiency, the rest to increased acreage (much poached off the commons). Fourth, enclosure dealt a fatal blow to a long-established lower-class domestic economy, in which access to fields and commons had given families a small stake in the land and enabled the resourceful poor to piece together a living. A striking but typical instance of rural collapse following enclosure is the village of Wigston Magna in Leicestershire, enclosed in 1765. Long before enclosure, the inhabitants were already highly unequal in wealth; only three tenths of the villagers owned land and, of those, five owned more than 200 acres each, while two thirds had less than 50 acres. Yet within sixty or seventy years of enclosure practically all the small owner-occupiers had disappeared. The lower orders had lost all ownership of the means of rural production and had become rural labourers or framework-knitters. In Wigston, pauperism became for the first time a grave problem.

In 1754 just £95 had been spent on the poor rate. By 1802 the charge was £1,776.

Most observers believed that those rural poor who continued to have a stake in the land were better-off. Arthur Young wrote revealingly of the inhabitants of the unenclosed Isle of Axholme in Lincolnshire: 'Though I have said they are very happy, yet I should note that it was remarked to me, that the proprietors work like negroes and do not live so well as the inhabitants of the poor house: but all is made amends for by possessing land.'

Enclosure cast long shadows. The profile of the dispossessed rural proletariat, especially in central southern England, at the turn of the nineteenth century is of a group not merely impoverished but sinking – a charge on ratepayers and increasingly moving towards desperate guerrilla war against the propertied, culminating in poaching, rick-burning, riot, incendiarism, and rebellion. Dispossessed cottagers from Dorset, Cambridgeshire, and Lincolnshire were not driven into northern factories. Indeed their tragedy was compounded by the fact that they tended to stay put, immobilized partly by the poor law and partly by apathy. The nineteenth-century poor, however, were certainly haunted with a vision of repossessing the land.

During the first forty years of the eighteenth century, society and economy remained in self-adjusting equilibrium, and there were no great pressures towards destabilization. Employment opportunities were restricted, marriage was late, reproduction was regulated. The rise of population was slow, and severe epidemics at times reversed the process. From about the 1740s, however, the economy started to grow, and this growth accelerated, fuelled in part by population pressure. Economic expansion increased the national product, and the 'haves' – farmers, property-owners, rentiers, and capitalists from small masters right up to plutocrats – could all count on benefiting from rising prosperity. This was particularly so as consumer prices had been low since the beginning of the century, and price inflation did not begin to pinch till the last decades. Acceleration of economic change, however, was a mixed blessing for the 'have-nots', the mass of the working people. Population rise destabilized the terms of labour. Growing competition for jobs began to slice wage-rates, particularly on the land, and undermined customary work organization and restrictive practices. The old working life pattern in which the apprentice could hope to become a master was increasingly challenged by the rise of wedges of less skilled, less organized labour. A proletariat, and a lumpenproletariat, were forming. Yet, where manufactures were advancing, there was a brisk demand for labour, and wages had to be competitive. Without economic growth, England could not have supported her newly booming population, though it was a population in which the spreading base was condemned to lives of toil and poverty as wage-labourers.

6. Having and Enjoying

It was argued in the last chapter that the economy of eighteenth-century England was an abrasive one, scouring the face of the country, bringing some parts up bright:

Great towns decay, and small towns rise [wrote Defoe]; new towns, new palaces, new seats are built every day; great rivers and good harbours dry up, and grow useless; again, new ports are open'd, brooks are made rivers, small rivers navigable ports, and harbours are made where none were before, and the like.

But how, and how far, did economic change and rising national wealth affect the ways people lived, their material belongings and surroundings, their life-style? Four main currents of development stand out. First, there was a growth of well-being filtering down, however unequally, to improve the standards and quality of living of much of the population (though in turn heightening contrasts between the 'haves' and the 'have-nots'). Second, much of this additional wealth was being converted into personal goods, raising many households from levels of subsistence to comfort and style. Third, spare cash was often laid out on entertainment and enjoyment. Easy-come, easy-go attitudes towards spending were widespread: people liked to take their pleasures noisily, effusively, and in public (later snootily deemed more a characteristic of working-class culture). Last, entertainment, art, letters, and culture were becoming increasingly commercially organized, angling for wider audiences. This opened up new vistas of material enjoyment, as well as problems of coexistence between traditional and elite culture.

Not everything changed, not everybody benefited. Prosperity for some meant impoverishment for others. Yet, for many, the effect of economic buoyancy was that there were more sovereigns in the purse, or more halfpennies, to be spent. Of course, this did not instantly revolutionize the quality of life. Surplus income generally went on more of the same old things: new clothes, another foaming quart of ale, half-a-dozen oysters (then a cheap snack, rather like crisps today). Material life remained the same in many of its fundamental dimensions. In 1800 as in 1700 (or 700) the fastest mode of locomotion – except perhaps for intrepid balloonists and their kittens – was still the horse. In 1800 affluent houses were still lit by candles, and hovels by rushlight and starlight. In these, as in other basic matters, dramatic change was just around the corner. Gas lighting, the steam printing press, and then railway engines, horse-trams, and the telegraph made the early decades of the nineteenth century times of bold change in everyday living and perception.

In fundamental matters, the life-styles of the 'haves' and 'have-nots' were very distinct, and these distinctions were not eroded. Take housing. A shockingly large mass of the urban poor were still occupying shanties and cellars, and the rural poor shacks made of wattle, turf, and road-scrapings (to discourage poor-law settlements, many parishes demolished cottages and refused permission to build new ones). 'Mud without and wretchedness within,' was the Hon. John Byng's verdict on housing at Warminster. At Bridgnorth the poor lived troglodite existences in homes gouged out of the cliff face. With timber shortage and enclosure, many could not even afford a fire. 'Humanity shudders,' observed Thomas Davis, steward to the Marquis of Bath,

at the idea of the industrious labourer, with a wife and five or six children, being obliged to live or rather to exist, in a wretched, damp, gloomy room, of 10 or 12 ft square, and that room without a floor; but common decency must revolt at considering, that over this wretched apartment, there is only *one* chamber, to hold all the miserable beds of the miserable family.

Styles of town and country housing for the higher orders did not alter out of recognition. Tidy-fronted brick-terraced town houses with vertical lines, handsome doors, classical mouldings and fittings, and sash windows held sway. In other necessities, such as diet, the distinctions stayed much as before. Food ate up the bulk of the poor's budget. About two thirds of a working family's income would go on food and drink, the rest struggling to cover rent, fuel, clothes, and boots. Labourers' diets were at least as meagre and monotonous in 1800 as in 1700, bread and cheese predominating. The common people could afford little meat, and that was mainly fat bacon. Adulterated tea, used over and again, tended to replace milk and beer (home brewing got more difficult, and fewer cottagers could keep cows). Yet the spread of potatoes improved nutrition and even the poor had their aspirations to a better – or more fashionable – diet, such as a taste for white over brown bread, particularly in the South ('rye and barley bread are looked on with horror even by poor cottagers,' commented Arthur Young in 1767). The higher in the social scale, the larger the amount of meat eaten, especially the patriotic roast beef, carnivores lording it over granivores. As with architecture, eating habits diversified somewhat. Prejudices against fruit and vegetables relaxed: pulses and greens were more widely eaten, and strains of fruit improved. Imported provisions such as coffee, tea, and sugar ceased to be seen as luxuries, and suppliers' lists show handsome ranges of spices, exotic fruits, and fish. But the boards of the rich remained mountainous and unsubtle. French cooks were rare and rather despised. Patriotism in *haute cuisine* meant loading your belly. As the Swedish visitor Pehr Kalm saw it in 1748, 'The art of cooking as practised by most Englishmen does not extend much beyond roast beef and plum pudding.' 'BLESSED BE HE THAT INVENTED PUDDING,' bantered the Frenchman Henri Misson, *à propos* of English *goût*, 'for it is a Manna that hits the Palates of all Sorts of People: a Manna better than that of the Wilderness, because the People are never weary of it. Ah, what an excellent Thing is an *English Pudding! To Come in Pudding Time*, is as much as to say, to come in the most lucky moment in the world.'

Satisfying a hearty appetite was the soul of hospitality. Parson Woodforde recorded his annual tithe dinner in 1783:

I gave them for Dinner a Leg of Mutton boiled, and Capers, some Salt Fish, plenty of plumb Puddings and a Couple of boiled Rabbitts, with a fine large Surloin of Beef rosted. Plenty of Wine, Punch and strong Beer after Dinner till 10 o'clock. We had this Year a very agreeable meeting here, and were very agreeable – no grumbling whatever. Total recd. this Day for Tithe 286. 15. 0.

Alcohol consumption was high among all ranks. Liquor (even brandy, when smuggled) was cheap, sealed bosom companions, and spelt out cheer and health. The tombstone of Rebecca Freeland (d. 1741) read

> She drank good ale, good punch, and wine
> And lived to the age of ninety nine.

In any case, water supplies were often contaminated. Early in the century 11.2 million gallons of spirits were being drunk in London a year (about seven gallons per adult), sold from 207 inns, 447 taverns, 5,875 ale-houses, and 8,659 brandy shops. Northampton, with a mid-century population of 5,000, had sixty inns and 100 ale-houses, and there were about 50,000 inns and taverns throughout the country. Though the Gin Craze eviscerated mainly the dregs, the rich liked their glass too. In 1774 the Lord Mayor's dinner at the Mansion House polished off 626 dozen bottles of wine. In 1733 Robert Walpole's household consumed over 1,000 bottles of White Lisbon wine alone: perhaps its thirst had been raised by the 1,200 lb. of chocolate he ordered a year.

Nevertheless, some real changes in consumption patterns were afoot, most notably amongst people faring well, from craftsmen up to professionals and farmers. Growing purchasing power was being laid out on greater ranges of goods, beyond mere necessities, which could be afforded partly because they were becoming *cheaper*. Prices dropped by some 10–15 per cent between 1700 and 1750. Sugar got cheaper: 200,000 lb. were consumed in 1690, 5,000,000 lb. in 1760. Tea halved in price over that period. Real wages moreover were going up early in the century because the stagnant population gave skilled labour a strong bargaining position. A family could survive on 10s. a week, but craftsmen such as printers or Spitalfields silk-weavers were earning £2–£3 a week (and family income would be topped up by women and children). Soame Jenyns reflected in mid-century on these rising material comforts: 'The consumption of everything is also amazingly increased from the increase in wealth in our metropolis, and indeed in every corner of this Kingdom, and the manner of living, throughout all ranks and conditions of men, is no less amazingly altered.' The dice were loaded for spending rather than saving. Easy credit, low interest rates, and lack of legal security for bank and friendly society savings took some of the joy out of deferring gratification. In any case, the emulative urge to have something to show for one's work was strong. 'Every man now,' wrote Defoe,

be his fortune what it will, is to be doing something at his place, as the fashionable phrase is, and you hardly meet with anybody who, after the first compliments, does not inform you that he is in mortar and heaving of earth, the modest terms for building and gardening. One large room, a serpentine river, and a wood are become the absolute necessities of life, without which a gentleman of the smallest fortune thinks he makes no figure in his country.

Commentators – some enthusiastic, others reproachful – remarked how rising standards and expectations were feverishly chasing each other's tails. It was said in the 1770s of provincial shopkeepers: 'Their tables are served as well as rich merchants were a hundred years ago: their houses good and ornamented. What formerly was a downfall gable end, covered with thatch, is now brick and tile.' A commentator from mid-century Nottingham wrote:

People here are not without their Tea, Coffee and Chocolate, especially the first, the use of which is spread to that Degree, that not only Gentry and Wealthy Travellers drink it constantly, but almost every Seamer, Sizer and Winder will have her Tea in a morning . . . and even a common Washer woman thinks she has not had a proper Breakfast without Tea and hot buttered White Bread!

Moralists berating lower-class luxury switched their thunder from beer- to tea-drinking. As the very proper Dissenting minister Richard Price lamented in 1773, 'The lower ranks of the people are altered in every respect for the worse, while tea, wheaten bread and other delicacies are necessaries which were formerly unknown to them.'* Yet others saw the economic

* Ironically, wheaten bread might have been healthier than rye, because less subject to ergotism.

benefits of keeping up with the Joneses. Asking rhetorically, 'Is not the creation of wants the likeliest way to produce industry in a people?', Bishop Berkeley approved of the fact that householders were now purchasing items previously only within reach of their betters: ceramic tableware (perhaps Spode or Royal Derby) to replace pewter mugs and platters; metal knives and forks supplanting wooden implements; iron hobs and grates, cushioned chairs, Axminster and Wilton carpets, kitchen ranges, wallpaper, framed prints on their walls, the latest delicate Sheraton furniture (no one wanted antiques), and brass ornaments. Argosies of fabrics enticed housewives into the shops. In 1774 one draper had for sale:

Dutch ratteens, duffles, frizes, beaver coatings, kerseymeres, forrest cloths, German serges, Wilton stuffs, sagathies, nankeens, Silisia Cambricks, Manchester velvets, silks, grograms, double allapeens, silk camblets, barragons, Brussels camblets, princes stuffs, worsted damasks, silk knitpieces, corded silks and gattias, shagg velvets, serge desoys, shalloons and allapeens.

Even artisans came to have quite well-appointed houses. Witness the inventory of a Colchester weaver in 1744 (she was significantly being removed to the workhouse):

Two Bedsteads 2 Beds 1 pair of Curtains 7 Sheets 3 Blanketts 2 Coverlids 4 pillows 4 pair of Cases 2 Bolsters 2 Pair of Drawers 3 Tables 1 Copper Saucepan and Cover 1 small Boyler 1 Iron pot 1 Iron Kettle 2 Box Irons and heaters 2 Iron Candlesticks 1 Looking Glass 2 Jugs 1 pair Bellows 12 pictures 3 glass Ditto 1 pair Tongs Sifter poker and Fender 1 Frying pan 2 Chamber pots 1 Iron Tramell 3 Basketts 2 Earthern pots 1 Wash tub 1 pail 2 Bowl dishes 9 Glass Bottles 3 Dishes 16 plates 9 Basons 4 Tea pots 16 Cups and Saucers 2 Silver Spoons 3 Quart pots 1 Trunk 1 Sweeping Brush 3 pewter Measures half pint Quart D° and ½ quart Ditto 1 Bird Cage 14 Gallon Cask 1 Bay [etc.].

Furnishings underwent a spring-clean. The architect John Wood Senior thought that traditional interiors – stately, sombre, built to last – were being scrapped. Now

The floors were laid with finest clean deals, or Dutch oak boards; the rooms were all winscotted and painted in a costly and handsome manner; marble slabs, and even chimney pieces, became common; the doors in general were not only made thick and substantial, but they had the best sort of brass lock put on them; walnut tree chairs, some with leather, and some with damask or worked bottoms supplied the place of such as were seated with cane or rushes; the oak tables and chests of drawers were exchanged, the former for such as were made of mahogany, the latter for such as were made either with the same wood, or with walnut tree; handsome glasses were added to the dressing tables, nor did the proper chimneys of any of the rooms long remain without framed mirrors of no inconsiderable size; and the furniture of every chimney was composed of a brass fender, with tongs, poker and shovel agreeable to it.

Similarly the designer Robert Adam noted in 1773

a remarkable improvement in the form, convenience, and relief of apartments ... The massive entablature, like the ponderous compartment ceiling, like the tabernacle frame, almost the only forms of ornament formerly known in this country, are now universally exploded, and in their place we have adopted a beautiful variety of designs, gracefully formed, delicately enriched and arranged with propriety and skill. We have introduced a great diversity of ceilings, friezes, and decorated pilasters, and have added grace and beauty to the whole by a mixture of grotesque stucco and painted ornaments, together with the painted rainceau with its fanciful figures.

All that lagged was sanitation; in these new interiors, plumbing changed little; except for aristocratic mansions, few houses had baths installed, and urban back-to-backs had to share pumps and privies.

For artisans, stone or brick houses increasingly replaced cob, lathe and plaster dwellings (very heaven for vermin). In the 1780s Gilbert White noted that all the villagers in Selborne now had brick and stone cottages. Georgian terraces have lasted well: little built previously in vernacular materials has survived. Tens of thousands of standardized, two-up, two-down, sash-windowed houses were erected, costing from as little as £150, and building societies were floated to help small men to build and buy. Expectations about acceptable standards of comfort, cleanliness, and decency were rising. Dr Johnson could

remember when people in England changed a shirt only once a week. Formerly, good tradesmen had no fire but in the kitchen; never in the parlour, except on Sunday. My father, who was a magistrate of Lichfield, lived thus. They never began to have a fire in the parlour, but on leaving off business or some great revolution of their life.

Pride in better material conditions was mirrored in domestic spruceness. Foreigners thought English houses cleaner than anyone else's – except the Dutch. 'The amount of water English people employ is inconceivable, especially for the cleansing of their houses,' thought César de Saussure in the 1720s:

> Though they are not slaves to cleanliness, like the Dutch, still they are remarkable for this virtue. Not a week passes by but well-kept houses are washed twice in the seven days, and that from top to bottom; and even every morning most kitchens, staircase, and entrance are scrubbed. All furniture, and especially all kitchen utensils, are kept with the greatest cleanliness. Even the large hammers and the locks on the door are rubbed and shine brightly. English women and men are very clean; not a day passes by without their washing their hands, arms, faces, necks and throats in cold water, and that in winter as well as in summer.

The Duc de La Rochefoucauld, touring England in the 1780s, agreed: 'People take the greatest possible pains to maintain the standard of cleanliness.' That ordinary people could afford not just necessities but 'decencies' and novelties also impressed continental visitors, unused to this amongst their native peasantry. De Saussure, for example, was amazed that artisans – even, he claimed, shoe-blacks – lounged about browsing the papers in London coffee houses. Pastor Moritz found his London landlady read Milton and other classics of English literature: 'The English national authors are in all hands, and read by all people, of which the innumerable editions they have gone through are a sufficient proof.' Once a year this widow treated herself to a visit to Ranelagh in Chelsea to stroll round the gardens and rub shoulders with the nobs. Out in rural Oxfordshire Moritz was impressed by the living standards of countrymen dressed 'not as ours [that is, the Germans] are in coarse frocks, but with some taste, in fine good cloth; and were to be distinguished from people of the town not so much by their dress as by the greater simplicity and modesty of their behaviour'. Madame du Bocage thought the same about husbandmen: 'they have their houses

well furnished, are well-dressed and eat well; the poorest country girls drink tea, have bodices of chintz, straw hats on their
heads and scarlet cloaks upon their shoulders.'

Pulpits might thunder but the flood of pinchbeck consumer
goods, and the surplus to buy them, drove the wheels of emulation and tyrant fashion faster and faster. 'The labourer and
mechanic will ape the lord,' complained Jonas Hanway in 1752,
and other sourpusses had a field day, finding (as did John
Trusler in 1796) 'the great degree of luxury to which this
country has arrived within a few years . . . not only astonishing,
but almost dreadful to think of. Time was, when those articles
of indulgence, which now every mechanic aims at possession
of, were enjoyed only by the Baron or Lord of a district.'

But advertising and salesmanship shamelessly exploited envy.
Josiah Wedgwood opened London and Bath showrooms for his
tableware, laying out tempting dinner sets, ready to eat off.
Consumer psychology was tapped by manipulators of fashion.
For promoting sales, thought Wedgwood, '*Fashion* is infinitely
superior to *merit* in many respects; and it is plain from a thousand
instances that if you have a favourite child you wish the public
to fondle and take notice of, you have only to make choice of
the proper sponsors.' Wedgwood played on cultural aspirations
by promoting neo-Classical designs in his Etruscan ware,
modelled on finds from newly discovered Herculanaeum.
Everyone connived at the envy game. Newspapers, magazines,
and tea-table conversation lingered over the last detail of
material possessions, especially spotlighting the new. Fops man-
nequinned fashionable outfits and accessories in public (it was a
peacock society). Fashion-conscious travellers scoured stately
homes, anxious to discover the latest in motifs, cabinets, fabrics,
and wallpaper (197,000 yards were sold in 1713, 2,100,000 yards
by 1785).

The urge to 'improve' and 'arrive' was irresistible. The people
consciously mimicked their betters. The Hon. John Byng reported in 1795:

I remember in Bedfordshire an old tenant of my brother's, who
wore the same coloured coarse cloth all the year round, and tied his
shoes with thongs; his son in succession, when I called upon him, in a
morning about nine years ago, ordered the maid servant to bring a

bottle of wine 'with black seal', and, pouring out a glass, said, 'There, colonel, perhaps there's as good a glass of claret as you ever drunk at St James's.'

Though moralists deplored how the 'effeminate' urge for comforts was sapping the nation's fibre, businessmen saw it as expanding trade by tapping wider markets. Furthermore, the well-off colluded. Gentlemen and ladies wanted their servants fashionably dressed as a garnish to themselves, and servants expected cast-offs. Dean Tucker wrote, with some exaggeration:

> Females of all Ages and Conditions hardly use any Woollens at present, except those of the finest Texture, and made of the finest Wools, Silks, Cottons, and Linens, combined in a thousand forms ... are now almost the universal wear, from her Grace in the drawing-room down to the lowest Scullion in the Kitchen.

Moreover, metropolitan fashions were sucked into the provinces. Many country areas had traditionally been isolated backwaters, Cobbett thus describing the Surrey of his infancy in the 1760s:

> As to politics, we were like the rest of the country people in England; that is to say we neither knew nor thought anything about the matter. The shouts of victory, and the murmur of defeat would now and then break in upon our Tranquility for a moment, but I do not remember ever having seen a newspaper in the house, and most certainly that privation ... did not render us less free, happy or industrious.

But provincials, spurred by newspapers and turnpikes and above all by the urge to shed their 'rustic' image, wanted to change all this.

Provincial towns put on London airs, London impresarios manipulating the impulse of provincial pacesetters to ape the metropolis. Better communications rushed London fashions into the regions, with results the smart found risible. As the *Connoisseur* condescendingly put it in 1756:

> Where the newest fashions are brought down weekly by the stage-coach, all the wives and daughters of the most topping tradesmen vie with each other every Sunday in the elegance of their apparel. The same genteel ceremonies all practised there as at the most fashionable churches in town. The ladies immediately on their entrance, breathe a

pious ejaculation through their fansticks and the beaux very gravely address themselves to the Haberdashers bills glued upon the linings of their hats.

Provincial towns christened their pleasure gardens Ranelagh and Vauxhall, their theatres Drury Lane. John Wood the Elder laid out grounds in Bath 'in imitation of the Ring, in Hyde Park, near London'. Burghers made Handel the staple of regional musical life after his oratorio triumphs in London and Dublin. Edinburgh, Bath, Cheltenham, and Bristol all built show-case new towns, abandoning vernacular styles and materials, and promoting autocratic international Classicism. From early in the century reading societies and gentlemen's clubs were set up in market towns such as Peterborough and Boston to imbibe the *Spectator*. Genteel provincials suppressed their dialects and affected London catch phrases, cant, and euphemisms. Always the eye was on the capital. 'The theatrical performances here,' announced the *Bristol Guide* of 1801, 'are little (if any) inferior to those in London,' and even the Bath Penitentiary for Reformed Prostitutes modelled itself proudly on its London prototype.

Sophisticated shops sprang up – seedsmen, gunsmiths, high-class booksellers. Visiting Halifax in 1781 Thomas Twining was surprised: 'I should not have expected to meet with a bookseller (Mr Edwards) in Halifax who is one of the best and most elegant binders in England, and has a valuable collection of books and prints.' Eyeing London, provincials set up circulating libraries, theatres, concert-seasons, subscription balls, coffee houses, musical societies, assembly rooms, and free-masons' lodges, and the elite put on a philanthropic face, managing charities, infirmaries, and dispensaries. Not least, alongside slums and sewage stench, townscapes were improved with new utilities and amenities: squares and walks, bridges, paved and lit roads, piped water, pleasure gardens and new street plans, not to mention grids of elegant town houses.

Plenty and panache of this kind were new to the provinces. In 1761 the fey Horace Walpole delivered his verdict on the citizens of King's Lynn: 'their language is very polished since I lived among them [1741]. I attribute this to their more frequent intercourse with the world and the capital, by the help of good roads and post-chaises, which, if they have abridged the King's dominion, have at least tamed his subjects.' John Byng, by contrast, rued innocence corrupted: 'the country is only improved in vice and insolence by the establishment of turnpikes' – 'I meet milkmaids on the road with the dress and looks of Strand misses.'

Georgian society took pride in material objects. Inventories even of ordinary people's belongings reveal hosts of items: tongs, bellows, prints, trunks, clocks, fenders, pans, copper kettles, saddlery, firescreens, trinkets, toys. Many of these went beyond the timeless necessities that never wore out which were found in the ancestral cottage, and there were more articles of fashion and amusement, from family games to magazines. In the 1750s Thomas Turner, the Sussex grocer, was bringing home scientific toys: 'I entertained my sister Sally, and my brother's wife, with the sight of the Modern Microcosm, which I think is a very pretty curious sight, for we see the whole solar system move by clockwork, in the same manner as they do in the heavens.' The stout heirloom Bible was now shelved alongside tatty novels which soon fell apart (few have survived). There was more impulse buying: there were more ephemera to buy.

But as yet few manufactures were standardized as they became in the next century. Individual craftsmanship still prevailed. People were not yet dwarfed by possessions: the clutter of furniture and domestic bric-à-brac came with Victorian mass-production and sentimentality about home. Georgian taste still favoured clean lines, simplicity, sparseness. The Georgians were certainly fascinated by objects: they loved poring over factories, inspecting machinery, peering down microscopes, going to galleries, collecting curios. But they were mobile at heart, valuing the freedom money gave them to buy and do things, and enjoying being out of doors and on the move. 'Home sweet home' is a sentiment meaning little until near the end of the century.

In Georgian England, the social life of the common people had an out-of-doors atmosphere. Trades were carried on in

yards, open-fronted workshops and booths looking out on to
the world. People did their business, discussed their politics, and
took their pleasures in public. They milled around in streets
bustling with flower-girls, pie-men, milkmaids (selling adulterated milk), patterers and ballad-mongers, street vendors,
street-walkers, street-criers, street-urchins. Home had fewer
attractions. Blessed were the convivial. Solitary people were
pitied and diagnosed as morose, melancholic, boorish: sociability integrated people, invigorated the faculties, and knocked off
rough edges. Dr Johnson had no doubts: 'The true felicity of
human life is a tavern.'

Two powerful currents were tugging on the moorings of
social life. First, the public domain was growing increasingly
secular, independent of the Church. Second, many forms of
culture and enjoyment, once private and exclusive, were becoming more open.

The Church's once crucial place in communal life was being
eroded. In previous centuries church had been the only place in
many settlements housing paintings, books, and learning, the
chief forum for news, discussion, and community action
(weapons were stored there). Vicars had dispensed herbal remedies and taught the ABC, and schoolmasters were generally
clergymen. In the eighteenth century, churches continued to
fulfil these broad roles, especially perhaps for inward-looking
Dissenting and Catholic congregations. The English continued
to enjoy listening to a wholesome sermon. But churches met
alternatives and competition. Religious pluralism and toleration
meant that no single place of worship could bring whole communities together. With growing religious indifference, people
looked elsewhere. Privately owned, non-denominational
schools sprang up, run by laymen. Hundreds of communities,
even in small villages, set up their own secular book clubs,
which for a guinea or two a year gave subscribers access to
scores of volumes. Proprietary libraries were founded in Liverpool in 1768, Sheffield in 1771, Hull in 1775, and Birmingham
in 1779. The English were still religious in their culture: witness
the popularity of sacred music. Yet this was being divorced
from worship. Handel's biblical oratorios were often performed not in church but at a concert and without liturgical

function. The *Messiah* was sung at fund-raisers at the Foundling Hospital.

As an assembly place the church faced rival venues. With magistrates frowning on church ales, the church became less of a place of merriment. Coffee houses blossomed, over 2,000 having been set up in London by 1700. Goldsmith wryly described clergymen snug in coffee houses penning sermons; doctors used them for consultations; Addison wrote *Spectator* papers from Button's Coffee House. Some even had educational aspirations – William Hogarth's father set one up where Latin was to be spoken: *non floruit*. If the Puritan chapel had been the citadel of seventeenth-century freedoms, by the eighteenth the coffee house was – in Prévost's words – the 'seat of English liberty' – because of its open political discussion. Unlike churches, they were open to all denominations (though few admitted women).

Pursuit of pleasure became more respectable. Calvinist taboos against indulgence were sloughed (Cromwellian Puritans became caricature killjoy stormtroopers). Not many seventeenth-century fathers would have advised a son, as Lord Chesterfield now did, 'Pleasure is now, and ought to be, your business.'

Travelling, if not for business, had once been holy, as religious pilgrimage, or therapeutic, for exercise to recover broken health. Now jaunts were blossoming in their own right, partly because better roads, inns, and coaches made it more pleasurable. Bath – called by Defoe 'the resort of the sound rather than the sick' – became the cynosure of elegance and one of the top ten towns, its population of 2,000 in 1700 shooting up to 34,000 by 1800. 'Taking the waters' for medicinal reasons was the excuse, but in reality it was a holiday spa. Visitors flocked in to idle away time, ogle the exquisite, haggle matches for their daughters, and above all gamble. Unlike Restoration Tunbridge Wells, Bath was not a hotbed of sexual debauchery, possibly because Beau Nash, the *arbiter elegantiarum*, was heedful to preserve Bath's reputation and took a rake-off from gambling. Indeed, Bath was so properly organized as to be dull. 'The only thing one can do one day one did not do the day before,' confessed Elizabeth Montagu, 'is to die' – though for his part the Methodist Charles Wesley called the town 'the headquarters of

Satan'. Bath was imitated all over the country: Malvern Wells, Cheltenham, Buxton, Harrogate, Scarborough, all offered glimpses of glamour for the more homespun. 'Here was the same specimen of company as usual,' complained the bilious John Byng about Cheltenham, 'widows wanting husbands, old men wanting health, and misses wanting partners.'

The coach tour also came into vogue as a secularized pilgrimage (the walking holiday was to be a discovery of the Romantic poets). Abroad, grand tourists flocked to France and Italy, high altars of European history, culture, and civility. At home, the Peak fed the new love of natural sublimity until it was rivalled by the Lake District and the Welsh Mountains towards the end of the century. Like other delights, travelling was now being indulged by a broader cross-section. 'Life has not many things better than this,' Boswell was informed by Dr Johnson as they bowled along the Stratford road. He hankered after spending his life, Johnson confided, 'driving briskly in a post-chaise with a pretty woman'. Even stick-in-the-mud Johnson visited the Hebrides.

Travelling became more agreeable partly because coaches improved in comfort, being sprung and upholstered. Chaises could be hired, but the Englishman's dream was to own his own (Regency bucks popularized the phaeton, the sports car of the horse age):

In everything that concerns the stables [commented Arthur Young], the English far exceed the French; horses, grooms, harness, and change of equipage; in the [French] provinces you see cabriolets undoubtedly of the last century; an Englishman, however small his fortune may be, will not be seen in a carriage of the fashion of forty years past; if he cannot have another, he will walk on foot. It is not true that there are no complete equipages at Paris, I have seen many; the carriage, horses, harness, and attendance without fault or blemish; but the number is certainly very much inferior to what are seen at London. English horses, grooms, and carriages have been of late years largely imported [into France].

The sea-side holiday was invented. Sea water was prescribed originally for its therapeutic properties by Dr Russell of Brighton, who recommended that it should be *drunk* for health. Then sea-bathing was offered as a cure, but soon it came into its own as a pleasure. George III patronized Weymouth, where he loved taking the salute. John Byng by contrast detested its affected vulgarity:

a sandy shore, being excellent for bathing, has first induced the neighbours to come; and since, by fashion, and by the Duke of Gloucester's having built a house, is become the resort of the giddy and the gay: where the Irish beau, the gouty peer, and the genteel shopkeeper blend in folly and fine breeding.

The Prince Regent popularized Brighton, where he built the pavilion and raced chariots with his friends along the strand. Londoners flocked to Margate, northerners to Scarborough. 'One would think that the English were ducks,' remarked Horace Walpole, 'they are for ever waddling to the waters.' At resorts commercial opportunities were seized, from hotels (though most people hired lodgings) and scheduled coaching services down to souvenir shops, bathing machines, and their attendants ('dippers'). Beneath the gentry, most who could afford holidays stayed with friends and relations. Londoners of slenderer means strolled out on a Sunday picnic to Bagnigge Wells, Sadlers Wells, or Hockley-in-the-Hole, where there were ornamental gardens, ponds, fishing, teas, glasses of purgative waters, and sometimes sport such as bear-baiting. The urban poor got away by going harvesting and hop-picking.

Leisure time was thus being spent in less religious ways. The second great change was that many forms of enjoyment previously private, elitist, and monopolized by the very rich were becoming public and more shared: 'It is evident,' observed Madame Roland, 'that man, whatever he may be, is here reckoned something, and that a handful of rich does not constitute the nation.'

During Tudor and Stuart times, the centre of gravity for poetry, music, and theatre lay within exclusive cliques and especially the Court. Individual noblemen had patronized their own consort of viols or company of players, or even had their jesters. Restoration gentlemen had written and performed their own plays. In the absence of a sustaining general public, artists and performers, thinkers, and poets had an eye to patrons' hospitality. Great philosophers such as Hobbes and Locke did time as domestic savants, tutors to gentlefolks' children; Dryden received pensions of £200 a year as Poet Laureate and Historiographer Royal.

But this changed. Market forces – affluence, leisure, the book trade – led to high culture becoming available if not to the masses at least to the many. One no longer needed to be a gentleman proprietor to saunter round ornamental gardens, because Vauxhall, just south of the river at Westminster, and Ranelagh at Chelsea, made pleasure grounds available to Londoners at a small charge. Now you did not have to own paintings to appreciate them, because public art exhibitions were held – from 1768, by the Royal Academy. Commercial galleries were common in London by the second half of the century (though the state was hardly involved: the National Gallery dates from the nineteenth century). Cheap engravings of Old Masters sold briskly in the print shops which were springing up everywhere.

The popularization of what had once been reserved for the cognoscenti often developed by stages. For instance, in the seventeenth century, collections of antiquities and natural history had been privately owned, but their owners had displayed them to select visitors armed with letters of introduction. By 1759 the British Museum had been opened, at the bequest of Sir Hans Sloane, as the first publicly owned, free-entrance museum in Europe. The second half of the century saw privately run museums opening their doors as commercial ventures in London and the provinces. Sir Ashton Lever's in Leicester Square took £13,000 at the door between 1775 and 1784. Similarly, all England's stately homes were of course private domiciles, yet proud proprietors threw them and their grounds open to visitors, strangers included. Some even sold teas, prints, guidebooks, and souvenirs to visitors. At Wentworth, Arthur Young found Lady Strafford so obliging as to retire from a room so he could view it.

In poetry and drama the domestic and private sectors of course continued: the Duke of Richmond was famous for his private theatricals, and many polite families – Jane Austen's for instance – staged plays: texts of plays were bestsellers. Yet the performing arts spread more into the public arena – a shift speeded by the Court's decline as a show-case and a forcing-

house of the arts. Charles II had been a friend of the arts, and
many Restoration wits – Wycherley, Sedley, Etherege, Roch-
ester, Vanbruch – were gentlemen at Court. Restoration Court
culture had been intimate, innovative, *risqué*. Court art was lively
art. But amongst the early Hanoverians Court taste was staider.
The Georges liked gardens and built up high quality picture
collections, but they were no great patrons of literature. The
first two Georges were known as Dunce the First and Dunce
the Second. George III's taste was dull too. He disliked Shakespeare (though reading *King Lear* when mad), but he paid
Benjamin West a handsome £34,000 for sixty-four paintings.
Hanoverian Court dress trailed fashion. The edge of artistic
innovation and *avant garde* taste swung away from the Court
and towards the public (significantly, styles were named not
after monarchs but after craftsmen and designers – Sheraton,
Hepplewhite, Chippendale, Adam – and in any case, the English
crown never had regulated the arts and intellectual life to anything like the degree to which, for example, Bourbon monarchs
did from Versailles, via institutions such as the Académie
Française).

The theatre of bold wit, intimate allusion, and in-jokes declined. The commercial playhouses of Georgian London were
huge (in 1794 Drury Lane held 3,611), and even Norwich's
theatre seated more than a thousand. Popular playwrights –
Cibber, Goldsmith, Colman, Lillo – wrote for middle-brows,
their hits being simple, moral, sentimental, with elements of
pantomime, farce, and music-hall.

What were the implications of culture becoming more
secular and publicly oriented? First, the arts became *commercialized*, leisure a trade. Anyone who could pay could play, could
join the audience. As the disdainful Gibbon put it, 'The pleasures of a town life, the daily round from the tavern to the play,
from the play to the coffee-house, from the coffee-house to the
— are within the reach of every man, who is regardless of his
health, his money, and his company.'

Casanova's view was more enthusiastic: 'In London, everything is easy to him who has money and is not afraid of spending
it.' No fewer than 12,000 of the culture-hungry paid 2s. 6d.
each to hear a rehearsal of Handel's *Fireworks Music* at Vauxhall.

London had at least sixty-four pleasure gardens where for a small admission fee one could take the family, have tea, listen to music, gawp at macaronis, and keep assignations. Subscription concerts were pioneered in London, music festivals in the provinces (the Three Choirs Festival dates from 1724). Alongside traditional rough-and-tumbles such as Bartholomew Fair, scores of diversions were opened to paying customers in London and elsewhere: prize-rings, masquerades, waxworks, magic-lantern shows, cock-fights, panoramas, hippodromes, puppet-theatres. From 1730 Walsh was issuing cheap part-music scores in large quantities. Fashion plates and fashion dolls for clothes came in, keeping people abreast of the latest Parisian modes. Pattern books, such as John Wood's *Series of Plans for Cottages*, and magazines, such as *The Fashions of London and Paris* and *The Gallery of Fashion*, published plates of the latest modes in households and clothes. You could ornament your house with ready-made Adam motifs – fluted fans, plaques, wheat-ear drops, festoons, scrolls.

Opening up such events to whoever could pay produced a very mixed company. Admission fees were great levellers. Foreigners were astonished to find the petty bourgeois rubbing shoulders with peers at the ridotto or regatta (pick-pockets had a jubilee). Mixing was made less fraught because John Bull knew he was as good as his betters, and young bloods still liked blood sports such as boxing and bull-baiting and the roar of the crowd. Louis Simond noted that English stage-coaches were 'crammed with passengers of all sexes, ages, and conditions'. Pastor Moritz asked himself what was so special about St James's Park. 'It is the astonishing medley of people.' César de Saussure wondered the same about cricket, and answered: 'Everyone plays it, the common people and also men of rank.' All sorts went to Ranelagh rotunda – 'You can't set your foot without treading on a Prince of Wales or Duke of Cumberland,' mock-complained Horace Walpole: 'The company is universal: from his Grace of Grafton down to children out of the Foundling Hospital – from my Lady Townshend to the kitten.'

As well as gouty lords, Bath attracted *nouveaux riches* (and *nouveaux pauvres* too, hoping to recoup fortunes), as Smollett describes:

Clerks and factors from the East Indies, loaded with the spoil of plundered provinces; planters, negro-drivers, and hucksters, from our American plantations, enriched they know not how; agents, commissaries, and contractors, who have fattened, in two successive wars, on the blood of the nation; usurers, brokers, and jobbers of every kind; men of low birth, and no breeding, have found themselves suddenly translated into a state of affluence, unknown to former ages.

The etiquette of Beau Nash, the master of ceremonies, ensured that, once arrived in Bath, all ranks were regimented equally. No one was to wear a sword, and all were to minuet in strict rotation, defying aristocratic precedence.

As commerce increased its stake in culture, myriad new ventures sprang up, set fair to turn a penny. Though total literacy spread only slowly, readers devoured whatever publishers could issue. Pastor Moritz ran across a saddler in Derbyshire who struck up a conversation about Homer and Virgil: 'He quoted lines from them moreover, in a way I should have thought possible only in a doctor or a master of arts from Oxford' (Moritz had just visited Oxford). He commented, 'German authors are hardly read [in Germany] outside learned circles except by a few of the middle classes. Yet the common people of England read their English authors. You can tell it, among other things, from the number of editions of their works.'

Slaking this thirst for print, newspapers flooded on to the market. By 1790 there were fourteen London morning papers. In 1788 the first London evening paper appeared; in 1799 the first Sunday paper – 'everyone who reads at all,' exaggerated Southey in 1812, 'reads a Sunday newspaper.'

Up to 1700 all newspapers had been printed in London, being sped down to the provinces by coach. But a provincial press was soon challenging the metropolitan. The *Norwich Post* began in 1701, the *Bristol Postboy* in 1702, and within the century almost every district got its own paper. 50,000 copies of provincial papers were sold a week in 1700, 200,000 in 1760; sales doubled by 1800. By 1760, thirty-five provincial papers were in business, selling for about 1½d. Each had a sale running from a few hundred to a couple of thousand, but a readership probably five to ten times that number (and many more picked up the contents by word of mouth). Provincial newspapers publicized local events, carried scores of local commercial advertisements, and conveyed military, political, and financial intelligence from London, all important symptoms of the health of trade. Contemporaries believed that newspapers were the whipcrack of civilization; in Dr Johnson's words, 'The mass of every people must be barbarous where there is no printing and consequently knowledge is not generally diffused. Knowledge is diffused among our people by the news-papers.'

Before the eighteenth century almost no printing presses were licensed in the provinces, where there had been few specialized book stores (Samuel Johnson's father ran one in Lichfield, but it was not a success). By the end of the century, every town had its printer and bookshop.

The output of prints, pamphlets, cartoons, and ballads swelled but never saturated the market. Magazines such as Addison and Steele's *Spectator* created an enduring taste for light and polite literature, Addison wishing to 'bring philosophy out of closets and libraries, schools and colleges, to dwell in clubs, and assemblies, at tea-tables, and in coffee-houses'. By uniting entertainment and instruction, he taught ease and affability to squireens and the commercial classes with leisure on their hands. Magazines had a circulation of up to a few thousand copies: the *Spectator* early in the century about 3,000, the *Gentleman's Magazine* from the 1730s up to 10,000. Mainly monthly and selling at about 6d., they branched into more specialized readership. There were soon journals for ladies, for provincials, for fashion; some focused on politics, some were illustrated, many were religious, a few pornographic, some had quizzes, others dress patterns. By 1800, 250 periodicals had seen the light of day, including the *Matrimonial Magazine*, the *Macaroni*, the *Sentimental Magazine*, the *Westminster*.

Books remained quite dear – though that does not seem to have damaged sales (anyway, cheaper pirated editions could not be suppressed and you could buy secondhand copies at auctions). A novel would cost at least 7s. 6d., a work of history or *belles lettres* a guinea. Even so, Henry Fielding's *Joseph Andrews* sold 6,500 copies in 1742. Enterprising publishers brought books out serially, in parts, at about 6d. a time, to spread the cost (Smollett's *History of England* sold 13,000 in serial form). And in any case, the works that were really popular were cheap political pamphlets, sermons, penny dreadfuls, ballads, and slim octavos of verse. The floating of circulating libraries, moreover, made thousands of books available to subscribers at a guinea or two a year. By 1800 there were 122 circulating libraries in London, 268 in the provinces. Though critics condemned them as 'evergreen trees of diabolical knowledge', others, such as the bookseller James Lackington, saw their value as a home university library, especially for ladies:

... circulating libraries have greatly contributed towards the amusement and cultivation of the other sex; by far the greatest part of ladies now have a taste for books ... Ladies now in general read, not only novels, although many of that class are excellent productions, and tend to polish both the heart and the head; but they also read the best books in the English language, and may read the best authors in various languages; and there are some thousands of ladies who frequent my shop, and that know as well what books to choose, and are as well acquainted with works of taste and genius as any gentleman in the kingdom, notwithstanding they sneer against novel readers, etc.

For those who could not afford literary classics, abridgements were available. Novels were boiled down into chapbooks. John Wesley condensed *Pilgrim's Progress*, pricing it at 4d., alongside his nine-page *Short English Grammar* and his 144-page *Complete English Dictionary*. His *Primitive Physick*, a do-it-yourself guide to health, had gone through twenty-three editions by 1791. 'The sale of books in general,' wrote James Lackington in 1792,

has increased prodigiously within the last twenty years. According to the best estimation I have been able to make, I suppose that more than four times the number of books are sold now than were sold twenty years since. The poorer sort of farmers, and even the poor country people in general, who before that period spent their evenings in relating stories of witches, ghosts, hobgoblins etc., now shorten the winter nights by hearing their sons and daughters read tales, romances etc., and on entering their houses you may see *Tom Jones*, *Roderick Random*, and other entertaining books stuck up on their bacon racks.

Traditional culture was continually being infiltrated from above by entrepreneurs of the arts and the elite. Sports such as marbles and cheese-rolling, enjoyed by local communities time out of mind and often linked to calendar festivities, went on as before, but many sports and pastimes were now glamorized to suit celebrity and fashion. Cricket might be moved from the village green to the estate (Lord Chesterfield instructed his son, 'You will desire to excel all boys of your age at cricket'). As befitted the age of reason, cricket, like other sports, had its rules codified (the leg-before-wicket rule, for example, dates from 1774). The MCC was founded in 1787 at Thomas Lord's ground in Marylebone. Hitherto chiefly for participants, cricket (like others) became a spectator sport: 20,000 watched Kent play Hampshire in 1772. By the early nineteenth century, some top players were professionals. The sport's enormous popularity lay in its being tailor-made for gambling. Teams themselves competed for high stakes, but thousands of guineas were wagered at the ground in betting on the result, leading to games-manship and bribery. Bets were also placed on individual innings, and even on particular balls and strokes. Horace Mann thought nothing of staking £1,000 on a match. A later, prim-mer, age rejected the commercial paternity of organized cricket: bookies were banned from Lords in 1825.

Prize-fighting developed in the same way. Earlier there had been no illustrious prize-fighters because boxing was not profes-sional. Under George III and the Regency, however, boxing stars, such as Jem Belcher, Dutch Sam, Bill Stevens the nailer, Tom Crib, and the superstar Daniel Mendoza, emerged. They were backed by glittering publicity (Mendoza mugs and plaques, and instruction books; later, memoirs were big busi-ness). Boxing journalism pumped up interest, immortalizing fighters as Homeric heroes in a patois all its own (the sport was termed 'the fancy'). Mendoza himself wrote *The Art of Boxing*, opened an academy, and teamed up with Philip Astley, the hippodrome proprietor. Tens of thousands of guineas were staked on big bouts. Successful fighters became rich, set up their own gymnasia, and 'gentrified' bruising into the science of pugilism.

It was the same with horse-racing. At the Restoration the

turf had been exclusively aristocratic, the sport of kings; Ascot was Queen Anne's own estate. But under the Georges many towns got their races: Norwich held them regularly from 1710, Warwick from 1711, the sport becoming so popular that grandstands had to be built to corral the rich away from the crowds. The turf became big business. The Jockey Club was set up in 1752, the horse-dealers, Tattersalls, in the 1770s. Professional trainers and jockeys took the initiative. The successes of thoroughbreds such as Eclipse gave rise to blood-stock pedigrees and equine ancestor-worship. 'Classic' races such as the St Leger (from 1778), the Oaks (1779), and the Derby (1780) created the racing calendar. And once again, betting made the wheels go round.

Even hunting (thanks to the game laws, the most select of sports) became organized and commercial. Traditionally favourite forms of killing wild animals – hawking, trapping, and netting – were fairly solitary; but these gave way to scientific warfare and a rational approach. Birds were now bred and protected by gamekeepers and flushed out by beaters for the mass shoot, the *battue*. Shooting became competitive, with glory for the biggest 'bags'. Above all, fox-hunting as we know it was a Georgian invention, with horses bred specially for speed and jumping and packs of hounds for scent. The chase, which in Stuart times had been more stop-and-start, increasingly went at the gallop. Permanent packs with national reputations, such as the Pytchley, the Belvoir, the Cottesmore, and the Quorn in Leicestershire, date from the 1770s. Although fox-hunting was aristocratic ('the only chase in England worthy of the taste or attention of a high bred sportsman'), hunting clubs with yearly subscriptions became commercial speculations. Whoever could afford the fees – even London plutocrats – could join.

England was gripped by gambling fever. Men bet on political events, births and deaths – any future happenings. For a few pounds challengers galloped against the clock, gulped down pints of gin, or ate live cats. A common wager was to take out insurance policies on *other* people's lives. When George II led his troops against the French in 1743 you could get four to one against his being killed. Cards were the opium of the polite. Parson Woodforde regularly played: 'Mr and Mrs Custance drank Tea with us in the Afternoon with their eldest Son. After Tea we all got to Loo at which I won o. 6. o. Nancy also won at Loo this evening o. 6. o.' Gambling itself became nationalized. The state ran a lottery from 1709 to 1824, national institutions, from the British Museum to Westminster Bridge, being partly funded out of the proceeds. But gaming was also the life blood of London clubs such as Almack's, White's, and Boodle's, and astronomical sums flew around. Charles James Fox had lost £140,000 by the age of twenty-five. At White's, Horace Walpole reported, 'Lord Stavordale, not yet one-and-twenty, lost eleven thousand last tuesday, but recovered it by one great hand at hazard: he swore a great oath – "Now, if I had been playing *deep* I might have won millions".'

Outdoor sports were big attractions, partly because they brought together lords and commons, traditional recreation and profit. Peers – sport's first sponsors – were prepared to share pleasures such as horse-racing with the people, celebrating their own supremacy as patrons. Bucks backed bruisers and ran their own cricket teams. Classic races commemorated noble names ('The Oaks' was the name of Lord Derby's Epsom house). Sport was mimic warfare and a version of pastoral for the Regency toff. The crowd liked the touch of class that lordly presences lent and the business they created for tapsters, porters, and hawkers, and could see peers as men of the people when Lord Sackville batted for a Kent side captained by Rumney, his head gardener. And aristocratic protection was vital for prize-fighting, since technically it was illegal.

The more culture became commercialized, the more box office appeal dictated taste. Playhouses sprang up everywhere. The Nottingham theatre was built in 1769, the Manchester Theatre Royal opened in 1775, and by the end of the century even small towns such as Wisbech and Bury St Edmunds could boast spacious playhouses, where London stars such as Mrs Siddons would tour. And there were smaller barns to be stormed by strolling players. But the fare served up was what the customers wanted. Shakespeare was made easy. *A Midsummer Night's Dream* was turned into *The Fairies*; *King Lear* was given a happy ending. Farces, ballads and recitations, pantomimes and tragedies, jostled on the same bill: something for everyone. In Birmingham the stage developed into a proto-music-hall. Amongst the shows of London, freaks, midgets, women gladiators (such as 'Bruising Peg'), contortionists, and mathematical pigs were sure-fire money-spinners. Likewise Jeremiahs rued how circulating library shelves groaned under sentimental and titillating gothick novels, supposedly devoured by impressionable teenage girls.

Capitalizing on these commercial opportunities, the culture trade was revolutionized by outstanding entrepreneurs, ready to anticipate, stimulate, and satisfy demand. These included actor-managers such as John Rich, who first staged *The Beggar's Opera*, Colley Cibber, and David Garrick, the grand-master of publicity, who floated the Stratford Shakespeare Jubilee in 1769. Philip Astley developed his bare-back stunt riding into a stunning hippodrome spectacle. The printer Edward Cave, proprietor of the *Gentleman's Magazine*, created a readership by pioneering parliamentary reporting. Later in the century, speculators opened galleries in London decked with paintings of scenes from Shakespeare, the Bible, and English history. The capital's effervescent musical life was orchestrated by Heidegger, Handel ('composer in ordinary to the Protestant religion'), and, later, Salomon. In 1791 Salomon gave Joseph Haydn £50 for each of twenty performances and a £200 benefit. Great landscape designers such as William Kent, Lancelot ('Capability') Brown, and Humphry Repton would produce environments to order. Enterprising publishers also seized their chances, quenching the readers' thirst for knowledge, diversion, news, education, sex. John Newbery poured out spelling books, primers, picture books, chapbooks, joke books, and fairy stories, as well as educational toys such as jigsaws. Catherine Hutton remembered reading as a child

all Mr Newbery's gilt books, as they were called for being covered with gilt embossed paper. They consisted of *Christmas Box*, *New Year's Gift*, *Goody Two Shoes* – nothing delighted me so much as the *Tale of the Fairies*. I no more doubted their truth than I did my own existence.

Publishers hit on cheap collected editions of British playwrights, poets, and essayists, Elizabeth Cooper putting out the first general anthology of English poetry in her *Muses' Library*

(1737). Certain publishers – Lintot, Strachan, Millar, Cadell, Johnson – struck up cordial terms with leading authors, selling their works in handsome editions. 'I respect Millar,' wrote Dr Johnson, 'for he has raised the price of literature.'

Scientific lecturers burst on the scene as the Enlightenment's answer to the itinerant preacher, trading on the new prestige of Newtonian science and the magic of experiments and dazzling apparatus (Adam Walker had a 20-foot orrery). Early in the century James Jurin, William Whiston, and others performed in London (Whiston was also an apocalyptic gospeller, prophesying the end of the world). Lecturers then went on the road, fanning out with their apparatus into provinces. Jurin lectured in Newcastle in 1710, Whiston in Bristol in 1724. James Ferguson (a canny Scot who had taken the high road south to London and become a leading text-book popularizer of science) lectured in Bath and Bristol in the 1760s and 1770s. By the end of the century most towns of any size had been milked by science lecturers offering courses of six or a dozen lectures, selling their books and instruments, puffing patent medicines, performing land surveys, and giving private tuition. 'Knowledge is become a fashionable thing,' announced a top lecturer, Benjamin Martin, 'and philosophy is the science 'a la mode' ('No man has been more anxious,' he flattered himself, 'to make the rugged paths to knowledge plain and easy and the liberal arts more generally accessible').

Alongside impresarios of art and science, commercialization created *stars*, bathed in bubbly publicity. Some came up through recognized channels, such as the stage: Garrick (who had tramped to London to seek his fortune), Macklin, Quin, Mrs Oldfield, and Peg Woffington became household names. Others had to carve out their own legends – the Negro lion-tamer Macomo, or mountebanks such as the self-dramatizing magician, healer, and clairvoyant Cagliostro, or the mystic Katterfelto, with his black cats, lecturer on the 'Philosophical, Mathematical, Optical, Magnetical, Electrical, Physical, Chemical, Pneumatic, Hydraulic, Hydrostatic, Proetic, Stenographic, Blaencical, and Caprimantic Arts'. The sex therapist James Graham (flanked by nymphs, one of whom was the future Emma Hamilton) unveiled a Celestial bed in his Temple of Venus at the Adelphi, hired out at £50 a night to reinvigorate the impotent, and titillated society with his erotic lectures. Unorthodox healers, such as Mrs Mapp the bone-setter, were nine-day wonders in chic society. Samuel Foote, the farceur, Henry Angelo, founder of London's premier fencing academy, Cadman, the rope-walker, to Grimaldi, the clown – all had their fans. And for jaded palates there was 'the amazing Learn'd English Dog' on circuit in the North West which

reads, writes, and casts Accompts, by Means of Typographical Cards, in the same Manner that a Printer composes; and, by the same Method, answers various Questions in Ovid's Metamorphosis, Geography, and History; knows the Greek Alphabet, reckons the Number of People present, if not above 30 ... solves small Questions in the four Rules of Arithmetick, tells by looking on any common Watch of the Company, what is the Hour and Minute.

Beneath impresarios and stars, the commercialization of culture needed production-lines, drudges, and managers (Hogarth complained of 'picture-jobbers'). To cope with the insatiable demand for culture, supply was mechanized. 'Grub Street' became literature's conveyor belt, employing hacks such as 'Sir' John Hill willing to pen instant copy on any subject for a fee. Defoe wrote in 1725:

writing is become a very considerable part of the English commerce. The booksellers are the master manufacturers or employers. The several writers, authors, copyers, subwriters, and all other operators with pen and ink are the workmen employed by the said master manufacturers.

Meeting the demand for pulp reading meant penal servitude for many hireling writers (hence the Grub Street joke advertisement: 'An author to be let'), but for others a big readership meant freedom, and the chance to be a man of the world. As the philosopher and essayist David Hume wrote:

It is with great pleasure I observe, that men of letters in this age have lost in a great measure that shyness and bashfulness of temper, which kept them at a distance from mankind; and, at the same time, that men of the world are proud of borrowing from books their most agreeable topics of conversation.

For many garret scribblers, poverty and anonymity; for the successful, new-found wealth. Pope made £4,000 each out of his *Iliad* and *Odyssey*, whereas half a century earlier Milton's reward for *Paradise Lost* had been £5 down and £5 at the end of the first edition. With the spread of the reading habit even journeymen of the Muses such as John Campbell made thousands a year – in his case, out of encyclopaedia writing, being, said Dr Johnson (a 'harmless drudge' of a lexicographer himself), 'the richest author who ever grazed the commons of literature'. Pot-boiling works of reference were now shrewd commercial speculations, as literature became just another trade. As Adam Smith saw it, 'Knowledge was now purchased in the same manner as shoes or stockings, from those whose business it is to make up and prepare for the market that particular species of goods.'

This age in which leisure and letters were gilded with commerce did not see the decline and fall of art, though William Blake prepared unsolicited graveside obsequies: 'Where any view of money exists, art cannot be carried on.' Blake believed that commerce killed creation, that his contemporary artists were traitors and that imagination's prophetic mission had been betrayed. But most writers demurred, thinking it natural that as in Augustan Rome or Renaissance Italy comfort should succour culture. The Liverpool banker William Roscoe wrote the life of Lorenzo the Magnificent to highlight the Anglo-Florentine entente between commerce and culture.

Leaving aside imponderables such as genius, artistic production and consumption blossomed in the Georgian age. Arts and crafts – such as cabinet-making in the hands of Chippendale and Sheraton, or interior decoration under the Adam brothers – reached exquisite pinnacles of elegance and delicacy. Elite taste had previously hired foreign painters, but now native talent – Hogarth, Reynolds, Gainsborough, Lawrence, Romney – nosed ahead. Continental skills still excelled in certain arts, but English working conditions and purses lured the maestros across the Channel. In music, Handel and J. C. Bach settled in England (they could do better freelancing than as foreign *Kapellmeister*), Mozart and Haydn did concert tours. Haydn, used to composing to Esterházy Court demands, valued London's artistic freedom: 'How sweet is some degree of liberty! I had a kind prince, but was obliged at times to be dependent on base souls. I often sighed for release and now have it in some measure.'

Everywhere people threw themselves into culture and expression, whether as performers or spectators, idling starers or cognoscenti. In many rural churches, wind bands still struck up the anthem, and tradesmen scraped together to play chamber music or sang out the people's muse: glees, catches, and bittersweet ballads of seduction. Lancashire textile communities became famous for their choirs, their craftsmen-composers of hymn-tunes and their fiddle-rounds for dancing. Exhibitions staged by Hogarth, raising money for the Foundling Hospital, drew huge crowds. And in high society, milord anglais on his Grand Tour pillaged the Continent for Old Masters (genuine, fake, or retouched), took an artist or two under his arm, and built and embellished at every opportunity. Frederick Hervey, prelate of Derry and creator of Ickworth, had such an itch for architecture that he was dubbed the 'edifying bishop'. Gentlemen of discernment clubbed together as connoisseurs of Antiquities in founding the Society of Dilettanti and lent their patronage when artists tried to raise their profession through bodies such as the Royal Academy. Lords put their personal stamp on the arts. The Earl of Burlington, returning from his Grand Tour, launched the English Palladian movement. In designing the grounds at Stowe, with their temples of Ancient and Modern Virtue and of British Worthies, Viscount Cobham used architectural motifs to construct a Whig pantheon to constitutional freedom. Horace Walpole, who devoted his life and fortune to the arts, experimented in taste – in his whimsical gothick home, Strawberry Hill, in his horror novel, *The Castle of Otranto* (1765), and in running his own printing press.

Art was rooted in opulence as in Medici Florence. England had a rich seedbed of skilled craftsmen: plasterers, stuccoists, woodcarvers, statuaries, gilders, etchers, plate-makers, and drawing-masters. Some blossomed into creative geniuses, and many leading artists started obscure. Gainsborough was the ninth child of a miller, Constable also a miller's son, Opie a carpenter's son. George Morland lived the life of a gipsy artist. Some got their training and breaks through being apprenticed to goldsmiths, cabinet-makers, or engravers. Hogarth, apprenticed to a silver-plate engraver, got going as a heraldic painter; Blake was schooled as an engraver. Many writers emerged out of other literary trades – Laurence Sterne was a clergyman and Samuel Richardson a master-printer turned author. And though precious connoisseurs liked to parade their discrimination, there was in fact no apartheid separating the fine and liberal arts from bread-and-butter craft skills, dividing pure art from commercial art. Top novelists such as Defoe and Smollett did not disdain hack-work: they could not afford to. Hogarth ranged from popular moralistic print series, such as *The Rake's Progress* and *Marriage à la Mode*, to noble portraits, as of the philanthropist Captain Coram.

Puritan animosity to art lost its edge. There were outbursts of High Church rage against the stage (spotlighted by Jeremy Collier), Evangelical thunder, and of course Dissenter scruples, but it was not an age of iconoclasm, nor was philistinism fashionable. Art was supercharged, every picture telling so many stories. For some, Hogarth's *Industrious* and *Idle Apprentices* were simply amusing, for others they really were wall-poster morality. Because visual images and the printed word were ubiquitous, and art was a mirror of life, all the world was a kind of stage. Street life was street theatre, for people played out their lives through rhetorical gesture and symbol, and saw life in fiction. The 'art' in the sashes and colours worn by mobs, the liberty caps, the symbolism of the British lion or the turnip (Jacobite shorthand for George I) paraded people's politics and faith. When theatre-goers heard Macheath in *The Beggar's Opera* exclaim, 'That Jemmy Twitcher should 'peach me, I own surprised me,' they saw mirrored there Lord Sandwich, betraying his former companion-in-rakery, John Wilkes. They did not just see it, but shouted it out, bringing the performance to a halt, and Sandwich was branded thereafter as Jemmy Twitcher. The hit success of *The Beggar's Opera*, of Hogarth's engravings, and of political cartoons in general lay in their being taken at different levels by a public used to reading between the lines.

The keynote of eighteenth-century art, its alliance with wealth, rang out in two main ways. First, craft-skill and artistry eddied all round material life: well-being meant there was more to read, more shows to go and see, more tutors, authors, performers, literati, all depending upon the public for their livelihood. Writers were less in the pockets of patrons. Patronage's decline was not due to the drying-up of private largesse. Rather the growth of an audience enabled the resourceful and talented to fare well without it. 'In the infancy of learning,' said Dr Johnson, 'we have some great men praised for it. This diffused it among others. When it becomes general, an author leaves the great, and applies to the multitude.' Hogarth declared his independence by penning a 'No Dedication' – 'Dedicated to nobody' – for a projected literary work. 'I paint for no lords,' asserted the truculent George Morland.

Livelihoods were in the offing. William Herschel, in his pre-astronomical career as a versatile professional musician in Bath in the 1760s, could make £500 a year out of composing, conducting concerts, and giving lessons. As a successful novelist Fielding pocketed £800 for *Amelia*. There was money in scholarship too. Dr Johnson received £1,575 for his *Dictionary*, William Robertson £4,500 for his *Charles V*, and Adam Smith £500 for the *Wealth of Nations*. Tobias Smollett became joint editor of a complete edition of Voltaire, panned books for the *Monthly Review*, and then in 1756 launched the *Critical Review*. He helped to prepare a seven-volume anthology of travel essays, for which he was to write 100 sheets in fifteen months at one and a half guineas a time. He contributed to *A Compendium of Voyages* for the same amount, and to the *Universal History*, and was involved in a *Complete History of England*, published between 1755 and 1758, for which he wrote 2,600 quarto pages in fourteen months for £2,000. Similarly, an ultra-fashionable painter such as Reynolds ('this man was hired to depress art', spat Blake) could receive a hundred guineas for a commission (as much as a small Old Master fetched). Dying worth over £100,000, Reynolds was buried in St Paul's with peers for pall-bearers.

Lions of culture were unashamed about turning art to advantage. Hogarth had a shrewd business nose, and Pope managed his own literary career, publishing a collected edition of his verse as early as 1717, collected editions of his letters in 1737 and of his prose in 1741, and editing Shakespeare in 1725. Even great writers had no compunction about conceiving of author-ship as a trade: 'No man but a blockhead,' dogmatized Dr Johnson, 'ever wrote, except for money.' The bid for profes-sional status amongst painters was marked by the founding of the Royal Academy in 1768.

Of course only the Olympians of the professions of the arts and letters got rich, but many got by. A competent professional painter could ask £15 or £20 for a head. Provincial towns such as Norwich and Birmingham began to support portrait painters, silhouettists, engravers, topographical print-makers, sign-writers, drawing-masters, enamelists, etc. By 1811 Bath had about twenty artists. Industry itself co-opted artists, Wedgwood employing talented draughtsmen such as Tassie. Top artists – Fuseli, Flaxman, Wright, Stubbs, and Blake himself – turned their hand to commercial and industrial art. Matthew Boulton believed industry's future hinged upon graceful design: with-out it manufacturers could not secure luxury markets.

Second, the power of the purse shaped the *content* of art and letters. Many commissions were to glorify rank, wealth, and status. Paintings of military and naval victories, sycophantic book dedications, heroic statues, funerary monuments, her-aldry, and monograms were art's tribute to riches (as Blake complained, 'portrait is everything'). The rich wanted their houses and grounds first designed and then painted, with rustics sentimentalizing the foreground. The taste, fostered by Capa-bility Brown, for more 'natural' landscaping reduced Nature herself, properly improved, to the property of the rich. William Kent's neat device of the ha-ha, the sunk fence round an estate's perimeter, made it look as though their lands went on for ever.

It was a halcyon age for production of top-quality decorative art for the wealthy – silverware, glass, plate, Delft, china. Yet the power of money itself stimulated aesthetic innovation. The century had begun with Classical canons entrenched in archi-tecture, verse, and drama, largely because aristocratic patrons and their intimate coteries lent their authority to such styles. Austere and dignified Augustanism and Palladianism clothed noble values. During the century, however, a wider moneyed clientele emerged, and – partly as a result – artists and writers themselves became more eclectic.

Classical rules crumbled at the edges; new tastes jostled alongside, making for 'neo-Classical' eclecticism and diversity. In architecture *nouveaux riches* nabobs, planters, and plutocrats splashed out into more ostentatious country-house styles. William Beckford, the rich and strange son of the City alderman, chose to construct (in collaboration with the architect Wyatt) a gothick abbey at Fonthill in Wiltshire, where he lived out a secluded fantasy life. Professional architects such as the Adam brothers, Chambers, or Wyatt, began to assert their own individual personalities. Grecian, Italianate, Chinese, Gothic, and crossbred amalgams of them proliferated. 'Decadent' asymmetry came into fashion. Landscaped gardens sprouted grottoes, follies, hermits' caves, and occasionally live hermits (one gave up the job after being pestered by tourists). *Fin-de-siècle* developers speculated in windswept hillside villas ('stareabouts'), mass-christened 'Belvedere', for merchants who wanted to be different. William Cowper noted a clergyman who 'enclosed his gooseberry bushes with a Chinese rail', and Horace Walpole's Strawberry Hill had 'embattled bookcases'. By 1800 more were building their own way.

In painting, regional styles asserted themselves. Joseph Wright of Derby created the genre of moonlit industrial scenes, East Anglian artists such as John Crome discovered clouds and atmosphere, exploiting the potential of water colours. Local styles sometimes rose to national importance, as in china ware. China manufactories were set up in 1745 at Chelsea, 1751 in Worcester and Derby, 1756 in Liverpool, 1768 in Plymouth, and 1771 in Bristol. Folklore, lays, and ballads became tear-jerking fads among the elite, Bishop Percy publishing his *Reliques* in 1765. Gothick tales of victims and horror, such as Matthew Lewis's *The Monk*, had their craze. By the end of the century, originality in art and appearance, traditionally condemned, found an eager audience. Novelty could even be hallowed as an expression of the English birth-right of Liberty, George Mason writing approvingly in 1768 of 'independency . . . in matters of taste, and in religion and government'. Fashions in clothes oscillated faster and further. The 1770s saw gargantuan head-pieces for women and macaroni styles for men. Yet in the wake of the French Revolution *citoyen* simplicity and ethnic garb were momentarily chic, whereas the Regency produced Beau Brummell's starched and austere dandyism.

The verso of this trend was greater self-expression and individuality on the part of the artist. Under patronage and within the code of Classicism the writer was expected to be self-effacing, adding his anonymous brick to the high cultural edifice of tradition. Time-honoured Classical forms and norms, such as the epic and mythological painting, had dictated expression: the writer was a kind of midwife. There was insistence not on uniqueness but on craft. As late as Dr Johnson's time, poets commonly polished up each other's verses. The rise of a wider, more varied and anonymous readership changed all that, encouraging writers and artists to carve distinctive niches. They were freer to experiment, because less often working to peer expectation or commission, but rather producing in anticipation of demand, even to satisfy their own sense of Creative Truth and personal authenticity. 'With patronage, what flattery! What falsehood!' said Dr Johnson. 'While man is in equilibrio, he throws truth among the multitude, and lets them take it as they please.' Yet freedom from noble patronage might take one out of the frying-pan into the fire. 'That a genius must write for a bookseller, or paint for an alderman!' shuddered Horace Walpole. By the end of the century, some – notably Romantic poets – were declaring independence from patrons and public alike, unable to bear servility any longer. 'The Enquiry in England,' huffed Blake, 'is not whether a man has talents and genius, but whether he is passive and polite and a virtuous ass and obedient to noblemen's opinions in art and science.' Blake despised toadying, consensus art: 'Without contraries, is no progression.'

Producing for an impersonal audience, writers explored their own sensibilities, dilemmas, and imaginations. Some cultivated proud, eye-catching eccentricity – such as Laurence Sterne, spinner of the solipsistic, sentimental, cock-and-bull fantasy, *Tristram Shandy*; others, such as the mawkish poet Cowper, found voice in a pre-Romantic introspection. Some began to identify with the poor and dispossessed, as did the impecunious Goldsmith in his anti-depopulation poem, *The Deserted Village*. Others, like the self-appointed artist-reformer Hogarth, strutted as moral missionaries. Yet Hogarth's career reveals the paradoxes of the artist flexing new muscles of independence. Embodiment of the Englishness of English art, Hogarth fumed at patronage and lordly taste, while courting it himself. He appealed to the public at large, yet despised it when it rejected him. Engraving for the many made him his fortune (*The Harlot's Progress* brought in £12,000), yet he sulked when connoisseurs found fault with his high art. Though raising burlesque to new heights, his ambition was to be regarded as a classical painter, master of the grand manner, hating yet envying creatures of the establishment such as William Kent.

The new audience, paying the piper and calling the tune, was broadly middle-class and middle-brow. For them drama shed the Frenchified gentlemanly-rakish taste of the Restoration, with its sly sexual innuendo, blasphemies, and cynicism (Addison had deplored 'the lewdness of the theatre'). Satire gave way to gentle and humorous comedy, sentiment replaced cynicism; morals and happy endings were wanted. A very English mongrel breed of musical comedy was born in plays such as George Colman's *Man and Wife*, *Man of Business*, and *Miss in her Teens* – light, domestic, and going with a swing. And kitchen-sink melodramas of bourgeois life, such as George Lillo's Hogarthian moral tragedy, *George Barnwell*, about an apprentice lured into murder by a drab, were staged. As Lady Mary Wortley Montagu complained, 'The heroes and heroines of the age are cobblers and kitchen wenches.' The emergent novel, with its psychological realism, its morality, and its sentiment, touched middle-class hearts.

For those above the poverty trap, the Georgian age was a tonic time to be alive. There were more goods and services available than ever before (the colonies and the poor helped to shoulder the cost). Things were cheap at least until the last third of the century. Popular culture's vigour was unflagging. Street life and the public domain remained vigorous and relaxed. New, capitalized forms of culture were growing up alongside, peddling commercialized art to wider audiences, but these had not yet supplanted or smothered older forms. Folk and elite, popular and patrician cultures were not rigidly stratified, nor did they become so. Polite society withdrew somewhat from

popular idioms into enclaves of its own, and some of course
exploited the superior pretensions of the polite. Thus the travelling scientific lecturer Benjamin Martin pandered to the elite
by portraying the mob as too dim to understand his performances:

> I remember, as my goods were once carrying into my lecture-room,
> at a certain town, the rabble crouded about the door, to know what it
> was; and one wiser than the rest immediately cries out, *'Tis a ZHOW
> come to town*; and what do we give to zee't? A GUINEA, replies the
> other. Z—nds, says the fellow, this is the D—l of a *Zhow*; why *Luck-
> man-zshure*, none but the *gentlevauke* can see this.

And, especially later in the century, magistrates began to throttle
certain popular enjoyments. But commercial entertainments
were by no means the kiss of death to folk ways and jollifica-
tions, and common culture resisted evisceration, having a
happy-go-lucky mind of its own. Ordinary people were able to
annexe those parts of high art and metropolitan life they valued.
When Lancashire artisans sang Handel, it was not a sell-out
to Culture, for they were moulding their own forms of musical
life. There was constant give-and-take between the popular
idiom and the cultural forms and technology of the polite.
In any case, folk culture never had been 'pure' and 'oral';
popular singers were as eager as any to have their music printed
and sold.

A neo-Puritan sobriety, the work-demon of industrialism,
and political panic were to come along and sap the cultured
stage and life out-of-doors of their exuberance and social com-
prehensiveness. But for most of the century these were just
clouds on the horizon.

7. *Changing Experiences*

Keeping your balance on the tightrope of life was tricky. The margins were slim between thriving and faltering, being reputable and being reprobate. Common folk were expected to obey superiors, look after themselves, and toe the economic and moral line; personal survival and the community demanded it. Misfits and failures could not count on sympathy or second chances, and the safety-net of the poor law, with its dependency and surveillance, could feel increasingly like a bed of nails. Yet sturdy independence was itself commonly prized. Working folks had to be self-reliant; and some made a virtue out of necessity and championed individualism, seizing opportunities in sectors of the make-or-break economy which provided scope for initiative, enterprise, and enrichment. There were lots of Robinson Crusoes who had made good and Moll Flanders who had married prudently. And, springing from the seedbeds of the Protestant conscience and the Enlightenment, values germinated saluting the sterling metal of individuality, conscience, and the rights of men – and of women and children.

To us, many aspects of Georgian England evoke a hard-bitten frontier post. The powers of the high and mighty were direct, self-defining, only sporadically checked by the state, little answerable to inspection or redress. It seemed a fact of life:

> How small, of all that human hearts endure
> That part which laws or kings can cause or cure

as Dr Johnson rued.

Though gentlemen were born with silver spoons in their mouths, he was a foolish commoner who thought he had a claim on society for a job, livelihood, or education. Owners, however, could expect to have free run of their property, fathers of their children, masters of their servants. The state did not deal in abstractions such as social justice, equality, or fraternity, though it was to protect positive legal rights. Indeed, the central offices of government were themselves cockpits of factional private interests. Laissez-faire ruled in many theatres of civil society long before it became the sacred cow of political economists. 'In England,' wrote Jeremy Bentham, 'abundance of useful things are done by individuals which in all other countries are done either by government or not at all' – for instance fire services, mad-houses, and even gaols were privately owned. If rough justice resulted, it was a price those who ruled the roost were willing that others might pay.

Foreigners found this society robust sometimes to a fault. Writing in 1725, the Swiss B. L. de Muralt thought the *mot juste* for the English was 'fierce'. It was assumed – if deplored – that holders of public office would be on the fiddle. After all, they had to buy the offices in the first place, and few were properly salaried. John Huggins bought the wardenship of the Fleet gaol in 1713 for £5,000 and milked it hard. It shocked no one that gaolers and lock-up keepers maltreated their charges, dunning them with exactions termed 'chummage' and 'garnish': 'pay or strip' was the watch-word to new prisoners. Public trustees such as grammar school or alms-house governors notoriously lined their pockets and promoted their relations. Discovering misappropriation of funds at a Winchester hospital, John Wesley commented, ' 'Tis a thing worthy of complaint when public charities designed for the relief of the poor are embezzled and depredated by the rich.' William Jones, vicar of Broxbourne, found his own parish clerk, a tailor, cutting up the parochial records to use the paper for taking measurements. But little was done to raise the standards of public life. Why? It was partly because reforming movements, such as the Societies for the Reformation of Manners, founded from 1699, failed to win public good-will. Resented for busy-bodying, they had declined by the 1740s. Before Evangelicals and Utilitarians gathered followers late in the century, there were no effective pressure-groups for probity, no popular clean-up-public-life brigades. In any case scruple in public life faced an uphill task. Public servants such as tipstaffs, turnkeys, or excise officers were either ill-paid or, like constables, unpaid. In many departments, the customs for instance, places and promotion went by nepotism and favour. No one would buy jobs such as that of gaol-keeper except to feather their own nests. It was left to a few private zealots, such as John Howard, to be scourges of prison and hospital conditions. (Howard, said Sir Samuel Romilly, 'made a visit to every prison and house of correction in England with invincible perseverance and courage'.) True, there were show-trials when enormities became too scandalous (as happened with Thomas Bambridge, warden of the Fleet prison in the 1720s, who took bribes to allow wealthy debtors to escape, and perpetrated cruelties) or when enemies came to power. And fickle public self-righteousness sometimes demanded scapegoats. In 1757, Admiral Byng was court-martialled and shot (*pour encourager les autres*) to assuage public wrath over the loss of Minorca. But there were few curbs on the powerful within their own bailiwicks, especially if they could pull strings in high places.

Respect for rights would not tolerate the sacrilege of 'interference'. A man's office, underlings, apprentices, or slaves, a general's regiment, were regarded as his property. This appeal to rights, liberty, and property often masked naked selfishness, and, as Goldsmith noted, could lead to a beggar-my-neighbour, devil-take-the-hindmost nihilism:

> That independence Britons prize too high
> Keeps man from man, and breaks the social tie;
> The self dependent lordlings stand alone,
> All claims that bind and sweeten life unknown.

And yet there was another side to the coin. It was in many ways an extraordinarily free and open society for those not too badly scarred by other people's freedom. Englishmen's championship of their freeborn rights ran deep and rang true. Foreigners were struck. 'I am here in a country which hardly resembles the rest of Europe,' wrote Montesquieu in 1729. 'This nation is passionately fond of liberty . . . every individual is independent.' He made the vital connexion: 'England has progressed the farthest of all peoples of the world in three important things: in piety, in commerce, and in freedom.' French philosophers, frequently unable to publish in their own country and occasionally imprisoned, envied English free-speech. Pastor Moritz contrasted English towns with Prussian: 'No walls, no gates, no sentries, no garrisons. You pass through town and village as freely and unhindered as through wide-open nature.' You could visit the Tower in London, but not the Bastille in Paris. Günerode observed: 'The Englishman breathes liberty, and anything that even appears to threaten this is an object of hatred to him and capable of driving him to all lengths!'

Law guaranteed Englishmen's freedoms and no one made light of its protection. The Revolutionary Settlement had confirmed parliamentary government, Habeas Corpus, and religious toleration. Statutory censorship of books and the press had ended with the lapse of the Licensing Act in 1695 (as late as 1683 Oxford University had publicly burned works by Hobbes, Baxter, and Milton). Characteristically, so far as the Government checked the press, it was not by direct censorship but by burdensome taxation following the Stamp Act of 1712. Admittedly in 1737, smarting from blistering satires against his regime, Walpole required that authors submit plays to the Lord Chamberlain for approval, and tried to close down all playhouses but Drury Lane and Covent Garden. But his ban was avoided – enterprising theatre managers instead staged 'concerts' with plays as interval pieces. From 1709 a succession of Copyright Acts guaranteed authors some property in their publications. The practice of parliamentary reporting in the press was pioneered from the 1730s, initially through the subterfuge of reporting on the 'Parliament of Lilliput'. In these and similar ways the individual could secure protection via the machinery of law.

Resistance to executive power was a reflex, localism the English creed. Schemes to extend standing armies and barracks, and centralize police and tax-gathering (such as Walpole's Excise Bill) often met ferocious and successful opposition: Dr Johnson defined excise as 'a hateful tax levied .. by wretches'. Foreigners were amazed at the obstreperousness of the common people in the face of their betters. On the highway, they would not melt before the rich. 'A man in court dress,' wrote Casanova, 'cannot walk in the streets of London without being pelted with mud by the mob, while the gentlemen look on and laugh.' The Prussian von Archenholz was offended:

The sentiment of liberty, and the ever-active protection of the laws, are the cause why the common people testify but little consideration for persons of quality, and even for persons in office, except they have gained their affection by affable and popular manners. That perfect equality which nature hath at all times established among men, presents itself but too forcibly to the minds of these haughty islanders, and neither dignity nor wealth are capable of effacing it. Even the Majesty of the Throne is often not sufficiently respected. The Englishman considers his sovereign only as the first of the magistrates in his pay.

Foreigners were surprised that the Quality actually paid respect to their inferiors, and in limited but significant ways were prepared to treat them man-to-man. In Madame du Bocage's epigrammatic exaggeration, 'In France we cringe to the great, in England the great cringe to the people.' Or as Madame Roland saw it:

The proudest Englishman will converse familiarly with the meanest of his countrymen; he will take part in their rejoicings. . . . It is true, that persons of higher rank find the common people necessary to realize their ambitious designs, and it is not uncommon, at elections, and those for members of Parliament especially, to see the lowest of citizens receiving letters from the most illustrious candidates, in which, in the most polite terms possible, they solicit the favour of their votes; and when these agree to their request, they are not long in receiving a letter, in which the candidate expresses his gratitude in the warmest terms. Have we not lately seen the Duchess of Devonshire lavishing, on such an occasion, not only gold, but kisses? That great popularity, enjoyed by the nobility which always so much astonishes strangers, is congenial to the constitution of a free state. Is it not the effects of this conduct in the English nobility that makes them the most enlightened of their rank in Europe?

Her account – however tendentious – contains a kernel of truth.

The English were passionately attached to their rights, enshrined in their law, Constitution, and political settlement. Historians, statesmen, and journalists constantly reminded them of the moral virtue of participation in a free commonwealth (even if, with diminishing electoral contests, few could directly do this). In Bishop Butler's words, 'In some other countries the upper part of the world is free, but in Great Britain the whole body of the people is free.' Or as Joseph Priestley, who as a Dissenter had a personal stake in the matter, put it:

> A sense of political and civil liberty, though there should be no great occasion to exert it in course of a man's life, gives him a constant feeling of his own power and importance, and is the foundation of his indulging a free, bold and manly turn of thinking, unrestrained by the most distant idea of control.

Moreover, the slogans of the age of reason, filtering down from the *literati*, fortified these freedoms. The thinkers of the Enlightenment championed individual affirmation and liberty. Liberal thinkers, from abstruse philosophers such as Locke to popularizers such as Addison and Goldsmith, spurned blind traditionalism, rejecting their fathers' Calvinist theology of original sin and the depravity of man, but equally despising 'Romish' irrationalism and prostration before Papal *ipse dixitism*. The intelligentsia's liberal and optimistic religion affirmed free-will, salvation for all, the goodness of mankind, and its capacity for progress. Each individual, they believed, had the right to moral autonomy and self-realization.

The well-tempered pursuit of happiness in the here-and-now became a leading theme of moral essayists. For many the trials of *Pilgrim's Progress* were over. The promised land of the pursuit of pleasure had been reached. Soame Jenyns intellectualized it:

> Happiness is the only thing of real value in existence: neither riches, nor power, nor wisdom, nor learning, not strength, nor beauty, nor virtue, nor religion, nor even life itself, being of any importance but as they contribute to its production.

Boswell experienced it: 'I felt a completion of happiness,' he wrote in 1772. 'I just sat and hugged myself in my own mind.'

Belief in the propriety of worldly happiness gave the leisured classes a licence to explore their own psyches. In some ways this was nothing new. From the Catholic confessional to anxious Protestant soul-searchings, Christianity had always required vigilant self-examination, the purging of sinful thoughts and the search for signs of grace. But traditional religious introspection had aimed to lead people out of this mire of egoism and slough of despond on to the straight and narrow of righteousness under priestly, ecclesiastical, or scriptural guidance. But when educated Georgian polite society examined itself, the tone was more subjective, even narcissistic. People dwelt more on their own psychological make-up, and indulged rather than quelled their humours and passions. Many of course found not the blueprint for bliss but the rich paradoxes of sentiment and an alluring but addictive melancholy (often called the English malady). Diary-keeping, silent reading, and perhaps greater privacy (as houses became subdivided into larger numbers of rooms) encouraged introspection.

More people rejected gloom and solemnity and affirmed the right to personal fulfilment. Georgian life bears witness to an infectious gaiety and sense of fun self-censored in certain ages. It was for example the apogee of humorous gravestones. Samuel Foote, the one-legged comedian, was thus memorialized in Westminster Abbey:

> Here lies one Foote, whose death may thousands save,
> For death has now one foot within the grave.

A social etiquette enjoining good humour was drummed home, the doctor Erasmus Darwin, for example, continually combating the 'drunkenness and hypochondriacism' of the idle rich and commending good spirits. 'In order to feel cheerful you must appear to be so.' When tedium threatened, the best therapy was activity. 'One must do something . . . otherwise one grows weary of life and becomes a prey to ennui.' For staving off the 'nihility of all things', work was – thought Darwin – 'an inexhaustible source of pleasurable activity'. Amongst Utilitarian moralists, virtue became reformulated as the 'greatest happiness' principle. Virtue and vice, argued Jeremy Bentham, are but 'the tendency of the action to promote or diminish the general happiness'.

The pursuit of personal gratification found expression in economic individualism, the dictum that each should use his own labour and capital to get on. 'The desire of bettering our condition,' commented Frederick Eden, 'is the predominant principle that animates the world,' which 'expanded into action, gives birth to every social virtue'. The economy was pictured as a hurly-burly of restless, ambitious men, eyes fixed on gain. As Nicholas Barbon had written in 1690:

> The wants of the mind are infinite. Man naturally aspires & his mind is elevated, his senses grow more refined & more capable of delight. His desires are enlarged, & his wants increase with his wishes, which is for everything which is rare, qualify his senses, adorn his body & promote ease, pleasure & pomp of life.

Seeing people as grasping and go-getting was nothing new. What was new was treating egoism and even greed not as sinful and anti-social but as natural and even admirable. Adam Smith, convinced of 'the uniform, constant & uninterrupted effort of every man to better his condition', believed that, providentially, by a hidden hand, untrammelled economic selfishness benefited the commonwealth. 'Private vices, public virtues': though Bernard de Mandeville's formula scandalized by its audacity, it was the secret rule by which many lived.

The overwhelming Christian and Classical sense of the depravity or limits of human nature melted into something more optimistic. Many cocked a snook at killjoy denunciations of the pleasures of the flesh, finding them morbid or splenetic. Puritans became Aunt Sallies in plays and novels, being seen not merely as ridiculous but as hypocrites (as, for instance, Joseph Surface in Sheridan's *School for Scandal*). Enlightenment England was for many a relaxed, emotionally frank breathing space after the strait-laced patriarchal solemnities of their parents' or grandparents' world (a brief interlude before the doubt, anxiety, and stridency which – though with some eighteenth-century roots – were to eat into the probity-conscious Victorians).

Most people took their pleasures in decent measured ways: in the quiet delights of a clay pipe or plum pudding, browsing through a sermon, tickling a trout, strolling with the family or paying calls on a Sunday, practising self-improvement, singing in a catch-club, patronizing a charity concert, or cultivating one's garden. But there was a tolerated hedonistic fringe. Shandyesque outlandishness had a free run. 'Surely our nation produces more originals than any other,' pondered Sir Horace Mann, aware that English eccentrics were proud of riding their hobby-horses. Major Peter Labeliere, dying in 1800, wanted to be buried head down, because the world itself had always been upside down. Edward Wortley Montagu, Jr, contracted two bigamous marriages, then turned Papist and Muslim (his father disinherited him). The trans-sexual Chevalier d'Éon was a welcome guest in polite homes. The rich built architectural follies and revived Druid cults.

There was an easy-going indifference to punctilio about English manners which foreigners found odd but attractive. Addison recommended an 'agreeable negligence' in matters of form (the Spectator Club was his parable, showing how men of divers humours could get along together). Later in the century Thomas Gisborne remarked how 'the stiffness, the proud and artificial reserve, which in former ages infected even the intercourse of private life, are happily discarded'. The German Moritz noted how when mixing in society officers 'do not go in uniform but dress as civilians'. Etiquette about dress became more relaxed. In the House of Lords, Lord Effingham had the appearance, according to Samuel Curwen, 'both in his person and dress of a Common Country Farmer, a great coat with brass buttons, frock fashion, his hair short, strait, and to appearance uncombed, his face rough, vulgar and brown, as also his hands'.

Personal relations became less suffocated by strict protocol. La Rochefoucauld observed:

Formality counts for nothing and for the greater part of the time one pays no attention to it. Thus, judged by French standards, the English, and especially the women, seem lacking in polite behaviour. All the young people whom I have met in society in Bury [St Edmunds] give the impression of being what we should call badly brought up: they hum under their breath, they whistle, they sit down in a large armchair and put their feet on another, they sit on any table in the room and do a thousand other things which would be ridiculous in France, but are done quite naturally in England.

Informality was aided by the metropolis's anonymity. 'There is no place in the world,' thought Pastor Wendeborn, 'where a man may lie more according to his own mind, or even his whim, than in London.' Hanoverian London was cosmopolitan, its migrant communities – Sephardic Jews, Huguenot refugees, Germans, Swiss – all finding their niche.

Amongst the affluent and leisured, sexuality thawed out.* The libido was liberated and erotic gratification was dissociated from sin and shame. Sex, thought Erasmus Darwin, is the 'chef d'œuvre, the masterpiece of nature', 'the purest source of human felicity, the cordial drop in the otherwise vapid cup of life'. John Wilkes's doggerel,

> Life can little else supply
> But a few good fucks and then we die

was glossed in Boswell's observation that there was no 'higher felicity on earth enjoyed by man than the participation of genuine reciprocal amorous affections with an amiable woman'. He practised what he preached. While a man-about-town in 1763 he performed many sexual feats, amongst others 'solacing his existence ... with a strong, plump, good-humoured girl called Nanny Baker' in St James's Park, and taking a whore (wearing a condom) on the recently opened Westminster Bridge:

At the bottom of the Haymarket I picked up a strong, jolly young damsel, and taking her under the arm I conducted her to Westminster Bridge, and then in armour complete did I engage her upon this noble edifice. The whim of doing it there with the Thames rolling below us amused me very much.

But sacrificing to Venus led to dosing with mercury, for Boswell contracted 'Signor gonorrhoea' at least seventeen times.

Sex was positively prescribed on medical and psychological grounds, for retention of semen was believed harmful. 'I was afraid I was going to have an attack of gout the other day,' wrote Lord Carlisle. 'I believe I live too chaste. It is not a common fault with me.' James Graham's Temple of Love at the Adelphi combined health club and brothel. Bagnios – high-class brothels – had the beneficial side-effect of getting wenching men to bathe.

Sex was on public view (its very earthiness perhaps forestall-ing the Romantic idealization of love which accompanies re-

---

* There is much less evidence for lower-class attitudes towards sexuality, as distinct from lower-class patterns of procreation and family formation.

pression and sublimation). The vicarious eroticism of bawdy songs and pornographic prints was part of the landscape, raising few eyebrows. Francis Place recorded the lewd songs common in his youth (though he thought these were disappearing by the early nineteenth century):

> One night as I came from the play
> I met a fair maid by the way;
> She had rosy cheeks and a dimpled chin
> And a hole to put poor Robin in.

The master-cartoonist, Rowlandson, engraved pornographic prints, some for the Prince Regent (Gillray drew obscene cartoons *of* the prince). Politicians suffered scatological satire without respite, Pitt the Younger being lampooned as the Bottomless Pitt, Walpole and George II, pictured with breeches down, farting and defecating. The leading feature of female fashion was a very conspicuous décolletage. Erotic literature multiplied almost unchecked, from John Cleland's *Fanny Hill* (which netted the publisher, Ralph Griffiths, £10,000) to sentimental titillating titles such as *The Innocent Adultress*, *Venus in the Cloister*, or *Cuckoldom Triumphant* and salty accounts of adultery trials. Newspaper advertisements peddled sexual services from gigolos to aphrodisiacs, VD cures, and abortifacients, and window-shopping gallants could buy prostitutes' directories, such as Jack Harris's *The Whoremonger's Guide to London*. Sexual prowess became a matter of public pride. The orgiastic demoniacs of the Hell-Fire Club, or Medmenham Abbey, who included Lord Sandwich and the Rev. John Kidgell, chaplain to the Earl of March, did not lose caste. 'Wilkes and libertinism' was as popular as 'Wilkes and liberty'. A Whitby collier of the 1760s was named *The Free Love*.

Sexual permissiveness was, of course, a man's world. Yet, at least in racy London society, ladies were assumed to possess strong sexual appetites and the right to their gratification. They were not kept prudishly innocent or ignorant, for sex manuals, such as *Aristotle's Masterpiece*, seem to have circulated widely amongst women (and maybe even youngsters: Francis Place read it while a schoolboy). London waxworks mounted 'educational' displays of female reproductive organs. And the

Nottingham Weekly Courant of 26 November 1717 had an advertisement for:

Any able young Man, strong in the Back, and endow'd with a good Carnal Weapon, with all the Appurtenances thereunto belonging in good Repair, may have Half A Crown per Night, a Pair of clean Sheets, and other Necessaries, to perform Nocturnal Services on one Sarah Y-tes, whose Husband having for these 9 Months past lost the Use of his Peace-Maker, the unhappy Woman is thereby driven to the last Extremity.

Whether spoof or genuine, Georgian frankness is unmatched. In this more relaxed atmosphere, sexual jealousies were held in check. High-society *ménages à trois* were quite common, wives and mistresses, lovers and wittols often maintaining studiously polite terms (a wife anxious not to conceive again might welcome her husband taking a mistress). The Duke of Devonshire had three children by the Duchess and two by Lady Elizabeth Foster, who lived under the same roof; for her part the Duchess had a child by Lord Grey. A man of the world did not automatically challenge his wife's lover to a duel, but he expected understanding from others. Horace Walpole wrote of Archbishop Blackburne:

I often dined with him – his mistress, Mrs Cruwys, sat at the head of the table, and Hayter, his natural son by another woman, and very much like him, at the bottom, as chaplain. Hayter was afterwards Bishop of London. I have heard, but do not affirm it, that Mrs Blackburne, before she died, complained of Mrs Cruwys being brought under the same roof.

One story I recollect, which showed how much he was a man of this world, and which the Queen herself repeated to my father. On the King's last journey to Hanover, before Lady Yarmouth came over, the Archbishop being with her Majesty, said to her: 'Madam, I have been with your minister Walpole, and he tells me that you are a wise woman, and so do not mind your husband's having a mistress.'

Polite society did not fear it was being eaten away by the worm of sexual intrigue (though it loved scandal).

There was a good deal of sexual promiscuity which didn't result in ostracism. It seems to have been taken for granted that maid-servants were fair game for advances; the gentlemen were thought gallants so long as they made arrangements for resulting bastards. Though women were clearly victims of unwanted attentions, many seem to have been compliant or active. Young William Hickey was first seduced at the age of ten by a maid, Nanny Harris. One of his early memories was of waking one morning to find himself between Nanny's legs, 'with one of my hands upon the seat of love where I have no doubt she had placed it'. Men such as Hickey and Boswell found no difficulty in getting sexual partners amongst respectable women, quite apart from prostitutes. Actresses and dancers were assumed to be sexually easy, and many women obviously felt better off being kept as mistresses by gentlemen than being servants or wives. Classy demi-mondaines and courtesans, such as Grace Dalrymple and Fanny Murray, won fame and respect, becoming much-prized models for leading painters. Women of easy virtue were not automatically pariahs. In the 1780s Francis Place's master was a London leather-breeches-maker, Mr France, who had three daughters.

His eldest daughter was and had been for several years a common prostitute. His youngest daughter, who was about seventeen years of age, had genteel lodgings where she was visited by gentlemen; and the second daughter ... was kept by a captain of an East India ship, in whose absence she used to amuse herself as such women generally do.

Evidently neither Place, nor France, nor the women were embarrassed by this situation. It was commonplace for public figures to keep mistresses and to walk out in public with them, as the Duke of Grafton did with Nancy Parsons.

Though bastardy still carried a stigma, bearing children out of wedlock could be winked at in smart society. Lady Mary Wortley Montagu wrote:

I deplore the unpopularity of the married state, which is scorned by our young girls nowadays, as once by the young men. Both sexes have discovered its inconveniences, and many feminine libertines may be found amongst young women of rank. No one is shocked to hear that 'Miss So and So, Maid of Honour, has got nicely over her confinement.'

Bastards were often brought up alongside legitimate children, publicly acknowledged by their fathers. The son for whom Lord Chesterfield wrote his letters was a bastard. Dr Erasmus

Darwin set up his two illegitimate daughters as the governesses of a school, noting that natural children often had happier unbringings than the legitimate line. The pious Joseph Addison sired a child on the Countess of Warwick, and Lady Harley reputedly had children by so many men that her brood was known as the Harleian miscellany. Similarly, the tenth Earl of Pembroke fathered children on two mistresses. His illegitimate son became close friends with his heir and with the Countess (who however insisted that the bastards should not take the family name of Herbert). Bastards might even marry well. The illegitimate daughter of Sir Edward Walpole married Lord Waldegrave, and on his death, George III's brother, the Duke of Gloucester.

Despite Hogarth's print sequence, not all harlots' progresses were tragic, Mrs Hayes, the society brothel keeper, retiring reputedly worth £20,000. Great men sometimes married their mistresses. The Earl of Coventry married Mary Gunning, and the Duke of Hamilton her sister, Elisabeth. The reverse even happened, though rarely. Lady Henrietta Wentworth, Lord Rockingham's sister, wed her footman.

When profligates were discreet and genteel, people turned a blind eye even to great vices. Mrs Theresa Berkeley ran a flagellants' brothel in Charlotte Street, and there was at least one female flagellants' club in late-century London. Though buggery remained a capital offence, it was no secret that London harboured sodomites' clubs and brothels ('molly houses') and well-connected male homosexual activity ran little risk of prosecution. Some notorious homosexuals, however, such as William Beckford, found it prudent to go abroad or to retire to rural privacy, and plebeian homosexuals, especially in the armed forces, risked being savagely punished (there were few cultural outlets for passionate attachments between males).

Masked balls, such as those staged in Soho by Casanova's one-time lover Mrs Cornelys, were well-known fronts for pick-ups - 'the whole Design of the libidinous Assembly seems to terminate in Assignations and intrigues'. London teemed with brothels and other pleasure domes such as Mrs Hayes's serail in Pall Mall, whose floor-show included a Tahitian 'Love Feast' between twelve nymphs and twelve youths, and naked dancing. Roués could get a whore for 6d., though Casanova thought that a night with a high-class courtesan at a bagnio cost 6 guineas. London had in excess of 10,000 prostitutes, openly plying in the theatre and on the street. 'Women of the town,' wrote John Macky

> seem to give the magistrates of London very little trouble. Yet they are more numerous than at Paris, and have more liberty and effrontery than at Rome itself. About nightfall they range themselves in a file in the foot-paths of all the great streets, in companies of five or six, most of them dressed very genteelly. The low-taverns serve them as a retreat, to receive their gallants in: in those houses there is always a room set apart for this purpose. Whole rows of them accost passengers in the broad day-light; and above all, foreigners. This business is so far from being considered as unlawful, that the list of those who are any way eminent is publicly cried about the streets: this list, which is very numerous, points out their places of abode.

Although disgruntled clients sometimes avenged themselves on pilloried bawds, attempts by Societies for the Reformation of Manners to hound whores off the streets got no general backing.

In this relaxed – or lax – society, in which neither state, Church, nor opinion was very vigilant in policing the morals of the urban and the moneyed, it was affluent males who enjoyed greatest latitude. But other people's claims to a place in the sun, reflected in such slogans as the birth-right of the free-born Englishman, the rights of man (and – as Mary Wollstone-craft claimed – of *woman*), and the greatest happiness of the greatest number, were also being acknowledged. Opinion-leaders liked to see themselves as humane and sympathetic, sensitive to the autonomy and feelings of others. There was a lot of breast-beating about the plight of underlings such as servants and unfortunates such as abandoned mothers. Where once there had been blanket stigmatization of malefactors, some observers instead put them under the microscope (*what* made people go to the bad?). Novelist and magistrate Henry Fielding argued it was beside the point to condemn young delinquents, for pauper boys become 'thieves from necessity', and 'their sisters are whores from the same cause ... Who can say these poor children had been prostitutes through vicious-ness? No. They are young, unprotected and of the female sex, therefore they become the prey of the bawd and the debauchee.' Following Rousseau, many vented disgust – some sincerely, some climbing on the band-waggon – at the gilded superficialities of smart society. The blessings of Nature, artlessness, and simplicity could be conjured up as counter-attractions – endorsing the common 'primitivist' view that the labouring classes were 'natural' souls, backs bowed under an artificial, corrupt civilization. Even the *Gentleman's Magazine* pondered in 1782:

The collier, the clothier, the painter, the gilder, the miner, the makers of glass, the workers in iron, tin, lead, copper, while they minister to our necessities or please our tastes and fancies, are impairing their health, and shortening their days.

Views such as these smoothed the path for philanthropists such as Jonas Hanway, campaigning on behalf of society's victims:

Let the subject be never so poor, humanity and religion do not therefore change their nature; and we ought no more to suffer a child to die for the want of the common necessaries of life, though he is born to labour, than one who is the heir to a dukedom.

Yet caution is needed. Tears for the exploited, the unfortunate, and the afflicted flowed freely, but sympathies were often more impressive in word than in deed; and words cost little. Pity proved the superior sensibilities of the tender-hearted and massaged the conscience. Acts of humanity were spiritual securities in an age of lax collective religious practice. Some were impressed: 'Religion in England,' wrote Prévost, 'in towns, and even in the smallest villages finds its expression in hospitals for the sick, homes of refuge for the poor and aged of both sexes, schools for the education of the children.' Yet tender-heartedness was often deflated as humbug. 'We live in an age when humanity is in fashion,' snarled Sir John Hawkins in 1787. But though contemporaries were not slow to indict the poverty of humanitarianism, attitudes and practices did change.

Children – the largest captive audience – were notably affected. Hitherto children had attracted little attention, despite or perhaps because of their vast numbers: about a quarter of the population was under ten. Childhood was traditionally a stage of life passed over without much notice. Calvinism had reckoned souls sinful from birth, needing to be beaten into obedience and reason. Not being civilized or rational, they were no company for adults. But this all changed. From Locke to Rousseau (whose educational writings got much lip-service) liberal religion and Enlightenment pedagogy argued for the natural innocence of children and hence their potential for rational thought and civilized behaviour. In polite society at least, children's feelings, cuteness, and wishes came to command some respect. Because within this model of childhood it would be society – if anything – that corrupted them, the psychology of parent-child and teacher-child relations needed care. Most important of all, affluent parents began taking pride in their offspring. For instance, child portraits became suddenly popular (families would pay Reynolds up to £150 for one). Couples became more child-oriented. 'If there could be found a fault in the conduct of my mother towards her children,' wrote 'Perdita' Reynolds, 'it was that of too unstinted indulgence, a too tender care.' Richard Steele said of his son, 'We are most intimate play-fellows.' Travellers such as Henri Misson found it remarkable:

They have an extraordinary Regard in *England* for young Children, always flattering, always caressing, always applauding what they do; at least it seems so to us *French* Folks, who correct our Children as soon as they are capable of reasoning, being of the Opinion, that to keep them in Awe is the best Way to give them a good Turn in their Youth.

Though groups such as Wesleyans kept faith with flogging, up-to-the-minute parents bullied their children less with the rod, trying reason, coaxing, and kindness. Infants were hugged and petted more. Affection moderated authority. Pastor Moritz noted, 'Parents here in general, nay, even those of the lower classes, seem to be kind and indulgent to their children; and do not, like our common people, break their spirits too much by blows and sharp language.' When Henry Fox was unhappy at his son's long hair, 'You gave me hopes that if I desired it, you would cut it,' he pleaded. 'I will, dear Ste, be much obliged if you will.' But Fox was notoriously liberal. When his son Charles James went to hurl his watch on the floor, 'If you must, I suppose you must' was his response. Lord Chesterfield began his letters to his son with the egalitarian and respectful 'Dear

Friend'. Symbolizing childhood's new privileged state, children came to be dressed less as miniature grown-ups, being allowed to wear looser, less formal clothes. Gentlefolks started addressing their little ones as Sukey, Jackee, or Dickee (though first-born were less likely to be given pet names). Jane Austen's father wrote at her birth in 1775, 'she is to be Jenny ... as like Henry or Cassy is to Neddy'. Children became important foci of consumption, the toy market in particular increasing by leaps and bounds. Books, playthings, and educational aids flooded on to the market. Old games such as hoops, trap-ball, and barley-break were joined by instructional toys such as Wallis's *Educational Cards for the Amusement of Youth* (1785), stuffed with morals such as:

> The rocking horse pursues the course
> Directed by your hand.
> Children should thus their friends obey
> And do what they command.

The new attention to children defies easy evaluation. Polite society 'discovered' childhood, but it was adults who did the discovering. In some ways children became merely superior pets and new objects of consumption for eager capitalists. The myth of childhood innocence developed ('where ignorance is bliss,' wrote Thomas Gray, ' 'tis folly to be wise'), but is it less pernicious than the idea of the child as originally sinful? The new myth made children childish and adults serious. Children, previously kept at arm's length by their parents, now had their lives invaded with intrusive grown-up ideas of what was good for them, such as Mrs Barbauld's prim learning books, full of 'geography and natural history', which – complained Charles Lamb – 'have banished all the old classics of the nursery'.

From the eighteenth century, children have become a focal point of attention, their differentness, autonomy, and rights acknowledged. The same is true for other groups. As the plight of the poor worsened and pioneer social investigators, such as Frederick Morton Eden, studied them, more concern was expressed. Making sport of the deformed and the mad became offensive: they were not for laughter, but for pity and treatment. Sophie von la Roche noted that whereas Damiens, the would-be assassin of Louis XV, was tortured to death in Paris, George III's attempted assassins were pronounced insane and stuck in Bedlam. The cult of the noble savage gained ground, especially when South Sea voyagers such as Captain Cook returned with such handsome prize specimens as Omai and reports of an Edenic Polynesia. Crude white Europocentrism was jolted by awareness of majestic civilizations such as the Chinese or Indian holding other values. A campaign was launched against the slave trade, bearing fruit in 1807. Wedgwood struck a medallion with the legend, over a chained blackamoor slave, 'Am I not a man and brother?' And the English, though already doting on their pets (one thinks of Hogarth's pug, of Gray's cat Selena, and of Dr Johnson keeping vigil, dosing his sick cat with oysters), at last began to question their heartless treatment of animals. In 1751 Hogarth produced a print sequence exposing cruelty to animals, about which he wrote:

The Four Stages of Cruelty were done in hopes of preventing in some degree that cruel treatment of poor animals which makes the streets of London more disagreeable to the human mind than anything whatever, the very describing of which gives pain ... It gratifies me highly and there is no part of my works of which I am so proud, and in which I feel so happy as in the series of the Four Stages of Cruelty, because I believe the publication of them has checked the diabolical spirit of barbarity which I am sorry was once so prevalent in this country.

Other barbaric prejudices were softening. Jew-baiting probably declined. Francis Place reported in the 1790s how Jews who within his memory had been 'hooted, hunted, cuffed, pulled by the beard and spat upon', now were 'safe', and he believed that 'the few who would be disposed to insult them merely because they are Jews would be in danger of chastizement from the passers-by and of punishment from the police'.

Yet evaluating this growing humanitarianism is complicated. In part, society's victims wrung fresh pity and guilt because they were being more savagely exploited than before. Work-beasts were driven harder and the slave trade became an abomination. In transit, sick slaves would sometimes be thrown overboard alive *en masse* for the insurance. Callousness caused needless suffering. Other nations cleaned chimney flues with brushes; England with climbing boys. Unguarded machinery in new factories reaped a grim harvest of young limbs. Moreover, as defenders of the *status quo* remarked, those who campaigned most righteously against the slave trade were often 'slave-driving' manufacturers at home, many of them Quakers.

For sympathy was selective. The labouring classes and the poor *en bloc* received little relief, whereas charities were directed to improve the lot of harmless sub-groups and token 'unfortunates', such as orphans, child prostitutes, or disabled servicemen, who, thus labelled, presented no complications. In any case, apart from certain laws safeguarding debtors, practically no *legislation* was passed to protect the weak.

And ironically humanitarianism, while apparently dignifying objects of pity, could demean them. Children of well-off families won attention, but at the cost of rococo miniaturization. Freed slaves were prettified as personal servants and imprisoned in condescending nicknames such as Zeno, Socrates, or Pompey. Care often meant surveillance and humanitarianism could often serve as a way of extending control.

As the century wore on, the English became more aware they were living through and participating in momentous and accelerating changes. Most were proud of what they saw (and seeing them they wanted them recorded: demand surged for prints of landscapes and townscapes, houses, prize bulls, and pedigree families). In the 1720s Defoe admiringly wrote:

In travelling thro' England, a luxuriance of subjects presents itself to our view. Wherever we come, and which way soever we look, we see something new, something significant, something well worth the traveller's stay and the writer's care . . .

(And as Hill has commented, with Defoe, 'We are already in the modern world, the world of banks and cheques, budgets, the stock exchange, the periodical press, coffee-houses, clubs, coffins, microscopes, shorthand, actresses and umbrellas.')

Times were changing. Harking back to Defoe, the *Gentleman's Magazine* noted in 1754: 'Were the same persons who made a full tour of England 30 years ago, to make a fresh one now they would find themselves in a land of enchantment.

England is no more like to what England was than it resembles Borneo or Madagascar.' The mask of Mars was shed: sword-wearing in public became less common, more a decoration. The gates of London – Cripplegate, Ludgate, Aldgate, Moorgate, Newgate – were demolished in the 1760s and 1770s to make room for the flood tide of traffic. Man conquered the air for the first time. In 1785 Horace Walpole nonchalantly observed, 'Three more balloons sail today' – it was the year of the first cross-channel flight, and soon express coaches were nicknamed 'balloon coaches'. Like everything else, ballooning was instantly commercialized, with admission fees charged for watching ascents. Needing to be up-to-the-minute, people became newsmongers. Ephemeral reading – newspapers, pamphlets, periodicals – jostled classics such as the Bible, Horace, and *Foxe's Book of Martyrs*.

Improvement was all around. In 1754 getting from Newcastle to London had taken six days; by 1783 it took just three. The four and a half days needed to get from Manchester to London in 1754 had been slashed to twenty-eight hours by 1788. And there was eager expectancy – with some, foreboding – about the future. In the 1790s Frederick Morton Eden thus saluted mechanical advances:

> With regard to mechanical knowledge, it is probable that we are still in our infancy, and when it is considered that, fifty years ago, many inventions for abridging the operations of industry, which are now in common use, were utterly unknown, it is not absurd to conjecture that, fifty years hence, some new contrivance may be thought of in comparison with which the steam engine and spinning jennies, however wonderful they appear to us at present, will be considered as slight and insignificant discoveries.

The English prided themselves on being practical and down-to-earth. 'Our business here,' Locke had taught, 'is not to know all things, but those which concern our conduct.' Inventions were introduced to abridge labour, speed production, and by-pass bottlenecks. Fertile brains such as Erasmus Darwin and Richard Lovell Edgeworth invented in the way others doodled: carriages, oil-lamps, agricultural tools, canal locks poured from their heads. Early in the century Charles

Povey conceived of a newspaper totally dependent on advertisements, a salvage corps, a water-bomb for putting out fires, and a typewriter. It was a remarkable century for technological change. In textiles there were the flying shuttle, the spinning jenny, the water frame, Crompton's mule, and Cartwright's power loom. Newcomen's sturdy steam pump drained mines, while Watt's steam engine, with its separate condenser, saved fuel and in its rotary form was adapted to providing power for driving machinery. Smelting iron with coke was one way abundant fossil fuels replaced scarce organic substances in production. Water-wheel engineering became a model of experimental efficiency, and John Smeaton perfected lighthouse design. In 1758 the 'Improved Birmingham Coach' had blazoned on its side 'FRICTION ANNIHILATED'. By 1801 Richard Trevithick had put a steam carriage on the road. Strides were also made in scientific instruments. John Harrison's marine chronometer solved the age-old navigational problem of gauging longitude.

Innovation was at a premium. In 1757 Josiah Tucker wrote about Birmingham, 'almost every Master & Manufacturer hath a new invention of his own, & is daily improving on those of others'. 'The English are great in practical mechanics,' wrote Louis Simond at the beginning of the nineteenth century. 'In no country in the world are there, perhaps, so many applications of that science, I might say, of that instinct of the human species.' As seer, William Blake by contrast distrusted the machine as all too emblematic of the modern world: 'it is destructive of humanity and of art: the word Machination'.

The most prophetic inventions were those multiplying power. In 1783 James Watt coined 'horse power' as a measure for his steam engines (significantly the horse was still the index of power), and his partner, Matthew Boulton, bragged to Boswell, 'I sell Sir what all the world desires: POWER.' 'The people in London, Manchester and Birmingham are all steam mill mad,' Boulton wrote in 1781. 1788 saw Symington's first workable steamship. Erasmus Darwin prophesied

> Soon shall thy arm, UNCONQUER'D STEAM! afar
> Drag the slow barge, or drive the rapid car;
> Or on wide-waving wings expanded bear
> The flying-chariot through the fields of air.

> – Fair crews triumphant, leaning from above,
> Shall wave their flattering kerchiefs as they move,
> Or warrior-band alarm the gaping crowd,
> And armies shrink beneath the shadowy cloud.

Scores of *domestic* gadgets also came in tow: lucifer matches, umbrellas, the modern tooth-brush (designed by William Addis), chimneys built not to smoke, patent kitchen ranges, alarm clocks which automatically lit candles, bell-pulls, dumb-waiters, ventilators, the argand oil-lamp (a French invention), clockwork cradles, Pears soap, Friar's Balsam, and Mr Schweppe's mineral waters – all found their way into the home. Tom Paine, later political revolutionary, experimented with smokeless candles and iron suspension bridges. Prototypes of fountain pens, telescopic candlesticks, roller skates, and patent exercisers appeared. Condoms were new to England. The heavy, dangerous, overhead London street signs were dismantled. From the 1770s, the numbering of houses began, and was insisted upon in London streets from 1805. In 1778 Joseph Bramah patented his superior ball-cock WC and had marketed 6,000 by 1797. In Nelson's house at Merton, each of the five bedrooms had a WC fitted in the adjoining dressing-room, together with a washstand and bowl, lead tank and tap, and a bath filled by servants.

The wealthy festooned their houses and grounds with exotica – pet monkeys, parrots, and goldfish, fuchsias, acacias, and pineapples; veronicas from the Falkland Islands, camellias from Japan, and jade ornaments from the Orient, imperial expansion also leading to experiments with clothes and building styles. Foreigners tasted delicacies unknown in England before, from sardines and kippers to Stilton cheese. The father of all convenience foods, the sandwich, appeared. 'The slices of bread and butter given you at tea are thin as poppy leaves,' drooled Pastor Moritz, in his most reverent Anglophile tone, 'but there is a way of roasting slices of buttered bread before the fire which is incomparable. One slice after another is taken and held to the fire with a fork till the butter soaks through the whole pile of slices. This is called *toast*.' In 1751 England introduced – at long last – the Gregorian Calendar. Old London Bridge was pulled down in 1760. Street lighting and sanitation improved. The

world's first iron bridge spanning a river was erected at Coal-
brookdale in 1776. The first national medical register appeared
in 1774. The Ordnance Survey was founded in 1791. English
increasingly replaced Latin as the language of administration.
From early in the century London had its own local penny post
and other towns followed. Ralph Allen pioneered a scheme of
crossroads to guarantee that all parts of the country were well
covered by the post. Later John Palmer replaced post-boys with
mail-coaches to ensure greater safety and punctuality. Change
was everywhere.

Accompanying this crescendo of inventions and improvements, a collective desire for advance – rational, technical, scientific, and industrial – caught the public imagination. Man's
conquest of Nature was trumpeted. Josiah Wedgwood the potter captured the faith in scientific method: 'Everything yields to
experiment.' His friend Joseph Priestley stressed science's practical side: 'Knowledge, as Lord Bacon observes, being power,
the human powers will in fact be enlarged; nature, including
both its materials and its laws, will be more at our command.'
Groups such as the Society of Arts (1754) were founded to
activate improvements. This voluntary society, subscribed to
by the fashionable, gave rewards to inventors on condition they
didn't patent their inventions. Prizes were offered mainly for
improvements in agriculture, the liberal arts, and handicrafts:
not until the last decades of the century did transforming heavy
industry seem so valuable. Agricultural improvement societies
sprouted – there were about fifty by 1800, awarding prizes for
improved tools, good management, and trusty labourers and
some publishing their own journals. Itinerant lecturers spread
the taste for scientific knowledge.

In the last third of the century, the Royal Society of London
was joined by new provincial scientific societies, such as the
informal Lunar Society of Birmingham and the Manchester
Literary and Philosophical Society (founded 1781), providing
a local forum for knowledge and culture, drumming up interest
in science and advancing manufactures. Their members (all
male) – such as James Keir the glass manufacturer and William
Withering the doctor – united amateur love of science and
involvement in practical improvements in manufactures, hus-

bandry, and medicine under the banner of a humanitarian ethos, which they saw best served by the spread of capitalist employment. Although in the metropolis the Royal Society dozed, up and down the country thousands of spare-time devotees made observations, collected, and experimented. In 1798 Malthus could celebrate the

great and unlooked for discoveries that have taken place of late years in natural philosophy, the increasing diffusion of general knowledge from the extension of the art of printing, the ardent and unshackled spirit of inquiry that prevails in the lettered and even unlettered world.

The eyes of earlier generations had been trained on the past – for visions of arcadian innocence, for authority and precedent, for the truths of the Apostolic Church or the prescriptions of the British Constitution. The eighteenth-century gaze focused much more upon the present – and then out into the future. Optimism mobilized faith in progress and human perfectibility, and made people eager to try new ways, from infant care to crop rotations, and sometimes novelty for its own sake. Even the fastidious Gibbon deigned to 'acquiesce in the pleasing conclusion that every age of the world has increased and still increases the real wealth, the happiness and knowledge and perhaps the virtue of the human race'.

Of course the dynamo of change had its diehard critics, who thought new-fangled ways were so much flam. 'The age is running mad after innovation,' fumed Dr Johnson over the abolition of public executions at Tyburn in 1783. 'All the business of the world is to be done in a new way. Tyburn itself is not safe from the fury of innovation.' (The main reason in fact for ending public hangings there was that Tyburn Tree adjoined the newly smart residential Mayfair, and swarming riff-raff lowered the tone.) And, of course, much didn't change at all, traditional ways retaining their vigour. Customs and folkways, magic and pagan practices remained deep-rooted. Belief in fate, evil spirits, spells, and omens made sense, particularly of countryfolks' lives, for the sophistries of polite culture had little to offer gnarled husbandmen (Wesley's hellfire meant more). Suicides continued to be buried at crossroads, stakes through their hearts. The Blundell family, Lancashire gentry though they

were, still cut their hair at full moon. Babies' cauls, used as
protective charms, still fetched high prices. Though social statistics and political arithmetic made headway, tabulating information on diet, income, and population, credulity still had its
day. In 1771 a newspaper reported a seventy-five-year-old gan-
der in Worcester. In any case complacent 'modernity' was often
only skin-deep. Sophisticated London panicked when minor
earth tremors struck in 1750 and 1755. Thousands fled the
metropolis, momentarily giving up their vices to placate the
angry God. George II called a public fast, and Bishop Sherlock's
Pastoral Letter, proving the quakes were divine punishment of
London's fleshpots, sold 100,000 copies.

In the absence of dramatic medical breakthroughs, old wives'
herbal medical wisdom survived – dung tea, crabs' eyes, vipers'
flesh, stewed owl, the eyes of pike as a specific for toothache.
'To Cuire t' Aguie,' scrawled James Brindley in his pocket
book, 'Drink your own Youren whan warm.' 'I drank snails'
tea for breakfast,' wrote the Hon. John Byng, 'for my chest is
very sore.' When Parson Woodforde had a stye on his eye, he
heard

that the eyelid being rubbed by the tail of a black cat would do it much
good, if not entirely cure it, & having a black cat a little before dinner
I make a trial of it, & very soon after dinner I feel my eyelid much
abated of the swelling.

(The cat had to be black because of residual witchcraft associations.) And, of course, there was no reason why the new should
surpass the old. Traditional female midwives were challenged
by the fancy new male *accoucheur*, armed with forceps: but
forceps, if dirty, or clumsily handled, did more harm than good.
Not all the 'new' was new anyway. Physicians 'discovered'
digitalis for treating heart conditions: as foxglove, it was a folk
remedy. Doctors in the Manchester infirmary took up cod-liver
oil, but it had long been used by Lancashire fishermen to combat
rheumatism. Many folk cures worked: dung *is* a good poultice.

Where traditional and new, popular and polite, culture con-
fronted each other, there was often objectively little to choose
between them. Some people refused to accept the Gregorian
Calendar when it replaced the Julian in 1751, afraid that 'losing'

eleven days would rob them of their wages. After the calendar switch, the *Salisbury Journal* reported:

Yesterday being Old Christmas Day, the same was obstinately observed by our Country People in general, so that it being Market Day (according to the order of our magistrates) there were but few at market, who combined the opportunity of raising their Butter to ninepence or tenpence a pound.

In need of personal guidance, the lower classes sought out wise women or consulted almanacs which printed horoscopes, made prophecies, and retailed proverbial advice: Old Moore's sold over 100,000 copies a year. The fashionable, for their part, began writing to the 'agony columns' of magazines (such as John Dunton's *Athenian Mercury*, founded in 1689) for answers to their intimate problems. Similarly, when sick, the wealthy hesitated whether to trust the physician or to try folk or quack remedies. Sir Robert Walpole ate soap by the pound for his stomach complaints. Patent medicine panaceas such as Daffy's Elixir and Dr James's Powder sold to people high and low.

The elite plumed themselves on pioneering more rational, liberal, and humane values. They rejected folklore as silly, cruel, and vulgar, and pooh-poohed traditional proverbial wisdom, preferring tags from the Classics. Unlike the French Bourbons, Hanoverian monarchs no longer 'touched for the King's Evil' (the plebs retaliated by clutching at the bodies of executed criminals, trusting to their thaumaturgical powers). The intelligentsia smiled at vulgar belief in a literal Hell and eternal punishment, in the Devil, guardian angels, hobgoblins and ghosts. Sensitive parents stopped frightening their children with threats of the bogey man, Maria Edgeworth, the immensely popular children's writer, asking 'Why should the mind be filled with fantastic visions instead of useful knowledge?' Sarah Trimmer was one of many superior children's writers who objected to fairy stories for being untrue and common. 'The histories of little Jack Horner, Cinderella, Fortunatus and other tales which were in fashion half a century ago,' she frowned, 'are full of romantic nonsense,' suggesting that solid factual works such as natural history combat such 'pernicious' rubbish. Fairy tales contained magic (which was contrary to science) and prejudiced children against wolves and step-mothers, and stories such as Dick Whittington gave them ideas about social climbing.

The debonair contrasted their own rationality with the stampeding passions of the herd, envisaging the progress of civilization as an evolution from 'rudeness' to 'refinement', from gut prejudice to reason. True taste, manners and morals, they emphasized, were matters of rational, even scientific, judgement rather than mere instinct or preference. The well-bred looked down on yokels, with their quaint speech and irrational folklore. As Henry Bourne reflected about folkways, 'though some of them have been of national and others perhaps of universal observance, yet at present they would have little or no being if not observed among the vulgar'. The elite gave the withering-away of folk customs a helping hand (though considerately recording them, somewhat expurgated, for scholarly posterity). The maypole in the Strand was felled in 1717.

Above all, polite society stopped believing in the reality of witchcraft, to the wrath of scriptural fundamentalists (for John Wesley, 'the giving up of witchcraft is in effect giving up the Bible'). From the late seventeenth century, the torchbearers of Enlightenment argued that so-called witches were just lonely, isolated, crabbed old women. As Joseph Addison put it in the *Spectator*:

When an old woman begins to doat, and grow chargeable to a parish, she is generally turned into a witch, and fills the whole country with extravagant fancies, imaginary distempers, and terrifying dreams. In the meantime, the poor wretch that is the innocent occasion of so many evils, begins to be frighted at herself, and sometimes confesses secret commerces and familiarities that her imagination forms in a delirious old age. This frequently cuts off charity from the greatest objects of compassion, and inspires people with a malevolence towards those poor decrepit parts of our species, in whom human nature is defaced by infirmity and dotage.

Magistrates became unwilling to sustain witchcraft allegations. After the 1680s no witch purge occurred, and in 1737 the witch laws were repealed, though throughout the century panicking villagers continued to take punishment into their own hands, meting out vicious and sometimes fatal lynch-law to suspected witches. Even then, gentlemen could supervene as guardians of the helpless: 'A few days ago,' the *Public Advertiser* reported in 1761,

one Sarah Jellicoat of this town [Wilton] escaped undergoing the whole discipline usually inflicted by the unmerciful & unthinking vulgar on witches, under pretence that she had bewitched a farmer's servant & a tallow chandler's soap, which failed in the operation, only by the favourable interposition of some humane gentlemen & the vigilance of a discreet magistrate, who stopped the proceedings before the violence thereof had gone to a great pitch.

'Spirits are lawful, but not ghosts,' punned the indignant Blake: 'especially Royal Gin is lawful spirit.' But how far did the elite onslaught on popular superstitions, on mystery and the spirit world go? Was it the secularizing thin end of the wedge of atheism? Certainly many 'rational' Christians no longer viewed the daily course of their lives as a succession of divine fingerposts. 'The doctrine of a particular providence,' lamented John Wesley in 1761, 'is absolutely out of fashion in England' (for many being 'provident' seemed more to the point). 'The influence of religion is more and more wearing out of the minds of men,' bewailed Joseph Butler, Bishop of Durham, in 1736. 'The number of those who call themselves unbelievers increases, and with their number, their zeal. The deplorable distinction of our age is an avowed scorn of religion in some and a growing disregard of it in the generality.' Religion seemed a shadow of its former self. John Wesley in fact rated it a most profane age:

Ungodliness is our universal, our constant, our peculiar character ... a total ignorance of God is almost universal among us – High & low, cobblers, tinkers, hackney coachmen, men and maid servants, soldiers, tradesmen of all rank, lawyers, physicians, gentlemen, lords are as ignorant of the Creator of the World as Mohametans & Pagans.

And it was said of Birmingham folk in 1788 that 'the great mass of the people give themselves very little concern about religious matters, seldom if ever going to church ... What religion there is ... is to be found amongst the Dissenters.'

Certainly secular views were supplanting Christian ones in many spheres. In the seventeenth century suicides were still religiously condemned as having committed wilful and mortal sin: men of the Enlightenment looked on them rather as sick people who had acted while their mind was disturbed. The rise of insurance (accompanied by probabilistic thinking) silently challenged belief in Providence. Popular almanacs contained fewer religious prophecies and more patriotic ones. Secular and Classical practices edged in where Christianity once had a monopoly. Plenty of Christians still saw the grave as the gateway to salvation, but others faced dying in new ways. For instance, the *Gentleman's Magazine* recorded the funeral of Mr John Underwood of Whittlesea in 1733:

At his Burial, when the Service was over, an Arch was turn'd over the Coffin, in which was placed a small piece of white Marble, with this Inscription, *Non omnis moriar*, 1733. Then the 6 Gentlemen who follow'd him to the Grave sung the last Stanza of the 20th Ode of the 2d Book of *Horace*. No Bell was toll'd, no one invited but the 6 Gentlemen, and no Relation follow'd his Corpse; the Coffin was painted Green, and he laid in it with all his Cloaths on; under his Head was placed Sanadon's *Horace*, at his feet *Bentley's* Milton; in his Right Hand a small Greek Testament ... After the Ceremony was over they went back to his House, where his Sister had provided a cold Supper; the Cloth being taken away the Gentlemen sung the 31st Ode of the 1st Book of *Horace*, drank a chearful Glass, and went Home about Eight. He left near 6000L. to his Sister, on Condition of her observing this Will, order'd her to give each of the Gentlemen ten Guineas, and desir'd they would not come in black Cloaths; the Will ends thus – *Which done I would have them take a chearful Glass and think no more of* John Underwood.

Gravestones and funeral tablets shed their macabre skulls and charnel-house carvings, and sprouted solacing urns and laurels.

Yet this does not amount to atheism. What many Georgians wanted was a basically secular life with certain religious fancy wrappings. Sacerdotalism was out. Benefit of clergy was curtailed, Convocation prorogued, the church courts reduced to a husk, the transcendental and mysterious elements of religion faded. And this was the way even the Anglican hierarchy wanted it, for their aim was not to be priestly at all, rather hoping to merge into county society, hobnobbing with the gentry. Pastor Moritz remarked: 'The English clergy, and I fear still more particularly those who live in London, are noticeably and lamentably conspicuous by a very free, secular and irregular way of life.' Louis Simond dubbed them 'free and easy'. The Rev. Henry Bate was not untypical of this breed: a prebendary of Ely Cathedral, he was a journalist, dramatist, formidable pugilist, art critic, and greyhound-breeder. His duels while editing the *Morning Post* earned him the nickname of 'the fighting parson', and in his seventies he led a troop of volunteers against rioters who had sacked the village of Littleport in Cambridgeshire. John Wesley was appalled by the worldly clergy he met. In 1743 he recorded in his *Journal*:

> While I was speaking, a gentleman rode up very drunk, and after many unseemly and bitter words, laboured much to ride over some of the people. I was surprised to hear he was a neighbouring clergyman. And this too is a man zealous for the Church! Ah, poor Church! if it stood in need of such defenders!

A fortnight earlier he had written:

> At our inn I found a good-natured man, sitting and drinking in the chimney corner; with whom I began a discourse, suspecting nothing less than that he was the minister of the parish. Before we parted I spoke exceedingly plainly. And he received it in love; begging he might see me when I came that way again.

Of course, many defended keeping a low religious profile as being truly civilized. Zeal would be vulgar, inflammatory, and smack of 'enthusiasm' (which Dr Johnson defined as 'a vain confidence of divine favour or communication'). Only a fully rational faith could command intellectual and scientific respect and, by encompassing free inquiry and scholarly method, be tested and proven true.

Endorsement of 'philosophical' religion, and of moderate behaviour in general, was one way the educated and propertied justified their own life-style against others (the 'vulgar'). What the elite considered rational they often backed with power: exposing the 'irrational' and 'traditional' often led to banning them. Thus calendar festivities were closed down, nominally because they were relics of paganism or popery which had outlived their usefulness. For, behind these rationalizations lay the desire to re-order society. It was indeed humane to end witch prosecutions, yet this step looks puny alongside the intensifying 'witch-hunts' against poachers, squatters, vagrants, and combining workers. The triumph of 'rationality' also meant rewriting the ground-rules in favour of the powerful, for the concept of reason that prevailed was theirs.

Many matters, traditionally ruled by custom, left to chance, or held sacred, were gradually brought under rational control. As the economy became more complex and investments greater the need grew to make life more regular and predictable. Weights and measures were standardized somewhat between regions, fighting men were put into uniform. Price tags – pioneered by the Quaker fair-price ethic – appeared in shops. The introduction of coach schedules and the royal mail led to the standardization of the time of day across the country. From the 1780s Cary's cheap road atlases helped people to find their way. Following an Act of 1773, more mile-posts and sign-posts were erected. Teach-yourself books told people the correct way to do things, as for example *The Country Housewife's Family Companion or Profitable Directions for whatever relates to the Management and good Economy of the Domestic Concerns of a Country Life. According to the Present Practice of the Country Gentleman's, the Yeoman's, the Farmers and Wives in the Counties of Hertford, Bucks and other parts of England, shewing How great Savings may be made in Housekeeping* (1750).

Zooming sales of calendars, diaries, ledgers, and account books suggest a desire to keep tabs on life. Newspapers' political and market information helped the commercial classes to cope with uncertainty and plan ahead. Dictionaries slowly led to more uniform spelling – yet what became standard written English was not the speaking voice, but rather elite orthography. Thus, though everybody said 'landskip' and most spelt it that way, it bowed out to 'landscape' – first in writing and then in speech. Yet even as late as mid-century a gentleman such as Henry Purefoy could still spell 'periwig' in three different ways (all wrong to us!) within one letter.

Hurly-burly human relations were taken under control in attempts to stabilize the environment, predict the future, and protect investments. Entrepreneurs imposed factory discipline on their workers, Wedgwood hoping to make 'such machines of men as cannot err'. Task-orientation giving way to time-orientation, factory time was introduced with bells and clocking-on. (Wedgwood's friend, John Whitehurst, designed special timepieces for the purpose.) Keeping good time mattered more – 'Everybody has a watch,' observed Misson in 1719 – for 'in a commercial country,' reflected Dr Johnson, 'time becomes precious'. Sir John Barnard gave homely advice: 'Above all things learn to put a due value *on Time* & husband every moment as if it were to be your last; in Time is comprehended all we possess, enjoy, or wish for; & in losing that we lose them all.' Even the leisured classes did not escape. Lord Chesterfield advised his son:

There is nothing which I more wish that you should know and which fewer people do know, than the true use and value of Time ... I knew a gentleman, who was so good a manager of his time, that he would not even lose that small portion of it which the calls of nature obliged him to pass in the necessary house, but gradually went through all the Latin poets in those moments. He bought, for example, a common edition of Horace, of which he tore off gradually a couple of pages, carried them with him to that necessary place, read them first and then sent them down as a sacrifice to Cloacina; that was so much time fairly gained, and I recommend you to follow his example ... it will make any book which you shall read in that manner very present in your mind.

The most systematic plan for the rational reorganization and policing of life was Jeremy Bentham's Utilitarian philosophy, in which all activity was to be remoulded on the basis of quantified calculations of costs and benefits, pains and pleasures. Bentham described his panacea for all social ills, the Panopticon, a total surveillance institution, as 'a machine for grinding rogues honest'.

The desire to extend control was put into practice in many areas of life. Landscape gardening exemplified dominion over Nature on a bijou scale. Landowners could redesign corners of creation, making it 'picturesque', like a picture. Urban amenities and utilities were improved, parks created, marshy ground drained. In London, the Thames was embanked, the Fleet Ditch was covered (in 1747), and sewerage improved:

Beneath the pavements are vast subterraneous sewers arched over to convey away the waste water which in other cities is so noisome above ground, and at a less depth are buried wooden pipes that supply every house plentifully with water, conducted by leaden pipes into kitchens or cellars, three times a week for the trifling expence of three shillings per quarter ... The intelligent foreigner cannot fail to take notice of these useful particulars which are almost peculiar to London.

Westminster Bridge was built in 1750, followed by Blackfriars in 1756.

Many embraced the Promethean myth that man should command his own destiny. There were admittedly few spectacular advances in medicine, though smallpox inoculation and subsequently vaccination were successful, and Cook showed how citrus fruits held scurvy at bay on trans-oceanic voyages. Yet doctors grew more confident that disease was a foe medical science could vanquish, Dr Erasmus Darwin loving 'to make war upon a pox or a fever'. Moreover medicine took on more public roles. Physicians had traditionally treated patients individually, concentrating on the bedside role, but some, such as Sir John Pringle, increasingly looked to social and preventative medicine – the health of the armed forces, or improved hygiene in industrial communities. Numbers of provincial doctors increased, Newcastle having eighteen practitioners by 1778. More doctors began to examine the relations between epidemics and environment, pressing for better public health provisions and legislation. Doctors were poised to become the new priests of the modern secularized world.

Illness came to be seen less as visitation, trial, or punishment, death less as fate or divine retribution. Increasingly, doctors hoped to cure, not just to relieve. Erasmus Darwin speculated on 'means of preventing old age', and James Graham promised to reveal 'the whole art of enjoying health & vigour of body & mind, & of preserving & exalting personal honour & loveliness or in other words of living with health, honour, & happiness in the world for at least a hundred years'.

'Humane Societies' were founded to teach artificial respiration and reduce deaths from drowning (of increased importance in the canal age). New optimism about coping with disease led to a mighty wave of hospital-founding. Traditionally hospitals had been 'hospices', places of 'hospitality' for the needy. Now they became centres of healing for the sick poor (the rich were nursed at home). Five great new London hospitals were founded through bequests and private philanthropy: the Westminster (1720), Guy's (1724), St George's (1733), the London (1740), and the Middlesex (1745). Provincial foundations followed. The first outside London was the Edinburgh Royal Infirmary in 1729, followed by Bristol (1735), Winchester (1736), York (1740), Exeter (1741), Bath (1742), Northampton (1743), and many others. Specialist hospitals, such as the Foundling Hospital for abandoned babies, lying-in hospitals, and hospitals for venereal diseases, were also set up. New dispensaries diagnosed and provided drugs for outpatients. By 1800 London dispensaries were treating 50,000 people a year. Like hospitals, these were financed philanthropically, with the needy as patients and the wealthy as subscribers.

Of course, hospitals and dispensaries provided valuable medical treatment for the common people, but while doing so they also served the interests of their masters. Trainee physicians and surgeons needed the poor to practise on. The poor were meant to show gratitude and in hospital would be less of a health risk to their betters (vital when so many of them were in-living servants). They would also form a captive audience for discipline and sermons – the Exeter Hospital was advertised as being 'of the greatest consequence not only for the health & welfare, but also to the religion & morals of the laborious poor'. Alured Clarke, founder of the Winchester Hospital, saw his mission as to 'instruct the sick and reclaim the bad'. The London Hospital gave discharge certificates only to those patients who had attended chapel to give thanks for their recovery. Hospitals were charity prudently dispensed.

Whether hospitals actually did much to heal the sick is another matter. It was the policy of most of them not to take chronic or highly infectious cases – nothing could usefully be done for these. Hospitals wrought no spectacular cures, particularly as in the age of agony before antiseptics and anaesthetics surgery was limited to simple, quick, or desperate operations, such as amputations, removing bladder-stones, and setting fractures. But the view that hospitals were 'gateways to death' is probably exaggerated.

The change in therapies for lunatics is a spectacular barometer of rising optimism – and its ironies. Before the eighteenth century, madness was commonly seen as spiritual derangement (in some cases, demonic possession), or as recidivism to animality. It was not expected that lunatics could generally be cured. Partly for this reason, there had been almost no institutions for the insane, outside London's Bethlem Hospital (Bedlam), where the mad suffered degrading zoo-like physical confinement, being chained up, lashed, and exposed to gawping, paying visitors. All this began to change. Enlightened physicians came to see madness as a *disease* of the body and later as one of the mind. The mad were neither brutes nor possessed by devils, but were sick and therefore amenable to treatment and cure. But the right environment would be needed – preferably asylums in rural surroundings, set apart from hubbub and anxiety. Privately run madhouses were founded for those who could afford it (the mad poor either remained at large or were cooped in houses of correction and poor-houses). Instead of confinement, punishment, terror, or sedative medicine, psychological management was championed. Late in the century, 'kindness' became the watchword for a new 'moral therapy'. Rational approaches to madness certainly led to more considerate treatment for patients. In 1766 Bedlam closed its doors to visitors, and St Luke's Asylum, founded in London in 1751, never exposed inmates to public gaze. Early in the nineteenth century, Louis Simond, visiting the prestigious York Retreat, found humanity the keynote:

There is near York a retreat for lunatics, which appears admirably managed, and almost entirely by *reason* and kindness: it was instituted by Quakers. Most of the patients move about at liberty, without noise and disorder, and by their demure and grave deportment shew they have not quite forgotten to what sect they belong.

But the optimism induced by the new asylums sowed its own problems. They were often used as lock-ups for troublesome relatives; confinement of a wife or a child as insane could be the first step to laying hands on a fortune. Patients had little legal protection. The growing popularity of madhouses perhaps also indicates warning social tolerance of misfits and simpletons around the household and the community.

A similar tale could be told in many walks of life. Reason

and control brought order and care, but also more segregation, more social engineering, greater expectation of conformity. In polite society, greater consideration towards the young meant fencing childhood off as an age of innocence, in turn inducing overprotective parental anxiety. Parents became more concerned with toilet-training and building up moral backbone by cold baths and psychological conditioning. Protectiveness demanded that childhood sexuality be stamped out. Moralists began to expose masturbation as an evil, books such as *Onania, or the Heinous Sin of Self-Pollution* 'proving' that it led to physical and psychic degeneration, even madness. James Graham prophesied that it caused

debility of body and of mind, – infecundity, – epilepsy, – loss of memory, – sight, and hearing, – distortions of the eyes, mouth and face, – feeble, harsh and squeaking voice, – pale, sallow and blueish black complexion, – wasting and tottering of the limbs, – idiotism, – horrors, – innumerable complaints – extreme wretchedness – and even death itself . . .

Doctors hence set about eradicating it by medical, physical, and moral treatment.

Belief in improvement through organization, system, and surveillance was making inroads elsewhere. Educating platoons of children in charity schools with few masters created logistic problems analogous to those of factory discipline. In answer, Andrew Bell and Joseph Lancaster mapped out factory methods of teaching, in a schooling system to be dubbed 'the steam engine of the moral world'. By division of labour, student monitors were to funnel instruction down from a single teacher to the pupils. 'Such is the intellectual organ,' wrote Bell in 1797,

which puts the whole scholastic machine in motion; such . . . the principle on which every *schoolroom, factory, workhouse, poorhouse, prison house*, the *administration* of the poor laws, and every public or even private institution of any magnitude should be conducted.

Lawbreakers felt the wind of change most keenly. Traditionally felons were executed, transported, or whipped to satisfy community wrath. Except for debtors, prisons had chiefly been transit places where the accused awaited trial. Long gaol sentences had been very rare. Even in the early 1770s, only 2–3 per cent of judges' sentences at the Old Bailey were for gaol, and then stretches were short. Internally gaols had been open-plan dens of disorder, drunkenness, corruption, and disease, as John Howard's visits revealed. But in the last third of the century reformers – both secular, such as the Utilitarians, and religious, such as Quakers – cast doubt upon corporeal retribution, deeming it both cruel and inefficacious. Thus branding was abolished in 1779. In the new penology, vengeance yielded to correction. Reformers developed alternative schemes of minutely controlled and supervised punishment centred on prison, aimed at deterring and (a new emphasis) reforming. The anarchic self-governing gaol with its own robust sub-culture was on the way out. The new penitentiaries, it was hoped, would become 'total institutions' under public scrutiny, with clear chains of expert command from above. Courts had traditionally sought to empty prisons: now the answer was to fill them. Purpose-built gaols would commit prisoners to regimes of discipline and hard labour. Prisoners were for the first time cooped in solitary confinement in cells, where they would repent and learn how to lead useful lives.

Such were the schemes. From the 1780s several such prisons were actually constructed (though most remained as before). Gloucester got a new gaol in 1792 at a cost of £40,000 (instantly dubbed 'The Gloucester Bastille'). Fanny Burney was impressed:

> This jail is admirably constructed for its proper purposes – confinement and punishment. Every culprit is to have a separate cell; every cell is clean, neat and small, looking towards a wide expanse of country, and (far more fitted to his speculation) a wide expanse of the heavens. Air, cleanliness and health are all considered, but no other indulgence. A total seclusion of all commerce from accident, and an absolute impossibility of all intercourse among themselves, must needs render the captivity secure from all temptation to further guilt, and all stimulus to hardihood in past crimes, and makes the solitude become so desperate that it not only seems to leave no opening for any comfort save in repentance, but to make that almost unavoidable.

The reforming vision was humane, with its stress on improved hygiene and healthy exercise, and its clamp-down on intimidation. Yet 'humanitarianism' tightened the screw – and designedly so. As the Gloucestershire philanthropist Sir George Onesiphorous Paul put it, 'I am not of the number of those who from a misplaced tenderness of heart would unbind the just terrors of the law. I am far from thinking that prisons should be places of comfort ... they should be places of real terror.' Now felons were to be gaoled for longer terms and psychologically racked. The new prison was a harbinger of a new species of planned punitiveness: long-term institutional control, using new disciplines and drills and new mechanical aids such as the treadmill – all in specially designed buildings. Jeremy Bentham planned a custodial institution, the Panopticon, which maximized surveillance by means of a central omniscient gaze. As he described it:

> Morals reformed – health preserved – industry invigorated – instruction diffused – public burthens lightened – economy seated as it were upon a rock – the gordian knot of the Poor Laws not cut but untied – all by a simple idea in Architecture.

The perils of neglect were superseded by the pains of attention. Moreover the pioneer new institutions did not fulfil expectations. There was never enough money, they became overcrowded; prison labour, like workhouse toil, never paid its way, and dedication was not a strong point of Georgian warders. And they failed to reform. When they didn't solve the problem, the response was to set up more, giving a further twist to the spiral of institutionalization. The age was just dawning when, alongside new wealth, new freedoms, and new powers, labour was being subordinated to machine time, and society's misfits (paupers, the mad, the ill, the criminal) were being set apart, drilled to conform under the management of 'experts'. The eighteenth century, however, saw only the beginnings. The central state did little. New hospitals and prisons were built on local and private initiatives; Bentham's Panopticon was not constructed. Yet the ball had started rolling. The modern, the rational, the humanitarian, had its more sombre face; the Enlightened mind forged its own manacles.

The complexion of power in Georgian society was at bottom rough-and-ready, *sauve qui peut* its legend. Authority was

backed by physical terrors, from the gamekeeper's blunderbuss
to the gallows. Yet these were not sure *deterrents* against riot and
crime: at best they were sporadic, angry, clumsy retribution. In
village England where social discipline was strong, the poor law
was a powerful agent of stabilization. But the central state did
not possess the grinders of control available in other countries:
censorship, Inquisition, judicial torture, administrative justice,
education run by religious orders, a secret police. Hence, to
maintain public order, rulers had to bank heavily upon inertia
and the restraints of traditional society: scarcity, paternal discipline, community opinion, dependency, hostility to outsiders,
and so forth.

Fears mounted that these time-honoured corsets of repression
were beginning to fray. Labour shortage and rising real wages
in the first half of the century sparked incessant employers'
complaints about truculence and eroded work discipline. Commercial expansion was giving labour bargaining power in
growth industries. 'When we strike, the masters cannot help
themselves,' boasted an Old Bailey witness in 1765. Profitability
required a well-heeled work-force.

Authorities are always haunted by the spectre of the masses
answering back, but this dread was now especially acute because
the national Church could not awe them and (unlike later)
central Government could command little direct local police
power. To fill this vacuum voluntary initiatives were taken
to coax the people into quietness. In floating these, urban
moneyed interests were most prominent. Westminster did little;
Parliament passed more hanging statutes, but these were ineffective if not counter-productive. Nor did the Anglican Church
corporately act, being weakest where the risks of disorder were
worst, in the boom towns. Grandees for their part could afford
to be a bit nonchalant. Dependency still bound Hodge on their
own country estates, and they might have much to lose in
informal influence from the setting-up of a national police
responsible to the executive. Aristocrats had no desire for a
regulated, bureaucratic society: they had too great a stake in
personal power. They also had a shrewd confidence in the
rock-solid stability of landed society, a faith in horse-whipping,
and a steady nerve. As politicians, grandees learned to live with

occasional disturbances, since they often made capital out of agitation out-of-doors themselves.

Those itching to clean society up were rather the affluent, anxious, and assertive *haute bourgeoisie*: men such as John Bellers, the Quaker London cloth merchant, Thomas Guy, the London bookseller (who gave £220,000 from his Bible-printing monopoly to found his hospital), William Wilberforce, scion of a Hull trading family, or Robert Raikes, a Gloucester printer, newspaper proprietor, and pioneer of Sunday schools. For such people, everything was at stake. They aimed at asserting themselves above the herd as right-minded, responsible, and successful, and impressing their worth upon their social betters, including God. They wanted a collective voice. Lacking direct string-pulling power in national politics, the vocal bourgeois chose not to challenge the aristocratic political machine, but rather to build up their own parallel moral authority, to be stamped on their inferiors. *The World* magazine thus reflected on their claims to moral superiority:

There are certain vices which the vulgar call 'fun' and the people of fashion 'gallantry' but the middle rank, and those of the gentry who continue to go to church still stigmatize them by the opprobious names of fornication and adultery.

Prominent amongst those who thus led with their moral fists were the Dissenters, who figured so prominently in movements to sanitize and patrol the masses. Contemptuous of the profligate heathenish eminences who excluded them from the state, they made a parade of their own superior piety. Women – for instance, Hannah More and Elizabeth Fry – were also conspicuous among philanthropists. In a society which barred women's managerial energies from professional life, charity offered one of their few outlets.

Townsdwellers had to thread their way through crime, drunkenness, ale-house brawls, and prostitution more than the grandees did. As employers, their profits were drained by absentee, feckless, and pilfering workers, and as vexed ratepayers they bore the brunt of poor relief and unpaid local office. In reforming the manners of the poor, duty and advantage converged and the appeal to personal self-interest was an underground stream which often surfaced. 'If compassion cannot move you,' preached William Sharp in 1755,

let considerations of interest prevail with you. For neglect this poor man's numerous family, leave them to follow their own imagination and to make what wretched shift they can, and experience the sad consequence. They will soon grow up to public nuisances, infect your families with their idle disorderly behaviour, fill your streets with vice and violence; break in upon your comfort and your security: take the same persons under your patronage, teach them what is right and hear how you will be repaid. They will be serviceable to you in many ways by themselves, and by their examples, Industry, Sobriety, Good Order and Good Manners will get ground among you. Your city will be stocked with honest laborious ingenious artisans, some of the most useful members of a community; wealth will increase.

The sincerity of reformers of manners is not at issue (though the scathing Blake saw to the heart of the matter: 'They reduce the man to want and then give with pomp and ceremony'). Men such as Jonas Hanway and John Howard devoted their lives and fortunes to such work, and superintending the poor was a prime duty to earnest men of condition. As Bishop Butler said:

God has distributed men into these different ranks ... has formally put the poor under the superintendency & patronage of the rich. The rich then are charged by natural providence as much as by revealed appointment with the care of the poor.

The Dissenting Liverpool physician James Currie agreed: 'The labouring poor', he declared,

demand our constant attention. To inform their minds, to repress their vices, to assist their labours, to invigorate their activity, and to improve their comforts: – these are the noblest offices of enlightened minds in superior stations.

Many launched into reform out of disgust for the luxurious, money-crazed self-seeking society festering around them. Young Elizabeth Gurney (later Fry), brought up within a lax ('gay') Quaker household, turned idealistic and puritanical, rejected her easy-going family, and cleansed herself with philanthropy. Above all, Christian humanitarians were aghast that the poor vegetated in pagan ignorance of Scripture.

Moral reformers wanted to improve life, but in line with their own blueprints, and on their own terms, for they were absolute against indiscriminate alms. They sought not the transformation of society's structure but the alleviation of personal distress amongst the deserving and the conquest of vice. They wanted to make the poor not equal or affluent but virtuous, and above all God-fearing. 'Children fed by charity', wrote the chilling Sarah Trimmer, 'ought in a more special manner to be clothed in humility.'

Most philanthropists were sworn enemies of political radicalism, and were to detest the spirit of the French Revolution. As Hannah More saw the matter,

Who can forbear observing and regretting ... that not only sons, but daughters, have adopted something of that spirit of independence and disdain of control, which characterizes the times? The rights of man have been discussed, till we are somewhat wearied with the discussion. To these have been opposed ... the rights of women. It follows that the world will next have – grave descants on the rights of youth – the rights of children – the rights of babies!

Rather moralists looked to charity as a prophylactic against, or an antidote to, mutinous grassroots stirrings. As the Quaker John Bellers delicately hinted, 'It is the interest of the rich to take care of the poor.'

The campaign to moralize the poor took an organized form in voluntary associations, to which individuals subscribed sums which bought them shares in the management. The turn of the eighteenth century saw 'joint stock religion' in bodies such as the Societies for the Reformation of Manners (founded from the 1690s) comprising eminent merchants, full-time philanthropists, and a halo of higher clergy. Such movements were Protestant but inter-denominational: combating irreligion and disciplining the poor were more urgent than dogmatic niceties. They channelled deep-seated puritan compulsions into social and legal expression, in many ways supplementing the declining church courts by laying prosecutions before the civil courts for vice offences, above all swearing, drunkenness, gaming, sabbath profanation, blasphemy, keeping unlicensed ale-houses, pornography, prostitution, and homosexuality. Their vigilante smut-hounds brought many thousands of cases in the first third of the century – about 1,400 a year – before declining, having made themselves ridiculed and hated in the process. But their activities were taken up later by the Proclamation Society (1787) and then the Society for the Suppressing of Vice (1802), patronized by wealthy businessmen and a sprinkling of peers. Ambiguously known as the Vice Society, it was dubbed by the Revd Sydney Smith 'a corporation of informers supported by large contributions bent on suppressing not the vices of the rich but the pleasures of the poor': an unsympathetic but not inaccurate summary, for, as Smith wrote,

A man of £10,000 a year may worry a fox as much as he pleases, encourage the breed of a mischievous animal on purpose to worry it: & a poor labourer is carried before a magistrate for paying a sixpence to see an exhibition of courage between a dog and a bear.

Smith indeed thought the Vice Society misnamed: it should really have been called a 'Society for Suppressing the Vices of Persons whose income does not exceed £500 per annum'.

Vice societies and private prosecutions smothered popular culture in various ways. Popular sports, church ales, and fairs – the saturnalian solaces of plebeian life – were assailed, for such wanton mirth wasted money and led to idleness, while drunkenness and folk festivities, judged high-minded reformers, resulted in barbarities, such as killing cocks. Not least, they disrupted work rhythms, encouraged insubordination, and eroded deference. 'Should publicans be allowed' (it was asked in 1764),

to promote and even advertise such ridiculous diversions as horse, foot, or ass races, or any similar pastime for the populace, on the view of profit to themselves by the promotion of idleness & drinking: such proceeding I must consider as unlawful in their nature – How often do we see the whole inhabitants of a country village drawn from their harvest work, to see cudgel playing, or a cricket match?

Especially in the last third of the century, more and more popular recreations were suppressed, aided by the enclosure movement, which by abolishing commons often took the very ground away from under a fair or sports. In 1745 cock-throwing was banned in Worcester, in 1750 in Bewdley and Kid-

derminster, in Liverpool about 1778. The Rev. William Grimshaw put a stop to football and horse-racing at Haworth in the
1740s. In 1778 'the Minister, Church-wardens and principal
inhabitants' of Pebmarch prohibited the Midsummer Fair,
directing the constables to forbid merriments. Even the harmless
ceremony of the Dunmow Flitch, to find the most happily
married couple in the village, was axed. In 1772 the claimant of
the prize was turned away by the Lord of the Manor and future
attempts to revive the custom were foiled.

In London as early as 1709 May Fair was abolished (Mayfair
was getting fashionable) and by 1803 the Vice Society was
recommending that all fairs whatsoever be suppressed. In 1780
London magistrates closed skittle grounds outside taverns.
Looking back in 1801, the Rev. Richard Warner was pleased
to report some success. He bemoaned that 'the sports which
sufficiently satisfied our ancestors of the sixteenth and seventeenth centuries' had been

the pranks of mountebanks, the feats of jugglers, tumblers and dancers,
the jests of itinerant *mimes* or mummers, and the dangerous amusement
of the quintane, diversified occasionally by the pageant and the masque,
or the *elegant* pastimes of bullbaiting, cock-fighting, cock-scaling, pig-
racing, bowling, football, grinning through a horse-collar, and swal-
lowing scalding hot frumenty . . . But [he reported] as national manners
gradually refined, the ideas of elegance were proportionally enlarged,
and public amusements insensibly approximated to the taste and splen-
dour which they at present exhibit; balls, plays, and cards, usurping
the place of those rude athletick sports, or gross sensual amusements,
to which the hours of vacancy had before been devoted.

Alongside bans, philanthropists offered baits. They showered
working people with sermons and pamphlets, charities such as
the Society for the Promotion of Christian Knowledge (1699)
and the Society for Distributing Religious Tracts among the
Poor (1782) gushing the holy waters of Christian truth. The
SPCK issued 15,000 copies of the *Soldier's Monitor* to Marlborough's army. Societies for the Reformation of Manners distributed *Kind Cautions against Swearing* to hackney-carriage
drivers, mindful, doubtless, of the delicate ears of the passengers.
Sermons and admonitions were supplemented by the edifying
doggerel and uplifting tales penned by such do-gooders as

Hannah More in her cheap *Repository Tracts.* Worldly and heavenly reward – thus went their moral – would in time repay labouring families who were meek and did what they were told. For the rest there was *The Story of Sinful Sally:* obstreperous folks, who drank and cursed their lot, went to the bad. Snowing down throughout the century, these tracts became a blizzard raised by the chilling gusts of the French Revolution.

School complemented Church for indoctrinating the masses' children. Charity and Sunday schools were set up in dozens. Some were staffed by lady bountifuls. ('At Windsor,' wrote Robert Raikes, 'the ladies of fashion pass their Sundays in teaching the poorest children.') But lesser mortals – blacksmiths and tradesmen – taught as well. By 1788 Manchester Sunday schools boasted 5,000 pupils. By 1797 across the country there were 1,086 Sunday schools with 69,000 pupils, some of them adults. They taught reading (but less frequently writing: 'Reading will help the people's morals,' Jonas Hanway had written, 'but writing is not necessary'), Scripture, piety, drill, and elementary manual skills. Catechizing was the key activity. Mrs Sarah Trimmer wrote edifying dialogues for them:

Instructor: There is one kind of dishonesty which is often practised without thought by workmen, and that is wasting the time for which they are paid and the materials belonging to the Trade or Manufacture they work at. Of the same nature with this is the crime of many household servants who take every opportunity of being idle and who make no scruple of wasting provisions or giving them away without leave …
Question: Is it honest for workmen to waste and destroy the materials and implements which they make use of?
Answer: No.
Question: Who do these things belong to?
Answer: Their Master.
Question: Whose eyes see you when your master is not by?
Answer: God's.

Sunday schools were clever inventions because they ensured that children who worked from Monday to Saturday were instructed on their day off. As the Bishop of Chester put it,

By this wise expedient, that most desirable *union,* which has been so often wished for in Charity Schools, but which it has been generally found so difficult to introduce, is at length accomplished, the union of *manual labour* and *spiritual instruction*. These are by means of the Sunday schools both carried on together and the interests both of this life and the next so consulted, as not to interfere with or obstruct each other.

Better still, the schooling was cheap; the reassuring bishop added: 'The whole expence of instructing twenty children, including books, rewards, and every other charge, will not amount to five pounds a year; a sum so trifling and so easy to be raised that it cannot create the smallest difficulty.'

The dream of colleges of industry (work-schools) for poor children had a lustre no set-backs could tarnish. Their promoter, Quaker John Bellers, spelt out their rationale: 'therein is 3 things I aim at: first Profit to the Rich (which will be life to the rest); Secondly a plentiful living for the poor, without difficulty; Thirdly a good education for youth, that may tend to prepare their souls.' As Bellers stressed, investing in colleges of industry should yield better returns than mere alms-giving. He was confident that private-enterprise institutions for the poor must be more efficient than the public poor law.

Alongside schools, however, many other bodies were set up to help out, or buy off, the troublesome classes. Refuges such as the Magdalen Hospital were founded to rescue penitent prostitutes. The Marine Society for Educating Poor Destitute Boys to the Sea took waifs off the streets to turn them into sailors, each boy receiving a copy of *Christian Knowledge Made Easy*. The Foundling Hospital (opened in 1741) aimed to save the lives of abandoned babies (most were bastards). The National Truss Society and the Society for the Ruptured Poor were to help men whose physiques had been broken by heavy labour to keep working. The Philanthropic Society, dating from 1788, was to reform criminal children. Spiralling inflation from the 1780s led to the Society for Bettering the Conditions and Increasing the Comfort of the Poor (1790), teaching them to go and drink soup, and publishing recipes showing how they could feed more nutritiously upon much less. Local dearth and disasters usually led to relief subscriptions and charitable doles.

As pauperism worsened, new charities were founded: ten

were launched in London from 1771 to 1780, eighteen from 1781 to 1790, and thirty from 1791 to 1800. Two goals were always prominent. First, the desire to make the lower orders God-fearing and deferential. They had to be habituated to hardship. 'Scarcity has been permitted', pontificated Panglossian Hannah More, 'by an all wise & gracious Providence to unite all ranks of people together, to show the poor how immediately they are dependent upon the rich, & to show both rich & poor that they are all dependent on Himself.'

And, second, there was the aim of encouraging in the labouring poor the petty bourgeois ethic of dedication to industry, thrift, sobriety, and self-help. The tireless philanthropist Jonas Hanway appealed to the poor,

though you are born to a humble estate in this world, let your AMBITION rise as high as heaven itself: there direct your hopes – But you can hardly be honest unless you are industrious – & would you be a good man, you must add to industry & religion good nature or a happy temper. Thus you will insure happiness.

Backing the poor law and the courts, in this way Georgian England saw philanthropic gestures by their betters to reform the lives of the lower orders. But how penetrative this encroachment on plebeian life from above was is difficult to gauge. Sermonizers and snoopers met with catcalls, hecklers, and stones, doles were mistrusted, and popular spokesmen were suspicious – thus Cobbett condemned village schools: 'Nothing is taught but the rudiments of servility, pauperism and slavery.' Property, thought Cobbett, would have done more than propaganda: 'A couple of flitches of bacon are worth 50,000 methodist sermons and religious tracts.'

Yet children flocked to charity and Sunday schools. Was this because uniforms and meals were often free? Or because of moral bullying? One set of ordinances for founding a Sunday school in 1786 states: 'Those parents who . . . obstinately refuse to send their children to the Sunday School shall be deemed improper objects to receive any Charity that shall in future be distributed to the parish of Curry Rivel.' And maybe such schools were a Pandora's box. Without philanthropic schools, where would Paine have got his hundreds of thousands of readers? Even Bible-reading was double-edged, for, as Thomas Laqueur has observed, 'working-class politics was largely the creation of people steeped in religion and the Bible'.

And yet there had been no united plebeian repudiation of hierarchy and capitalism up to the end of the century; the mills of the industrial revolution and Britannia's fleets and armies *were* manned. Had the lower orders absorbed the values they had been peppered with? Had they been embourgeoised? It is hard to say. Observers certainly held out hopes that the industrious poor were becoming more tractable. 'In the last century,' wrote Matthew Boulton,

Birmingham was as remarkable for good forgers and filers as for their bad taste in all their works. Their diversions were bull baiting, cock fightings, boxing matches and abominable drunkenness with all its train. But now the scene is changed. The people are more polite and civilized, and the taste of their manufactures greatly improved.

But Boulton attributed this transformation not to twopenny tracts but to trade.

Perhaps the cream of the lower classes was being skimmed. There were certainly able, articulate, and ambitious working men, such as Francis Place, who could see virtue in the values beckoning from above. Place rejected the beery, brutal ne'er-do-wells he grew up with in late-eighteenth-century London who tyrannized over their families and squandered their wealth and health. He advocated self-help, sobriety, education, getting-on. He got on himself, beginning as an apprentice cutter and becoming one of the largest tailors in the metropolis, with thirty-two journeymen under him and making £3,000 a year.

I never lost a minute of time, was never on any occasion diverted from the steady pursuit of my business, never spent a shilling, never once entertained any company. The only thing I bought were books, and not many of them. I adhered steadily to the practice I had adopted, and read for two or three hours every night after the business of the day was closed.

Place was a radical, an atheist, a birth-controller, a Painite, yet he also believed in self-advancement out of

the immorality, the coarseness, the obscenity, the drunkenness, the dirtiness and depravity of the middling and even of a large portion of the better sort of tradesmen, the artisans, & the journeymen tradesmen of London in the days of my youth. I cannot, like many other men, go to a tavern. I have attained my position *solely* by my own exertions. I left off everything which could in any way tend to impede my future progress in the world, or was in any way calculated to bring deserved reproach upon me or was likely to compel me on a close review of my conduct to reproach myself with injustice towards any one, or with having on any occasion acted meanly.

Offering ladders for the leaders perhaps did more for stability than converting the masses.

Moreover the pervasive propaganda conditioning had its effect on the masses too. Certainly there were village atheists and 'republican' agitators. Yet patriotism and xenophobia were etched on the brain, and droves would cheer for Church and king (often paying off scores against the lofty Dissenting tradesmen to whom they were in debt). And many working people took pride in vegetating in surly independence. Frederick Eden thus paid tribute to the lives of two Surrey farm-workers, James Strudwick and his wife Anne:

He worked more than threescore years on one farm; and his wages, summer and winter, were regularly a shilling a day. He never asked more: nor was he ever offered less. Strudwick continued to work till within seven weeks of the day of his death; and at the age of fourscore, in 1787, he closed, in peace, a not inglorious life; for, to the day of his death, he never received a farthing in the way of parochial aid. His wife survived him about seven years; and though bent with age and infirmities, and little able to work, excepting as a weeder in a gentleman's garden, she also was too proud either to ask or receive any relief from her parish. For six or seven of the last years of her life, she received twenty shillings a year from the person who favoured me with this account, which he drew up from her own mouth.

With all her virtue, and all her merit, she yet was not much liked in her neighbourhood; people in affluence thought her haughty, and the paupers of the parish, seeing, as they could not help seeing, that her life was a reproach to theirs, aggravated all her little failings.

Even this paragon, however, ultimately proved a disappointment to her betters. Eden reported:

A more serious charge against her was, that, living to a great age, and but little able to work, she grew to be seriously afraid that, at last, she might become chargeable to the parish (the heaviest, in her estimation, of all human calamities); and that thus alarmed, she did suffer herself more than once, during the exacerbations of a fit of distempered despondency, peevishly (and, perhaps, petulantly) to exclaim that God Almighty, by suffering her to remain so long upon earth, seemed actually to have forgotten her.

Whatever the impact of philanthropy upon its recipients, it served the benefactors well. Merchants and manufacturers in particular were often uncomfortable about their own station and *mœurs*. Steering between the pedigrees of the swells and the animality of the *canaille*, they needed to find self-respect. Though it was Dissenters who were most directly debarred from public life, many other solid bourgeois remained disqualified from voting until 1832. Their own course of life, in business, shepherding and investing their own capital, trying to establish a family line, bred insecurity and required prudence. Thus situated, they put trust in their own virtues, their 'credit'. Philanthropy enlisted the ambitious bourgeois in a moral mission, a vindication of their own worth. As Hannah More unctuously said of Mendip colliery villagers, 'they have nothing human to look to but us'. In any case, as Bishop Horne pointed out, charity was 'the most exquisite luxury'.

But moral seriousness was not exclusive to the commercial classes. Many propertied families emerged shell-shocked from the Stuart legacy. Political extremism – from Stuart tyranny to regicides – had been mirrored by religious bigotry, from Fifth Monarchists to Papist traitors. One king had been executed, another deposed. Public morals had swung from the Zeal-of-the-land business of Cromwellian saints and major-generals to the libertines of Charles II's Court (where not having a mistress was reputedly a stumbling block to advancement). Neither was readily stomached by the 'silent majority' of substance who thought themselves the backbone of the nation. With parties and sects still at each other's throats, and families divided amongst themselves, the danger was real that if men remained so factionalized, hot-tempered, and dogmatic, civil society would cannibalize itself. Furthermore, strains on the life-style of propertied society were intensifying as a result of alluring new prospects for enrichment, speculation, and high living (punctuated by nightmares of overreaching, of bankruptcy). *Nouveaux riches*, whose egoism had known no manners, needed to win acceptance. Beset by bewildering change, temptations, and anxieties, many people of substance sought anchorage by putting their own houses in order. Moderation, decorum, and accommodation were needed. 'Romping, struggling, throwing things at one another's head,' Lord Chesterfield advised his dullard son, 'are the becoming pleasantries of the mob, but degrade a gentleman.' The *dolce vita* was to be enjoyed, but only through behaviour which was liberal, polite, and genteel. When so many of the propertied had been splenetic boors, bigots, braggarts, and drunkards, and their sons profligates, the Spectatorial call to gentility was not foppish tinsel, but crucial to personal and social adjustment, the best resource for ensuring respect for the propertied and for securing the world for their enjoyment. Restraint, control, and propriety were vital if society was not to blow up in their face.

After his drinking bouts, Thomas Turner, the Sussex grocer, was all Boswellian remorse: 'Oh! with what horrors does it fill my heart, to think I should be guilty of doing so, & on a Sunday too!' Some thought it wiser to refrain from hard liquor altogether. 'I drink only water,' boasted Erasmus Darwin, 'and am always well.' Though there was no total abstinence movement, there were a few staunch teetotallers, such as the prison reformer John Howard – also a vegetarian, severe in dress, and austere in morals. Cliques such as the bluestockings tried to wean their friends on to tea evenings, and William Cowper penned his own tribute to

> ... the cups
> That cheer but not inebriate.

Bluestockings also tried to cut card-playing ('that hun, whist'), encouraging conversation instead.

Sectors of affluent society (though less so the aristocracy) were indeed becoming starchy as the age of Jane Austen approached. Joseph Farington noted, from about 1770.

a change in the manners and the habits of the people of this country was beginning to take place. Public taste was improving. The coarse familiarity so common in personal intercourse was laid aside, and respectful attention and civility in address gradually gave a new and better aspect to society. The profane habit of using oaths in conversation no longer offended the ear, and bacchanalian intemperance at the dinner-table was succeeded by rational cheerfulness and sober forbearance.

For many, propriety meant retreating from 'coarseness'. Addison and Steele had themselves deplored the vulgarity of their times, but – if Jane Austen's *Northanger Abbey* is a guide – even their own writings caused blushes a century later. Grandfather's everyday colloquialisms became obscenities. 'Piss' was a vulgarism from about the 1700s, and the four-letter words were kept out of blunt Dr Johnson's *Dictionary*. Terms such as 'stink' and 'sick' began to offend polite ears. Bob Acres in Sheridan's *The Rivals* (1775) explained that nowadays one had to go in for 'sentimental swearing': 'Damns have had their day.' Leigh Hunt, born in 1784, recalled that his mother instilled in him a blind horror of swearing. Etiquette also was attended to. Greater use was made of table napkins and clean sheets, helped by the replacement of dear linens by cheap cottons. Eating with one's hands and spitting were condemned as boorish.

Accompanying self-restraint, greater value was laid upon *sociability*, the ability to mix, and sink political, religious, and family differences in common company. The arts of conversation and the tea-table graces were spruced up. 'Good manners', in Swift's definition, were 'the art of making those people easy with whom we converse'. Education was oriented to groom the young for society (and Enlightenment educationists believed that, because the mind was originally like a lump of wax, it was malleable enough to be moulded to society's requirements). Locke and his followers stressed that education should be geared towards living, not just learning, and Lord Chesterfield, in his instructions to his son, preached the cardinal importance of being agreeable. 'Pleasing in company is the only way of being pleased in it yourself.' Politeness and good breeding would open life's doors. 'By the art of good breeding,' Fielding wrote, 'I mean the art of pleasing, or contributing as much as possible to the care & happiness of those with whom you converse.' In a world intimate enough for personal power still to count yet mobile enough to be increasingly anonymous, form and address were crucial visas. The finesses of etiquette helped to secure entrée and advancement in a world of social nicety. Life was a stage on which good actors would shine: courtesy books, dancing masters, and elocutionists abounded to teach the parts. Not too much of the inner self was to be exposed.

Politics, religion, and a thousand and one material interests divided men: culture, it was hoped, might re-unite them. And so the Town devoted itself to cultivating *taste*. 'The Graces, the Graces, remember the Graces! Adieu!' Chesterfield urged his son. The pure breath of Olympian culture would invigorate the elite mountain above the plebs, booby squires, and mere moneybags (yet taste could also baptize wealth). True taste in the arts, people began to stress, should not be flash or racy, but modest and decent, riding pillion with goodness. Addison and Steele thus sought to end 'the long divorce of wit from virtue' which had tarnished cynical Restoration culture. 'I shall endeavour', Addison wrote, 'to enliven morality with wit, and to temper wit with morality, that my readers may, if possible, both ways find their account in the speculation of the day.'

Refinement would polish a person's true mettle, for art, after all, was nature refined, just as the civilized man was the natural man burnished. The *Spectator* advertised itself as a 'work which endeavours to cultivate and polish human life', aiming 'to establish among us a taste of polite writing'. 'Refine or perish' became the watchword, attractive to top people who wished to be *le dernier cri*, to fustian squires who wanted to impress, and to parvenu farmers and tradesmen who aimed at gentrifying themselves. Not least, it was the chorus of everyone in the booming culture business. Encouraging Manchester manufacturers to join its Literary and Philosophical Society, the secretary, Thomas Henry, argued 'a taste for polite literature, and the works of nature and art, is essentially necessary to form the gentleman', quoting Addison's view that learning gave a gentleman 'a kind of property in everything he sees'.

In a parallel way, Lord Chesterfield urged his son to refine his sexual tastes. Polite sex had real advantages, being more erotic and also less risky to health. He recommended him to win his sexual spurs with a genteel Parisian lady rather than with a streetwalker because it was more educative:

> *Un arrangement*, which is, in plain English, a gallantry is in Paris as necessary a part of a woman of fashion's establishment as her house ... A young fellow must therefore be a very awkward one to be reduced to, or of a very singular taste to prefer, drabs and danger to a commerce (in the course of the world not disgraceful) with a woman of health, education and rank.

Alongside manners and taste, morals needed attention. Georgian essayists, tutors, and parents were longwinded on the need to cultivate virtue precisely because the old sheet anchors of morality – the Christian commandments and the authority of tradition – had had their cables cut. In Georgian polite society virtue came to have two particular resonances. First, a disposition of *benevolence* towards self and others, leading to actions productive of happiness. In the amused and ironical worldly atmosphere of affluent society, traditional moral precepts enjoining hair-shirt self-denial were beside the point. People wanted to do good but also to do well. Few were as nakedly pragmatic as Archdeacon Paley, whose touchstone was that 'whatever is expedient is right', or as Jeremy Bentham, for whom the only test of good or evil was the greatest happiness of the greatest number. But in blander form, similar sentiments echoed down the corridors of society.

Second, there was a growing emphasis on the culture of the heart, on sensibility, and on private moral judgement. In this more liberal and patriarchal world, where the Church no longer gave commandments and authority was toned down, the shrine of morality moved within the self. For those, women especially, rich enough to enjoy the luxury of a conscience, goodness became a more introspective, and even aesthetic, matter, involving cultivating and exercising finer, more sensitive feelings. 'Delicacy in pleasures', wrote Steele, 'is the first step people of condition take in reformation from vice.' The quiet sociable virtues – friendship, forbearance, loyalty, cheerfulness – moved to the centre of the stage. Tender-heartedness towards the suffering and the unfortunate became a barometer of sensibility, sometimes collapsing into mawkishness, melancholia, and perhaps *anorexia nervosa*.★ Thus on the death of her father, Abigail Gawthern, a prosperous Nottingham widow, reflected in her diary on her outward mourning and inner grief:

That the sable trappings of woe too often cover the heart divested of every *exquisite feeling* is certain, but the truly delicate and sensible mind depends not upon the mere semblance of affliction. The dingy shade of a garment can neither add to or diminish the sensations of *dear and unfading regret*; heartfelt and unaffected grief turns with disgust from the hackneyed display of ostentatious sorrow whilst it enjoys a *secret luxury* which the hardened and unfeeling mind can *never experience*.

In the latter part of the century virtues of a more private and domestic nature were championed, especially among the middling people, spurred by the example of the faithful, frugal, home-loving George III, who reputedly toasted muffins by the fire while Queen Charlotte fried the sprats. Some repudiated the *beau monde*, cultivating a pre-Romantic preference for peace and quiet and cosy retreat. As Mrs Montagu, queen of the blues, wrote, 'I often think that those people are happiest who know nothing at all of the world & sitting in the little empire of the fireside, where there is no contention or cabal, think we are in a golden age of existence.' Hannah More agreed. 'As to London,' she wrote in 1790, 'I shall be glad to get rid of it; the old, little parties are not to be had; everything is great and vast and late and magnificent and dull.' The Dissenting moralist Mrs Barbauld wrote a work characteristically called *Evenings at Home*.

Especially towards the close of the century moral rearmament became a clarion call for certain groups. Consciously pursuing virtue was one way the swelling ranks of the self-made moneyed could come to terms with the temptations and paradoxes of their own success. New wealth needed to be consecrated by goodness. Bankers and dealers well knew that enduring financial well-being rested upon their good name and credit. Being 'good' took on greater importance with young ladies. Having an impeccable reputation helped them to secure some leverage

---

★ 'We Hypochondriacks', wrote Boswell, 'may console ourselves in the hour of gloomy distress, by thinking that our sufferings make our superiority.'

against family pressures, now many were claiming greater personal choice in the business of marriage. For other women introspection and delicate concern with purity of heart helped them to cope with their lack of external control over lives lived under oppressive parents or husbands. In households where the religion of the heart and soul took a hold, these effects were intensified.

Moral eagerness made itself felt especially amongst certain professional and business strata and at the strident, alienated margins of the intelligentsia: there was no lack of corruption and materialism to feel alienated from. In real life no less than in maudlin novels, refined ladies and sentimental gentlemen suffered agonies of heartache and became tearful over thwarted love, the death of children, cruelty to dumb animals. Sincerity and simplicity became badges of personal identity and integrity. Missions overseas and purity campaigns at home were launched. For some, sabbath-keeping became a touchstone. George III abolished Sunday Court dinners, and the Sunday Observance Society was founded in 1775.

Such people were also anxious to remove 'indecency' (sex) from public life. Delicacy (desexualization) became a matter of moment, especially to protect women. As John Bennett wrote in 1789: 'Delicacy is a very general and *comprehensive* quality. It extends to everything where woman is concerned. Conversation, books, pictures, attitude, gesture, pronunciation should all come under its salutary restraints.'

Sparing the blushes of the innocent knew no bounds for those who saw lasciviousness and smut everywhere. Codpiece Row (next to Breeches Yard in London) had to be renamed Coppice Row. Some would no longer call a bitch a bitch, but rather a 'mother mastiff'. Women no longer were 'big with child' but 'pregnant'. 'Bellies' became 'stomachs', and 'smocks' and 'shifts' 'chemises' (yet poetic diction had long been full of euphemisms). To meet changing taste, Reynolds draped his statues with togas. Protests – as yet hardly effectual – grew against nude bathing. Thomas Bowdler's castrated Shakespeare was first published in 1802 (Doll Tearsheet exited from *Henry IV*).

Of the many manifestations of the flesh, sexuality was the most sinister, sinful, and insidious. Bowdlerism, Grundyism, prudery, repression, anxiety, and shame were all summoned up to button sexuality back in its rightful place. Sensuality came to be the antonym of respectability. By association, cleanliness became a cardinal virtue. For Wesley it was next to godliness, yet Hannah More rated it a higher priority, at least for the poor: 'The necessity of going to church in procession with us on the anniversary, raises an honest ambition to get something decent to wear, and the churches on Sunday are now filled with very cleanlooking women.' All in all, 'Victorianism' was already casting its long shadows in the age of Victoria's grandparents. 'By the beginning of the nineteenth century,' wrote G. M. Young, 'virtue was advancing on a broad, invincible front.'

The vanguard of this drive, largely in moneyed society, for self-esteem through self-censorship was specifically Christian, the Evangelical Movement within the Church of England. The Evangelical Revival had multiple sources – for example Charles Simeon in Cambridge, or John Newton, the reformed slave-trader – but it was galvanized above all by a plutocratic elite in London, the so-called Clapham sect, headed by merchants and bankers such as William Wilberforce, Zachary Macaulay, and John Thornton and his sons. The 'Saints' rejected Latitudinarian religion, renouncing reason for faith, and easiness for the conquest of sin by muscular, crusading struggle; the call to seriousness repudiated what Wilberforce called 'the universal corruption and profligacy of the times, which taking its rise amongst the rich and luxurious has now extended its baneful influence and spread its destructive poison, through the whole body of the people'. The 'Spiritual Barometer' (opposite), printed in the *Evangelical Magazine* in 1800, tabulated the columns of sin and salvation, showing how urgent was excising Satan from society.

Thus, almost all the cultural developments of the Georgian century, from Vauxhall to novels, were beneath contempt and salvation. 'Novels,' thundered the *Evangelical Magazine* in 1793, 'generally speaking are instruments of abomination and ruin. A fond attachment to them is an irrefragable evidence of a mind contaminated, and totally unfitted for the serious pursuits of study, or the delightful exercises and enjoyments of religion.'

Wilberforce's aim was practical, crusading religion: 'God has

set before me as my object the reformation of manners.' The
'Saints' set out to re-Christianize the great, fitting them for their
duty of leadership. Starting with the home, and thus setting the
pattern for nineteenth-century family life, they were not much
concerned to work through legislation, preferring voluntary
action. Thus the Grays, a York Evangelical family, were prominent in setting up spinning schools, Sunday schools, friendly
societies, and charity schools. They drew up cheap diets for the
poor and helped the campaign against the slave trade.

In the tense world of self-made riches surrounded by growl-
ing disaffection, Evangelicalism offered what many patriarchs

70 — Glory: dismission from the body.

60 — Desiring to depart to be with Christ; patience in tribulation; glorying in the cross.

50 — Ardent love to the souls of men; followed hard after God:
Deadness to the world by the cross of Christ.

40 — Love of God, shed abroad in the heart; frequent approach
to the Lord's Table; meeting for prayer and experience.

30 — Delight in the people of God; looking to Jesus.

20 — Love of God's house and word; daily perusal of the Bible
with prayer; vain company wholly dropped.

10 — Evangelical light; retirement for prayer and meditation;
concern for the soul; alarm.

0 — Indifference; family worship only on Sunday evenings;
private prayer frequently omitted; family religion wholly
declined.

10 — Levity in conversations; fashions, however expensive or
indecent, adopted.

20 — Luxurious entertainment; free association with carnal
company.

30 — The theatre; Vauxhall; Ranelagh, etc.; frequent parties of
pleasure; home of God forsaken; much wine, spirits, etc.

40 — Love of novels, etc.; scepticism; private prayer totally
neglected; deistical company prized.

50 — Parties of pleasure on the Lord's day; masquerades;
drunkenness; adultery; profaneness; lewd songs.

60 — Infidelity; jesting at religion; sitting down in the chair of
the scoffer.

70 — Death; perdition.

The Spiritual Barometer (from the *Evangelical Magazine*, 1800)

and their families needed – a stern, steely clear-cut, personal
creed to stabilize and energize the demanding calls of business,
minimize insecurity, and win respect. Each man took paternalistic responsibility for himself and his family, aiming to build
characters that were reliable, hard-working, sober, used to deferring gratification. Evangelicalism gave respect to parvenu
manufacturers such as Peel as Methodism did to artisans, and
renewed the moral authority of peers such as the Earl of Hardwicke. Respectability – a word first used in 1785 – was beginning its meteoric career.

The Georgian age gave plenty of scope to those living com-
fortably above the breadline to explore new life-styles. The low
profiles of Church and state, continued internal peace and security, the generally relaxed moral atmosphere, economic opportunities, and optimism about the future all spurred worldliness,
individualism, and pluralism. This freedom, however, also
threw back burdens upon the personality. Success or failure
hinged upon dexterity in negotiating and manipulating testing
codes of conduct and social rituals. Great premium came to be
placed upon self-management and presentation. In the bewildering clamour of individualism, many struggling souls
looked for beacons of clear religious and moral ideals to guide,
illuminate, and inspire their lives – and others'. With a more
intricate economy, and where social disturbances arose, certain
groups and occasionally the state were beginning to press for
reform or greater control. This was rarely due to industrialization as such (indeed where industrialization was precocious
reforming movements were less urgent). But capitalism was
generating substantial material wealth for large sectors of the
population who, indulging in a more refined life-style, felt
increasingly threatened by the *hoi polloi*. Property-owners had
more to preserve – more to lose – and a greater stake in order,
in finding ways to make the world safe for capital and self-
advancement. Moreover secular outlooks, the rationalism and
pragmatism of the Enlightenment, the vision of human educa-
bility, improvement, and new technological wizardry – all were
fuelling a Promethean myth that regulated change was necessary, possible, and desirable. Ambition, power, and control
were the brood of the Georgians.

8. *Towards Industrial Society*

In the last quarter of the century, economic activity and population began to soar. 'After 1782,' wrote T. S. Ashton,

almost every available statistical series of industrial output reveals a sharp upward turn. More than half the growth in the shipments of coal and the mining of copper, more than three-quarters of the increase of broadcloths, four-fifths of that of printed cloth and nine-tenths of the exports of cotton goods were concentrated in the last eighteen years of the century.

Real national output, growing at about 1 per cent per annum between 1749 and 1780, was increasing by about 1.8 per cent between 1780 and 1800. From 1780, pig-iron output doubled every eight years. Whereas the years from 1660 to 1760 had seen 210 patents for inventions between 1760 and 1789, 976 new patents were taken out. Economic expansion and population rise generally went hand-in-glove. For despite certain labour-saving machinery, economic growth needed more hands, yet without rising output (not least of food) more mouths would have created subsistence crises, similar to those in nineteenth-century Ireland. Keeping nationally in step, both continued pressing on to qualitative and irreversible change, the birth of industrial society. After centuries of precarious balancing of targets of food supply, family size, and employment opportunities within an agriculture-based cottage-industrial economy, a watershed was surmounted.

Economic change in motion is a juggernaut, yet it is the sum of millions of individual choices. Towards the end of the century, more of these were involving bets upon a buoyant future. In industrializing areas people were marrying younger and having larger families (heeding Arthur Young's advice: 'Away! my boys; get children; they are worth more than ever they were'). Entrepreneurs were risking heavier investment in plant, anticipating the forging of new markets. As grain prices and profits reached dizzy heights, farmers put hill-slopes under the plough. Canal mania set in. Not all risks came off: many canals yielded scant profit; competition caused cotton-spinners to crash. But the gambles on expansion paid off often enough – despite the troughs of the trade cycle, multiple bankruptcies, inflation, mounting social distress and pauperism – to allow momentum to gather. The astute and the serendipitous made fat killings: a big textile factory could spin profits of 100 per cent or more. The entrepreneurial whales of the Industrial Revolution, such as the Arkwrights and the Peels, became rich beyond the dreams of cautious industrialists a couple of generations earlier, such as the Darbys of Coalbrookdale. Furthermore, although its consequences were disruptive and its rewards unevenly distributed, industrialization meant that a much larger aggregate national work-force could be supported.

England was the original soil of the Industrial Revolution. How far was the fact that England staged such a revolution at all, and was the first nation to do so, due to the particular quality of its society? Naturally, rapid industrialization did not have only one cause; it depended on the felicitous chemistry of numerous disposing elements, many related only obliquely to social features. Conveniently sited and easily extractable natural resources were indispensable. Coal and iron ore were often cheek by jowl, as in South Yorkshire or the Black Country. Cornish copper and tin could readily be shipped for smelting with South Wales coal. The abundant streams of Pennine and Peak provided washing water and water-power for textiles. Through the war years (1793–1815) and even during Napoleon's blockade the Royal Navy enabled island England to slip an absolute stranglehold on the import of vital raw materials from overseas, above all the increasingly important raw cotton. Growing export outlets to foreign markets were also crucial. Exports, averaging about £9 million a year in 1780, had shot up to £22 million by the end of the century. Iron and steel shipments, running at 16,770 tons in 1765–74, almost doubled to 30,717 in 1795–1804. Over the same period export of woollens went up from £4,356,000 to £6,323,000, and of cottons from

£236,000 to £5,371,000. During Napoleon's European block-ade manufacturers' ability to sell to the colonies and to create markets such as Latin America kept the imperilled English ship of state afloat. How far it was limitless export horizons that impelled industrial expansion remains controversial. Certainly about two thirds of the output of the fastest-growing industry, cotton, was exported.

Many of these advantages were 'natural', 'fortuitous', or 'external'. Yet the capacity to *exploit* them was enhanced by developments in the socio-economic infrastructure. Thus, the new web of navigable waterways and canals was greatly easing and cheapening carriage of bulky natural resources such as minerals, explaining why it was not until late in the eighteenth century that many timeless 'natural' advantages could be con-veniently utilized.

In certain industries, the vast late-eighteenth-century surge in output was achieved thanks largely to technological break-through. In cottons, inventions such as Arkwright's water frame (1769) and Crompton's mule (1779) dramatically boosted pro-ductivity per operative, proportionately slashing unit costs. In spinning cotton yarn, elements of cost shifted as follows:

	1779	1784	1799	1812
Raw cotton	2s.	2s.	3s. 4d.	1s. 6d.
Capital and labour	14s.	8s. 11d.	4s. 2d.	1s.
Total	16s.	10s. 11d.	7s. 6d.	2s. 6d.

This cheapening was largely because technology speeded operations. To process 100 lb. of cotton, an Indian hand-spinner took 50,000 operative manhours, a Crompton mule (1780) took 2,000, a 100-spindle mule (1790) took 1,000, a power-assisted mule (1795) took 300, and by 1825 Roberts's automatic mule took 135.

In the metal industries, widespread adoption of smelting cast-iron by coke ended the stricture which the growing shortage and rising price of charcoal was creating. Henry Cort's reverberatory furnace and the process of purifying iron by 'puddling' made mass use of wrought-iron a practical proposi-tion. Not least, by the end of the century, rotatory steam engines were just beginning to become attractive for driving mills –

flour mills in London, cotton mills in Lancashire, Derbyshire, and Nottinghamshire. Steam power enabled spinning factories (once confined to out-of-the-way up-country river valleys) to move into town centres such as Manchester. By vastly increasing productivity, technological change cheapened products.

England led in technological application not because she had the most brilliant or scientific inventors. Advanced textile machinery and canal technology had been available much earlier in Italy, and in certain fields, such as warship design, France continued to excel. Certainly France had more scientifically trained professional engineers than England. England scored rather in transforming the germs of inventions into industrial application. Central bureaucratic control of industrial processes and standards linked with guild powers probably stifled the innovative drive on the Continent. State patronage in France, Austria, and Russia lured scientists and engineers away from manufacturing industry towards teaching, administration, or military service. In England the paucity of state support for science and engineering ironically encouraged by default the close working partnerships between scientific, technical, and entrepreneurial talents found for instance in the members of the Lunar Society of Birmingham. With legal regulation of industry withering, there were no outside impediments to technological change (except perhaps the patent laws; Arkwright's and Watt's patents probably retarded diffusion of their inventions for some years).

Alongside technological explanations, narrowly economic accounts have sometimes been put forward to account for England's industrial surge. For instance it has been argued that industrialization shot ahead when capital formation or investment crossed certain critical thresholds. Others have claimed that the exponential growth of cotton acted as a 'leading sector', boosting the rest of the economy by a multiplier effect. These views, however, are tripped up by the evidence. Capital investment in manufactures did not rise very significantly. It didn't need to. Because plant remained generally small-scale, fixed capital requirements were not huge. Credit, loans, partnerships, and sleight of hand saw entrepreneurs through. Though many individual capitalists failed, English industry at large was never choking from a capital drought. What was required could be raised privately; there was no need for an industrial stock exchange. The sum total in any case was modest. By 1815, £20 million had gone into canals, but governments raised fifty times as much to finance the Napoleonic wars. Neither did cotton mobilize the rest of the economy. In 1800 it was still largely using wooden machinery and water-power. Unlike the iron industry's products, those of the cotton industry were not the plant and hardware required for tooling further basic industries.

The character of English society was critical to industrialization. Trends in society at large provided the potential for industrialization, particular features of it facilitated rapid economic expansion, and one group master-minded it. Without an expanding population which could be drilled into a supple labour force, rapid industrialization would soon have faltered. For even the introduction of spectacular labour-saving machinery in certain trades, notably cotton-spinning, created the need for more operatives in others, such as weaving. Stocking-knitting, the metal trades, transport, building, and all the processing, distributive, and service industries soaked up more hands. Fresh employment opportunities sustained the population's steep climb: from 5.7 million in 1750 to 8.6 million in 1800 and 11.5 million in 1820. Migration into industrial areas quickened. Most of it, such as that from the Pennines and the Lake District into lowland Lancashire, was creeping, though Irish and Scots flocked into the cotton towns. The fact that many of these extra hands were themselves skilled operatives and their children eased their absorption into the work-force. Technological innovation admittedly sometimes met powerful labour resistance. In March 1792 there was an attack on Grimshaw's factory in Manchester, the first to use Cartwright's power loom. Only two years after it had opened the factory was burnt down by hand-loom weavers, and its destruction inhibited power-loom weaving in the area for several years. Even so, the scale of physical opposition to mechanization was trivial compared with the transformations taking place. Outside areas of old craft industrial towns where guilds and combinations dug their heels in, technical innovation usually proceeded without continuing disruption. This was partly because English workers were already used to wage labour. Many had been brought up from infancy in industrial by-employments, which could easily become full-time. Women and children had long been working at carding and spinning within cottage industry. Migrating to mill towns, they were readily integrated into the new textile factories (unlike, it is said, dispossessed Scottish highlanders, who kicked against factory discipline).

Furthermore, English artisans were able to adapt to and even promote rapid change in crafts such as the wheelwright's because they possessed proud and proven traditions of resourceful workmanship – a fact which impressed foreigners throughout the century, such as Abbé le Blanc:

'Tis not in great works alone that the English excel, the most common trades here seem to partake of the perfection of arts. ... With regard to the neatness and solidity of work of all kinds they succeed better in the least towns of England, than in the most considerable cities of France. I have seen here, in country places, common hands work and put together the several parts of a piece of joiner's work with a degree of exactness and propriety which the best master-joiners of Paris would find it difficult to come near.

The English artisan has the quality, extremely commendable, and peculiar to him, which is, never to swerve from the degree of perfection in his trade which he is master of: whatever he undertakes, he always does as well as he can. The French workman is far from deserving this commendation.

However exaggerated, this view has a ring of truth because so many other commentators thought likewise. Though industrialization created a swelling residuum (largely of women and children) in de-skilled, machine-minding jobs, in other trades, such as puddling iron, fitting machine parts, or painting pottery, highly skilled and well-paid jobs multiplied.

Vital, of course, was agriculture's capacity to feed the booming population. This it did, partly through greater productivity per unit and partly by enclosing common and waste (involving ploughing up downland, chiefly in the South, and converting pasture to arable). Corn output rose from 17,353,000 quarters in 1770 to 21,102,000 in 1800. Greater demand, bad harvests, runaway inflation, and wartime conditions meant that grain and bread prices shot through the roof in the 1790s. A quartern loaf, traditionally costing about 7d., was at 1s. 2d. by 1796. Neophytes to laissez-faire, governments did little to peg prices, for it was precisely these rocketing prices and mushroom profits which made it worth farmers' while to keep boosting output (poorer consumers, heavily dependent on bread, footed the bill of rapid change).

As well as possessing a tractable labour force swelling to meet the demands of industry, England boasted a socio-economic infrastructure well adapted to manufacturing expansion. Systems of credit, bill-broking, and banking permitted growth in scale; road, river, and sea links and haulier services speeded distribution. Chains of wholesalers, middle men, and shops threaded supply to demand. In most respects the entrepreneurs of the Industrial Revolution needed neither to build nor to equip their own macro-economic houses; they could rent them ready-furnished. Turnpikes, often originally built to serve local interests (for conveying agricultural produce to market, for instance), could be commandeered by industrialists moving merchandise cross-country. Similarly in many districts banking facilities had originally been developed largely to serve property-owners investing savings in the Funds; yet later it was increasingly entrepreneurs who capitalized on their credit and bill-redeeming services. Manufacturers were beneficiaries of the fact that great landed proprietors had long behaved as capitalists, deploying surplus wealth in profitable ways, an elite who themselves gained vastly from industrialization. And just as there was no serious economic hindrance to industrialization from High Society (however much snootiness about parvenus), so neither did the state lay obstacles. England's Industrial Revolution generated its own steam, without centralized state economic bellows or dampers. Yet tariff walls throughout the century had given home industry a breathing space. Liquid capital – like profits – escaped direct taxation and its deployment was little hampered.

Broadly distributed affluence growing among the swelling middling ranks created vital demand for increased commodity output. As many observed, there were more comfortable master-craftsmen, petty bourgeois and farmers, spinsters and widows, living off invested income in England than elsewhere. Their ability to enjoy a role as consumers was critical to the expansion of many trades. 'The English,' noted Josiah Tucker,

have better conveniences in their houses, & affect to have more in quantity of clean, neat furniture, & a greater variety such as carpets, screens, window curtains, chamber bells, polished brass locks, fenders, etc. - things hardly known abroad among persons of such a rank - than are to be found in any other country in Europe, Holland excepted.

Thus, he concluded, 'the people of Great Britain may be considered as the customers to or the manufacturers for each other.' It has been suggested that the 'average family' was buying £10 worth a year of British-made goods in 1688, £25 worth in 1750, and £40 worth in 1811.

Consumer demand, for instance, stimulated the rise of the pottery towns, as earthenware and china replaced pewter. Similarly, much of the late-eighteenth-century expansion in the iron and metal trades was not (unlike later) in heavy capital goods - plant, urban utilities, ships, pipes, bridges, track, etc. Machinery, even water-wheels and steam engines, was still made largely of wood. Rather it was in agricultural implements, horses' harnesses, and domestic hardware such as locks, pots and pans, fenders, fireplaces, carriages and household fittings, and ornaments.

There could have been no industrializing sprint without such *nationwide* elements of economic 'fitness' as profitable agriculture, a penetrative distributive system, and a broadening consumer market. Yet it was in only a *small* number of regions that concentrations of heavy industry and factory employment had clustered by the end of the century. New manufactures were localized and extremely unevenly distributed. The metropolis and most country market towns were essentially unaffected, and across most of the countryside the prospect was not scarred by industrialism until the coming of railways in Victoria's reign. A countryman such as William Cobbett could stand without incongruity as the mouthpiece of working people during the Regency before ever visiting an inferno of new industrialism.

Not only was primitive industrialization highly localized but its locations were far flung, and in traditionally 'dark corners' of the land. Peninsular Cornwall had an abnormally highly industrialized work-force because of its key importance in extracting tin, copper, lead, and china clay. Coal-mining and smelting were booming in the narrow valleys of South Wales, in Ebbw Vale and around Merthyr Tydfil, where the Dowlais iron-works were. Tinplate-works developed at Pontypool, copper at Neath. Massive chemical and iron plant such as the Carron works sprouted around the Firth of Forth. Lead-works clustered in lonely settlements high in the Pennines, such as Wharfedale, High Teesdale, and Alston Moor. The Parys copper 'mountain' brought prosperity to Anglesey – Thomas Williams, the 'Copper King', had up to 1,500 workers there. Coal pits expanded on England's distant perimeter in Cumbria, beyond the Lakes. All this was dictated by the geography of raw materials – ore, coal, water – for the critical first phase of industrialization lay in maximizing primitive extraction. To some degree entrepreneurs planted factories – a bit like slave plantations – where labour was unregulated and rivalry least. This sudden, highly localized, and uneven development was what shocked visitors who found belching industrial works poised like giant military encampments deep amidst sublime scenery (most did not see them as blots on the landscape). Early industrialization involved the ultra-rapid transformation of relatively under-developed areas, above all Lancashire, South Wales, and Clydeside, rather than the steady expansion of regions such as Devon, Gloucestershire, or London where regulated trades and workshop industry had been rooted for centuries.

Though an open race was on for riches, the Industrial Revolution had its own sprinters, the entrepreneurs. Challenged to organize staggering new concentrations of production, they were a remarkable breed. Most were essentially self-made and had started small. A high proportion – for example the Peels, Wedgwoods, and John Kay, one of twenty-two children – came from the yeomanry or had begun as small tradesmen, like Arkwright, a barber and wig-dresser who shrewdly got out when wigs went out of fashion. William Radcliffe described his own rise to become a manufacturer:

Availing myself of the improvements that came out while I was in my teens, by the time I was married [aged twenty-four, in 1785], with my little savings, and a practical knowledge of every process from the cotton-bag to the piece of cloth, such as carding by hand or by the engine, spinning by the hand-wheel or jenny, winding, warping, sizing, looming the web, and weaving either by hand or fly-shuttle, I was ready to commence business for myself; and by the year 1789 I was well established, and employed many hands both in spinning and weaving, as a master manufacturer.

By 1801 he had command of over a thousand weavers.

Successful iron-masters generally rose through small work-shops: Aaron Walker began as a nailer, William Hawks of Newcastle and John Parker of Staffordshire as blacksmiths; George Newton of Thorncliffe was a spade maker; Benjamin Huntsman came to steel from clock-making. Samuel Garbett began life as a brass-worker; John Roebuck's father was a Sheffield maker of small wares; William Reynolds was the son of a Bristol iron-trader. Great brewers, such as Courage and Strong, began as inn-keepers. Much of industrialization was launched with small master skills on small master capital.

From these acorn beginnings they came to run hitherto unimagined industrial capitals, plants, and work-forces, exercising local power as great as any noble proprietor's. They innovated spectacularly in work organization, labour discipline, management, and merchandising (the scale of their operations demanded constant innovation). Like modern Hong Kong or Taiwan they banked on selling basic goods in vast quantities to new markets at low unit costs, risking slim profit margins.

Entrepreneurs of course did not, God-like, create the Industrial Revolution on their own, out of nothing. Yet they were forgers of a new world, and their personal innovating role was decisive. Whereas City merchant princes played for fortunes within the well-rutted practices of the Exchange, entrepreneurs were ploughing virgin fields, having to be capitalist, financier, technocrat, works manager, engineer merchant, and salesman all in one. Only in England did entrepreneurs become so prominent so early. On the Continent aspiring *bourgeois gentilhommes* to a much greater extent continued to seek office, professional, or rentier status.

Max Weber suggested long ago that the English entrepreneurs emerged out of the crucible of Calvinism, justifying themselves to God by industry, frugality, and sober living, their secret being that profits did not get dissipated but was ploughed back. There were indeed many entrepreneurs who were Dissenters, such as John Wilkinson and the Quaker Darbys (though few were strictly Calvinists). But many others, such as the Peels and Arkwrights, were Anglicans, and some, like Robert Owen, were no friends of orthodox Christianity. Nonconformists *were* prominent as entrepreneurs, not however because of their creed, but because (like the Jewish community) they formed a close-knit, 'marginal' group spared the fashionable world of dissipation – Quakers in particular shut themselves off from landed High Society. They aimed to dignify the world left open to them, business, with success.

In some ways the formative years of the Industrial Revolution lived off the legacy of the past, generating expansion within a familiar economic framework but at accelerating rates. Production even of goods made by time-honoured processes soared: between 1785 and 1800 commodity output increased as follows:

strong beer 33%	soap 41%	spirits 73%
small beer 30%	tobacco 58%	tea 97%
tallow candles 33%		

What became the great firms of the early Industrial Revolution were not vast combines, floated on landed, City, or finance capital, under the eye of established merchant princes, but minnow enterprises which had seized opportunities to keep growing. And a small works could get going almost for a song. Workshops were to be had at low rates:

Suitable for a beginner in Trade in the sailcloth manufacture and other branches in Linen and Cotton [ran an advertisement from Prescot]. Shops for 8 or 10 Hacklers, two Rooms for laying up Hemp, Flax, etc., one Shop with 8 Sail Cloth Looms, one ditto for six Starching Frames, one ditto for Warping, counting Yarn, etc., the Mill ready fix'd, a large Boukhouse, with plenty of good Water, and a Croft of a proper Size adjoining, the present rent of the whole only £16 per Annum.

Even a steam engine could be purchased for a couple of hundred pounds. Used machinery was readily up for sale. In 1792 a second-hand 'forty-spindle jenny of the best sort' could be had for £6; a large scribbling or carding machine could sell at £50. A small factory would cost no more than £2,000. In 1741 Abraham Walker set up his Sheffield ironfoundry on £600 (by 1801 the business was worth £235,000). In 1793 Jedediah Strutt's mill at Belper, one of the giants, cost £5,000 for the building, £5,000 for the machinery, and £5,000 for the materials; William Marshall's first flax-spinning mill in Leeds cost about the same (a stately home could swallow up to £100,000).

Capital was privately raised (bankers were not eager to make long-term loans to industry for plant, preferring to lend 'short'), and capital burdens were often pooled between partners in an infant firm. Early in the century Abraham Darby had joined three others to set up the Vale Royal Furnace in Cheshire, each contributing materials, skills, or money. Every Monday the pig-iron produced was shared out between the four in proportions dictated by the partnership agreement. In 1759 the Dowlais iron-works in South Wales was built on £4,000 put up by eight partners. Sometimes labyrinthine sub-contracting and sub-letting arrangements were devised to share the capital load around. When Robert Owen set up his first factory, he had to sub-let almost the whole of it.

Furthermore, because most of the money needed to set up in business was not fixed but circulating capital, it might be largely 'illusory', floated chiefly by credit (that is, in effect footed by other people). The ratio of fixed to working capital was often in the region of 1 : 4. By 1800 no more than £2 million in fixed capital had gone into the cotton industry (little more than what rebuilding Bath had cost). In short, in the early days of the Industrial Revolution it was remarkably easy for a modest man, indeed a beginner, to start up a business of enormous expansive potential even without owning much capital. The shrewd entrepreneur accelerating from nowhere might leave the second son of an earl in the dust. The man who a generation earlier had rested content with a workshed might now be king of a factory.

It was easy to set up businesses because so much machinery was actually cheap, simple, and traditional. In manufacturing industry steam-power remained almost superfluous. Most steam engines were used for draining mines rather than driving wheels. Even in textiles, the move from stream-power to steam-power came slowly, for water-wheels were cheap, durable, and highly efficient, though vulnerable to drought and ice. Not till 1785 was steam harnessed to a cotton mill (at Popplewick in Nottinghamshire), and in 1800 the horses in London and Middlesex still outnumbered all the steam 'horsepower' in England and Wales. There were only 490 Watt steam engines (the meticulous Boulton and Watt assembled about a dozen a year). Steam's chief advantage lay in giving a geographical mobility which water-power lacked.

Yet because of fierce competition, technological transformation, frontierism in the market, and financial panics even the biggest guns (including Lancashire spinners such as Horrocks or McConnels) could go broke. Whereas peers by blood could strut through chronic indebtedness, when aristocrats of manufacturing were caught short for want of funds, it was serious; they had no lands to mortgage. Even Matthew Boulton was continually cadging from his friends to tide him over bad times, and he dragged his heels about repaying.

Industrialization involved a revolution in relations of production. The concentrated work-place, employing several hundred men, women, and children, ceased to be a freak characteristic chiefly of dockyards and became an integral feature of employment. Not all large works were multi-storey factories housing serried ranks of identical machines fed from a single belt or power shaft. Some were really highly organized chains of distinct workshops engaged on multifarious processes. In Birmingham the Soho foundry of Matthew Boulton was an interlocking range of workshops, each serially engaged on a segment of the metal processes – casting, assembly, stamping, burnishing, etc. Boulton spatially located each operation in his flow-line to minimize movement, time-wastage, and transport. He maximized the division of labour, silently endorsing Adam Smith's view that 'the greatest improvement in the productive powers of labour and the greater part of the skill, dexterity & judgment with which it is anywhere directed, or applied, seem to have been the effects of the division of labour'.

But the centrally powered factory was the herald of the future. Though the first real English factory was the silk mill set up in 1719 by Thomas Lombe in Derby (in six storeys, housing 300 workers, driven by a central water-wheel), cotton-spinning was the vector in which factories paid dividends. Kay's flying shuttle (1733) and Hargreaves's spinning jenny (1767) had been cheap and compact enough for use in cottage industry. But from Arkwright's water frame (1769) onwards, efficient spinning machinery was too costly to be owned by individual out-workers, too bulky to be housed at home, and increasingly harnessed to mechanical sources of power. Arkwright further-more stipulated that his frame should be used in 1,000 spindle units, to pre-empt evasions of his patent. The new factories were purpose-built. Industrialists experimented with fire-proof cast-iron frames, steam-heating, and later gas-lighting to facili-tate round-the-clock shifts.

For centuries, putting-out and sub-contracting had made good sense for capitalists as appropriate modes of industrial organization. They escaped heavy investment in central plant or even tools; workers could be instantly laid off, and mainten-ance of the work-place, work discipline, collecting and deliver-ing materials were the workers' problems. It was a flexible system, minimizing employers' responsibilities. Now, with artificial power and labour-saving technology promising sky-rocketing output, concentrating the work-force came to have the edge. Behind the walls and under the roof of a factory, it was easier for a manufacturer to protect advanced and secret machinery from industrial espionage, a trauma haunting the most technologically sophisticated entrepreneurs (who never-theless also appreciated the selling power of visibility, showing visitors over public parts of their works). One of Boulton's aims in dividing up his premises into separate workshops was to prevent information leakage amongst the work-force, crafts-men being banned from all shops except those where their trade lay. Employers threatened no quarter to workers who spilt trade secrets. Inside a factory it was easier to ensure that hands worked the maximum number of hours a week, like clockwork, every hour, every workday, every week. Moreover, within handicraft organization, employers had had little check upon their materials (what employers called pilfering, workers saw as lawful perks). Inside the factory, owners could reduce losses to a minimum.

Factories employing platoons of workers needed new labour relations. In the first place, owners needed to create a work-force. Workers were wooed in newspapers, as for instance by this advertisement placed by Strutt and Arkwright in the *Derby Mercury*:

Cotton Mill, Cromford, 10th Dec. 1771
Wanted immediately, two journeymen clock-makers, or others that understand tooth and pinion well. Also a smith that can forge and file. Likewise two wood turners, that have been accustomed to wheel-making spoke-turning, etc. Weavers residing at the mill, may have good work. There is employment at the above place for women, children etc. and good wages.

Adults were lured by prospects of secure work and higher wages, but until 1816 many manufacturers conscripted their child labour by contracting with parish authorities to take infant paupers off their hands as apprentices. 'It is a very common practice,' wrote Samuel Romilly,

with the great populous parishes in London to bind children in large numbers to the proprietors of cotton-mills in Lancashire and Yorkshire, at a distance of 200 miles. The children, who are sent off by wagon loads at a time, are as much lost forever to their parents as if they were shipped off for the West Indies.

Between 1786 and 1805, Cuckney Mill in Nottinghamshire secured juvenile workers as follows:

from 24 parishes in Notts. and the adjacent parts of Derby-shire and Yorkshire	63
from 26 parishes in London and the adjacent parts of Middlesex and Essex	498
from 4 other parishes	44
Total sent by parishes	605
from 3 philanthropic organizations	98
from parents, relatives and private individuals	77
	780

Child and female labour was prized by new masters, being more tractable and less militantly organized, and drawing lower wages than men. In 1793, 18 per cent of Robert Owen's work-force was under nine years old.

This new labour force needed to be tamed and trained. Out-workers had been used to pacing their own work by the piece, not by the clock, chatting, drinking, and larking on the job. Punctuality, regularity, and accuracy by contrast were demanded by the metronome tempo of the new factory.

Ambrose Crowley had battled against resistance to labour discipline early in the century:

> Some have pretended a sort of right to loyter, thinking by their readiness and ability to do sufficient in less time than others. Others have been so foolish to think bare attendance without being imployed in business is sufficient ... Others so impudent as to glory in their villany and upbrade others for their diligence ...

It was an endemic problem. As the hosier Cookson put it in 1806:

> I find the utmost distaste on the part of the men, to any regular hours or regular habits ... The men themselves were consistently dissatisfied because they could not go in & out as they had been used to do; & were subject during after hours, to the ill natured observations of other workmen to such an extent as to completely disgust them with the whole system.

This was partly because entrepreneurs sought to impose longer hours. Crowley had stipulated,

> To the end that sloath and villany should be detected and the just and diligent rewarded, I have thought meet to create an account of time by a Monitor, and do order and it is hereby ordered and declared from 5 to 8 and from 7 to 10 is fifteen hours, out of which take 1 for breakfast, dinner, etc. There will then be thirteen hours and a half neat service ...

This service, Crowley insisted, must be calculated 'after all deductions for being at taverns, alehouses, coffee houses, breakfast, dinner, playing, sleeping, smoking, singing, reading of news history, quarrelling, contention, disputes or anything foreign to my business, any way loytering'. Cotton operatives were regularly having a thirteen- or fourteen-hour day thrust upon them. Adults kicked against the discipline. Many left, or were dismissed (plenty more were queuing at the gates). McConnel and Kennedy in Manchester had a work-force turnover of 100 per cent a year.

Employees hankered after traditional holidays. Josiah Wedgwood fumed in 1772, 'Our men will go to the Wakes if they were sure to go to the D...l next. I have not spared them in threats & I would have thrashed them right heartily if I could.' It was for him a continuing problem. Four years later he complained, 'Our men have been at play 4 days this week, it being Burslem Wakes. I have rough'd and smooth'd them over & promised them a long Xmass, but I know it is all in vain, for Wakes must be observed though the world was to end with them.' He wanted to end such atavism and make craftsmen go like clockwork. Southey commented in 1806: 'In commerce, even more than in war, both men and beasts are considered merely as machines, and sacrificed with even less compunction.'

Labour discipline was injected in various ways. Supervision was tightened – for Boulton workmen must be 'under our eyes & immediate management – everyday & almost every hour'. Many entrepreneurs set up schools to break in the very young. Wedgwood tried to yoke workers within long-term contracts. Swingeing fines punished malefactors – those who were late or out of position, who dozed, talked, or slacked. The iron-master William Reynolds drew up 'Rules for the Preservation of good order in the works of William Reynolds and Co.'. Wedgwood's rule-book stipulated:

Any workman striking & likewise abusing an overlooker, to lose his place.
Any workman conveying ales or liquor into the manufactory in working hours, forfeit 2/-.

But exemplary workers were also rewarded – with bonuses, special clothes, promotion. Wedgwood, John Christian Curwen, and other employers set up compulsory, contributory sickness benefit and pension schemes for their workers, to give them a lasting interest in the firm. Matthew Boulton founded the Soho Society, to which workers contributed between ½d. and 4d. a week, receiving up to 80 per cent of their earnings when sick. Contemporaries believed attention to labour discipline and personnel management paid off, one remarking about Soho:

> The rules of this Manufactory have certainly been productive of the most laudable and salutary effects, and besides the great attention paid to cleanliness and wholesome air etc., this Manufactory has always been distinguished for its order and good behaviour and particularly during the great riots at Birmingham.

Entrepreneurs had to be titans and tyrants, because of the sheer scale of their operations. By 1793, Reynolds' iron-works were valued at £138,000. In 1770 Boulton had about 700 workers at Soho and by 1795 Peel was employing a work-force of 15,000. Their sights rose and rose. 'I shall ASTONISH THE WORLD ALL AT ONCE,' wrote Wedgwood to his partner Bentley, 'for I hate piddling you know.' Becoming 'vase-maker general to the universe', he died worth £½ million. By way of self-commemoration John Wilkinson the iron-founder stipulated burial in an iron coffin (prudent protection also against body-snatchers).

The labours involved in the relentless enterprise of nursing large-scale industry from the cradle were Herculean. Some – like Wedgwood – saw scientific management as the philosopher's stone: understanding cash-flow better, promoting time-and-motion efficiency, and making accountancy more rigorous. Marketing policy was also crucial. Wedgwood, aided by his faithful merchant partner, Thomas Bentley, put his cards on psychological snobbery, pioneering brand names and show-rooms. Matthew Boulton also recognized the economics of reaching the broadest markets:

> Though you speak contemptuously of Hawkers, Pedlars, and those who supply *Petty Shops*, yet we must own that we think they will do more towards supporting a great Manufactory, than all the Lords in the Nation. We think it of far more consequence to supply the people than the nobility only.

Others, such as John Marshall, the Leeds flax-spinner, trusted to the nitpicking business of enforcing exact order:

> In Marshall's every man chases his business ... the hands have very particularly printed instructions set before them which are as particularly attended to ... so strict are the instructions that if an overseer of

a room be found talking to any person in the mill during working hours he is dismissed immediately – two or more overseers are employed in each room, if one be found a yard out of his own ground, he is discharged. No overseer is allowed to touch a tool or shift a pinion with his own hands, on pain of dismissal – everyone, managers, overseers, mechanics, oilers, spreaders, spinners and reelers, have their particular duty pointed out to them, and if they transgress, they are instantly turned off as unfit for their situation.

Richard Arkwright's entrepreneurial successes were achieved by bulldozing. Though his interest in technological innovation waned, his opportunism remained acute. Still others, like the Strutts, kept up religiously with every minuscule technical wrinkle. The great entrepreneurs kept tabs on their empires, monarchs of all they surveyed, down to the last petty operation. Wedgwood strode around his works smashing 'rejects' with his wooden leg. If the owner didn't bother, no one else would, for there were no boards of directors, and trusty middle managers were rare as rubies.

A proprietor, like a king, would pray for an heir to inherit the family business (though sons as often as not became absentees and prodigals).

Entrepreneurs were the frontiersmen of the new industrial world, colonizing virgin corners of the land. Factories straddled the fast-flowing streams of rural Derbyshire, Lancashire, and Yorkshire. Arkwright set up his works at obscure Cromford, Belper, Milford, Birkacre, and Holywell, far from the old cities and guilds. Hence they needed not just to drill labour *inside* their own factories but also to create a total community environment from scratch. They ran up terraces of cottages, lodging houses, shops, roads, bridges, weirs, chapels, drains, and schools. Youths working for Strutt and Arkwright had to attend school for four hours on Saturday afternoons and Sundays to 'keep them out of mischief'. Angling for loyalty, the bluff Arkwright built an inn at Cromford, whereas the sober Strutts set grounds aside for kitchen gardens. John Farey praised 'the vast numbers of neat and comfortable cottages ... erected by the late Sir Richard and by the present Mr Richard Arkwright, by Messrs Strutts, Mr Samuel Oldknow and numerous others of the cotton spinners and manufacturers'.

Where parish aid was rudimentary they established benefit clubs and health schemes (they had first created industrial disease and accidents). Aping paternalist grandees, bosses organized sports and feasts, inventing works loyalties and traditions (as in Japanese industry nowadays, ballads were sung toasting success to the works). When Matthew Boulton's son came of age, he staged a jamboree for 700 workers. Works bands and choirs soon followed.

Captains of industry had to create willy-nilly a new environment. With the exception perhaps of colonial governors, they had unequalled scope to dictate the shape of things to come, and some had shining new views of society, the most remarkable embodiment being the New Lanark Mills, where Robert Owen was to attempt by paternalism a cooperative utopia.

Owen himself epitomizes the new world of the manufacturers. Son of a Welsh saddler, at the age of ten he tramped to London with forty shillings in his pocket, later working behind a haberdasher's counter for £25 a year. At eighteen he set up in business in Manchester manufacturing spinning-mules by borrowing £100 from his brother. His first year's profit was £300. At twenty-eight he married into the Dales, a wealthy Scottish textile family, finally buying up his father-in-law's mills for £60,000. Once rich, his attention turned from making money to making utopian socialism, for having created an environment for his own work-force he came to believe that people were creatures of environment. Social perfection was then a matter of social engineering. Industrialization, within a socio-economy of cooperation and communism, would conquer poverty and end the curse of labour.

Certain industries – iron, for example – spurted ahead in the last part of the century. Iron had not hitherto been the key metal trade (brass, tin, copper were more prominent, and much iron was imported from Sweden). But the introduction of the new technology of coke-smelting, the puddling process for wrought-iron (it boiled off the sulphur), and rolling- and-slitting mills relieved bottlenecks. No charcoal furnace was built after 1775. Output shot up from 17,350 tons in 1740 to 68,300 in 1790 and 125,019 in 1796. Iron was beginning to replace wood for machine parts, tools, and screws. Iron pillars, beams and girders were being tried in buildings (including Wesleyan chapels): they were admirably fire-proof. John Wilkinson developed precision boring for cannon and steam-engine cylinders. The first iron bridge, over the Severn, was constructed in 1779, the first iron ship in 1787. More durable than wood, iron was preferable where wear and tear were heavy (for instance for gears, for the rails within pit workings and for the waggon-ways on which colliery trucks ran down to canals and quays). From 1793 war gave a blank cheque to the metal trades. Whereas in 1700 charcoal furnaces had been small and sited in the rural woodlands (the Weald in Sussex, for instance) where firing was available, by the end of the century blast furnaces were complex and costly, many needing steam engines to provide the jet of air. Close on 90 per cent of iron production was by then centred on the coalfields, confirming Arthur Young's observation that 'All the activity & industry of this land is fast concentrating where there are coal pits.'

In the cotton industry, the same thing happened. Up to mid-century cottons had been rather insignificant (total sales amounting to perhaps £600,000 a year in 1760). They were not cheap, the price of raw cotton being higher than for wool. Indian calicoes and muslins were better in quality. Most English 'cottons' were linen mixtures: and as fine fabric, linen, though expensive, was preferred.

Output of English cottons began to pick up from the 1760s, largely by breaking into and expanding continental and colonial markets. Imports of cotton wool, at 2.8 million lb. in 1750, shot up to 14.8 in 1780 and 59.5 in 1800. Paul's carding machine and Kay's flying shuttle speeded carding and weaving so dramatically that by the 1760s it required numerous spinners to supply a weaver (Arthur Young claimed as late as 1780 that 'they reckon twenty spinners and two or three other hands to every weaver'). The spinning jam was solved by Hargreaves's jenny (developed 1767, patented 1770), which began with about sixteen spindles but by the end of the century was taking up to a hundred, and then by Arkwright's water frame (1769), which produced a yarn strong enough to be used as both warp and weft, inaugurating English pure cotton fabrics. Once

Arkwright's patents had been cancelled in 1785, the way was open for the general introduction of huge factory steam-spinning. By the early nineteenth century, one spinner was as productive as 200 had been seventy years earlier. In the words of the manufacturer William Radcliffe, 'Cotton, cotton, cotton has become the almost universal material for employment.'

Between 1780 and 1800, imports of raw cotton went up eightfold. Handicraft weaving ceased to be largely a winter fall-back by-employment, becoming a lucrative and quickly learnt full-time occupation. The industry which had rated barely a mention in Adam Smith's *Wealth of Nations* (1776) was accounting for some 7–8 per cent of Britain's national income by the early nineteenth century, employing about 100,000 spinners. The twenty spinning factories of 1770 had increased to 150 by 1790. By 1788 there were forty cotton mills in South Lancashire alone, and spinning was busying some quarter of a million weavers in cottage and workshop industry up and down the country. There seemed no ceiling to demand, not least because prices tumbled.

Other industries shared in the rapid late-century expansion, chemicals assuming particular importance. The wealth-multiplying consequences of expansion produced euphoria: 'It is impossible,' wrote Patrick Colquhoun just after the turn of the century,

to contemplate the progress of manufactures in Great Britain within the last thirty years without wonder and astonishment. Its rapidity, particularly since the commencement of the French revolutionary war, exceeds all credibility. The improvement of the steam engines, but above all the facilities afforded to the great branches of the woollen and cotton manufactories by ingenious machinery, invigorated by capital and skill, are beyond all calculation; and as these machines are rendered applicable to silk, linen, hosiery and various other branches, the increased produce, assisted by human labour, is so extensive that it does more than counter-balance the difference between the price of labour in this, and other countries – the latter cannot enjoy the same facilities without those extensive capitals, skill, and experience which the British manufacturers have acquired, and which cannot be transferred to foreign nations without those requisites (capital and skill) which they will probably not possess for a long series of years, and which very few of them can ever hope to enjoy.

What was the wider social impact? Industrialization had drastic *long-term* consequences, which those living through it knew very well: sooty Coketowns made up of barrack-like back-to-backs; grime, fog, sulphureous smoke, choking chemical wastes; the Great Exhibition in the Crystal Palace; the horrors of factory accidents and industrial diseases, cholera, the triumphs of the railways, cheap cottons, cheap books, cheap travel, Marx's vision of class conflict, a revolutionary bourgeoisie facing an alienated proletariat; affluence and effluents. As the economy industrialized, individual capitalists and operatives felt waning control over their own destinies, becoming the puppets of market forces and the trade cycle. Even the greatest might go to the wall. But what had industrialization changed by 1800?

Romantics were already assailing stony materialism and wasteland blight, the scandal of child labour, the tyranny of lucre, the robot system in which 'getting and spending we lay waste our power'. Yet such criticisms of commercialism and alienated labour had been expressed throughout the eighteenth century: indeed since Biblical times. Equally we must stress that many sectors of the economy – even many manufactures – had been hardly touched by new industrial technology, and that by no means all rapid change was due to the manufacturing system. 'London is, I am certain, much fuller than ever I saw it,' observed Horace Walpole in 1791: 'I have twice been going to stop my coach in Piccadilly [to inquire what was the matter] thinking there was a mob, and it was only nymphs and swains, sauntering and trudging.' London expanded, but not because of the Industrial Revolution.

Until the end of the century, the face of industrialization impressed more than it horrified (though John Byng thought it 'destroyed the course and beauty of nature'). Forges and chimneys belching flame into the night had their own sublime majesty, qualities picked out by artists such as Joseph Wright of Derby, more endearing to tourists than choking residents. Iron bridges and canal viaducts (with barges sailing through the air) were new wonders of the world. Industrial towns appeared businesslike, thronging with activity. Productive labour was a heart-warming sight. The desolate lunar landscapes of mineral slag, abandoned workings, and chemical pollution in Lancashire, the Black Country, and South Yorkshire were largely for the future. The worst slums were not in new centres of dense industrialization, but in overcrowded cottage-industry villages, ports, and ancient cities such as Bristol. Before the turn of the century, however, overburdened sanitation was breeding decimating waves of feverous diseases in Manchester,* Bury, Bolton, Ashton, and other parts of industrial Lancashire, and tuberculosis and rickets worsened.

What had industrialization done for the people up to 1800? It certainly hadn't uniformly elevated living standards amongst the working population. Industrializing trades of course needed to offer attractive wages. Thus whereas in 1700 wage-rates in under-developed Lancashire had been below those of the rural South (between 8d. and 1s. a day as compared with about 1s. 2d.) they outran them as industrialization proceeded. But the replacement of male by female and child labour in textile factories took its toll on family incomes (women's pay was about two thirds that of men). And with roaring inflation even rising wages failed to keep pace with the rocketing cost of food, particularly during the 1790s. The pressure of demand, exacerbated by harvest crises in 1783, 1792-3, 1795-6, and 1799-1800, pushed bread to staggering prices. Wheat cost 48s. a quarter in 1760, 36s. in 1770, 54s. in 1780, 75s. in 1790, and a record 113s. a quarter in 1800. The cost of living almost doubled between 1770 and 1795 and went up by as much again by 1800.

There were, however, rich pickings in certain trades. With unlimited demand for cloth, and enormous expansion in output of spun yarn, hand-loom weavers shot up in numbers, and were enjoying a spectacular Indian summer before their catastrophic demise in the teeth of power-weaving from the 1820s. A Lancashire or Derbyshire hand weaver could command £3 a week or more at the turn of the century (an agricultural labourer was probably on less than ten shillings). Up to the end of the century there had been no general crisis of technological obsolescence for out-workers. Even businesses with large turnovers such as West Riding worsteds long continued on strictly traditional small-

*Manchester failed to cope with a rising population of 27,000 in 1773, 39,000 in 1780, and 75,000 in 1801.

master lines. In some areas, however, staple industries (Devon worsteds for example) had been hit by competition.

Had industrialization already spelt a revolution in conditions of life? Generalization is hazardous and of course the bulk of the labour force had been barely touched. (The number of nailers, for instance, trebled between 1770 and 1810, but they were all domestic workers.) In many trades, industrialization had certainly eroded independence. Mechanization diminished workers' bargaining over production processes and introduced new health dangers. Steam pumps allowed deeper coal-mining, resulting in more explosions (the introduction of the Davy 'safety' lamp from 1815 further multiplied hazards since it encouraged the reworking of abandoned 'unsafe' pits). Dry grinding in the cutlery trades, paint-making, and the use of lead glazes in the potteries were often lethal. Josiah Wedgwood proved stubborn even when informed of the dangers – to consumers and workers alike – of lead in his glazes. Unguarded machinery in textile factories, into which exhausted children had to crawl while it was still running to pick up broken threads, made mutilations commonplace. Factory labour was extremely long, often over twelve or thirteen hours a day, six days a week. Factories were stifling, machine-minding was dead-end soul-destroying work (though also comparatively light, all-the-year-round, and fairly secure). Above all, factories drastically reduced operatives' control over their work (in Owen's words, under this system, 'to support life you must be tyrant or slave'). In the family-oriented work-where-you-live economy typical amongst craftsmen and out-workers, the group (whether barge crew or family workshop) customarily regulated its own work practices (though within the wider constraints of necessity). This was dramatically curtailed within the martinet discipline of the factory, where even talking was suppressed. Yet family life adjusted rapidly to the widespread migration and new patterns of work involved in factory towns. Many migrants moved to districts where they already had friends and kin; grandparents and aunts minded children while mothers were out at work (though most female factory hands were unmarried), and strong neighbourly support cared for the sick and out-of-work. Migrants in new manufacturing communities re-asserted their roots through ale-houses, friendly societies, parades, union activities, and chapels; the works themselves became a focus of loyalty.

By contrast, labour sometimes united to resist the installation of new machinery. Arkwright's carding factory at Birkacre in Lancashire was attacked in 1776 when

a most riotous and outrageous Mob assembled in the Neighbourhood, armed in a warlike Manner, and after breaking down the Doors of the Buildings, they entered the Rooms, destroyed most of the Machinery, and afterwards set fire to and consumed the whole Buildings, and every Thing therein contained.

Responses to new conditions of production differed however from place to place. In 1787 the attempt to apply Arkwright's roller principle to worsted-spinning in Leicester led to riots, the death of the mayor, and the smashing of the machinery; but the process was accepted in Nottingham. In Coventry there was such successful resistance to the mechanization of ribbon-weaving that the trade became uncompetitive and died off.

For the individual worker, industrialization involved a complex profit-and-loss account. What industrialization was doing as a whole however was multiplying toil (seemingly a paradox given the growth of 'labour-saving' technology). Artisans in traditional manufactures may not have received larger wages, and many trades had been – and remained – sweated. But they had been accustomed to flexible work hours, to fringe benefits, and to time off for fairs, holidays, or anniversaries. With industrialization came the iron cage of working six days a week, every week. Holidays and leisure were squeezed; fatigue stared out from unsmiling faces. As Godwin pointed out, mechanization, which should have made machines the servants of men, freeing them to enjoy new commodities, was actually making them the slaves of work – the slaves of machines – more than ever before.

Many believed that in industrializing districts the faces of Nature and of society were becoming more opulent, sprucer, and more civilized. ('The general diffusion of manufactures throughout a country,' thought Robert Owen, 'generates a new character in the inhabitants.') Visiting Stoke in 1781, John Wesley commented on the effects of the rise of the Potteries:

How the whole face of the country has changed in about 20 years, since which inhabitants have continually flowed in from every side – the wilderness is literally become a fruitful field. Houses, villages, towns have sprung up; & the country is not more improved than the people.

Josiah Wedgwood invited his young workers to consider the benefits industry had brought:

... ask your parents for a description of the country we inhabit when they first knew it; and they will tell you that the inhabitants bore all the marks of poverty to a much greater degree than they do now. Their houses were miserable huts, the land poorly cultivated and yielded little of value for the food of man or beast, and these disadvantages, with roads almost impassable, might be said to have cut off our part of the country from the rest of the world, besides rendering it not very comfortable to ourselves. Compare this picture, which I know to be a true one, with the present state of the same country, the workmen earning near double their former wages, their houses mostly new and comfortable, and the lands, roads, and every other circumstance bearing evident marks of the most pleasing and rapid improvements ... Industry has been the parent of this happy change.

Against this, however, there was John Aikin's verdict in 1795 on the festering mill town of Manchester:

... the poor are crowded in offensive, dark, damp, and incommodious habitations, a too fertile source of disease! ... In some parts of the town, cellars are so damp as to be unfit for habitations ... The poor often suffer from the shattered state of cellar windows. This is a trifling circumstances in appearance, but the consequences to the inhabitants are of the most serious kind. Fevers are among the most usual effects; and I have often known consumptions which could be traced to this cause. Inveterate rheumatic complaints, which disable the sufferer from every kind of employment, are often produced in the same manner ... I have often observed, that fevers prevail most in houses exposed to the effluvia of dunghills in such situations.

Workers were nostalgic for rusticity and remained so throughout the coming century. Yet no new laws of settlement were needed to corral the proletariat within the new industrial towns. Labouring men colluded in the creation of the new economy. For what the Hammonds called 'the curse of Midas' had its two sides. Now cheap cotton garments were easier to clean and more hygienic – but smoky atmospheres dirtied them faster (and lungs can't be washed). Factories paid good wages but denied labourers the small perks and pleasures gleaned by country-dwellers. Above all no one took overall responsibility for the new world captains of industry were creating. Though entrepreneurs were kings in their own bailiwick they lacked a collective voice and social vision, and competition amongst them was fierce. After the swift demise of the General Chamber of Manufactures (1785) no parliamentary lobby spoke for them as a whole.

Already by the end of the eighteenth century, industrialization was lending its weight to tilting the economy (though it was tilting quite slowly). Distribution of Gross National Product shifted towards the town and manufacturing:

	1700 (% GNP)	1800
Agriculture	40	33
Industry	20	24
Services	35	44
Urban %	c. 22	c. 30

Economic change, however, had wrought an unparalleled transformation of social *geography* during the century. In 1700 the major centres of population, wealth, and industry had lain within a southern triangle of which Bristol, London, and Norwich were the points. By 1800 the triangle had rotated northwest to become contained by Bristol, Hull, and Preston. Many of the conurbations of modern England – Birmingham, Manchester, Bradford, Huddersfield, Preston, etc. – had been but sprawling villages in 1700 but were great towns by 1800, the change being largely due to industrial developments. The classic mill towns were shooting up near the end of the century. By 1801 Wigan had a population of 10,989, Bury 7,072, Oldham 12,024, Blackburn 11,980, Bolton 12,549, Preston 11,887, and Stockport 14,850. These totals are about as high as those of any town (London, Norwich, and Bristol excepted) in 1700. Areas of England lightly peopled in 1700 were fast becoming densely populated industrial regions, the West Riding of Yorkshire and Lancashire in particular:

| | *Estimated population per square mile* | | |
	1700	1750	1801
Lancashire	127	179	253
Yorks, West Riding	91	122	212
Worcestershire	141	139	189
Cheshire	92	105	174
Staffordshire	111	133	210
Warwickshire	112	152	236

In 1700 Norfolk, Somersetshire, and Lancashire all had comparable populations (242,000, 214,000, and 238,000 respectively). The first two had climbed steadily by 1800 (to about 282,000 each). Lancashire had shot up to 694,000.

The destiny of this new geography of industrialization still lay unresolved in 1800. The burgeoning new mill towns of Lancashire, Cheshire, Derbyshire, and the West Riding, as well as the mining and foundry centres dotted about the country, still lay on the fringes of established society, the nation of parliamentary boroughs, grandees' seats, assize towns, cathedral cities, public schools – and above all the metropolis. Almost none had a corporation. They lacked churches, hospitals, and other civic amenities. Sparseness of local gentry meant that there were few active JPs on the spot, a crucial factor in responses to radical disturbances from the 1790s. How these 'gold-rush towns' would eventually relate to the traditional nation – its political interest and representation, its social elevators, its sources of power and prestige, its ecology of local communities – was still entirely open-ended. And two thirds of the population still lived in the countryside, more people worked on the land than elsewhere and domestic service was employing an ever-growing sector. Yet the proportion of the Gross National Product attributable to industry and commerce was steadily rising; Britain was becoming the workshop of the world.

9. Conclusion

This book has highlighted three main aspects of eighteenth-century English society. First, the fundamental strength and resilience of its social hierarchy. It was presided over by a super-confident oligarchy, swimming with the tide, without an exposed Achilles' heel, whose dominion was consolidated early in the century and never – at least not till the 1790s – seriously challenged, let alone jeopardized. Magnates' grip on power – capital, economic leverage, office, local influence, pervasive manipulation of patronage in state, Church, and armed forces – was tightening. Crown and magnates saw more eye-to-eye, and the no-holds-barred sectarian and party antagonisms amongst the officers which had threatened throughout the Stuart age to capsize the ship of state were tamed into ritual in-fighting. The English ruling class knitted itself together.

National stability could be maintained – despite endemic pockets of local disorder – because the economy worked well enough to profit the rich, to keep practically everyone alive, to prevent sudden subsistence crises, and to give prospects of individual improvement. The parochial poor law muffled acute distress. There was no nationwide politics of famine or panic, hedgerows were not crawling with beggars and bandits. Crucially Albion was uniquely successful in war, conquest, and colonization, eupeptic patriotism and profit being heads and tails of Britannia's golden guinea. Moreover, financing government by borrowing meant that the tax burdens of empire-building were not utterly crippling, and debt finance secured the loyalty of the widening circles of fund-holders. Many layers of society became modestly more affluent, and none which could topple the oligarchs was suddenly or chronically disrupted. (Religious Dissenters, the Stuart century's crusading saints, fought amongst themselves, becoming introspective.)

The traditional disciplines of family and work-place, prudential morality, natural beliefs, and religious taboos continued to guide reproduction of the generations and renewal of the cyclical rhythms of the workaday world. Even rapid industrial change or the abrupt disruption to ingrained patterns of rural life that enclosure could bring did not produce Jacqueries or *une grande peur*. Labour steadily became more fully absorbed within the wage nexus.

In its socio-political stability England was (superficially at least) characteristic of most contemporary European nations. Before the cataclysm of the French Revolution, *ancien régime* society appeared more secure than in the preceding centuries of Reformation, Counter-Reformation, the great inflation, the Thirty Years' War, and the so-called 'general crisis'. Peasant share-cropping, serf-labour, seigneurial exactions, and privilege continued like the seed time and the harvest. Yet, in the event, the English hierarchy proved uniquely tough. In France the bones of the old order's skeleton, after all, proved brittle and broke, and the Netherlands, Italy, and many German principalities succumbed to French invasion and the enforced 'rationalization' of their regimes. By contrast, menaced by the contagion of the French Revolution and the upheavals of continental wars, the English body politic, clad in its protective armour of government, held up, despite the prophecies of Painite radicals that the walls of power and privilege would tumble before the trumpet-blasts of Reason and Liberty. Not only that, but English industrialization romped ahead despite the python-coils of blockade and war.

My second theme has been this: though the social hierarchy was inegalitarian and oozing privilege (some of it hereditary), it was not rigid and brittle. There was continual adaptiveness to challenge and individual mobility, up, down, and sideways. Money was a passport through more frontiers than in other nations. English society was not frozen into immobilized, distended, and archaic forms by the mortmain of law, courts of heralds, nobiliary protocol, or the pantomime pageantry of absolutist courts. Men could not be parted from their property, capital was allowed to ferret where it would, and new riches could be manicured into respectability. Private gain was expected to lead, thanks to the magic of the invisible hand, to public benefit. For those above the poverty line, goods, services, and opportunities multiplied. The consuming public – the nation of shopkeepers – broadened and made its stake in prosperity felt. Peace and well-being allowed relaxation of punitive authoritarianism and religious terrors, or at least their displacement into substitute bogeys, such as Francophobia. Compared with most contemporary nations, and its own recent past, Georgian England was an unintrusive relaxed society in which ordinary toes were relatively infrequently trodden on by central officials and priests. Many congratulated themselves that prosperity, freedom, confidence, knowledge, and happiness were marching on together, arms linked. Looking back in 1800 on the dying century, the *Annual Review* reflected:

On a general recollection or review of the state of society or human nature in the eighteenth century, the ideas that recur oftenest, and remain uppermost in the mind, are the three following: the intercourses of man were more extensive than at any former period with which we are acquainted; the progression of knowledge was more rapid, and the discoveries of philosophy were applied more than they had been before to practical purposes ... This present age may be called an age of humanity.

For this editor, as indeed later for Marx, the dynamo of the market was the secret of this change:

Whence this happy change? Not from the progressive effects of moral disquisitions and lectures; not even from the progressive effects of preaching, trimmed up by the artifices of composition taught by professors of rhetoric; but from the progressive intercourses of men with men, minds with minds, of navigations, commerce, arts and sciences.

But at what price? For many feared that in this market society, where money was the *lingua franca* and everyone had his price, social cohesion, public virtue, justice, authority, respect, and compassion would drown in a maelstrom of greed and envy. In this Mandevillian world – moralists worried – public well-being was being corroded by private ambition, statesmen seduced and suborned by executive graft. Yeomen were abandoning native hearths for the fleshpots of London, and servants had become choosy about their masters. Profit, not fair prices, ruled exchange. The Church was feeding itself, not its sheep. Disturbances and violent crime, knaves and thieves, were rampant. Incensed preachers and sentimental novelists warned the rich that through their reckless greed and neglect of duty they were digging their own graves:

Noblemen and gentlemen have almost abandoned the country, so amongst the first great people now residing there may be reckoned the innkeepers, the tax gatherers and the stewards of great estates who with the lawyers rule the country ... the poor must plunder because not provided for ... corporations are venal; trade and manufactories are overstrained; banks and bankruptcies in and over every town; laws, from being multiplied beyond comprehension, cannot be enforced ... and as that increasingly when the metropolis must be fed the body will gradually decay – why then there will come a distress, a famine and an insurrection; which the praetorian guards, or the whole army cannot quell; or even the parliament pacify; the latter because they have connived at the (now general) alarm, from having been constantly employed in struggles for power; and regardless of the peace and interior happiness of their country!

Thus, on the eve of the French Revolution, wrote the Hon. John Byng, but the country he wrote about was England. Recent historians have agreed with Byng that the ruling classes wanted to have their cake and eat it:

A fundamental contradiction lay at the heart of English agrarian society in the period of the Industrial Revolution [write Eric Hobsbawm and Rudé]. Its rulers wanted it to be both capitalist and traditionalist and hierarchical. In other words, they wanted to be governed by the universal free market of the liberal economists (which was inevitably a market for land and men as well as for goods) but only to the extent that suited nobles, squires and farmers; they advocated an economy which implied mutually antagonistic classes, but did not want it to disrupt a society of 'ordered ranks'.

Many warned that English society was corrupt and rushing lemming-like to the precipice. And meanwhile, from below rose the wail of the oppressed, Blake's 'marks of weakness, marks of woe' in London's chartered streets.

The ruling order was, however, alert to the problems of

maintaining order within the fluid and to some extent polarizing society they presided over, recognizing that they had to find ways to continue cracking the whip of capitalism without the work horses rearing up. So the third focus of this book has lain on their attempts to secure consensus within this acquisitive, restless society. Resort to brute force could not be more than local, specific, and sporadic. Sailors were routinely lashed, but (children apart) labouring men were not slaves to be frog-marched into the fields or factories. Feuding private, sectarian interests, particularism, and gentry heel-digging against executive *diktat* meant that military might was generally neither on tap nor acceptable. Towards the end of the century, schemes were being mooted to renew social discipline through exemplary institutions such as purpose-designed prisons deploying solitary confinement. Thus, between 1776 and 1800 boom-town Liverpool built a new lunatic asylum, bridewell, and gaol. Such were the ominous harbingers of a more therapeutic, surveying, controlling state, but until the end of the century they remained but prototypes. Rather, the Georgian battle was mainly for the mind. The hope was to win acquiescence and endorsement by influence and persuasion – bluster, grandeur, liberality, promises, show and swank, the open door held just ajar. Those in power and their media mouthpieces dangled before people's eyes ambition, self-respect, new enjoyments, polite values, and fashionable life-styles. Certain of these goals, such as education, Methodism or New Dissent, with their gratifications of inner-light, self-improvement, and a Heaven in prospect, were spiritual. Jesus would save even if the labouring poor could scarce afford to. Other prospects, such as promotion and prosperity through toil and sobriety, leading to shares in material well-being and gentility, were worldly. In offering self-betterment (through 'Bibles, religious tracts, gospel shops, itinerant tub-men and national schools', as Cobbett sardonically dubbed them) lay the aim of creating an English dream a divided people could share.

Society did not polarize into bristling camps. The bloody internecine wars of religious truth of Stuart times slowly subsided into pamphlet polemics, bitter though these remained. Anglicans and Dissenters coexisted. It wasn't only Voltaire who observed how business overrode confessional fences. The political spoils-system and the civil list got men to kowtow to crown and ministry. The swelling, prosperous middle ranks of brokers, shippers, wholesalers, hauliers, and dealers, down to retailers, petty manufacturers, and superior craftsmen, gave society a stout midriff and prevented simple class dichotomies. In any case much of society was still encased in small face-to-face communities. In 1800, fewer than one person in five lived in towns of more than 20,000 inhabitants.

In the last third of the century seismic rumblings served notice of growing social tension. With fiercer spokesmen such as Richard Price and Joseph Priestley, Protestant Dissenters flexed their muscles and renewed campaigns against the civil disabilities of the Test and Corporation Acts ('So long as we continue Dissenters,' declared Priestley, 'it is hardly possible that we should be other than friends to civil liberty'). Government 'tyranny' in waging war against the Thirteen Colonies, and its incompetence in losing it, gave opposition a sitting target and strengthened agitation – especially among the trading classes – for efficiency and retrenchment. The War of American Independence proved a watershed, acutely dividing the political nation on a constitutional issue and making many City merchants and tradesmen side with His Majesty's enemies.

Americans' demands for representation were echoed by vote-less taxpayers at home, and fears of executive and Court machinations undermining the Constitution were rekindled. From the 1760s political grievances fanned into flame – though fitfully – out of doors: groups such as the Society of the Supporters of the Bill of Rights (1769) began assailing the citadels of power, seeking to 'restore the constitution', John Wilkes providing an anti-ministerial hero and martyr. Redistribution of seats to restore due weight to stout county opinion was demanded by Christopher Wyvill's Yorkshire Association (1779) and the Society for Constitutional Information (1780). Agitation mounted for the relief of Irish Catholics. The swelling ranks of middling men voiced ever more scathing criticisms of privilege, corruption, and aristocratic hauteur.

This triggered soul-searching within well-bred breasts. The Evangelical movement within the Church, growing from the

1770s, sought to purge profligacy and debauchery from the hearts of high-livers. Liberals questioned subscription to the Thirty-Nine Articles, and a few noble spirits such as John Jebb in Cambridge proposed university reform. Jeremy Bentham embarked on his life-long single-handed Utilitarian labour the Augean stables of cleansing law and redesigning the machinery of administration head to foot. Even Establishment figures such as Archdeacon William Paley doubted whether the distribution of wealth and power brought the greatest possible happiness. Within Westminster itself in the 1780s, Lord Shelburne and Pitt the Younger were prepared to tinker with reforms (though the effect of this was actually to split the radicals). Radical and Dissenting journalists frothed against corruption, imperialism, and arbitrary power, and a new wave of preachy novelists such as Mrs Inchbald and Robert Bage prescribed the knife for the cancers of pride, privilege, and superciliousness which infected high society. Lord George Gordon, fearing subversion of true reformed faith, founded the Protestant Association, and William Blake began to prophesy Doom. For Blake and others the bugbears all around gave the lie to the diabolical house the Georgians had built: hunger stalking in the midst of the smarmy self-congratulators who mouthed pieties and doled out philanthropic halfpennies, while denying life, love, and joy to God's innocents.

As growing criticism lashed corruption, strains in the social and administrative fabric became more visible. The surge of industry and population outran local government and left the distribution of parliamentary seats grotesque. Cornwall had twenty-one boroughs, Lancashire six. With an electorate of barely 250,000, the enfranchised proportion of the population (about 3 per cent) had dwindled lower than since before the Civil War. The provinces were showing signs of an autonomous counter-life and problems of their own, a second nation erupting in the midst of the old.

Polite society [writes R.E. Schofield], by state and custom established, might still be concerned with land and title, they might still spend their time disputing in an unrepresentative Parliament, discussing literature and the arts in London coffee shops, and drinking and gambling at White's; but the world they knew was a shadow. Another society, in which position was determined by an ungenteel success, was creating a different world more to its liking.

Other social rifts were indeed widening. Polite society, growing more fastidious, was distancing itself more from the dirty, pungent, and sometimes dangerous world of the *hoi polloi*, withdrawing from village and community activities, and emasculating the culture of its inferiors.

And yet, until the dawn of the French Revolution, these portents were but straws in the wind. The Wilkite movement was a spectacle of stage thunder and lightning, a gala performance for the greater glory of John Wilkes himself. With its concentration on the defence of individual legal rights, but indifference to social change, the movement left an ambiguous legacy. Wilkes – who soon described himself as 'an extinct volcano' – later became alderman and mayor, siding with the City authorities against the Gordon Riots and living to be a friend of Dr Johnson and an enemy of the French Revolution. The Gordon Riots of 1780 persuaded parlour liberals that those who brandished the torches of popular agitation got their fingers burnt. The disastrous American war over, Wyvill's parliamentary reform movement had dwindled to shadow-boxing by 1784. In the countryside enclosure awards sparked no château-burning, and the building of the first great factories of the Industrial Revolution produced no concerted defiance.

Whether or not to be young was very heaven, the 1790s were certainly a new dawn. The tocsin of *Liberté*, *Égalité*, and *Fraternité* gave fresh heart to normally insular radicals and liberals this side of the Channel. Apocalyptic visions of a clean slate swam before the eyes of sober parliamentary reformers, such as Horne Tooke, of Godwin (with his wish for the 'true euthanasia of government'), and of Blake:

> The fields from Islington to Marybone
> To Primrose Hill and St John's Wood
> Were builded over with pillars of gold
> And there Jerusalem's pillars stood.

Within Westminster, events in France had the sympathy of patrician radicals and vanguard Whigs, at least until 1792.

Artisan radicals harangued meetings and set up reform societies, hoping, especially after Tom Paine's *Rights of Man* (1791), to plant the liberty tree. 'Frenchmen, you are already free,' declared the London Corresponding Society in 1792, 'but the Britons are preparing to be so.' From 1793 war against revolutionary France – with crippling taxes, inflation, press-gangs, trade disruption, anti-war protests, and (in 1797) naval mutinies and the counteracting waves of loyalist bullying – created unparalleled antagonisms within English society. About a third of the century's strikes occurred in this decade.

Through the 1790s the margins by which Government, magistrates, and loyalists battened down the hatches against the seething waters of unrest were often slim. It was not just hawks and paranoid squires who dreaded that Anarchy stalked the land. Republican whispers grew more audible, and for the first time since the Civil War, plebeian radicals were organizing their own, independent political programme. Corresponding Societies now linked agitation from town to town and planned their own shadow government, the Convention. In retaliation, Pitt, during his 'white terror', suspended constitutional freedoms, such as Habeas Corpus (1794, 1798), passed the Treason and Sedition Act (1795), the Unlawful Oaths Act (1797), and the Corresponding Societies Act (1799), banned public meetings, and recruited gaggles of spies and informers. Radical leaders such as Thomas Hardy, secretary of the London Corresponding Society, had their premises raided, and were arrested and put on trial. The administration bought up newspapers and posted troops through the country in specially constructed barracks.

The prospect of civil strife and even bloody revolution in the 1790s was sudden and traumatic. It was obviously made *possible* by a long-term build-up of stress-points, such as the concentration of disaffected and literate artisans in northern and Midland towns which were weak links in the chain of local government. But it was not *precipitated* by these developments. It was, rather, a sudden conflagration, sparked from outside. Rights of Man radicalism, republican toasts, dark mutterings about peers and priests being strung up – all of course tapped a libertarian rage flowing largely underground since the collapse of the Puritan revolution. Yet without the example, success, and wild-fire spread of revolution abroad, their explosive expression would have been unthinkable. The refrain of most eighteenth-century English plebeian protest had, after all, been local, piecemeal, and traditional, drawing on notions of community within the framework of custom, common law, and Constitution. The working man's voice had traditionally been to call his betters to their duties. Tom Paine – seasoned American then French Revolutionary – had quite another song: 'The present age will hereafter merit to be called the Age of Reason,' he proclaimed, 'and will appear to the future as the Advent of a new World.'

Yet though the *ideology* was new, Painites could build on foundations laid earlier. Working men had got used to running their own micro-republican friendly societies and combinations. Debating societies, such as London's Robin Hood Club, had given tub-thumpers practice in para-political invective. Methodism and popular Dissent had loosened fiery tongues which could switch from religious to political scores. The spread of printing presses, brave publishers, literacy, and the reading habit made it remarkably easy to read radical pamphlets and Tom Paine (hundreds of thousands of copies were sold). Newspapers had attuned the provinces to the political key of the capital.

Political radicalism spread in the regions alongside economic disturbances, the two often being mutually reinforcing, though never ultimately losing their separate identities. Grain riots worsened as prices rocketed in the mid-1790s. Unemployment grew, and antagonism between rich and poor got more menacing. John Byng witnessed this:

It is from neglect and despair that Democracy, that Anarchy, spring: ... while the unaided paupers of the country will look at a dogkennel with envy, and the starvers of the town are to peer down without hope upon the blazing displays of cookery – I will say, 'something is rotten in the State of Denmark'.

Furthermore, initially at least the impact of the French Revolution was to split the establishment. The Revolution won ringing plaudits amongst Whigs and Dissenters (though only one bishop supported it). 'How much the greatest event that has ever happened in the world,' exclaimed Charles James Fox at the fall of the Bastille. Erasmus Darwin, the Midlands physician, thought it 'the dawn of universal liberty'; Theophilus Lindsey, aspiring reformer of the Church of England, pronounced, 'The Revolution in France is a wonderful work of Providence in our days, and we trust it will prosper and go on and be the speedy means of putting an end to tyranny everywhere.' Most Dissenters supported it, as did strata of professional and commercial opinion eager for reform at home, and above all the intelligentsia. Even staid burghers walked around on air for a while, addressing each other as 'citizen'. Joseph Priestley caught this mood in urging men to snatch the hour:

> While so favourable a wind is abroad, let every young mind expand itself, catch the rising gale, and partake of the glorious enthusiasm, the great subjects of which are the flourishing state of science, arts, manufactures, commerce . . . the abolishing of all useless distinctions which were the offspring of a barbarous age (producing an absurd haughtiness in some and a base servility in others), and a general release from all such taxes, and burdens of every kind, as the public good does require. In short, to make government as beneficial, and as little expensive and burdensome, as possible.

In the event, the talk about liberty, natural rights, and a new order fizzled out. The 1790s produced reform societies, a blizzard of pamphlets, and boisterous agitation. Revolutionary enthusiasms and Romantic ideals left scars on the hearts and minds of a generation of poets, artists, and thinkers. Many magistrates were paralysed with fear. But there were no co-ordinated large-scale assaults on the hierarchy, spontaneous or organized, in England (this is not true for Scotland and Ireland and less true of English radicalism between 1802 and 1820, which produced insurrections, assassinations, and conspiracies). No one stormed stately homes or cathedrals, or burnt Whitehall, St James's, or Newgate. No heads rolled. Most violence flared out of sudden impromptu flashpoints such as the activities of press-gangs; most agitation focused on practical issues:

> Peace and large bread
> Or a king without a head.

Certainly everyone saw with sobering clarity the people

ranged against the privileged and the possibility that the people might have Justice on their side. But there was not yet a mass proletarian consciousness (most popular agitation came from craftsmen), and the ideology of English Jacobinism remained individualistic. Even so, E. P. Thompson is right to see the 1790s as critical in the process of the formation of the English working class, for until then the wrath of injustice had been masked behind a show of deference and subordination. Now the lower orders were beginning to erupt on to the political scene as an articulate, disruptive, obdurate, avenging force in their own right. Sectors of them were to become truly menacing in the first decades of the next century. Moreover, it was to take a couple of generations of failure, repression, and discipline in the school of industrialism, and the articulation of gradualist political ambitions for them *within* the system, to ease them back again, by mid-century, into a stunned quiescence.

Yet there is no denying that the authorities, pummelled on the ropes, held up; Louis Simond was to observe, with astonishment and admiration, in the early years of the new century:

There is not another government in Europe who could long withstand the attacks to which this is continually exposed. The things published here would set on fire any other hearts in the world, but either from insensibility, reason, or habit, they make but little impression.

The old order battled through partly by unabashed repression. Civil liberties which were the toast of the Constitution – such as Habeas Corpus and freedom of association – were suspended by 'gagging bills'. Hundreds were arrested. Show trials were held of the 'seditious' (though in England, unlike Scotland, most were acquitted). Disturbances, in which national and local grievances reinforced each other, were quelled with unwonted violence. The toll-bridge riots in Bristol in 1793 left eleven protesters dead. In the Birmingham riots of 1791, 'Church and King' loyalist mobs, encouraged by magistrates, destroyed the property of Dissenters, Unitarians, and radicals. 'I cannot but feel better pleased', wrote George III to Henry Dundas, 'that Priestley is the sufferer for the doctrines he and his party have instilled.' The political nation saved its skin only by jettisoning its much-vaunted moderation and constitutional guarantees: its soul was barred.

The oligarchy held up, partly because of splits amongst its opponents. Faced by the execution of Louis XVI and the Terror, Whigs soon splintered into pro- and anti-Revolution factions, and, once divided, ceased to be a political challenge to the Government. Standard-bearers of revolution, such as Paine and Thomas Spence, sanguinely believed it would come about not by force of arms but by spontaneous rational Enlightenment. Radical intellectuals speechified and scribbled, but it was all sound and fury, for few had the stomach for killing and all feared mob extremism. Many, such as William Frend (stripped of his Cambridge fellowship for radicalism), campaigned for liberty, but did not see it in terms of direct *political* goals or bloody rebellion. Like the anarchist philosopher William Godwin (who was, in Hazlitt's thumb-nail sketch, the 'metaphysician engrafted on the Dissenting Minister') and many others, Frend chiefly desired the cultivation of individuality, wanting reason and freedom to have full play. Moral integrity meant more than the people wielding power. In any case, prosperous craftsmen radicals in Norwich and Sheffield did not see eye-to-eye with scarecrow proletarians, and insurrectionary artisans in the City did not agree with eloquent demagogues such as Major Cartwright and John Thelwall, of whose type Arnold Harvey has written:

The Westminster reformers were upwardly mobile, confident, re-silient: they had no need to seek consolation in millenarian fantasies. In Lancashire and the North Midlands, by contrast, where less sophisticated workers were more seriously affected by the economic crisis of the war years, religious enthusiasm and half-baked conspiracy seem to have taken a rather firmer hold.

But the *status quo* held up for other reasons too. Appeals to national defence split the opposition. Under invasion threat, patriotism was more popular than Paine. Cartoonists such as Gillray ridiculed the 'French disease' and native radicalism alike. War proved the ultimate rivet of the nation, restoring the virility of a ruling caste licking its wounds after the War of American Independence. The war years proved good for businessmen, farmers, speculators, and rentiers, too, and for commission-hungry younger sons seeking paths to glory in the forces.

Furthermore, the propertied closed ranks. There had never been much love lost between the squirearchy and City money-manipulators; paternalist magistrates had not always stood foursquare behind middle men against grain rioters; parvenu manufacturers were often despised by landowners (they competed for labour, raising its price). The Gordon Riots and the loss of the American colonies eroded the trading classes' confidence in Parliament's fitness to safeguard their vital interests. But the propertied were eager to sink their differences in the 1790s over the cardinal issues of the defence of property, the law, and the Constitution. The loyal toasts of the militia, yeomanry, and Volunteers brought squires' and merchants' sons together, tenantry mingling with 'employers on horseback'. Certain historians, such as E. P. Thompson, have argued that without the lucky accident or contrivance of war, aristocratic dominion would shortly have been assailed head-on by bourgeois challenge. This however is too catastrophic a view: the propertied always knew on which side their bread was buttered. Great manufacturers such as the Peels, Boultons, Arkwrights, and Strutts were already giving their vote of confidence to the old order by heading into land. Matthew Boulton bought up the lustrous estate of Great Tew, and Richard Arkwright was knighted and appointed High Sheriff of Derbyshire in 1787, in 1789 becoming Lord of the Manor of Cromford. For their part, shopkeepers and stock-holders formed loyalist groups and Associations for the Defence of Property. Agitation for parliamentary reform amongst middling men throttled back for a decade or two, while ministries and magistrates exorcised plebeian anarchy. As society closed ranks, radicalism's sting was drawn. The Dissenter-scientist Joseph Priestley might gravely warn that 'The English hierarchy . . . has equal reason to tremble at an air pump or an electrical machine.' Yet he was wrong, for science (like Romanticism and religion) could equally serve reaction. It was fashionable society that flocked to the Royal Institution, founded in 1799. Its wizard experimentalist, Humphry Davy, a poor Cornish boy made good, assured his glamorous audience that science proved 'society was necessarily and rightly grounded on property and inequality'.

Indeed, many of the propertied saw the light and recanted erstwhile liberal and Enlightenment credos, the 1790s producing more turncoats than any decade since the 1650s. Former Romantic utopians such as Wordsworth, Southey, and Coleridge, aghast at the Terror, went Tory. The execution of Louis XVI and the French declaration of war on England turned reaction into style, Samuel Romilly believing that their consequence was 'among the higher orders ... a horror of every kind of innovation'. Liberal sentiments, humanitarianism, optimism about human nature, sympathy for the aspirations of the weak, the have-nots, and the oppressed bowed to hard-bitten realism. Patriarchal attitudes were back, and in religion original sin was resurrected. 'Man is an apostate creature,' declared Wilberforce. 'It is a fundamental error,' echoed Hannah More, burying the Enlightenment commonplace, 'to consider children as innocent ... rather than as beings who bring into the world a corrupt nature and evil dispositions.' Other nostrums from the Enlightenment new deal, such as belief in inevitable progress, were tossed on the faggots.

It became urgent to reassert to the lower orders the politics not of consensus but of hierarchy and subordination. Burke styled them the 'swinish multitude', the Bishop of London could hardly believe 'the extreme depravity and licentiousness which prevails ... amongst the lowest orders of the people'. Didn't they know they were the lucky ones? Archdeacon Paley proved it, showing that 'frugality itself is a pleasure'. Bishop Horsley applied casuistry to deprivation: 'Poverty ... can be nothing more than an imaginary evil of which the modest will never complain.' Yet the 'evil of poverty' was also 'a public good'. In any case, the poor needed to be told what was what. Twopenny repository tracts ('Burke for beginners') deluged from the presses, 300,000 copies being printed in 1795 alone. Hannah More wrote a pamphlet for the poor sub-titled *Half a Loaf Is Better Than No Bread*, waxing ecstatic about the joy of going without:

And though I've no money, and tho' I've no lands
I've a head on my shoulders and pair of good hands.

> So I'll work the whole day, and on Sundays I'll seek
> At Church how to bear all the wants of the week.
> The gentlefolks too will afford us supplies
> They'll subscribe – and they'll give up their puddings and pies.

Outrage against the grumbling lower orders grew more shrill. Bishop Watson, renegade liberal, called country labourers 'perverse, stupid, and illiterate' and town artisans 'debauched, ill-mannered'. In 1795 in soup-kitchen mood, *The Times* gave the poor more mealy-mouthed (and anti-canine) advice:

THE WAY TO PEACE AND PLENTY

Rules of the Poor
1. Keep steadily to your work, and never change masters, if you can help it.
2. Go to no gin-shops, or alehouse: but lay out all your earnings in food, and clothes, for yourself, and your family: and try to lay up a little for rent and rainy days.
3. Avoid bad company.
4. Keep no dogs: for they rob your children, and your neighbours.
5. Go constantly to church, and carry your wives, and children with you, and God will bless you.
6. Be civil to your superiors, and they will be kind to you.
7. Learn to make broth, milk pottage, rice-pudding, etc. One pound of meat, in broth, will go further than two pounds boiled or roasted.
8. Be quiet, and contented, and never steal, or swear, or you will never thrive.

The rich would do their bit.

Rules for the Rich
1. Abolish gravy soups, and second courses.
2. Buy no starch when wheat is dear.
3. Destroy all useless dogs.
4. Give no dog, or other animal, the smallest bit of bread or meat.
5. Save all your skim-milk carefully, and give it all to the poor, or sell it at a cheap rate.
6. Make broth, rice-puddings, etc., for the poor, and teach them to make such things.
7. Go to church yourselves, and take care your servants go constantly.
8. Look into the management of your own families, and visit your poor neighbours.

9. Prefer those poor who keep steadily to their work, and go constantly to church, and give nothing to those who are idle, are riotous, or keep useless dogs.

10. Buy no weighing meat, or gravy beef: if the rich would buy only the prime pieces, the poor could get the others cheap.

The rich would thus considerately buy only the best cuts of meat and oversee the poor to keep them good. Smiling Old Leisure had become poker-faced. Cobbett noted this new mood soon afterwards:

Never did we, until these days, hear of millions of 'Tracts, Moral and Religious' for the purpose of keeping the poor from cutting the throats of the rich. The parson's sermon, once a week or a fortnight, used to be quite sufficient for the religion and morals of a village. Now we had a busy creature or two in every village, dancing about with 'Tracts' for the benefit of the souls of the labourers and their families. The gist of the whole of the 'Tracts' was to inculcate content in a state of misery! To teach people to starve without making a noise! What did all this show? Why, a consciousness on the part of the rich, that the poor had not fair play; and that the former wished to obtain security against the latter by coaxing.

Eminent Georgians preserved themselves. They did so by pinching the lower orders, many of whom were pauperized or pressed into the army or navy. A few were transported or gaoled. The elite maintained itself at the price of putting on ice its more conciliatory, accommodating poses. The Enlightenment dream that there was indeed a hidden hand, which without human effort, united 'self love and social', creating a natural identity of economic interests, faded with the new century's dismal Malthusian and Ricardian visions of ineradicable class antagonism, population explosion, the iron-law of starvation wages, and crises of over-production. For many, optimism about rational progress was now pie in the sky, for society seemed gripped by forces – international trade cycles, inflation, demographic pressure, continental war – beyond the power of individuals or governments to regulate. Certain of these forces, however – the laws of political economy – did require the canonization of private property, for the one freedom not called in doubt but endlessly endorsed was that of capital. As a Commons Committee put it in 1806:

The right of every man to employ the capital he inherits, or has acquired, according to his own discretion, without molestation or obstruction, so long as he does not infringe on the rights or property of others, is one of those privileges which the free and happy Constitution of this Country has long accustomed every Briton to consider as his birthright.

The same fate met the easy-going morals of the Georgians. Though still paraded by real swells, these now appeared scandalous and inflammatory to the more tight-lipped spokesmen of the insecure respectable classes. Stricter family discipline, paternal authority, and sexual propriety were all urgently needed. 'Do not luxury, corruption, adultery, gaming, pride, vanity, idleness, extravagance and dissipation prevail too generally?' thumped the outraged Thomas Bowdler. 'Every man,' reflected Lady Frances Shelley, 'felt the need recently for putting his house in order.'

Underwriting all these came a grand-scale religious revival. 'The churches were well attended, and sometimes even crowded,' reflected the *Annual Review* just after the outbreak of the French Revolution:

It was a wonder to the lower classes, throughout all parts of England, to see the avenues to the churches filled with carriages. This novel appearance prompted the simple country-people to inquire what was the matter.

Evangelicalism won converts, even amongst old roués such as the Duke of Grafton. 'Vital religion' would spiritualize crumbling social relations. Religion's political message was not lost: it was 'to the decline of religion and morality', wrote Wilberforce,

that our national difficulties must both directly and indirectly be chiefly ascribed ... my only solid hopes for the well-being of my country depend not so much on her fleet and armies, not so much on the wisdom of her rulers, or on the spirit of her people, as on the persuasion that she still contains many who in a degenerate age love and obey the Gospel of Christ; on the humble trust that the intercession of these may still be prevalent, that for the sake of these Heaven may still look upon us with an eye of favour.

'The true Christian,' Arthur Young insisted, 'will never be a Leveller and will never listen to French politics or to French philosophy.' Cobbett replied that Evangelicalism was a bid 'to keep the poor from cutting the throats of the rich, to starve without making a noise'. In Lucy Aikin's phrase, 'the precepts of Christianity have been pressed into the service of a base submission to all established power'. The light of 'Reason' was too glaring. As Canning jingled in the *Anti-Jacobin Review*:

> Reason, Philosophy, 'fiddledum, diddledum'
> Peace and Fraternity, higgledy, piggledy
> Higgledy piggledy, 'fiddledum, diddledum'.

'Instead of casting away our prejudices, we cherish them,' boasted Burke. 'From liberty, equality and the rights of man,' sighed Hannah More, 'Good Lord deliver *us*.'

He did. English society nosed into the nineteenth century immensely richer than in 1700, every day generating new wealth. As a parliamentary report put it in 1806,

> The rapid and prodigious increase of late years in the Manufactures and Commerce of this Country is universally known, as well as the effects of that increase on our Revenue and National Strength; and in considering the immediate causes of that Augmentation, it is principally to be ascribed to the general spirit of enterprise and industry among a free and enlightened People, left to the unrestrained exercise of their talents in the employment of a vast capital.

Yet, as John Burnett has noted, that wealth was 'being built upon a sub-structure of poverty more extensive than it has been for centuries past'. Those standing on the shoulders of the poor, however, were set fair to do very well. At the top, the Bedfords, Bridgewaters, Devonshires, and Northumberlands were all netting more than £50,000 a year by 1800.

This increase in wealth and the prospect of its acceleration had become a kind of master-key, the ideological open-sesame of society. The view from above was that nothing ought to stand in the way of the triumphal procession of capital. Viewed from below, it was profit and credit which ground the faces of the poor. As Cobbett saw it, 'England had long groaned under a commercial system which is the most oppressive of all possible systems, and it is, too, a quiet, silent and smothering oppression that it produces which is more hateful than all others.' It was

British finance that had won her wars and proved her imperial destiny, and the fundamental political ideology (as Marx was to recognize) was becoming political economy. Even the 'paternalist' Burke thought government could do nothing to relieve the poverty which the laws of nature decreed. 'The laws of commerce,' he argued, 'are the laws of nature, and consequently the laws of God.' Sectors of the politically excluded (including substantial bourgeois) could console themselves with the thought that wealth gave them local influence, understudying for some future national stage.

Political and economic opportunism tided the ruling classes over into the nineteenth century intact, and buoyed the rest of the propertied with them. Landed incomes and peers' rent-rolls were shooting up especially fast (many rents doubled during the war years), and aristocrats were not just richer than ever, but even more secure in the driving seat of power. In 1800, no fewer than six out of twenty-six bishops were peers' sons, and whereas in 1734 there had been seventy-five peers' sons in the Commons, by 1812, 143 had blue blood (the peerage itself had expanded). In the 1790s some ninety MPs were returned effectively at the nomination of peers, and another 120 with their influence. Pitt's wartime ministry was entirely composed of peers and their sons. The wartime cynicism of the Regency was soon to see grandees, headed by George III's own sons, pursuing luxury and vice more nakedly, more grossly, than ever. Cruikshank's satire 'The Court of Love' starred the Duke of York (boasting 'I am proud to say that the greater part of my life has been passed in the commission of adultery') and the Duke of Clarence ('I have lived in adultery with an actress for 25 years and have a pretty number of illegitimate children'). The age of Crockfords, Harriet Wilson, Brighton pavilion, and Beau Brummell's dandyism was dawning. And down the road from Piccadilly many others were getting a lick of the jampot: 'The people are better dressed, better fed, cleanlier, better educated in each class respectively, much more frugal, and much happier' thought Francis Place, early in the nineteenth century:

Money which would have been spent at the tavern, the brothel, the tea-garden, the skittle yard, the hurly burly and the numerous other low-lived and degrading pursuits, is now expended in comfort and conveniences, or saved for some useful purpose.

The THING – as Cobbett dubbed the monstrous nerve centre of establishment power, patronage, clientage, wealth, machin-ation, and corruption – had survived. A smaller percentage of people held the franchise than in 1700, and because grandees were still able to forestall hustings contests, even they were able to exercise their rights infrequently. Aristocratic dominion had come under fire, and the offices, sinecures, and rake-offs of state had been slightly slimmed down in the cold sweat induced by radicalism. But privilege was still alive and flourishing. In his *Political Justice* (1793) William Godwin demanded *Götter-dämmerung*: an end to kings, lords, priests, taxes, and govern-ments. Yet his anarchism was a response to the fact that all of these were more securely entrenched than ever. Central govern-ment, spending £3.2 million in 1700, handled £51 million in 1800, its debts having risen from £14.2 million to £456.1 million (yet debts were its strength). It is remarkable how, even under pressure, so few reforms had been needed. Up to the beginning of the nineteenth century, no sweeping changes had been passed to modernize the state to cope with the new scale of population, wealth, and power. There was still no central police, no modernization of local government, no new man-darin bureaucracy, appointed on talent. Generals and admirals retained great freedom of command (Sandhurst was a nineteenth-century invention). There was no English *levée en masse*. Men of property prized 'independence' above all else. Even in 1811, John William Ward could write:

They have an admirable police at Paris, but they pay for it dear enough. I had rather half-a-dozen people's throats to be cut in Radcliffe Highway every 3 or 4 years, than be subject to domiciliary visits, spies, and all the rest of Fouché's contrivances.

Derek Jarrett is of course right to state that 'by making them-selves the richest nation on earth the English created in their own country problems which could no longer be solved by the old easy-going methods of local management' – hence 'the age of neglect gave way to the age of supervision'. But only in the longer run. In the short term, the English, precisely by making themselves the richest nation on earth, were able to *avoid* confronting the obsolescence of the devolved, traditional methods. Ingrained inequalities, self-help, high hopes, work discipline, twopenny tracts, and a whiff of grapeshot saw the propertied through. The Georgians created vast problems they left for others to solve.

And landed society, with its entourage of plutocrats and fund-holders, pamphleteers, preachers, and flunkeys, was still in undivided possession of the THING. England stood on the threshold of the nineteenth century successfully – and unparadoxically – as the foremost capitalist society in Europe, yet the one most resistant to pressure for violent change. It was business as usual.

Statistical Tables

Table 1: Population of England

	total (millions)	% growth per decade
1681	4.930	− 1.06
1691	4.931	0.02
1701	5.058	2.58
1711	5.230	3.40
1721	5.350	2.29
1731	5.263	− 1.63
1741	5.576	5.95
1751	5.772	3.52
1761	6.147	6.50
1771	6.448	4.90
1781	7.042	9.21
1791	7.740	9.91
1801	8.664	11.94
1811	9.886	14.10

Reproduced with permission from E. A. Wrigley and R. Schofield, *The Population History of England 1541–1871: A Reconstruction* (Edward Arnold, London, 1981).

Table 2: Population Distribution in 1801

County Population			
Yorkshire	858,892	Durham	160,861
Middlesex	818,129	Sussex	159,311
Lancashire	672,731	Northumberland	157,101
Devon	343,001	Nottingham	140,350
Kent	307,624	Worcester	139,333
Somerset	273,750	Northampton	131,757
Norfolk	273,371	Leicester	130,081
Surrey	269,049	Cumberland	117,230
Gloucester	250,803	Dorset	115,319
Stafford	239,153	Oxford	109,620
Essex	226,437	Berkshire	109,215
Hampshire	219,656	Buckingham	107,444
Suffolk	210,431	Hertford	97,577
Lincoln	208,557	Cambridge	89,346
Warwick	208,190	Hereford	89,191
Shropshire	197,639	Bedford	63,393
Cheshire	191,751	Monmouth	45,582
Cornwall	188,269	Westmorland	41,617
Wiltshire	185,107	Huntingdon	37,568
Derby	161,142	Rutland	16,356

Chief Provincial Towns in 1801

Over 50,000			10,000–20,000 (contd)	
Manchester/Salford	84,000		Stockport	15,000
Liverpool	78,000		Shrewsbury	15,000
Birmingham	74,000		Wolverhampton	13,000
Bristol	64,000		Bolton	13,000
Leeds	53,000		Sunderland	12,000
			Oldham	12,000
20,000–50,000			Blackburn	12,000
Plymouth	43,000		Preston	12,000
Norwich	37,000		Oxford	12,000
Bath	32,000		Colchester	12,000
Portsmouth/Portsea	32,000		Worcester	11,000
Sheffield	31,000		Ipswich	11,000
Hull	30,000		Wigan	11,000
Nottingham	29,000		Derby	11,000
Newcastle upon Tyne	28,000		Huddersfield	11,000
			Quick	11,000
10,000–20,000			Warrington	11,000
Exeter	17,000		Chatham	11,000
Leicester	17,000		Carlisle	10,000
York	16,000		Dudley	10,000
Coventry	16,000		King's Lynn	10,000
Chester	15,000		Cambridge	10,000
Dover	15,000		Reading	10,000
Great Yarmouth	15,000			

Table 3: Distribution of Population in 1801

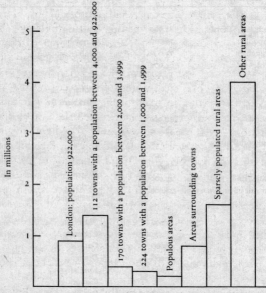

Reproduced with permission from D. Marshall, *Industrial England 1776–1851* (Routledge and Kegan Paul, London, 1973).

Table 4: Indicators of Economic Growth

	Retained imports of raw cotton (m. lb.)	Raw and thrown silk		Flax (rough) imports (000 cwt.)	Linen yarn (raw) imports (m. lb.)	Scottish linen stamped for sale (m. yards)	Bar-iron imports (000 tons)	London coal imports (000 London chaldrons)	Cornish copper ore production (000 tons)	Cornish tin production (tons)	Tin retained for home use (tons)	Strongbeer production (000 barrels)	Wood imports (£000)
		Imports (000 lb.)	Retained imports (000 lb.)										
1695–1704	1.14	525	—	34	2.1	—	16.4	327	—	1,323	232	3,446	114
1700–1709	1.15	499	—	34	2.1	—	16.0	339	—	1,426	308	3,673	114
1705–14	1.00	482	—	34	2.1	—	16.3	355	—	1,476	174	3,387	112
1710–19	1.35	557	—	42	2.8	—	17.3	389	—	1,453	194	3,483	115
1715–24	1.68	629	—	44	3.1	—	19.0	433	—	1,396	326	3,744	135
1720–29	1.55	675	—	48	2.7	—	19.7	468	—	1,482	333	3,669	146
1725–34	1.44	685	—	66	2.7	3.87	21.5	475	6.6	1,632	345	3,588	143
1730–39	1.72	645	—	80	2.7	4.53	25.5	475	7.7	1,667	278	3,606	138
1735–44	1.79	563	—	74	2.8	4.81	24.2	484	7.4	1,691	290	3,512	136
1740–49	2.06	552	—	79	3.1	5.68	22.5	480	6.3	1,744	251	3,536	140
1745–54	2.83	607	—	98	3.6	7.50	26.6	492	9.1	2,159	474	3,679	153
1750–59	2.81	670	—	113	4.2	9.04	29.3	508	13.8	2,658	937	3,777	168
1755–64	2.57	777	—	119	4.9	10.82	33.0	527	16.7	2,669	1,023	3,818	176
1760–69	3.53	906	—	127	5.2	12.42	39.7	582	19.5	2,728	913	3,775	203
1765–74	4.03	946	—	129	6.5	12.58	44.9	634	25.2	2,851	990	3,744	239
1770–79	4.80	950	—	131	8.4	12.84	44.5	653	28.8	2,751	1,089	3,957	248
1775–84	7.36	1,083	—	125	9.1	14.68	43.0	666	29.7	2,657	808	4,220	249
1780–89	15.51	1,132	—	132	9.0	17.49	44.1	709	33.3	2,958	918	4,329	275
1785–94	24.45	1,177	1,093	—	—	19.38	—	771	37.1	3,327	945	4,690	
1790–99	28.64	1,181	1,094	242	8.7	20.89	49.9	825	46.7	3,245	822	5,278	489
1795–1804	42.92	1,128	1,041	317	8.8	21.42	43.0	875	52.9	2,881	861	5,407	558

Reproduced with permission from P. Deane and W. A. Cole, *British Economic Growth 1688–1959* (Cambridge University Press, 1967).

Table 5: Gregory King's 'Scheme of the income and expense of the several families of England ... for 1688' compared with Joseph Massie's 'Estimate of the social structure and income, 1759-1760'

KING				MASSIE	
Number of families	Heads per family	Number of persons	Classification	Number of families	Annual income or expenses
					(£)
160	40	6,400	Temporal lords		
26	20	520	Spiritual lords		
800	16	12,800	Baronets		
600	13	7,800	Knights		
3,000	10	30,000	Esquires		
12,000	8	96,000	Gentlemen		
			(Massie does not	10	20,000
			distinguish the top	20	10,000
			ranks by status,	40	8,000
			but by financial	80	6,000
			turnover per	160	4,000
			family per annum)	320	2,000
				640	1,000
				800	800
				1,600	600
				3,200	400
				4,800	300
				6,400	200
5,000	8	40,000	Persons in greater offices and places		
5,000	6	30,000	Persons in lesser offices and places		
			Civil officers	16,000	60
2,000	8	16,000	Eminent merchants		
8,000	6	48,000	Lesser merchants		
			Merchants	1,000	600
			,,	2,000	400
			,,	10,000	200
			Master manufacturers	2,500	200
			,, ,,	5,000	100
			,, ,,	10,000	70
			,, ,,	62,500	40
10,000	7	70,000	Persons in the law	12,000	100
2,000	6	12,000	Eminent clergymen	2,000	100
8,000	5	40,000	Lesser clergymen	9,000	50
40,000	7	280,000	Freeholders, better sort		
120,000	5½	660,000	,, lesser sort		
			,,	30,000	100
			,,	60,000	50
			,,	120,000	25

KING				MASSIE	
Number of families	Heads per family	Number of persons	Classification	Number of families	Annual income or expenses
150,000	5	750,000	Farmers	5,000	150
			,,	10,000	100
			,,	20,000	70
			,,	120,000	40
15,000	5	75,000	Persons in liberal arts and sciences	18,000	60
50,000	4½	225,000	Shopkeepers and tradesmen		
			Tradesmen	2,500	400
			,,	5,000	200
			,,	10,000	100
			,,	20,000	70
			,,	125,000	40
60,000	4	240,000	Artisans and handicrafts		
			Manufacturers of wood, iron etc. Country 9s. per week	100,000	22.5
			London 12s.	14,000	30
			Manufacturers of wool, silk etc. Country 7s. 6d.	100,000	18.75
			London 10s. 6d.	14,000	26.25
5,000	4	20,000	Naval officers	6,000	80
4,000	4	16,000	Military officers	2,000	100
50,000	3	150,000	Common seamen		
			Seamen and fishermen	60,000	20
364,000	3½	1,275,000	Labouring people and outservants		
			Husbandmen (6s. per week)	200,000	15
			Labourers, country 5s.	200,000	12.5
			Labourers, London 9s.	20,000	22.5
			Innkeepers, alesellers	2,000	100
			Alesellers, cottagers	20,000	40
			,, ,,	20,000	20
400,000	3¼	1,300,000	Cottagers and paupers		
35,000	2	70,000	Common soldiers	18,000	14
		30,000	Vagrants, as gypsies, thieves, beggars, etc.		
Total		5,500,520			

Reproduced with permission from W. Speck, *Stability and Strife* (Edward Arnold, London, 1977).

Table 6: Social Structure: P. Colquhoun's Estimates Based on the Census Returns of 1801 and the Pauper Returns of 1803.

No. of heads of families		Persons in each family	Aggregate of persons	Yearly income per family averaged	Aggregate income of each rank
				£	£
287	Temporal peers and peeresses, including princes of the blood	25	7,175	8,000	2,296,000
26	Bishops	15	390	4,000	104,000
540	Baronets	15	8,100	3,000	1,620,000
350	Knights	10	3,500	1,500	525,000
6,000	Esquires	10	60,000	1,500	9,000,000
20,000	Gentlemen and ladies living on incomes	8	160,000	700	14,000,000
2,000	Persons in higher civil offices (state and revenue)	7	14,000	800	1,600,000
10,500	Persons in lesser civil offices (state and revenue)	5	52,500	200	2,100,000
2,000	Eminent merchants, bankers, &c.	10	20,000	2,600	5,200,000
13,000	Lesser merchants trading by sea	7	91,000	800	10,400,000
11,000	Persons of the Law (judges, barristers, attorneys, clerks, &c.)	5	55,000	350	3,850,000
1,000	Eminent clergymen	6	6,000	500	500,000
10,000	Lesser clergymen	5	50,000	120	1,200,000
40,000	Freeholders of the better sort	5½	220,000	200	8,000,000
120,000	Lesser freeholders	5	600,000	90	10,800,000
160,000	Farmers	6	960,000	120	19,200,000
16,300	Liberal arts and sciences (medical, literary, and fine arts)	5	81,500	260	4,238,000
74,500	Shopkeepers and tradesmen	5	372,500	150	11,175,000
445,726	Artisans, handicrafts, and labourers employed in manufactures, building, and works of every kind	4½	2,005,767	55	24,514,930

PERSONS NOT INCLUDED IN GREGORY KING'S ESTIMATE

No. of heads of families		Persons in each family	Aggregate of persons	Yearly income per family averaged	Aggregate income
				£	£
1	The Sovereign, household, &c.	50	50	200,000	200,000
5,000	Shipowners, letting ships for freights only	5	25,000	500	2,500,000
25,000	Manufacturers employing capital in all branches, wool, cotton ...	6	150,000	800	20,000,000
500	Principal warehousemen selling by wholesale	6	3,000	800	400,000
300	Persons employing capital in building and repairing ships and crafts, &c.	6	1,800	700	210,000
25,000	Persons employing capital as tailors, mantua-makers, milliners, &c., including Army clothiers	5	125,000	150	3,750,000
5,000	Persons employing professional skill and capital as engineers, surveyors, master-builders of houses	5	25,000	200	1,000,000
30,000	Clerks and shopmen to merchants, manufacturers, shopkeepers, &c., &c.	5	150,000	75	6,750,000
2,500	Clergymen regularly ordained, dissenting from the established Church	5	12,500	120	300,000
500	Persons educating youth in universities and chief schools	4	2,000	600	300,000
20,000	Persons employed in the education of youth of both sexes and generally employing some capital	6	120,000	150	3,000,000

Table 7: Index Numbers of Real Output (1700 = 100)

	Export industries (18)	Home industries (12)	Total industry and commerce (30)	Agriculture (43)	Rent and services (20)	Government and defence (7)	Total real output (100)	Average real output
1700	100	100	100	100	100	100	100	100
1710	108	98	104	104	103	165	108	105
1720	125	108	118	105	103	91	108	105
1730	142	105	127	103	102	98	110	108
1740	148	105	131	104	102	148	115	113
1750	176	107	148	111	105	172	125	119
1760	222	114	179	115	113	310	147	130
1770	256	114	199	117	121	146	144	119
1780	246	123	197	126	129	400	167	129
1790	383	137	285	135	142	253	190	134
1800	544	152	387	143	157	607	251	160

Reproduced with permission from P. Deane and W. A. Cole, *British Economic Growth 1688-1959* (Cambridge University Press, 1967).

Table 8: National Wealth and State Expenditure

Year	National debt (cumulative) £m.	Total debt charges £m.	%	Military expenditure £m.	%	Civil government £m.	%	(Education) £m.	%	Total £m.	%
1700–1709	19.1	1.3	21	4.0	66	0.7	12	—	—	6.1	100
1710–19	41.6	2.7	35	4.2	55	0.8	10	—	—	7.7	100
1720–29	52.1	2.8	47	2.1	36	1.0	17	—	—	5.9	100
1730–39	46.9	2.1	39	2.3	43	0.9	17	—	—	5.4	100
1740–49	77.8	2.4	25	6.2	65	0.9	9	—	—	9.5	100
1750–59	91.3	2.9	33	4.9	55	1.1	12	—	—	8.9	100
1760–69	130.3	4.5	33	8.1	59	1.1	8	—	—	13.7	100
1770–79	153.4	4.8	38	6.3	49	1.2	9	—	—	12.8	100
1780–89	244.3	8.4	39	11.5	53	1.4	7	—	—	21.6	100
1790–99	426.6	11.6	35	19.4	58	1.9	6	—	—	33.4	100
1800–1809	599.0	20.0	33	35.3	59	4.6	6	(0.1)	0	60.6	100

Reproduced with permission from P. Mathias, *The First Industrial Nation* (Methuen, London, 1969).

Table 9: Prices

Year	Consumers' goods	Consumers' goods other than cereals	Producers' goods	Wheat prices (shillings per quarter)	Bread prices: London (pence per 4 lb. loaf)
1700–1704	101	101	102	29.80	4.8
1705–9	95	92	98	38.02	5.7
1710–14	112	105	100	40.21	5.7
1715–19	98	97	90	34.64	4.9
1720–24	95	94	89	30.05	4.8
1725–9	100	94	93	37.29	5.7
1730–34	89	88	91	25.68	4.5
1735–9	90	86	83	29.79	5.3
1740–44	97	91	94	26.81	4.6
1745–9	92	92	88	27.32	4.9
1750–54	92	87	85	31.25	5.1
1755–9	100	92	96	36.54	5.6
1760–64	98	93	102	32.95	4.9
1765–9	106	94	97	43.43	6.6
1770–74	112	99	97	50.20	6.8
1775–9	113	101	103	42.80	6.3
1780–84	119	108	114	47.32	6.7
1785–9	119	108	110	44.92	6.1
1790–94	126	114	114	49.57	6.6
1795–9	151	134	132	65.67	8.8
1800–1804	186	156	153	84.85	11.7

index 1701 = 100

Reproduced with permission from P. Mathias, *The First Industrial Nation* (Methuen, London, 1969).

Further Reading

The following lists give an indication of the works which have influenced me most in writing this book and which can be recommended for follow-up reading. I confine myself here almost wholly to *books* (whose publication place is London unless otherwise indicated). Lists of periodical articles, and more extensive reading suggestions, can be found in the bibliographies of many of the books below. The standard if dated bibliography of the period is S. Pargellis and D. J. Medley, *Bibliography of British History: The Eighteenth Century 1714–1789* (Oxford, 1951). Copious listings of new works in socio-economic history are published annually in the *Economic History Review*. Helpful reference works and source books include two volumes in the *English Historical Documents* series, ed. David C. Douglas: VIII (1660–1714), ed. Andrew Browning (1953), and IX (1714–1783), ed. D. B. Horn and Mary Ransome (1957); E. N. Williams, *The Eighteenth Century Constitution 1688–1815* (Cambridge, 1960); and C. Cook and J. Stevenson, *British Historical Facts 1760–1830* (1980).

General

The best general chronological over-views of the period are J. H. Plumb, *England in the Eighteenth Century* (1950), J. Carswell, *From Revolution to Revolution: England 1688–1776* (1973), D. Jarrett, *Britain 1688–1815* (1965), D. Marshall, *Eighteenth Century England* (1962), and J. B. Owen, *The Eighteenth Century 1714–1815* (1974). J. Kenyon, *Stuart England* (1978), is an important revision of the Stuart background.

More thematic interpretations of society are Christopher Hill, *Reformation to Industrial Revolution* (1969), D. Jarrett, *England in the Age of Hogarth* (1974), W. Speck, *Stability and Strife, England 1714–1760* (1977), E. N. Williams, *Life in Georgian England* (1962), G. M. Trevelyan, *English Social History* (rep. 1977), P. Earle, *The World of Defoe* (1976), and M. D. George, *England in Transition* (1953). The first chapters of J. H. Plumb's *Sir Robert Walpole*, Vol. 1 (1956), offer a succinct and penetrating introduction to early-eighteenth-century society. For cultural and literary perspectives see A. R. Humphreys, *The Augustan World* (1955), B. Willey, *The Eighteenth Century Background*

(1950), A. S. Turberville (ed.), *Johnson's England* (2 vols., Oxford, 1933), J. L. Clifford (ed.), *Man Versus Society in Eighteenth Century Britain* (Cambridge, 1968), and P. Rogers, *The Augustan Vision* (1974). See also L. Namier, *England in the Age of the American Revolution* (1930), and R. J. White, *The Age of George III* (1968).

Anthologies etc.

Useful collections of extracts from contemporary material include M. D. George, *England in Johnson's Day* (1928) (as is her *Hogarth to Cruikshank: Social Change in Graphic Satire* (1967)), J. Hampden, *An Eighteenth Century Journal. Being a Record of the Years 1774–1776* (1940), A. Briggs, *How They Lived, 1700–1815* (Oxford, 1969), A. F. Scott, *Every One a Witness: The Georgian Age* (1970) and his *The Early Hanoverian Age 1714–1760* (1980), E. R. Pike, *Human Documents of Adam Smith's Time* (1974) and *Human Documents of the Industrial Revolution* (1966), and C. Morsley (ed.), *News from the English Countryside 1750–1850* (1979).

Contemporary Foreign Writings about England

Foreigners' views have been discussed in M. Letts, *As a Foreigner Saw Us* (1935), and F. M. Wilson, *Strange Island: Britain Through Foreign Eyes* (1955). Writers frequently referred to in the present book include J. von Archenholtz, *A Picture of England* (Dublin, 1791), Casanova, *Memoirs* (8 vols., 1940), P. Kalm, *Account of a Visit to England*, trs. J. Lucas (New York, 1892), M. L. Mare and W. H. Quarrell, *Lichtenberg's Visits to England* (Oxford, 1938), H. Misson, *Memoirs* (1719), C. P. Moritz, *Journeys of a German through England in 1782*, ed. R. Nettel (1965), F. de la Rochefoucauld, *A Frenchman in England, 1784*, trs. S. C. Roberts (Cambridge, 1933), L. Simond, *An American in Regency England*, ed. C. Hibbert (1968), C. de Saussure, *A Foreign View of England in the Reigns of George I and George II*, trs. and ed. Mme van Muyden (1902), F. M. Voltaire, *Letters Concerning the English Nation* (1733), and Pastor Wendeborn, *A View of England* (2 vols., Dublin, 1791).

Contemporary English Writings

The tone of English social life is best captured by contemporary letters, diaries, and fiction. Ones I have most relied upon include T. Bewick, *A Memoir*, ed. E. Blunden (1961), J. Boswell, *Life of Dr Johnson*, ed. G. B. Hill (6 vols., Oxford, 1934), *The Yale Edition of the Private Papers of James Boswell*, ed. F. A. Pottle and others (1950–   ), F. Burney, *Diary and Letters*, ed. C. Barrett (1905), J. Byng, *The Torrington Diaries*, ed. C. B. Andrews (4 vols., 1934–8), W. Cobbett, *Rural Rides* (1912), *The*

Autobiography of William Cobbett, ed. W. Retzel (1933), *The Essential Works of Erasmus Darwin*, ed. D. King Hele (1968), D. Defoe, *Tour through the Whole Island of Great Britain*, ed. G. D. H. Cole (1962), *Selected Writings of Daniel Defoe*, ed. J. Boulton (Cambridge, 1975), E. Gibbon, *Autobiography*, ed. M. M. Reese (1970), W. Hickey, *Memoirs*, ed. A. Spencer (4 vols.), F. Macky, *A Journey through England* (1714), *Priestley's Writings*, ed. J. Passmore (1965), *The Purefoy Letters*, ed. G. Eland (2 vols., 1931), R. Southey, *Letters from England*, ed. J. Simmons (1951), J. Tucker, *A Collection of his Economic and Political Writings*, ed. R. L. Schuyler (New York, 1931), T. Turner, *The Diary of Thomas Turner of East Hoathley, 1754-65*, ed F. M. Turner (1925), H. Walpole, *Letters*, ed. W. S. Lewis (39 vols., New Haven, Conn., 1937-79), J. Wesley, *Journal* (4 vols., 1904)), and James Woodforde, *The Diary of a Country Parson 1758-1802*, ed. J. Beresford (5 vols., Oxford, 1924-31). See also *The Diary of Abigail Gawthern of Nottingham 1751-1810* (Nottingham, 1980). Invaluable insights are offered by publications such as the *Spectator* and the *Gentleman's Magazine*.

1. *Contrasts*

The situation and changing position of women within the family have been most recently discussed in L. Stone, *The Family, Sex and Marriage in England 1500-1800* (1977), and R. Trumbach, *The Rise of the Egalitarian Family* (New York, 1878). For bluestockings see M. A. Hopkins, *Hannah More and Her Circle* (New York, 1947). C. Tomalin's *The Life and Death of Mary Wollstonecraft* (1974) is an illuminating biography. For women's work see I. Pinchbeck, *Women Workers and the Industrial Revolution* (1969). Far the best discussions of scholarship on women's place are in B. Kanner (ed.), *The Women of England* (1980). On wife-sales, see S. P. Menesee, *Wives for Sale* (Oxford, 1981). See also *Letters from Lady Mary Wortley Montagu*, ed. R. Brimley Johnson (1906), The Duchess of Northumberland, *Diaries of a Duchess*, ed. J. Grieg (1926), and D. Monaghan, *Jane Austen in a Social Context* (1981).

The socio-economy of England in 1700 is well covered in H. C. Darby (ed.), *A New Historical Geography of England* (1973), W. G. Hoskins, *The Making of the English Landscape* (1970), L. A. Clarkson, *The Pre-Industrial Economy in England 1500-1750* (1971), D. C. Coleman, *The Economy of England 1450-1750* (1977), and B. A. Holderness, *Pre-Industrial England: Economy and Society 1500-1750* (1976). For its cultural implications see R. Williams, *The Country and the City* (1973). Provincial life is explored in E. Hughes, *North Country Life in the Eighteenth Century* (2 vols., Oxford, 1952-65), E. Moir, *The Discovery of England* (1964), D. Read, *The English Provinces c. 1760-1960* (1964), and W. G. Hoskins, *Provincial England* (1963). For London see M. D.

George, *London Life in the Eighteenth Century* (1925), and J. Lindsay, *The Monster City: Defoe's London 1688–1730* (1978); for Scotland, H. G. Graham, *A Social Life of Scotland in the Eighteenth Century* (Edinburgh, 1901), and J. Rendall, *The Origins of the Scottish Enlightenment 1707–1776* (1976); for Ireland, C. Maxwell, *Dublin under the Georges* (1956); and for Wales, D. Moore (ed.), *Wales in the Eighteenth Century* (Swansea, 1976). For imperial expansion in general see A. Calder, *Revolutionary Empire* (1981). The definitive discussion of English demography, from which all the population figures in this book are taken, is now E. A. Wrigley and R. Schofield, *The Population History of England 1541–1871: A Reconstruction* (1981). Contemporary evaluations of the social structure by Gregory King and Joseph Massie etc. are discussed in P. Mathias, *The Transformation of England* (1979).

2. The Social Order

Important discussions of social structure and its interpretation are to be found in D. Marshall, *English People in the Eighteenth Century* (1956), H. Perkin, *The Origins of Modern English Society* (1969), and E. P. Thompson, 'Patrician Society, Plebeian Culture', *Journal of Social History* (Summer 1974), 382–405, and his 'Eighteenth Century English Society: Class Struggle Without Class?', *Social History* (1978), 133–65, newly reviewed in R. S. Neale, *Class in English History 1680–1850* (Oxford, 1981).

The best treatments of the world of the landowners are G. E. Mingay, *English Landed Society in the Eighteenth Century* (1963), his *The Gentry* (1976), H. Habbakuk's essay in A. Goodwin (ed.), *The European Nobility in the Eighteenth Century* (1953), and M. Girouard, *Life in the English Country House* (1979). See also R. Bayne-Powell, *English Country Life in the Eighteenth Century* (1937), and E. W. Bovill, *English Country Life 1780–1830* (1962).

On middling men, there is much of interest in M. J. Reader, *Professional Men* (1966), R. B. Westerfield, *Middlemen in English Business 1600–1760* (1915), T. S. Willan, *An Eighteenth Century Shopkeeper: Abraham Dent of Kirkby-Stephen* (Manchester, 1970), and R. G. Wilson, *Gentlemen Merchants: The Merchant Community in Leeds 1700–1830* (Manchester, 1971). *The Autobiography of Francis Place*, ed. M. Thale (Cambridge, 1972), *The Life of William Hutton*, ed. L. Jewitt (1869), and J. Lackington, *Memoirs* (13th edn, 1810), also make fascinating reading.

On the lower orders see W. Hasbach, *A History of the English Agricultural Labourer* (1908), J. L. and B. Hammond, *The Town Labourer, 1760–1832* (1917), *The Village Labourer 1760–1832* (1919), and *The Skilled Labourer 1760–1832* (1919); and J. J. Hecht, *The Domestic Servant*

Class in Eighteenth Century England (1956). For work and the working man see J. Rule, *The Experience of Labour in Eighteenth Century Industry* (1980), C. R. Dobson, *Masters and Journeymen* (1980), and R. W. Malcolmson, *Life and Labour in England, 1760–1780* (1981). For the poor see D. Marshall, *The English Poor in the Eighteenth Century* (1926), and J. R. Poynter, *Society and Pauperism* (1969).

An unrivalled profile of the structure of a village community at the beginning of our period is Richard Gough's *History of Myddle*, written in 1700, now edited by D. Hey (1981). See also P. Horn, *A Georgian Parson and His Village: The Story of David Davies (1742–1819)* (Abingdon, 1981).

3. Power, Politics, and the Law

The role of public violence in English society is discussed in G. Rudé, *The Crowd in History* (1964), and also his *Paris and London in the Eighteenth Century* (1952) and *Wilkes and Liberty* (1962); in J. Brewer and J. Styles (eds.), *An Ungovernable People* (1980), E. P. Thompson, 'The Moral Economy of the English Crowd in the Eighteenth Century', *Past and Present*, no. 50 (1971), and J. Stevenson, *Popular Disturbances in England, 1700–1870* (1979). See also J. Castro, *The Gordon Riots* (1926).

For power, politics, the state, and the grip of oligarchy see J. H. Plumb, *The Growth of Political Stability in England* (1967) and his *Sir Robert Walpole*, 2 vols. to date (1956–), W. A. Speck, *Tory and Whig 1701–1715* (1970), G. S. Holmes, *British Politics in the Age of Anne* (1967) and his *Britain after the Glorious Revolution 1689–1714* (1969), L. Namier, *The Structure of Politics at the Accession of George III* (rev. edn, 1957) and his *England in the Age of the American Revolution* (1930), B. Kemp, *King and Commons 1660–1832* (1959), R. Pares, *George III and the Politicians* (1954), and for constitutional beliefs J. Brewer, *Party Ideology and Popular Politics at the Accession of George III* (1976). Commentary on these is to be found in J. Cannon (ed.), *The Whig Ascendancy* (1981). On financing government see P. G. M. Dickson, *The Financial Revolution in England 1688–1756* (1967). For monarchy see J. H. Plumb, *The First Four Georges* (1956), J. M. Beattie, *The English Court in the Reign of George I* (1967), and R. Hatton, *George I* (1979).

The most thorough works on local government remain S. and B. Webb, *English Local Government from the Revolution to the Municipal Corporation Act* (9 vols., 1906–29). These should be supplemented with D. Marshall, *The Old Poor Law 1795–1834* (1968), M. E. Rose, *The English Poor Law 1760–1830* (Newton Abbot, 1971), G. Taylor, *The Problem of Poverty, 1660–1834* (1969), U. Henriques, *Before the Welfare State* (1979), and B. Keith Lewis, *The Unreformed Local Government*

System (1980). For London local government see G. Rudé, *Hanoverian London* (1971). See also F. M. Eden, *The State of the Poor* (1794).

The fundamental discussion of the criminal law is L. Radzinowicz, *A History of English Criminal Law* (1948–). Discussion of the law in its social context may be found in Brewer and Styles and S. and B. Webb listed above, and also in E. P. Thompson, *Whigs and Hunters* (1975), D. Hay and others (ed.), *Albion's Fatal Tree* (1975), and J. S. Cockburn (ed.), *Crime in England 1550–1800* (1977). A. Macfarlane, *The Justice and the Mare's Ale* (Oxford, 1981), is a case-history of a crime in Westmorland in 1680.

4. *Keeping Life Going*

The leading discussions of population and family life are E. A. Wrigley, *Population and History* (1969), E. A. Wrigley (ed.), *An Introduction to English Historical Demography* (1966), P. Laslett, *The World We Have Lost* (rev. edn, 1971) and *Family Life and Illicit Love in Earlier Generations* (1978), P. Laslett, K. Oosterveen, and R. M. Smith, *Bastardy and Its Comparative History* (1980), and for a brilliant survey M. Anderson, *Approaches to the History of the Western Family 1500–1914* (London, 1980). For the economic dimensions see D. Levine, *Family Formation in an Age of Nascent Capitalism* (1977), and for bold over-views see E. Shorter, *The Making of the Modern Family* (1976), and Stone and Trumbach, cited above. The memoirs of Samuel Bamford, *Early Days* (1849), are interesting.

The best broad survey of education is J. Lawson and H. Silver, *A Social History of Education in England* (1973). For universities see L. Stone (ed.), *The University in Society* (2 vols., Princeton, N.J., 1975), and W. R. Ward, *Georgian Oxford* (Oxford, 1958); for grammar schools, R. S. Tomson, *Classics or Charity? The Dilemma of the Eighteenth Century Grammar Schools* (Manchester, 1971), and W. A. L. Vincent, *The Grammar Schools 1660–1714* (1969). For Dissenting education, H. McLachlan, *English Education under the Test Acts: The History of Non-conformist Academies 1662–1820* (Manchester, 1931). For discussion of popular education see N. Hans, *New Trends in Education in the Eighteenth Century* (1951), V. E. Neuberg, *Popular Education in Eighteenth Century England* (1972), M. G. Jones, *The Charity School Movement* (Cambridge, 1938), and B. Simon, *Studies in the History of Education* (1960). For ideals of culture see C. Strachey (ed.), *The Letters of the Earl of Chesterfield to his Son* (2 vols., 1932).

Surveys of religious developments include A. D. Gilbert, *Religion and Society in Industrial England* (1978), N. Sykes, *Church and State in the Eighteenth Century* (Cambridge, 1934), and S. C. Carpenter, *Eighteenth Century Church and People* (1959). Trends in religious thought are covered in R. N. Stromberg, *Religious Liberalism in Eighteenth Century England* (1954), and G. R. Cragg, *Reason and Authority in the Eighteenth Century* (Cambridge, 1964). The history of Nonconformist sects is handled in M. R. Watts, *The Dissenters* (Oxford, 1978), and their social significance in I. Grubb, *Quakerism and Industry before 1800* (1930), R. Vann, *The Social Development of English Quakerism 1655-1750* (Cambridge, Mass., 1969), E. D. Bebb, *Nonconformity and Social and Economic Life 1660-1800* (1935), and A. Raistrick, *Quakers in Science and Industry* (1950). On the radicalization of Nonconformity, see A. Lincoln, *Some Political and Social Ideas of English Dissent, 1763-1800* (Cambridge, 1938). Amid the vast literature on Methodism see M. Edwards, *John Wesley and the Eighteenth Century* (1955), and R. F. Wearmouth, *Methodism and the Common People of the Eighteenth Century* (1945). For Catholics, J. Bossy, *The English Catholic Community* (Cambridge, 1975), for enthusiasts see J. F. C. Harrison, *The Second Coming* (1979), and for hostility to such movements, R. Knox, *Enthusiasm* (1950).

5. Getting and Spending

For the relations between wealth, economic growth, and population see C. H. Wilson, *England's Apprenticeship 1603-1763* (Cambridge, 1965), T. S. Ashton, *Economic Fluctuations in England 1700-1800* (Oxford, 1959), and his *An Economic History of England: The Eighteenth Century* (1961); P. Deane and W. A. Cole, *British Economic Growth 1688-1959* (1967), and J. D. Chambers, *Population, Economy and Society in Pre-Industrial England* (1972). For agriculture see E. L. Jones and G. E. Mingay, *Land, Labour and Population in the Industrial Revolution* (1967), E. Kerridge, *The Agricultural Revolution* (1967), E. L. Jones, *Agriculture and the Industrial Revolution* (Oxford, 1974), E. L. Jones (ed.), *Agriculture and Economic Growth in England 1660-1815* (1967), P. Horn, *The Rural World 1780-1850* (1980), and J. D. Chambers and G. E. Mingay, *The Agricultural Revolution 1750-1880* (1966). For enclosure see M. Turner, *English Parliamentary Enclosure* (1980), and J. M. Yelling, *Common Fields and Enclosure in England 1450-1850* (1977). A local study is W. G. Hoskins, *The Midland Peasant* (1957). For communications see E. C. R. Hadfield, *British Canals* (1966), W. Albert, *The Turnpike Road System of England 1663-1840* (1972), E. Pawson, *Transport and the Economy: The Turnpike Roads of Britain* (1977), and D. Hey, *Packmen, Carriers and Packhorse Roads* (Leicester, 1980). For finance see P. G. M. Dickson, *The Financial Revolution in England 1688-1756* (1967), and L. S. Pressnell, *Country Banking in the Industrial Revolution* (Oxford, 1956), and amongst the many historians of particular industries see P. Mathias, *The Brewing Industry in England 1700-1830* (Cambridge, 1959), M. W. Flinn, *Men of Iron: The Crowleys in the Early Iron Industry* (Edinburgh,

1962), T. S. Ashton, *Iron and Steel in the Industrial Revolution* (Manchester, 1924), W. H. B. Court, *The Rise of the Midland Industries 1600–1838* (Oxford, 1938), H. Heaton, *The Yorkshire Woollen and Worsted Industries* (Oxford, 1920), and A. P. Wadsworth and J. de L. Mann, *The Cotton Trade and Industrial Lancashire 1600–1780* (Manchester, 1965). For a stress on the importance of distribution see E. Pawson, *The Early Industrial Revolution* (1979). J. D. Chambers, *The Vale of Trent 1660–1800* (Economic History Review Supplement no. 3, 1957), is a masterly regional study. National wealth is assessed in S. Pollard and D. Crossley, *The Wealth of Britain* (1968). See also G. E. Mingay, *Arthur Young and his Times* (1978).

6. *Having and Enjoying*

Some indication of basic styles and standards of living can be got from J. C. Burnett, *The History of the Cost of Living* (1969), J. Drummond and A. Wilbraham, *The Englishman's Food* (1957), D. Davis, *A History of Shopping* (1966), C. W. Chalklin, *The Provincial Towns of Georgian England 1740–1820* (1974), and J. H. Plumb, *Georgian Delights* (1980). For clothes see A. Buck, *Dress in Eighteenth Century England* (1979).

For the spread of commercial culture and its relations to the popular idiom see J. H. Plumb, *The Commercialization of Leisure in Eighteenth Century England* (Reading, 1973), R. Malcolmson, *Popular Recreations in English Society 1700–1850* (Cambridge, 1975), R. Elbourne, *Music and Tradition in Early Industrial Lancashire 1780–1840* (Woodbridge, Suffolk, 1980), H. Cunningham, *Leisure in the Industrial Revolution* (1980), R. Paulson, *Popular and Polite Art in the Age of Hogarth and Fielding* (1979), and more broadly U. P. Burke, *Popular Culture in Early Modern Europe* (1978). For the provinces see J. Money, *Experience and Identity: Birmingham and the West Midlands 1760–1800* (Manchester, 1977), G. Jackson, *Hull in the Eighteenth Century* (1972), A. Barbeau, *Life and Letters at Bath in the XVIII century* (1904), R. S. Neale, *Bath: A Social History 1680–1850* (1981), and G. A. Cranfield, *The Development of the Provincial Newspaper 1700–1760* (Oxford, 1962). For London see W. Boulton, *The Amusements of Old London* (1900), and R. D. Altick, *The Shows of London* (1978). For particular artistic, cultural, and sporting forms see I. Watt, *The Rise of the Novel* (1957), A. Nicoll, *A History of Eighteenth Century Drama 1700–1750* (Cambridge, 1925), *1750–1800* (Cambridge, 1927), J. Ashton, *The History of Gambling in England* (1898), R. Longrigg, *The English Squire and his Sport* (1977), A. Ellis, *The Penny Universities: A History of the Coffee Houses* (1956), J. A. R. Pimlott, *The Englishman's Holiday* (1947), and E. D. Mackerness, *A Social History of English Music* (Toronto, 1964).

For the position of artists and performers see A. S. Collins, *Authorship in the Days of Johnson* (1927), J. Saunders, *The Profession of English Letters* (Toronto, 1964), P. Rogers, *Grub Street* (1972), M. Foss, *The Age of Patronage: The Arts in Society 1660-1750* (1972), and D. Jarrett, *The Ingenious Mr Hogarth* (1976). For changing artistic styles see T. Fawcett, *The Rise of English Provincial Art* (Oxford, 1974), F. D. Klingender, *Art and the Industrial Revolution* (1947), K. Clark, *The Gothic Revival* (1928), B. Sprague Allen, *Tides of British Taste 1619-1800* (Cambridge, Mass., 1937), Sir J. Summerson, *Georgian London* (1945), and N. Pevsner, *The Englishness of English Art* (1956). See also J. Barrell, *The Dark Side of the Landscape* (Cambridge, 1980), W. Blake, *Complete Writings*, ed. G. Keynes (1972), and J. Bronowski, *William Blake and the Age of Revolution* (1972).

7. Changing Experiences

The fundamental, and arguably growing, individualism of English society has been brought out in very different ways by D. Jarrett, *England in the Age of Hogarth* (1974), A. Macfarlane, *The Origins of English Individualism* (Oxford, 1978), and L. Stone, *The Family, Sex and Marriage in England 1500-1800* (1977). The Enlightenment dimensions of such ideas are stressed in Roy Porter, 'The English Enlightenment' in Roy Porter and M. Teich (eds.), *The Enlightenment in National Context* (Cambridge, 1981); for other perspectives on the Enlightenment in England see E. Halévy, *The Growth of Political Radicalism* (1928), J. Redwood, *Reason, Ridicule and Religion* (1976), and L. Stephen, *A History of English Thought in the Eighteenth Century* (1876). Political aspects of freedom are treated in G. Rudé, *Wilkes and Liberty* (1962). For the growth of philanthropy see D. Owen, *English Philanthropy 1660-1960* (Cambridge, Mass., 1965), B. Rodgers, *Cloak of Charity: Studies in Eighteenth Century Philanthropy* (1949), and F. J. Klingberg, *The Anti-Slavery Movement in England* (New Haven, Conn., 1926). See also J. H. Hutchins, *Jonas Hanway, 1712-86* (1940). For changing attitudes towards children see J. H. Plumb, 'The New World of the Children in Eighteenth Century England,' *Past and Present*, no. 67 (1975), 65-95, and I. Pinchbeck and M. Hewitt, *Children and English Society*, Vol. 1 (1969). For a survey of sexual attitudes see P. G. Boucé (ed.), *Sexuality in Eighteenth Century England* (Manchester, 1982). See also J. Cleland, *Memoirs of a Woman of Pleasure* [Fanny Hill] (1977).

Aspects of change, modernization, rationalization, and secularization are covered in K. Thomas, *Religion and the Decline of Magic* (1971), A. Briggs, *The Age of Improvement* (1959), J. Roach, *Social Reform in England 1780-1880* (1978), and B. Capp, *Astrology and the Popular Press: English Almanacs 1500-1800* (1979). Science and technology are discussed by R. E. Schofield, *The Lunar Society of Birmingham* (Oxford,

1963), A. E. Musson and E. Robinson, *Science and Technology in the Industrial Revolution* (Manchester, 1969), and G. S. Rousseau, 'Science', in P. Rogers (ed.), *The Context of English Literature: The Eighteenth Century* (1978). D. King-Hele's *Doctor of Revolution: The Life and Genius of Erasmus Darwin* (1977) is a biography of a leading scientist-doctor. Particular fields of 'rational' change are analysed in M. Ignatieff, *A Just Measure of Pain* (1978), A. Scull, *Museums of Madness* (1979), W. Ll. Parry-Jones, *The Trade in Lunacy* (1972), J. Woodward, *To Do the Sick No Harm* (1974), and G. Williams, *The Age of Agony: The Art of Healing c. 1700–1800* (1975).

Movements in the second half of the century to police popular culture more effectively, refine patrician culture, and introduce respectability are dealt with in R. W. Malcolmson, *Popular Recreations in English Society 1700–1850* (Cambridge, 1973), E. J. Bristow, *Vice and Vigilance: Purity Movements in Britain since 1700* (Dublin, 1977), T. Laqueur, *Sunday Schools and Working Class Culture 1780–1850* (1976), F. K. Brown, *Fathers of the Victorians: The Age of Wilberforce* (Cambridge, 1961), G. Rattray Taylor, *The Angel Makers: A Study of the Psychological Origins of Historical Change* (1973), M. J. Quinlan, *Victorian Prelude* (New York, 1941), M. Jaeger, *Before Victoria* (1956), and P. Fryer, *Mrs Grundy* (1963). See also R. Brimley Johnson, *The Letters of Hannah More* (1925), and O. Warner, *William Wilberforce and His Times* (1962).

8. Towards Industrial Society

General surveys of the early Industrial Revolution include P. Deane *The First Industrial Revolution* (Cambridge, 1965), E. Hobsbawm, *Industry and Empire* (1968), P. Mathias, *The First Industrial Nation* (1969) and his collection of essays, *The Transformation of England* (1979); T. S. Ashton, *The Industrial Revolution 1760–1830* (1948), D. Landes, *The Unbound Prometheus* (Cambridge, 1969), P. Mantoux, *The Industrial Revolution: The Eighteenth Century* (1928), D. Marshall, *Industrial England 1776–1851* (1973). Its historiography is discussed in R. M. Hartwell, *The Industrial Revolution and Economic Growth* (1971), and M. W. Flinn, *The Origins of the Industrial Revolution* (1966). An important regional study is W. Rowe, *Cornwall in the Age of the Industrial Revolution* (Liverpool, 1953), and studies of particular groups of workers include D. Bythell, *The Handloom Weavers* (Cambridge, 1969), and M. Thomis, *The Town Labourer and the Industrial Revolution* (1974). For debates about industrialization's effect on the standard of living and the quality of life see E. Gilboy, *Wages in Eighteenth Century England* (1934), M. Thomis, *Responses to Industrialization* (Newton Abbot, 1976), and

A. J. Taylor (ed.), *The Standard of Living in Britain in the Industrial Revolution* (1975). For studies of entrepreneurship see R. S. Fitton and A. P. Wadsworth, *The Strutts and the Arkwrights* (Manchester, 1958), H. W. E. Dickinson, *Matthew Boulton* (Cambridge, 1937), W. G. Rimmer, *Marshalls of Leeds* (Cambridge, 1960), and E. Roll, *An Early Experiment in Industrial Organization: A History of the Firm of Boulton and Watt, 1775–1805* (2nd edn, 1968). For an entrepreneur in his social context see B. and H. Wedgwood, *The Wedgwood Circle 1730–1897* (1980). See also J. T. Ward, *The Factory System*, 2 vols. (Newton Abbot, 1970).

9. Conclusion

Developments in the 1790s and early into the nineteenth century may be studied in C. Emsley, *British Society and the French Wars 1793–1815* (1979), and A. D. Harvey, *Britain in the Early Nineteenth Century* (1978). The roots of radicalism are discussed in G. S. Veitch, *The Genesis of Parliamentary Reform* (1913), and J. Cannon, *Parliamentary Reform 1640–1832* (Cambridge, 1973), radicalism itself in A. Goodwin, *The Friends of Liberty* (Manchester, 1979). Pre-Romantic disaffection is brought to life in J. Bronowski, *William Blake and the Age of Revolution* (1972). R. Soloway, *Prelates and People 1783–1852* (1969), charts growing religious rejection of the Georgian century and D. Cannadine, in *Lords and Landlords* (Leicester, 1980), indicates magnate strength and wealth. The issues of what kind of social structure the eighteenth century bequeathed to the nineteenth are discussed by R. J. Morris, *Class and Class Consciousness in the Industrial Revolution 1780–1850* (1979), E. P. Thompson, *The Making of the English Working Class* (1963), H. Perkin, *The Origins of Modern English Society* (1969), and E. Halévy, *A History of the English People in the Nineteenth Century:* Vol. I: *England in 1815* (1964). See also E. Hobsbawm and G. Rudé, *Captain Swing* (1969).

Index

Abbots Bromley, 167
Abigails, 102
Abortifacients, 41, 279
Académie Française, 249
Act of Toleration (1690), 187
Act of Union (1707), 48, 219
Acts of Parliament, private, 134, 142
Adam, Robert, 238, 249
Adam brothers, 260, 265
Addis, William, 291
Addison, Joseph, 34, 93, 118, 170, 172, 184, 185, 245, 252, 267, 274, 277, 296, 321, 322
Admiralty, 91
Admission fees, 250
Adultery, 39
Advertising, 206, 240
Agricultural improvement societies, 292
Agriculture, 57, 220-22, 334-5
    changes in geography of production, 222
    conditions in, 109-10
    economics of, 72, 210
    female labour in, 46-7
    improvements in, 221
    profitability of, 220, 229, 334
Aikin, Arthur, 98
Aikin, John, 196, 355
Aikin, Lucy, 376
Aislabie, John, 123
Alcohol consumption, 33-4, 235
Allen, Ralph, 292
Almack's club, 50, 172, 256
Amelia (Henry Fielding), 263
America, emigration to, 49
    See also Thirteen Colonies
American colonies, 50, 86, 363
American Independence, War of, 135, 223, 363, 370, 371
Amherst, Lord, 73
Analysis of Beauty (Hogarth), 263
Ancien régime, 359
Anglesey, 73, 337

Anne, Queen, 121, 129, 255
Annual Review, 360, 375
Anti-Jacobin Review, 376
Antinomians, 197
Anti-semitism, 116
Apothecaries, 90
Apprenticeship, 100, 101, 102, 103, 104, 159, 162, 167, 215, 217
Archenholz, J. von, 61, 206, 272
Archer family, 82
Architecture, 265
Argyll, Duke of, 72
Arianism, 197
Arkwright, Richard, 88, 103, 330, 331, 332, 337, 339, 342, 343, 347, 349, 354, 371
Army, 134
    recruitment to, 135
    sale of commissions in, 152
    size of, 23
Arrears, payment in, 101
Art exhibitions, 248
Art of Boxing, The (Daniel Mendoza), 254
Arts
    and nobility, 75, 87
    and wealth, 262
    commercialization of, 249-68 *passim*
    decorative, 264-5
Arundel, Sir Henry, 187
Ascot, 254-5
Ashton, T. S., 329
Asiento, 51
Associations for the Defence of Property, 371
Astell, Mary, 37
Astley, Philip, 257
Athenian Mercury (John Dunton), 295
Atlases, 300
Attorneys, 90
Audley End, 74
Austen, Jane, 38, 43, 44, 113, 180, 286, 320, 321
Austria, 22, 332

*More About Penguins
and Pelicans*

For further information about books available from Penguins please write to Dept EP, Penguin Books Ltd, Harmondsworth, Middlesex UB7 0DA.

In the U.S.A.: For a complete list of books available from Penguins in the United States write to Dept CS, Penguin Books, 625 Madison Avenue, New York, New York 10022.

In Canada: For a complete list of books available from Penguins in Canada write to Penguin Books Canada Ltd, 2801 John Street, Markham, Ontario L3R 1B4.

In Australia: For a complete list of books available from Penguins in Australia write to the Marketing Department, Penguins Books Australia Ltd, P.O. Box 257, Ringwood, Victoria 3134.

In New Zealand: For a complete list of books available from Penguins in New Zealand write to the Marketing Department, Penguin Books (N.Z.) Ltd, P.O. Box 4019, Auckland 10.

THE PELICAN SOCIAL HISTORY OF BRITAIN

General Editor: J. H. Plumb

Synthesizing the fruits of much recent research, this important new Pelican series will stand as a major survey of British society since the Middle Ages.

Already published:

BRITISH SOCIETY SINCE 1945

Arthur Marwick

From the military victory in the Second World War to economic and political impotence in the early 1980s; and from the high ideals and community spirit of 1945 to today's shoddy, market-oriented materialism – an essential theme in this new study is the question: 'What went wrong?'

High and popular culture; family, class and race relations; sexual attitudes and material conditions; science and technology – the main social developments in these areas are explored within a clear chronological framework. Special attention is given to the up-heavals of the sixties and the advent of, among other things, commercial television, pop culture and the Abortion Act. Finally, Arthur Marwick discusses whether 'stability' and 'consensus' really are integral – and fruitful – features of life in Britain today.

Titles in preparation:

SIXTEENTH-CENTURY ENGLAND

Joyce Youings

BRITAIN 1800–1870

V. A. C. Gatrell

BRITAIN 1870–1914

José Harris

The Pelican Economic History of Britain Volume Two

REFORMATION TO INDUSTRIAL REVOLUTION
Christopher Hill

The period 1530–1780 witnessed the making of modern English society. Under the Tudors England was a society of subsistence agriculture in which it was taken for granted that a fully human existence was possible only for the landed ruling class. In 1780 England was a national market on the threshold of industrial revolution, and the ideology of self-help had permeated into the middle ranks. A universal belief in original sin had been supplanted by the romanticism of 'Man is good'. And the first British Empire had already been won and lost. In this masterly study one of the great historians of the seventeenth century analyses the transformation of British society and the complex interaction of economic, cultural and political change in the period. In particular he stresses the political ferment of the seventeenth century and its influence on the revolutions in trade and agriculture, which in their turn prepared English society for the take-off into the modern industrial world.

'This formidable little book – its range of information is remarkable and it is stuffed with fruitful hypotheses – is rather a commentary than an analysis' – Peter Laslett in the *Guardian*

'There is clearly no lack of controversial matter here: Mr Hill has fulfilled an important function of a good social history' – *The Times Literary Supplement*

A Peregrine Book

THE ENGLISH PEOPLE AND
THE ENGLISH REVOLUTION

Brian Manning

'This excellent book restores sense to our understanding of the Civil War' – A. L. Rowse.

The English People and the English Revolution is a study of the decisive role played by the common people of England, and especially the London crowd, in precipitating the outbreak of the Civil War and thereafter in continuing the revolution. More often than is realized, says Brian Manning, the initiative was held not by the ruling gentry, but by the commons, led by 'people of the middle sort' and motivated by economic frustration and class hatred. It was they who split the House of Commons by their eruption onto the streets of Westminster; they who won many areas for parliament by preventing the King's Commissions of Array; they who did most of the fighting, and, when the fighting was over, provided the basis of the 'failed revolution' of the Levellers.

This book has a point to make about the nature of class relations in the seventeenth century and the economic causes of the Civil War, and in doing so it provides us with a magnificent picture of the excitement and tumult, misery and tragedy, of one of the most important moments in our history.

A Peregrine Book

WHIGS AND HUNTERS
E. P. Thompson

With *Whigs and Hunters*, the author of *The Making of the English Working Class*, E. P. Thompson, plunges into the murky waters of the early eighteenth century to cart the violently conflicting currents that boiled beneath the apparent calm of the time. His subject is the Black Act, a law of unprecedented savagery passed by Parliament in 1723 to deal with 'wicked and evil-disposed men going armed in disguise'. These men were pillaging the royal forests of deer, conducting a running battle against the forest officers with blackmail, threats and violence.

These 'Blacks', however, were men of some substance; their protest (for such it was) took issue with the equally wholesale plunder of the forest by Whig nominees to the forest offices. And Robert Walpole, still consolidating his power, took an active part in the prosecution of the 'Blacks'. The episode is laden with political and social implications, affording us glimpses of considerable popular discontent, political chicanery, judicial inequity, corrupt ambition and crime. Thanks to E.P. Thompson's superb writing and research, we are able to see and understand the major social tensions of the early eighteenth century.

'Outstanding for its skill in detection, in bringing alive and alight the violent social conflicts in the royal forests ... skilfully constructed and written with great panache' – J. H. Plumb

'Powerful, fascinating and endlessly suggestive ... the eighteenth century will never be the same again' – E. J. Hobsbawm in *New Society*

'Unrivalled among historians for his distinctive blend of biting irony, probing analytical intelligence, passionate moral commitment and sheer rhetorical skill' – Keith Thomas in the *New Statesman*

A Peregrine Book

ALBION'S FATAL TREE

Douglas Hay, Peter Linebaugh, John G. Rule, E. P. Thompson and Cal Winslow

The elegant *façade* of eighteenth-century England, with its land-scaped parks and polite culture, is what we chiefly remember of the age of Walpole and Pitt. We forget the backbreaking labour in field and forest and ignore the undergrowth of crime and cor-ruption: for the domestic peace of the Hanoverian age was seriously disturbed by gangs of wreckers, smugglers and poachers, while the apparent stability of the time was ensured by a criminal law of unexampled savagery.

It is this side of eighteenth-century life that the authors of this book have investigated. Douglas Hay deals with the role of the criminal law in maintaining the rule of the propertied classes, and in another essay shows it in action against the poachers of Cannock Chase, Staffordshire. John G. Rule and Cal Winslow tell of smug-glers and wreckers, showing how these activities formed a natural part of the life of the traditional communities involved. Together with Peter Linebaugh's piece on the riots against the surgeons at Tyburn, and E. P. Thompson's illuminating work on anonymous threatening letters, these essays form a powerful contribution to the study of social tensions in the eighteenth century.

'These two volumes [with E. P. Thompson, *Whigs and Hunters*, published simultaneously as a Peregrine] immensely advance our understanding both of Hanoverian England and of the relation-ship between law and society in general' – Keith Thomas in the *New Statesman*

'It is strange and wonderful that the five authors of *Albion's Fatal Tree* should jointly have produced a book at once so erudite in matter and so elegantly pungent in manner' – Claud Cockburn in *Bananas*

A Peregrine Book

LONDON LIFE IN THE EIGHTEENTH CENTURY

M. Dorothy George

The Industrial Revolution, it has been said, 'was like a storm that passed over London and broke elsewhere'. Whatever happened in other parts, it is clear that in the capital social conditions gradually improved. Between Defoe and Wordsworth, as it were, London progressed from gin and brutality to tea and temperance.

On this period of London's development Dorothy George's exhaustive study is now a standard work, as balanced in its judgements as it is comprehensive in its sources. The observations of such well-known figures as Johnson, Wesley, and Place, of Henry Fielding and his half-brother John, who were so intimately involved with London's poor, are filled out here with evidence from contemporary reports and newspapers, sessions papers and county records, pamphlets and memoirs by foreign travellers.

Certainly no more complete survey has ever been made of the place and the period in which the idea of progress began to become a reality.